Understanding Econometrics

DENNIS HALCOUSSIS

California State University, Northridge

THOMSON
™
SOUTH-WESTERN

Australia · Canada · Mexico · Singapore · Spain · United Kingdom · United States

Understanding Econometrics
Dennis Halcoussis

VP/Editorial Director:
Jack W. Calhoun

VP/Editor-in-Chief:
Michael P. Roche

Publisher:
Michael B. Mercier

Senior Acquisitions Editor:
Peter Adams

Developmental Editor:
Bob Sandman

Senior Marketing Manager:
John Carey

Production Editor:
Chris Hudson

Technology Project Editor:
Peggy Buskey

Media Editor:
Pam Wallace

Manufacturing Coordinator:
Diane Lohman

Production House:
Lachina Publishing Services

Printer:
Quebecor Printing
Kingsport, Tennessee

Art Director:
Chris Miller

Cover Images:
© Getty Images

Brief Contents

Contents

Dedication

This book is dedicated to my bride of 6 years, Donna Driscoll. Her gentle encouragement and proofreading skills were essential to me for completing this book.

Preface

Many students find econometrics to be intimidating. Most textbooks are full of complicated equations, mathematical notation, and dry examples. The writing can seem to be in a foreign language, because it contains so much jargon. The first time I taught econometrics, students complained that they couldn't understand the text I was using. I discovered that my students would give up on reading the textbook after the first couple of weeks. They had trouble understanding the material, because there was nothing in their experience that they could relate it to; econometrics was different from anything they had seen before. Students need to be introduced to both theory and practice in a way that is accessible to them without losing rigor. I wrote this book to meet demand for a text that uses a down-to-earth approach in presenting undergraduate econometrics without skipping topics or neglecting theory.

ACCESSIBILITY

Understanding Econometrics is an introductory econometrics text that uses a new, understandable approach. Econometric theory will be explained intuitively in English, not through a series of mathematical derivations. The book is written assuming readers do not have a strong background in math or statistics. Using this approach, instructors can eliminate prerequisites, making the course accessible to more students.

Students need to learn both theoretical and applied econometrics. Theory alone makes it hard to see how to use the material, and students become bored and frustrated. Alternatively, if students are taught only how to run regressions on software without any theoretical background, they won't really understand what all the results mean or how to interpret them properly. All the theory you would expect at the undergraduate level is included in the text. However, *Understanding Econometrics* does not present all the mathematics found in traditional econometrics texts. Instead, the theory behind econometric practice will be taught in clear English with a minimum of mathematical notation. The text also calls careful attention to the interpretation of regression results. All econometric students can benefit from knowing how to read and interpret regression results correctly, even if they never come across an opportunity to run a regression during their careers.

READABILITY

Understanding Econometrics is written in a lively and engaging style. To get an idea of how the writing style of this text differs from that of other econometric textbooks, compare the table of contents of this book to any other undergraduate econometrics textbook. Please take a look at Section 5-1, the introductions of Chapters 7 and 8, or any other part of the book that interests you. I believe the readability of this text will keep students engaged, helping them to learn the material.

All econometrics texts have examples. For an example to have meaning, students need to see the connection between the example and the theory being taught. The text focuses on examples that connect theory with practice. These examples are integrated into the text throughout the book. For an example, please see the Concert Tour Model used in Chapter 8 or pick any other chapter. The book is written to be used with the student version of EViews, so that students can practice what they have learned. EViews is very easy to use, so students don't have to worry about learning how to use the software; they can concentrate on the econometrics. However, there is nothing in the text that precludes an instructor from using different software.

OVERVIEW OF THE TEXTBOOK

The text includes all the standard topics usually covered in an undergraduate text, as well as two special features. Chapter 9 covers estimation of pooled time-series cross-section models. The use of panel data is an important topic that, unfortunately, is omitted from many undergraduate texts. Also, *Understanding Econometrics* features a unique chapter entitled "Econome-'tricks': Misleading Uses of Econometrics." Students will like this chapter, because they value learning what to look out for and how to spot deceptive results.

Every chapter starts off with a set of learning objectives that lets the reader know the main lessons of the chapter. Each chapter is followed by a point-by-point summary and a set of questions for the student to answer. The questions vary from those that test the student's knowledge of theory to those that require the student to run regressions and interpret the results.

Below, you will find a concise description of each chapter:

- **Chapter 1** explains what econometrics is, introduces the simple regression model, and shows how intercept and slope estimates are found for the simple regression model. The derivation of the ordinary least squares estimators for the simple regression model is presented in an appendix.
- **Chapter 2** brings in the multiple regression model and explains how to interpret multiple regression results. The classical assumptions and the Gauss-Markov theorem are covered here as well.
- **Chapter 3** presents common statistics used in regression analysis, such as the t-statistic, the F-statistic, R^2, and adjusted R^2. Even though some students may have

taken a statistics class before, I have found that many have only a "cookbook" understanding of hypothesis testing. A more meaningful, intuitive approach to hypothesis testing is included in the chapter.

- **Chapter 4** starts off with an explanation of how to choose a topic for an econometrics project and how to do a literature review. Next, some basic modeling issues are discussed. This is followed by an important section concerning objectivity and ethics in econometrics. The last two sections include some advice on finding and using data, and a suggested format for writing an econometrics paper.

- **Chapter 5** explains dummy variables, interaction variables, different kinds of F-tests (including the Chow test), polynomial models, and log models.

- In Chapters 6 through 8, a medical analogy is used to present common estimation problems. **Chapter 6** covers multicollinearity. Special care is taken to make sure students realize that many regressions have at least some multicollinearity and that the degree of multicollinearity must be considered before deciding whether to take further action.

- **Chapter 7** presents the autocorrelation problem, how to use the Durbin-Watson statistic to test for first-order autocorrelation, and different approaches to treating the autocorrelation problem.

- **Chapter 8** covers heteroskedasticity, the Park and White tests, and different methods of tackling heteroskedasticity.

- **Chapter 9** explains how to estimate regressions using panel data. Fixed effects models and random effects models are covered, as well as seemingly unrelated regression. The chapter ends with a comparison of the three different methods to help the student see when the use of each is appropriate.

- **Chapter 10** discusses simultaneous-equation systems and includes coverage of the identification problem, instrumental variables estimation, and the Hausman test.

- **Chapter 11** delves into time-series models and is the most challenging chapter in the text for students. Koyck lags, autoregressive and moving average models, the unit-root problem, forecasting, and testing for causality (Granger causality) are explained. An appendix presents the math behind the Koyck lag model.

- **Chapter 12** explains qualitative choice models. Knowledge of qualitative choice models allows the student to expand his or her application of econometrics to situations they might not have thought of previously. Both binary and multiple choice models are covered. Censored and truncated data are discussed as well.

- **Chapter 13** is a special chapter that shows how econometric results can sometimes be misleading. Each of the first seven sections presents an example with misleading results, along with an explanation. Each section has a different theme, such as "statistical significance does not prove causality" (Section 13-1) or "the self-selection problem" (Section 13-6). The final section of the chapter, Section 13-8, provides a large table that summarizes many of the situations and estimation problems that have been described throughout the text. For each situation or problem, the table lists how the situation can be recognized, whether it is a violation of a classical assumption, the solution (and 2nd best solution) to the problem, and where the situation or problem appears in the book.

RESOURCES

Instructor's Manual (ISBN 0-03-034813-7)

The Instructor's Manual contains answers to all the end-of-chapter exercises in the text-book. There are also comments on the material, organized by chapter. The answers for the exercises are a bit longer and more complete than those provided in most instructor's manuals. The answers are written for students so that instructors do not have to supplement them; the answers can be distributed to the students as they are, if desired.

Instructor's Resource CD (ISBN 0-324-31935-5)

This CD contains the Instructor's Manual in Microsoft Word files and data set files in three formats: EViews, Excel, and ASCII.

Text Website

The text website is located at http://halcoussis.swlearning.com. All data used in the text are available at the website *free of charge* and available to both students and instructors. Qualified instructors can also download the Instructor's Manual.

South-Western/Thomson Learning also provides useful online resources as follows.

TextChoice: Economic Issues and Activities

TextChoice is the home of Thomson Learning's online digital content. TextChoice provides the fastest, easiest way for you to create your own learning materials. South-Western's Economic Issues and Activities content database includes a wide variety of high-interest, current event/policy applications as well as classroom activities designed specifically to enhance economics courses. Choose just one reading or many—even add your own materials—to create an accompaniment to the textbook that is perfectly customized to your course. Contact your South-Western/Thomson Learning sales representative for more information.

Economic Applications (e-con @pps) Website

Complimentary access to South-Western's **e-con @pps** website (http://econapps.swlearning.com) is included with every new copy of this textbook. (Students buying a used book can purchase access at the site.) This site includes a suite of highly acclaimed and content-rich dynamic web features developed specifically for economics classrooms: EconNews Online, EconDebate Online, and EconData Online. Organized and searchable by key economic topic for easy integration into your course, these regularly updated features are pedagogically designed to deepen students' understanding of theoretical concepts through hands-on exploration and analysis of the latest economic news stories, policy debates, and data.

ACKNOWLEDGMENTS

I was very fortunate to have had an outstanding group of reviewers for the text. Their careful reading of the manuscript and excellent suggestions were extremely valuable. I thank the following reviewers for all their work and insight:

Susan Averett
Lafayette College

Keith R. Criddle
Utah State University

Bruce K. Johnson
Centre College

Hannah McKinney
Kalamazoo College

I thank the dedicated team at South-Western/Thomson Learning, especially my editor, Peter Adams; developmental editor, Bob Sandman; production editor, Chris Hudson; and editorial assistant, Steve Joos. I also thank Tom Gay for his contributions during the early part of the process.

I am indebted to Donna Driscoll for careful proofreading and valuable discussions about the text. I am also indebted to Linda Johnston, M.D., who helped me develop the idea of using a medical analogy to explain estimation problems. Dr. Johnston also provided me with insight into the book-writing process. I thank Heather Martin, Amy Blossom Dinkfeld, Paul Chang, and Rania Sullivan for discussions about econometrics that helped me write this book.

Dennis Halcoussis
Department of Economics
California State University, Northridge

1

An Introduction
to Ordinary Least Squares

In this chapter, you will learn:

- What econometrics can do.
- How to set up and estimate a simple econometric model.
- How the estimation process works.

Welcome! Econometrics is a valuable subject to understand and use. Even if you do not do econometrics as part of your career, a solid understanding of this widely used subject gives you a competitive advantage in the workplace. If you are presented with proposals or forecasts based on econometrics, you will be better able to evaluate their worth—and less likely to be bamboozled by misleading results.

Econometrics can be used to study all types of interesting topics. For example, econometrics can be used to study what factors influence box office receipts for movies. Is it more important to use a big budget to bring well-known stars on board, or is it better to spend the money on expensive special effects? If the film is nominated for an award, how much does that help? Econometrics can also be used to look at what factors determine professional athletes' salaries. Are individual performance statistics all that matter? Will an outstanding athlete on a losing team make just as much money as one on a winning team? Econometrics can help answer such questions.

Econometrics is also used for forecasting. You can build an econometrics model to forecast a company's sales, for example. Such a model will help you learn what factors affect the firm's sales figures, and why. Never forget, however, that econometrics cannot really tell you what is going to happen in the future. It's a way to use the available information to make the best, most scientific guess possible, but it is still just a guess.

Econometrics is all about measurement. It measures how much something changes. Econometrics is often used to test whether a theory holds up in real life and also to see how much change occurs. Basic economic theory tells us that when the price of a good increases, the quantity demanded decreases, keeping other factors constant. Economic theory does not tell us how *much* the quantity demanded will decrease, though. That depends on the particular product and situation. Econometrics is often used to estimate a demand curve for a specific product. It can confirm that quantity demanded will decrease when the price of a good rises, and it can estimate the amount of the decrease.

1-1 YOU ALREADY USE ECONOMETRICS EVERY DAY

You already use a casual version of econometrics every day, you just don't call it econometrics. Econometrics uses existing data to estimate relationships between different variables, and you routinely use your past experiences to do the same thing. An **econometric model** is one or more equations that are used in econometrics to estimate the relationship between different factors or variables. For instance, an econometric model can be used to estimate the number of hours you need to study to do well on an exam. You already know that the amount you study and how you do on an exam are related, and you probably have a reasonable idea of how long you need to study to get a good grade. You simply haven't formalized the relationship. You can't ever know exactly how much to study because of unknown factors (such as the difficulty of the exam), but your experiences as a student help you make an estimate. Econometrics is a more formal method of making this estimate. That is, it uses *data* (number of hours studied, test scores, and other important factors) to *estimate* how much study time you'll need.

Suppose that every weekday you buy a sandwich for lunch at the Captain Hero sandwich shop. As you have noticed, the time it takes you to get your sandwich once you walk in the door differs. You could construct an econometric model to study the situation, to estimate the relationship between different variables or factors and the time you have to wait for your sandwich. The number of people in line and the number of people working behind the counter might both be part of the model, because these factors seem likely to influence the time you have to wait for your sandwich. Using econometrics to estimate this model will give you estimates of how each variable, such as the number of people in line, is associated with how long you have to wait. Because you go to Captain Hero every day, you've already estimated this model casually in your head. So, when you walk in and see a long line (and perhaps notice there are no extra people behind the counter), you know that they're busy and it will take longer for you to get your sandwich.

Econometrics is a statistical method that uses data to estimate relationships between variables. Once you have used econometrics to estimate the Captain Hero shop model, you can use the results to make conclusions about the model, such as how line length and number of workers behind the counter affect the time you have to wait for your sandwich. All of us use our experiences to make guesses about what's going to happen in the future. Data are just numbers that reflect what has happened in the past, so econometrics is a more formal, scientific way of using past experiences to see if you can predict what will happen. So, you already use an informal version of econometrics every day without realizing it.

1-2 A SIMPLE REGRESSION MODEL: COLLECTING DVDS

A Theoretical Regression Line

Quinn has a passion for film and enjoys collecting DVDs, but she is also a student and has to watch her budget. She knows she can't spend too much money on DVDs, so the amount she spends on them each month depends on how much she earns at her part-

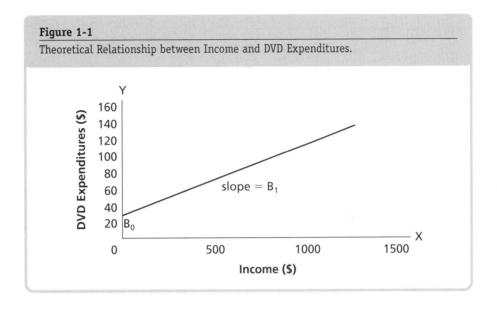

Figure 1-1

Theoretical Relationship between Income and DVD Expenditures.

time job. Quinn believes that the relationship between her income and the amount she spends on DVDs can be expressed as a straight line. She imagines it looks something like Figure 1-1.

The line in Figure 1-1 can be written as an equation, where Y is Quinn's DVD expenditures and X is her income.

$$Y = B_0 + B_1X \tag{1-1}$$

B_0 is the intercept of the line. The intercept tells you the value Y will take if X is zero. If B_0 is equal to 30, it means that when Quinn's monthly income is zero, she will still spend \$30 on DVDs. (*Note*: The estimation of an intercept should not be given too much importance. We will examine this idea in more detail in Section 1-3.) Always include a term for the intercept; otherwise the line will be forced through the origin on your graph, as if the intercept was automatically zero. This changes the rest of the line and gives you misleading results.

B_1 is the slope of the line. The slope shows the change in Y that occurs for a one-unit change in X. Suppose B_1 equals $\frac{1}{4}$. If X increases by 1, Y will increase by $\frac{1}{4}$. This is the same as saying that if Quinn's income increases by a dollar, her DVD expenditures will increase by 25 cents. B_0 and B_1 both represent constant numbers. If B_0 is 30 it stays at 30 every month; it doesn't change. Likewise, if B_1 is $\frac{1}{4}$, it will remain $\frac{1}{4}$ month after month. B_0 and B_1 are called **coefficients** to indicate they represent constant numbers. We don't know what B_0 and B_1 are equal to in this example, but we expect B_1 to be bigger than zero. A negative B_1 would mean that an increase in Quinn's income is associated with a decrease in her DVD expenditures. We expect B_1 to be positive, showing that she'll spend more on DVDs when she has more income.

The values of X and Y change each month in our example, so X are Y are both called **variables** because they are not constant. Y is the **dependent variable** because the equation implies that the value of Y depends on the value of X; the equation is an attempt to explain why the Y variable takes on the values that it does. X is an **independent variable** because the values of X are considered to be independent of the rest of the equation; the equation does not explain why X takes the values it does. X is also called an **explanatory variable** because it helps explain or predict the values of Y.

However, the econometric techniques we use in this book cannot *prove* that changes in X actually cause Y to change. Any change may be a coincidence, or there may be some other factor that causes Y to change that is not accounted for in the model. An example from the history of economic theory illustrates this idea. In the 1870s, William Jevons noticed that the movements of spots on the sun seemed to happen during changes in the business cycle. He concluded that sunspots caused changes in the business cycle! It was probably a coincidence, if it was true at all.[1] That two variables tend to change at the same time, if they are correlated, doesn't prove that one variable causes the other to change. This idea is often expressed by an old saying, "correlation does not prove causation."

The Error Term

Equation (1-1) depicts a theoretical relationship between the independent and dependent variable. The equation makes it seem that if we know the intercept B_0, the slope B_1, and a particular month's income X, we can calculate *exactly* how much Quinn will spend on DVDs that month. In real life, however, it is very unlikely that Quinn's DVD expenditures and income each month will line up exactly as shown in Figure 1-1. This means that Equation (1-1) won't work perfectly. In any month, the amount Quinn spends on DVDs, Y, is unlikely to be exactly equal to $B_0 + B_1X$. There will be an error. The proper equation for Quinn's model is

$$Y = B_0 + B_1X + e \qquad (1\text{-}2)$$

where e is an error term. Equation (1-2) represents a **simple regression model.** We call it "simple" because it contains only one independent variable; it is a regression model because it includes an error term [as opposed to Equation (1-1), which is the mathematical equation for a line, not a regression line, since it does not include an error term]. The error term e is **stochastic**, which means it is random. Thus, e must be included to account for the part of the Y value that is not explained by the rest of the model, the line $B_0 + B_1X$. The error term is not a constant number. In our example here, it will be different for each month. It is also a random variable, meaning that it changes in an unpredictable fashion. Even if a model is set up and estimated correctly, there are still three reasons for the existence of an error term:

1. Sometimes there is measurement error; the variable isn't measured accurately. (Perhaps, when tracking her DVD expenditures, Quinn forgot about a purchase; this would make the Y value for that month lower than it should be.)
2. There will always be small or secondary factors that influence the dependent variable that are too small to measure and include in the model.

---

[1] William Stanley Jevons, *Investigations in Currency and Finance* (London: MacMillan, 1884), pp. 194–243.

3. Random variation is a fact of life. Human behavior cannot be predicted perfectly by any model. There is always a random aspect to it. This is also true for many types of natural phenomena, such as weather.

Since e is a random variable, and $Y = B_0 + B_1X + e$, then Y consists of two parts: the part that is explained by the model, $B_0 + B_1X$, and the part that is random and comes from the error term e. Because part of the dependent variable Y is random, Y itself is a random variable, along with the error term e.

The Theoretical Regression Line Cannot Be Observed: It Must Be Estimated

Equation (1-2), $Y = B_0 + B_1X + e$, represents a *theoretical* regression line that cannot be observed. This means that B_0, B_1, and e cannot be observed. B_0 and B_1 are often called the true values of the intercept and coefficient, because they represent the values we would find if we recorded every single data point possible and used them to find the regression line. Usually we just have a sample, or some of the data points available. We want to use econometrics to estimate B_0 and B_1 so that we can estimate the regression line. To do this, we must first find sample values for X and Y.

Over the past year, Quinn has kept track of how much she spent on DVDs and also what she earned each month. There is an income number and a DVD expenditure number that go together for each month; each month can be called an observation. In general, an **observation** is a set of numbers for different variables that work together; they can be for one time period, person, country, firm, or other entity. For each month Quinn has collected data, there is an income number and an amount she spent on DVDs that make up each observation. The 12 months of data represent a sample from the months that have gone by since Quinn got her DVD player. This information is plotted in Figure 1-2.

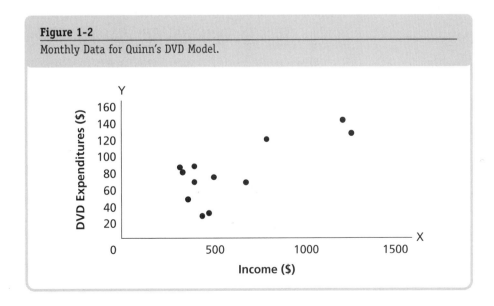

Figure 1-2

Monthly Data for Quinn's DVD Model.

These data are called **time-series data** because the data follow one person, country, firm, or other entity across different time periods.[2] **Cross-section data** give information for many people, countries, firms, or entities for the *same* period of time. If we wanted to build a model with cross-section data for this example, we would collect income and DVD expenditure data for different people in the same month.

There appears to be a positive relationship between income and DVD expenditures in Figure 1-2. That is, when one variable is larger, the other variable also tends to be larger, and when one variable is smaller, the other one tends to be smaller. Quinn's income and DVD expenditures seem to move together. This is what we expected. Quinn would like to understand this relationship between income and DVD expenditures more scientifically. To do this, we can estimate the regression line shown by Equation (1-2). That will give us the line that best fits the points as shown in Figure 1-2. This line can also be expressed as an equation:

$$\hat{Y} = \hat{B}_0 + \hat{B}_1 X \qquad\qquad (1\text{-}3)$$

The "hats" on $\hat{B}_0$ and $\hat{B}_1$ show that they are estimates of the true values of the intercept B_0 and slope B_1. (Recall that these true values cannot be observed.) The hat on $\hat{Y}$ indicates that $\hat{Y}$ is not the *actual* value of the dependent variable Y, but the value *predicted* for that observation by the estimated regression equation $\hat{B}_0 + \hat{B}_1 X$. $\hat{Y}$ is called the predicted value for Y ($\hat{Y}$ is read "Y-hat"). It is also called the fitted value because it fits exactly on the estimated regression line.

Figure 1-3 adds an estimated regression line for the points shown in Figure 1-2; it is drawn using the estimated intercept coefficient $\hat{B}_0$ and the estimated slope coefficient

---

[2] One piece of data is called a datum. Note that the word "data" is plural. It is incorrect to write "the data in Figure 1-2 is time-series data." It should be "the data in Figure 1-2 are time-series data" instead.

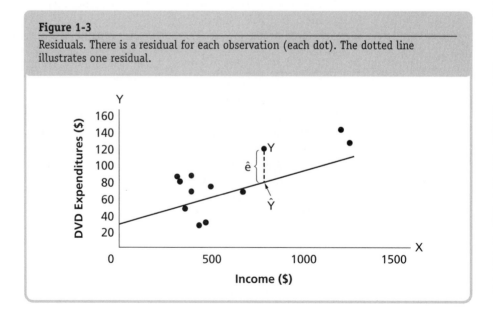

Figure 1-3

Residuals. There is a residual for each observation (each dot). The dotted line illustrates one residual.

$\hat{B}_1$. The estimated regression line shows a linear relationship between Quinn's income and DVD expenditures, but the relationship is not perfect. The data points do not all lie on the line; there are errors. The amount of expenditures predicted by the regression line is usually different from Quinn's actual expenditures. For each data point, the actual value of the dependent variable Y is shown by the height of the dot. This is the actual amount spent on DVDs when Quinn earned the amount of income shown on the X-axis. The height of the line shows the predicted value of DVD expenditures $\hat{Y}$ (the amount predicted by $\hat{B}_0 + \hat{B}_1 X$) given a value of X for that month or observation. The difference, $Y - \hat{Y} = \hat{e}$, is the observed error term, also called the **residual**. In Figure 1-3, if the data point lies above the estimated regression line, the residual $\hat{e}$ has a positive value. If it lies below the estimated regression line, $\hat{e}$ is negative. Residuals can be seen only after the regression line is estimated; think of them as observed values for the error term. Since the word *residual* means "left over," it is used here because the residual is that part of the dependent variable Y that cannot be explained by the regression line. It is left over.

1-3 ORDINARY LEAST SQUARES: THE BEST WAY TO DRAW THE LINE

The next step is to figure out the best way to draw the estimated regression line. We could plot the points and just eyeball the line, drawing the one that seems to fit the data points best. This would not be very scientific, though, and might not give us the best line. (It would also put all econometricians out of work!) It makes sense that the best line will be one that minimizes the size of the residuals, since residuals represent errors. The question is how to measure the size of the residuals across all observations for the whole regression. One simple way to do it would be to just add up the residuals and use this sum as a measure of how good the regression line is. A mathematical method could then be developed to pick the line that gives the smallest sum of residuals, and that would be considered the best estimated regression line for the data given. However, there's a big problem with this idea. Negative and positive residuals will cancel each other out. Suppose you have an estimated regression line with large positive residuals, but the line also has large negative residuals that are the same size. The sum of these residuals could come out close to zero, fooling you into thinking you have found the best estimated regression line when what you are really dealing with is large residuals.

Another possibility is to use the sum of the absolute values of the residuals. Doing this would turn all negative residuals into positive values, so that the negative and positive numbers would not cancel each other out. This makes sense, but because mathematics involving absolute values is complex, theoretical econometricians would have a tougher time as they try to discover new ways of doing things in econometrics.

A third possibility is to use the sum of the squared residuals to determine the best line. Since the value of a squared residual will always be positive, there is no problem with the positive and negative values of the residual canceling each other out, and there is no need to use the absolute value. The best estimated regression line is one that minimizes the sum of $\hat{e}^2$ ($\hat{e}^2$ summed over all observations). To find the best line, we need values for coefficient estimates $\hat{B}_0$ and $\hat{B}_1$ that minimize the sum of $\hat{e}^2$; this method of estimating regression lines is called **ordinary least squares (OLS)**. To see how this is done, we start with $\hat{e} = Y - \hat{Y}$. Next, using $\hat{Y} = \hat{B}_0 + \hat{B}_1X$ [Equation (1-3)], we substitute $\hat{B}_0 + \hat{B}_1X$ in for $\hat{Y}$ in to get $\hat{e} = Y - \hat{Y} = Y - \hat{B}_0 - \hat{B}_1X$. This means that

$$\hat{e}^2 = (Y - \hat{B}_0 - \hat{B}_1X)^2 \qquad (1\text{-}4)$$

Ordinary least squares finds the best estimated regression line by picking estimates $\hat{B}_0$ and $\hat{B}_1$ that minimize the sum of Equation (1-4) for all observations in the sample. This is the same as saying that OLS finds the line that minimizes the sum of the vertical $\hat{e}$ distances shown in Figure 1-3 when we square the distance for each observation.

Finding the OLS Slope and Intercept Estimates

Equations (1-5) and (1-6) show how the ordinary least squares method finds the slope estimate $\hat{B}_1$ and the intercept estimate $\hat{B}_0$ for a regression model that contains just one independent variable.

$$\hat{B}_1 = \frac{\text{sum of } (X - \overline{X}) \cdot (Y - \overline{Y}) \text{ added over all observations}}{\text{sum of } (X - \overline{X})^2 \text{ added over all observations}} \qquad (1\text{-}5)$$

$$\hat{B}_0 = \overline{Y} - \hat{B}_1\overline{X} \qquad (1\text{-}6)$$

Consider Equation (1-5) first.

- $\overline{X}$ and $\overline{Y}$ are the means of X and Y from the data sample.
- $(X - \overline{X})$ measures the distance or deviation that each X has from its mean.
- $(Y - \overline{Y})$ measures the same thing for Y.
- The numerator, $(X - \overline{X}) \cdot (Y - \overline{Y})$, measures the deviations of both X and Y.

Let's suppose that X and Y move together in the same direction. In this case, Y will tend to be greater than its average ($\overline{Y}$) at the same time X is greater than its average ($\overline{X}$), making $(X - \overline{X}) \cdot (Y - \overline{Y})$ a positive number. We are assuming that Y and X move together, so Y and X will both tend to be below their averages at the same time. Since a negative number multiplied by a negative number gives a positive number, once again $(X - \overline{X}) \cdot (Y - \overline{Y})$ will turn out positive. Therefore, when X and Y tend to move in the same direction, the top of Equation (1-5) will be positive for most observations. Since the bottom is squared and will always be positive, $\hat{B}_1$ will turn out to be a positive number.

Now suppose X and Y tend to move in opposite directions. Then one variable will tend to be above its mean when the other is below its mean. If $(X - \overline{X})$ is positive, $(Y - \overline{Y})$ will tend to be negative. If $(X - \overline{X})$ is negative, $(Y - \overline{Y})$ tends to be positive. This means that $(X - \overline{X}) \cdot (Y - \overline{Y})$ will usually be negative. When $(X - \overline{X}) \cdot (Y - \overline{Y})$ is summed over all observations in Equation (1-5), it will tend to be negative, and $\hat{B}_1$ will turn out to be a negative number.

The denominator in Equation (1-5), $(X - \overline{X})^2$, is the variance of X, and it measures whether X moves around its mean a lot or a little. It adjusts the value of $\hat{B}_1$ for the fact that if X varies around its mean by large amounts, then small movements in X and Y reflected in the numerator by $(X - \overline{X}) \cdot (Y - \overline{Y})$ are not as important. $\hat{B}_1$ will be smaller, compared to the case where the numerator is the same as before but X moves around its mean by smaller amounts.

Once a value for $\hat{B}_1$ is calculated, we use Equation (1-6) to find the intercept estimate $\hat{B}_0$. Equation (1-6) makes sure that the means of X and Y both fall on the estimated regression line. When Equations (1-5) and (1-6) are used to calculate $\hat{B}_1$ and $\hat{B}_0$ for a simple regression model (one independent variable), the sum of squared residuals will be minimized. The mathematics used to derive Equations (1-5) and (1-6) are set out in detail in Section 1-4 for those of you who are familiar with calculus.

The DVD model will be used to demonstrate how Equations (1-5) and (1-6) work. The only time you will see a regression calculated by hand is when you are just beginning your study of econometrics and are learning how ordinary least squares works. Regressions are not normally calculated by hand; that's what computers are for. However, seeing how we calculate the slope and intercept estimates without a computer will help you understand ordinary least squares.

Table 1-A gives the data for Quinn's DVD expenditures and her income; columns 4–7 will help us find $\hat{B}_0$ and $\hat{B}_1$. These are the same data that are plotted in Figures 1-2 and 1-3.

Table 1-A

Calculations for Quinn's DVD Expenditures Model

1	2	3	4	5	6	7
Month	Y (DVDEXP)	X (INCOME)	$Y - \bar{Y}$	$X - \bar{X}$	$(Y - \bar{Y})(X - \bar{X})$	$(X - \bar{X})(X - \bar{X})$
September	26.41	440	−52.71	−160	8,433.60	25,600
October	50.28	360	−28.84	−240	6,921.60	57,600
November	86.08	400	6.96	−200	−1,392.00	40,000
December	84.61	320	5.49	−280	−1,537.20	78,400
January	70.30	680	−8.82	80	−705.60	6,400
February	66.43	400	−12.69	−200	2,538.00	40,000
March	79.16	336	0.04	−264	−10.56	69,696
April	73.04	504	−6.08	−96	583.68	9,216
May	29.57	480	−49.55	−120	5,946.00	14,400
June	124.99	1,264	45.87	664	30,457.68	440,896
July	140.97	1,216	61.85	616	38,099.60	379,456
August	117.62	800	38.50	200	7,700.00	40,000
Sum	949.44	7,200	0	0	97,034.80	1,201,664
Mean	79.12	600	0	0		

Columns 2 and 3 give the data; Y and X are both summed at the bottom of their columns. These sums are then divided by the number of observations (12) to find the means of Y and X. Twelve observations is a small number for a regression; you will typically get better estimates from your regressions if you use larger samples.

First, we use Equation (1-5) to calculate $\hat{B}_1$. We need to calculate $(X - \bar{X}) \cdot (Y - \bar{Y})$ for each observation so that $(X - \bar{X}) \cdot (Y - \bar{Y})$ can be summed over all 12 observations for use in the numerator in Equation (1-5). Column 4 shows $(Y - \bar{Y})$ for each observation, calculated using the mean of Y from the bottom of column 2. Column 5 shows $(X - \bar{X})$ for each observation. Column 6 shows $(X - \bar{X}) \cdot (Y - \bar{Y})$, found by multiplying the entries for columns 4 and 5 for each observation. The sum of $(X - \bar{X}) \cdot (Y - \bar{Y})$ for all observations is shown at the bottom of column 6. It is this number (97,034.80) that is used in the top part of Equation (1-5) to calculate $\hat{B}_1$.

For the denominator of Equation (1-5), we need the sum of $(X - \bar{X})^2$ over all observations. This is shown in column 7; the entries in column 7 are found by squaring each entry in column 5. The sum of $(X - \bar{X})^2$ over all 12 observations is shown at the bottom of column 7. This number (1,201,664) is the bottom half of Equation (1-5), so we now have all we need to calculate $\hat{B}_1$.

$$\hat{B}_1 = \frac{\text{sum of } (X - \bar{X}) \cdot (Y - \bar{Y}) \text{ over all observations}}{\text{sum of } (X - \bar{X})^2 \text{ over all observations}} = \frac{97,034.80}{1,201,664} = 0.081$$

Now that we have an estimate for the slope, an estimate for the intercept can be found using Equation (1-6). $\bar{Y}$ and $\bar{X}$ are from Table 1-A.

$$\hat{B}_0 = \bar{Y} - \hat{B}_1\bar{X} = 79.12 - (0.081 \cdot 600) = 30.52$$

The estimated regression line can be expressed as

$$\hat{Y} = \hat{B}_0 + \hat{B}_1X = 30.52 + 0.081 \cdot X \tag{1-7}$$

This is the line shown in Figure 1-3. Here is what the 0.081 slope estimate means: If Quinn's income increases by a dollar one month, on average we would expect her DVD expenditures to increase by 0.081 dollars, or 8 cents.[3] The 30.52 intercept can be interpreted literally as meaning that we can expect Quinn to spend an average of $30.52, if she has no income that month (if X is zero). Do not put too much emphasis on this interpretation of the intercept, however. It would be a mistake to assume that the relationship between Quinn's income and her DVD expenditures will remain linear when her income is zero or approaches zero. In other words, the regression line will probably not predict the situation correctly in a low-income month. If you look at Table 1-A, the lowest income Quinn earned during the 12-month sample period was $320 (December). There

---

[3] Suppose the value of X_1 increases by one unit from one observation to the next. Because of the error term e, it is unlikely that the change in Y between the two observations will be exactly equal to B_1. That is why it's useful to think of B_1 as the *average* change in the dependent variable we can expect when X_1 changes by one unit.

was no month in which she had zero or close to zero income. Thus, it would be a mistake to think that the $30.52 gives us an accurate estimate of what she will spend on DVDs if she has no income, since that situation does not occur in this data sample. In general, the value of the intercept estimate should not be given much importance.

Now let's look at some predicted values or $\hat{Y}$'s. In April, Quinn earned $504. With that income, our estimated regression line predicts new DVD spending to be:

$$\hat{Y} = \hat{B}_0 + \hat{B}_1 X = 30.52 + 0.081 \cdot X = 30.52 + 0.081 \cdot 504 = 71.34$$

She actually spent $73.04 (see Table 1-A for April). The residual, or observed error term, for this observation is $\hat{e} = Y - \hat{Y} = \$73.04 - 71.34 = \$1.70$. The estimated regression line does a good job of predicting how much Quinn spent, given that she earned $504. Let's try another month, May, when Quinn's income was $480. Now the predicted value is

$$\hat{Y} = \hat{B}_0 + \hat{B}_1 X = 30.52 + 0.081 \cdot 480 = 69.40$$

Looking up May in Table 1-A, we see that Quinn actually spent $29.57 on DVDs. Here the residual is $\hat{e} = Y - \hat{Y} = \$29.57 - 69.40 = -\$39.83$. The model does not do a very good job predicting Quinn's DVD expenditures for May, even though it works well for April. (We will discuss statistics for measuring the overall performance of a regression model as well as forecasting for future time periods in later chapters).

In both November and February, Quinn's monthly income was $400. With a $400 income, the estimated regression line predicts her DVD expenditures will be

$$\hat{Y} = \hat{B}_0 + \hat{B}_1 X = 30.52 + 0.081 \cdot 400 = 62.92$$

Table 1-A tells us that Quinn spent $86.08 on DVDs in November and $66.43 in February, even though her income was the same for both months. This illustrates the point made earlier, that Y is a random variable. The randomness represented by the error term means that the dependent variable will not necessarily take the same value, even when X takes the same value in more than one observation.

Total, Explained, and Residual Sum of Squares

A regression model can explain some of the movement in the dependent variable, but not all of it. In Quinn's DVDs model, we can predict that Quinn will spend more on DVDs when she earns more income, and that she'll cut back her spending when she earns less. We even have an idea of how much her spending on DVDs will change as her income changes. We can use our model to explain movements in her DVD expenditures, but it doesn't work perfectly (as we saw earlier).

The movement or variation in the dependent variable can be broken into two parts: the part explained by the regression equation, and the rest, which is not explained (this part is captured by the error term). The total movement in the dependent variable is usually measured by $(Y - \bar{Y})^2$ summed over all observations; this is called the **total sum of squares (TSS)**. The total sum of squares can then be split into the two parts mentioned above: the movement in Y that is explained by the regression equation, called the **explained sum of squares (ESS)**, and the movement in Y that is not explained, called the **residual sum of squares (RSS)**.

$$\text{sum of } (Y - \overline{Y})^2 = \text{sum of } (Y - \hat{Y})^2 + \text{sum of } (\hat{Y} - \overline{Y})^2$$

$$\begin{array}{ccccc} \text{total sum of} & = & \text{residual sum of} & + & \text{explained sum of} \\ \text{squares (TSS)} & & \text{squares (RSS)} & & \text{squares (ESS)} \end{array}$$

(1-8)

where "sum of . . ." indicates that the term that follows is summed over all observations in the sample.

The total sum of squares $(Y - \overline{Y})^2$ is based on the distance between the actual value of Y for each observation and the mean value, $\overline{Y}$. Think of this $(Y - \overline{Y})$ distance as consisting of two parts: the distance from the actual value of the dependent variable to the predicted value $(Y - \hat{Y})$ and the distance from the predicted value of the dependent variable to the mean $(\hat{Y} - \overline{Y})$. These two parts add to $(Y - \overline{Y})$.

$$(Y - \hat{Y}) + (\hat{Y} - \overline{Y}) = (Y - \overline{Y}) \tag{1-9}$$

These distances, $(Y - \hat{Y})$, $(\hat{Y} - \overline{Y})$, and $(Y - \overline{Y})$, are shown in Figure 1-4 for one observation. Think of Figure 1-4 as a graphical representation of Equation (1-9).

The $(Y - \hat{Y})$ distance is the part of the total $(Y - \overline{Y})$ distance that is not explained by the regression equation. This makes sense because $(Y - \hat{Y})$ is also the definition of the residual; it is the difference between what actually happened and what the model predicts. The square of each $(Y - \hat{Y})$ is then summed for all observations to find the residual sum of squares.

As we noted earlier, the $(\hat{Y} - \overline{Y})$ distance is the distance Y takes from its mean that is explained by the regression equation. This makes the sum of $(\hat{Y} - \overline{Y})^2$ the *explained*

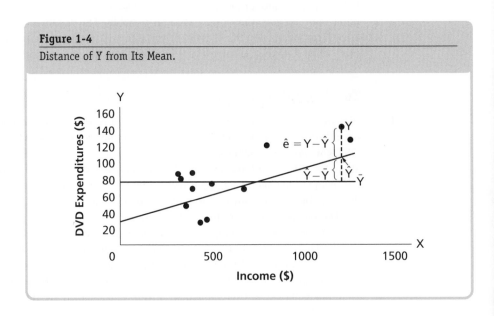

Figure 1-4

Distance of Y from Its Mean.

sum of squares. The total, explained, and residual sums of squares are useful for measuring the performance of a regression model, and we will used them in later chapters. You are asked to calculate these measures for Quinn's DVD model in an exercise at the end of this chapter.

SUMMARY

1. Econometrics uses data to estimate relationships between different variables.
2. A regression line can be written as $Y = B_0 + B_1 X + e$.
   - X are Y are both **variables** because they are not constant.
   - Y is the **dependent variable** because the equation implies that the value of Y depends on the value of X.
   - X is an **independent variable** because the values of X are considered to be independent of the rest of the equation; the equation does not explain why X takes the values it does. (X is also called an **explanatory variable** because it helps explain or predict the values of Y.)
   - B_0 and B_1 are called **coefficients** to indicate they represent constant numbers.
   - B_0 is the intercept of the line. The intercept shows the value Y will take if X is zero, but the intercept of a regression line should not be given much importance.
   - B_1 is the slope of the line. The slope shows the change in Y that occurs for a one-unit change in X.
   - The error term e shows that the regression line does not predict the value of the dependent variable Y perfectly. e must be included to account for the part of the Y value that is not explained by the rest of the model. The error term is not a constant number.
3. Even if a model is set up and estimated correctly, the error term e is necessary for three reasons:
   - Measurement error can occur—variables are not always measured accurately.
   - There will always be small or secondary factors that are too small to measure and include in the model, but they still influence the dependent variable.
   - Random variation is a fact of life.
4. Econometrics cannot *prove* that changes in X actually *cause* Y to change. Correlation may be coincidence, or the model may not be accounting for other factors that cause Y to change.
5. The theoretical regression line represented by $Y = B_0 + B_1 X + e$ cannot be observed. This means that B_0, B_1, and e cannot be observed. B_0 and B_1 are often called the true values of the intercept and slope. Econometrics is used to find $\hat{B}_0$ and $\hat{B}_1$, which are estimates of B_0 and B_1.
6. **Time-series data** follow one person, country, firm, or other entity across different time periods. **Cross-section data** give information for many people, countries, firms, or entities for the same period of time.
7. $\hat{Y}$ is the predicted value for Y. It is also called the fitted value because it fits exactly on the estimated regression line. It is found by using the equation $\hat{Y} = \hat{B}_0 + \hat{B}_1 X$.

8. $\hat{e}$ is the observed error term, also called the **residual**. It is found from $Y - \hat{Y} = \hat{e}$ and represents the difference between the actual value of the dependent variable and the value predicted by the regression equation.

9. Regression lines are typically estimated by finding estimates of B_0 and B_1 that minimize the sum of squared residuals. This method is called **ordinary least squares (OLS)**. The OLS slope and intercept estimates are found with Equations (1-5) and (1-6).

10. The **total sum of squares (TSS)**—total movement in the dependent variable—is found by summing $(Y - \bar{Y})^2$ over all observations. ($\bar{Y}$ is the mean of Y.) TSS can be broken into two parts: the **explained sum of squares (ESS)**, movement in Y explained by the regression model, and the **residual sum of squares (RSS)**, movement in Y not explained by the model. ESS is found by summing $(\hat{Y} - \bar{Y})^2$ over all observations. RSS is found by summing $(Y - \hat{Y})^2$ over all observations.

EXERCISES

1. Try to explain these terms without looking them up.
   - econometric model
   - coefficient
   - variable
   - dependent variable
   - independent variable
   - explanatory variable
   - simple regression model
   - stochastic
   - observation
   - time-series data
   - cross-section
   - residual
   - ordinary least squares
   - total sum of squares
   - explained sum of squares
   - residual sum of squares

2. In Quinn's DVD model, the slope estimate for the independent variable (income) is 0.081. How would you explain what this number means to someone who isn't taking the class?

3. In Chapter 2 we expand on Quinn's DVD model to include more than one independent variable. What other independent variables would you add to the model that might help predict Quinn's DVD expenditures? Explain why you think your variables might be important.

4. Think of something you do in your everyday life that you would like to estimate using a regression model. (Make sure it is different from the examples given in the chapter.) What is your dependent variable? What is your independent variable? (If more than one independent variable seems important, that's fine; Chapter 2 will show you how to set up regressions with more than one independent variable.)

5. Explain the difference between
    a. B_1 and $\hat{B}_1$
    b. e and ê
    c. Y and $\hat{Y}$
6. a. Why do regression models need an error term?
    b. See if you can write down the three main sources of the error term without looking in the text.
7. a. Suppose you've been tracking some data to use in the Captain Hero shop model discussed at the beginning of this chapter. You go to the same sandwich shop every day, and record the number of people in line and how long it takes you to get your sandwich. Use the data below to calculate the intercept and slope estimates for a regression model where Y is the time it takes to get your sandwich and X is the number of people ahead of you in line when you arrive at the shop. (Make a table similar to Table 1-A.).

Observation	Y	X
1	5	0
2	13	2
3	4	0
4	6	1
5	20	4
6	31	6
7	18	3
8	15	2
9	7	1
10	14	2

    b. What does the slope estimate mean?
8. a. What does "least" mean in the term *ordinary least squares*?
    b. What does "squares" mean in this term?
    c. Why does ordinary least squares work better than finding the line that minimizes the sum of the errors?
9. a. In the chapter, it is noted that the intercept estimate should not be given much importance. Why is this?
    b. If the estimate of the intercept is not important, why is it included in the regression equation? Draw a graph showing a regression line with an intercept and one without an intercept.
10. a. Use the data in Table 1-A to calculate the percentage of income spent on DVDs for the 12-month period.

    b. Equation (1-7) shows the estimate of the slope coefficient as 0.081. Why doesn't this estimate match your answer to part a?

11. It's easier to calculate an average than to estimate a whole regression model. In order to predict DVD expenditures or any other dependent variable, why not just calculate the average value for the variable, instead of running a regression model?

12. The data for Quinn's DVD model are time-series data, since the model tracks data for the same person at different points in time. Here are cross-section data for 30 different students who buy DVDs.

Observation	DVDEXP	INCOME
1	9.70	600
2	19.90	720
3	49.24	1120
4	9.26	455
5	30.94	974
6	38.39	880
7	33.10	422
8	26.76	1120
9	47.30	580
10	43.87	982
11	44.07	754
12	49.44	699
13	27.75	824
14	20.76	745
15	47.27	934
16	9.58	432
17	29.50	1023
18	14.30	623
19	22.73	798
20	24.61	687
21	26.47	987

Observation	DVDEXP	INCOME
22	18.09	863
23	42.44	642
24	15.30	475
25	38.19	685
26	32.66	865
27	50.93	983
28	27.24	465
29	30.24	783
30	30.67	854

    a. Estimate a DVD expenditure model using these cross-section data and an econometrics software program.

    b. How do the intercept and slope coefficients you found in part a compare to those found in this chapter?

13. a. Find fitted values and residuals for the 12 observations used in Quinn's DVD model.

    b. What is the mean residual?

14. a. Find the ESS, RSS, and TSS for the results from Quinn's DVD model.

    b. What part of the total sum of squares is explained by the regression model? (This concept, that the model explains a part of the total sum of squares, will be important in Chapter 3.)

APPENDIX

1-4 DERIVING OLS ESTIMATES FOR A SIMPLE REGRESSION MODEL

Our goal is to find equations that will give us a slope and intercept estimate that minimizes the sum of squared residuals. As discussed in Section 1-3, we need to find equations for $\hat{B}_0$ and $\hat{B}_1$ that minimize the sum of Equation (1-4), $\hat{e}^2 = (Y - \hat{B}_0 - \hat{B}_1 X)^2$, added over all observations in the sample. Calculus is useful here. By taking the partial derivative of the sum of $(Y - \hat{B}_0 - \hat{B}_1 X)^2$ with respect to $\hat{B}_1$, we can find the equation that gives us a value for $\hat{B}_1$ that minimizes the sum of squared residuals. This is where Equation (1-5) comes from. Similarly, Equation (1-6), the equation for finding $\hat{B}_0$, is derived by taking the derivative of the sum of $(Y - \hat{B}_0 - \hat{B}_1 X)^2$ with respect to $\hat{B}_0$. Below, the summation symbol Σ indicates that everything to the right of it is to be summed over all observations in the sample.

We start the derivation by taking partial derivatives and setting them equal to zero, as is usually done in calculus problems of this type [Equations (1-10) and (1-11)].

$$\frac{\partial}{\partial \hat{B}_0} \sum (Y - \hat{B}_0 - \hat{B}_1 X)^2 = -2 \sum (Y - \hat{B}_0 - \hat{B}_1 X) = 0 \qquad \textbf{(1-10)}$$

$$\frac{\partial}{\partial \hat{B}_1} \sum (Y - \hat{B}_0 - \hat{B}_1 X)^2 = -2 \sum X(Y - \hat{B}_0 - \hat{B}_1 X) = 0 \qquad \textbf{(1-11)}$$

Next, in Equations (1-12) and (1-13), both sides of both equations are divided by -2.

$$\sum (Y - \hat{B}_0 - \hat{B}_1 X) = 0 \qquad \textbf{(1-12)}$$

$$\sum X(Y - \hat{B}_0 - \hat{B}_1 X) = 0 \qquad \textbf{(1-13)}$$

When a constant number is summed over all observations, it is equal to the constant multiplied by the number of observations. For example, if there are 20 observations, and $\hat{B}_0 = 5$, then $\Sigma \hat{B}_0 = 20 \cdot 5 = 100$. In general, $\Sigma \hat{B}_0 = n \cdot \hat{B}_0$, where n is the number of observations. Also, when a variable is multiplied by a constant number, the constant can be taken outside the summation sign. For example, $\Sigma(5X) = 5\Sigma X$, so $\Sigma(\hat{B}_1 X) = \hat{B}_1 \Sigma X$. (Remember that $\hat{B}_0$ and $\hat{B}_1$ represent constant numbers.) Next, the summation sign Σ is applied to each term in Equations (1-14) and (1-15). Note that in Equation (1-15) the X, which was outside the parentheses in Equation (1-13), has been multiplied by all the terms inside the parentheses, making the parentheses unnecessary.

$$\sum Y - n\hat{B}_0 - \hat{B}_1 \sum X = 0 \qquad \textbf{(1-14)}$$

$$\sum XY - \hat{B}_0 \sum X - \hat{B}_1 \sum X^2 = 0 \qquad \textbf{(1-15)}$$

Moving the terms with negative signs to the right-hand side gives us Equations (1-16) and (1-17).

$$\sum Y = n\hat{B}_0 + \hat{B}_1 \sum X \qquad \textbf{(1-16)}$$

$$\sum XY = \hat{B}_0 \sum X + \hat{B}_1 \sum X^2 \qquad \textbf{(1-17)}$$

Equations (1-16) and (1-17) are called normal equations. Now we want to solve Equations (1-16) and (1-17) simultaneously for $\hat{B}_0$ and $\hat{B}_1$. Our first step is to multiply both sides of Equation (1-16) by ΣX. This gives us Equation (1-18).

$$\sum X \sum Y = n\hat{B}_0 \sum X + \hat{B}_1 \left(\sum X \right)^2 \qquad \textbf{(1-18)}$$

Then we multiply both sides of Equation (1-17) by n; this gives us Equation (1-19).

$$n\sum XY = n\hat{B}_0\sum X + n\hat{B}_1\sum X^2 \tag{1-19}$$

Now we subtract Equation (1-18) from Equation (1-19), which gives us $n\Sigma XY - \Sigma X\Sigma Y$ on the left-hand side. On the right-hand side we have

$$n\hat{B}_0\sum X + n\hat{B}_1\sum X^2 - \left[n\hat{B}_0\sum X + \hat{B}_1\left(\sum X\right)^2\right] = n\hat{B}_1\sum X^2 - \hat{B}_1\left(\sum X\right)^2$$

$$= \hat{B}_1\left[n\sum X^2 - \left(\sum X\right)^2\right].$$

The complete equation is

$$n\sum XY - \sum X\sum Y = \hat{B}_1\left[n\sum X^2 - \left(\sum X\right)^2\right] \tag{1-20}$$

In Equation (1-20), all the $\hat{B}_0$ terms cancel each other out, so we can solve for $\hat{B}_1$.

$$\hat{B}_1 = \frac{n\sum XY - \sum X\sum Y}{n\sum X^2 - \left(\sum X\right)^2} \tag{1-21}$$

Now we divide the numerator and denominator in Equation (1-21) by n.

$$\hat{B}_1 = \frac{\sum XY - \dfrac{\sum X\sum Y}{n}}{\sum X^2 - \dfrac{\left(\sum X\right)^2}{n}} \tag{1-22}$$

Using the definition of the mean ($\overline{X} = \Sigma X/n$ and $\overline{Y} = \Sigma Y/n$), along with some algebraic manipulation, Equation (1-22) becomes

$$\hat{B}_1 = \frac{\sum(X - \overline{X})(Y - \overline{Y})}{\sum(X - \overline{X})^2} \tag{1-23}$$

Equation (1-23) is the same as Equation (1-5), given earlier as the equation for $\hat{B}_1$.

Now to find $\hat{B}_0$, we start with Equation (1-16) and rearrange it so that the term with $\hat{B}_0$ appears by itself on the left-hand side.

$$n\hat{B}_0 = \sum Y - \hat{B}_1\sum X \tag{1-24}$$

Next we divide both sides of Equation (1-24) by n and use the definition of the mean to substitute for $\Sigma X/n$ and $\Sigma Y/n$.

$$\hat{B}_0 = \frac{\sum Y}{n} - \hat{B}_1\frac{\sum X}{n} = \overline{Y} - \hat{B}_1\overline{X} \tag{1-25}$$

Equation (1-25) is the same as Equation (1-6).

2

Ordinary Least Squares, Part 2

After reading this chapter, you will know:

- How to set up and interpret a regression model that contains more than one independent variable.

- The assumptions that must hold true for the OLS method to work well.

- The characteristics of ordinary least squares.

Most regression models have more than one independent variable. In the first section of this chapter we expand the simple regression model presented in Chapter 1 to include more than one independent variable. In Section 2-2 we present and explain the classical assumptions of ordinary least squares. These assumptions are really conditions that are necessary for the OLS method to work properly. When the assumptions hold true, ordinary least squares has some desirable characteristics; we discuss these characteristics in the final section of this chapter.

2-1 MULTIPLE REGRESSION MODELS: WHAT DO THE B's MEAN?

In Chapter 1 we set up a regression model that used Quinn's monthly income to explain her DVD expenditures. It's unlikely that Quinn's DVD expenditures can be predicted by her income alone; there are probably other factors we can include that would improve the model. Fortunately, we can add independent variables to our model to account for these other factors. A regression model with more than one independent variable is called a **multiple or multivariate regression model**. In general, it looks like

$$Y = B_0 + B_1X_1 + B_2X_2 + B_3X_3 + \cdots + B_kX_k + e \qquad \text{(2-1)}$$

The X's with subscripts 1–k are different independent variables. The letter k represents the number of independent variables in the model. The number of independent variables will differ from model to model. B_0 is the intercept, as before. All the other B's are slope coefficients. Each one represents the average change in the dependent variable we can expect when its independent variable changes by one unit, keeping the remaining independent variables constant.[1] Suppose we incorporate the average price of DVDs as another independent variable in our example so that the model is now $Y = B_0 + B_1X_1 + B_2X_2 + e$. ($X_1$ is Quinn's monthly income and X_2 is the average DVD price.) B_1 is the average change in the dependent variable that we can expect when X_1 (Quinn's monthly income) changes by one unit, keeping X_2 (the average DVD price) the same. B_2 is the average change in DVD expenditures we can expect when X_2 (average price) changes by one dollar keeping X_1 (Quinn's monthly income) the same. This idea—that we interpret each slope coefficient as measuring the isolated effect of its independent variable while keeping the other independent variables constant—is important. We will illustrate this key idea by adding other independent variables to our DVD expenditures model.

Let's think about what other independent variables might be important in determining Quinn's DVD expenditures. As mentioned above, the average price of DVDs is likely to affect the amount she spends on them. Quinn knows that she watches DVDs more often when it's raining, so in rainy months she also buys more DVDs. Therefore, the total monthly rainfall in Quinn's town is another likely candidate for an independent variable in our model.

Deciding which independent variables to use is an important part of creating regression models. We discuss this task in more detail in Chapter 4. Also, some regression models are more complicated than the linear models we've been using. Choosing which independent variables belong in a model, along with what form the model should take, is called the specification of the model.

The notation that is used to write the new version of our model can be simplified. It can get confusing to use X_1, X_2, X_3 to symbolize independent variables in a research paper or other work, because readers will forget what variable each X stands for. Here is a more convenient system: Give the dependent and independent variables nicknames that describe what they are. These nicknames are written in capital letters to signify that they are variables. So, Quinn's multiple DVD model can be written

$$DVDEXP = B_0 + B_1INCOME + B_2PRICE + B_3RAINFALL + e \quad \text{(2-2)}$$

where
> DVDEXP = amount Quinn spends each month on DVDs, in dollars
> INCOME = Quinn's monthly income, in dollars
> PRICE = average DVD price in dollars
> RAINFALL = total monthly rainfall in Quinn's town, in inches

It's important to define very precisely what each variable means, so that anyone reading your work will understand exactly what each variable measures. For the definitions of DVDEXP, INCOME, and PRICE, it is explicitly stated that they are in dollars because sometimes variables that involve money are also defined as being in hundreds

---

[1] Suppose the value of X_1 increases by one unit from one observation to the next, but the other independent variables don't change. Because of the error term e, it's unlikely that the change in Y between the two observations will exactly equal B_1. That is why it is useful to think of B_1 as the *average* change in the dependent variable we can expect when X_1 changes by one unit, keeping the other independent variables constant. This is the same idea as presented in Chapter 1, only now there are other independent variables in the regression that are being held constant.

Table 2-A

Data for Quinn's Multiple DVD Model

Month	DVDEXP	INCOME	PRICE	RAINFALL
September	26.41	440	28.98	3.0
October	50.28	360	27.98	0.8
November	86.08	400	17.99	4.7
December	84.61	320	21.69	4.0
January	70.30	680	21.24	3.7
February	66.43	400	26.49	5.5
March	79.16	336	16.48	4.5
April	73.04	504	18.99	1.9
May	29.57	480	23.99	2.4
June	124.99	1,264	23.46	5.7
July	140.97	1,216	17.99	4.1
August	117.62	800	22.99	4.5

or thousands of dollars. For example, a variable that represents the average house price might be defined in thousands of dollars. A variable that represents state population might be defined in millions of people. Equation (2-2) can be stated verbally as "DVD-EXP is regressed on INCOME, PRICE, and RAINFALL."

Table 2-A shows data for PRICE and RAINFALL that we will use along with the DVDEXP and INCOME data from Table 1-A to estimate the new version of the model. Quinn collected the PRICE and RAINFALL data for the same months as the DVDEXP and INCOME data. As noted in Chapter 1, we would probably get better estimates from our regression if we had more than 12 observations.

Estimating and Interpreting a Multiple Regression Model

A multiple regression model cannot be drawn as a line on a two-dimensional graph as done in Figure 1-3 for the simple regression model. Figure 1-3 plots the dependent variable on the vertical Y-axis, and the single independent variable on the X-axis. Now that our regression model contains several independent variables, there is no way we can plot it on a two-dimensional graph. Once a model has two or more independent variables, it is no longer a regression *line*; it's a regression *shape* that cannot be drawn in two dimensions. A model with two independent variables could be drawn as a shape

Table 2-B

OLS Results for Quinn's Multiple
DVD Model

Dependent Variable: DVDEXP

Variable	Coefficient
Constant	89.09
INCOME	0.064
PRICE	−3.18
RAINFALL	6.05

Observations: 12

in a three-dimensional graph. However, if the model has more than two independent variables (which is common), the shape can't be drawn even in a three-dimensional graph. We could instead draw a series of graphs, with the dependent variable on the vertical axis as always, and a different independent variable on the horizontal axis in each graph.

Intercept and slope estimates for multiple regression models cannot be calculated using the equations we used for simple regression models. Multiple regression models are estimated using a variety of econometric software programs. These programs find the intercept and slope estimates that minimize the sum of squared residuals, just as we did in Section 1-3, except that the mathematics used to find these estimates are more complicated. Table 2-B shows the results when we estimate Quinn's multiple DVD model [Equation (2-2)] using the data from Table 2-A.

Starting with the new variables, the estimated slope coefficient for PRICE, $\hat{B}_2$, is −3.18. The minus sign indicates that PRICE and DVDEXP are negatively related. When the average price of DVDs goes up, Quinn's DVD expenditures tend to go down. When the average price of DVDs goes down, Quinn's expenditures tend to go up. More specifically, if PRICE increases by one unit (a dollar), we can expect her DVD expenditures to fall by $3.18 on average, keeping INCOME and RAINFALL constant. If PRICE falls by a dollar, then DVDEXP increases by $3.18 on average, with INCOME and RAINFALL constant. Multiple regression allows us to look at the effect of PRICE on DVDEXP separately without the effects of INCOME and RAINFALL mixed in. Next, for RAINFALL, the estimated slope coefficient is 6.05. This means that if total rainfall for the month increases by one inch on average Quinn will spend $6.05 more on DVDs that month, keeping INCOME and PRICE the same.[2]

---

[2] It may seem that the 6.05 slope estimate makes RAINFALL more important than PRICE or INCOME, but that is not necessarily true, since a 1-inch change in monthly rainfall is not the same as a dollar change in price or income. We discuss this idea in Chapter 3.

The estimated slope coefficient for INCOME, $\hat{B}_1$, is 0.064. This means that if INCOME increases by a dollar, on average we can expect Quinn's DVD expenditures to increase by about 6 cents (0.064 dollar), keeping PRICE and RAINFALL constant. This estimated slope differs from the slope for our simple regression model where INCOME was the only independent variable. The slope estimate in that model was 0.081. The estimates come out differently because when PRICE and RAINFALL are included in the regression, the 0.064 INCOME slope estimate is estimated while keeping PRICE and RAINFALL constant. In the model in Chapter 1 where INCOME was the only independent variable, the 0.081 INCOME slope estimate was calculated *without* keeping PRICE and RAINFALL constant since PRICE and RAINFALL are omitted from the regression. When PRICE and RAINFALL are not included in the regression, some of the effects of PRICE and RAINFALL on DVDEXP get mixed in with the effects of INCOME. This means that the 0.081 slope estimate for INCOME in the simple regression model includes some of the effects of PRICE and RAINFALL in it.

Econometrics students sometimes believe (mistakenly) that they should run a set of regressions where each regression contains only one independent variable. In our current example, that would involve running three regressions, each with DVDEXP as the dependent variable—one regression with INCOME as its only independent variable, one with PRICE, and one with RAINFALL. People do this because they think it helps them measure the effect of each independent variable more accurately, but they are in fact doing the exact opposite. By leaving other relevant independent variables out of the regression, they fail to account for those variables. The effect, or explanatory power, that omitted variables may provide will be partially "absorbed" by the single independent variable in the model. For example, in the simple version of Quinn's DVD model, PRICE and RAINFALL are not included, so part of their power in explaining DVDEXP is being picked up by INCOME. In order to measure the effects of independent variables separately, you need to include them in the same regression model.

The estimate of the intercept $\hat{B}_0$ is 89.09, which seems like a lot to spend on DVDs every month, especially if we compare it to the actual DVDEXP numbers given in Table 2-A. Remember what the intercept means: B_0 is the amount Quinn would spend on DVDs if *all* the independent variables were set at zero. Interpreted literally, Quinn would spend $89.09 on DVDs if she doesn't earn a penny, the average DVD price is zero, and there is no rainfall that month. A moment's thought tells us that such a situation is highly unlikely. Yes, there is a *small* chance Quinn could lose her job and earn zero, and yes, one month's rainfall *could* be zero, but we also know that PRICE cannot be zero. (They don't give DVDs away!) And for B_0 to be taken at face value, all *three* independent variables must come up zero at the same time. Anyone who interprets the intercept estimate literally or thinks its value is important is making a dangerous gamble. They are betting that the relationship that held between the independent variables and the dependent variable within the sample of data we have will still hold even if every independent variable is zero. This is unlikely to be true, especially if there are few or no observations in the sample where the independent variables are close to zero. In general, it is not a good idea to rely upon regression estimates for situations in which the independent variables take values far from the values represented in the sample. This kind of **extrapolation**—projecting beyond the range of the sample—can lead to big mistakes.

We can find the predicted values in our new model the same way we found them in our simple regression model. The results of the multiple regression model shown in Table 2-2 can be written

$$\text{DV}\hat{\text{D}}\text{EXP} = 89.09 + 0.064 \cdot \text{INCOME} - 3.18 \cdot \text{PRICE} + 6.05 \cdot \text{RAINFALL} \quad \textbf{(2-3)}$$

Suppose we want to see what this model predicts for Quinn's expenditures in April. Table 2-A shows these observations for April: INCOME is \$504, PRICE is \$18.99, and RAINFALL is 1.9. These numbers can be substituted into Equation (2-3):

$$\text{DV}\hat{\text{D}}\text{EXP} = 89.09 + (0.064 \cdot 504) - (3.18 \cdot 18.99) + (6.05 \cdot 1.9) = 72.45$$

Our model predicts an April DVD expenditure of \$72.45, but Quinn actually spent \$73.04 on DVDs that month. The observed error term (residual) is $\hat{e} = Y - \hat{Y} = 73.04 - 72.45 = 0.59$. *Note*: You could also use values for independent variables that do not actually occur in the sample to predict how much Quinn would spend on DVDs in different situations. If you do this, make sure that the values you choose for the independent variables fall within or close to the range of values taken in the actual sample. Otherwise you will encounter a problem with risky extrapolation similar to what can happen with the intercept.

Degrees of Freedom

The **degrees of freedom** provide a measure of the amount of information that is available to estimate a regression model. They are equal to the sample size minus the number of coefficients that need to be estimated in the model, or $n - k - 1$. Here, n is the number of observations (sample size), and k is the number of slope coefficients in the model, one slope coefficient for each independent variable. One degree of freedom is subtracted off for the intercept, so that's why the -1 is there. Each observation provides some information for the regression procedure to use in estimating the coefficient. Each B that needs to be estimated uses up one degree of freedom. That's where the $n - k - 1$ comes from.

Think of each observation as a Ping-Pong ball being spun around by air blowers in a large container. Each coefficient in the model (including the intercept) needs to be estimated, and this estimation uses up one degree of freedom. For every coefficient in the model, imagine that one Ping-Pong ball is caught in a trap in the container so it can no longer move around. Now there are fewer Ping-Pong balls flying around, so there is less information available for estimating the coefficients. In general, the more degrees of freedom you have, the better. This means that a larger sample size adds information, increases the degrees of freedom, and allows the estimation process to work better.

The formula for degrees of freedom also tells us that if we try to estimate a model with a small sample size and a lot of independent variables, our estimates are unlikely to be good ones. In the multiple regression model for DVD expenditures, the number of observations is 12, and three slope coefficients need to be estimated, so the degrees of freedom are $12 - 3 - 1 = 8$. This is a very small number for degrees of freedom; it would be better if we could add more months to Quinn's sample. If we add additional independent variables to the model without increasing the sample size, the degrees of freedom will be even smaller.

2-2 ASSUMPTIONS OF THE CLASSICAL LINEAR REGRESSION MODEL

Ordinary least squares is the best procedure for estimating a linear regression model, but only under certain conditions. These conditions are referred to as the "**classical assumptions**"; they are classical because they are necessary for ordinary least squares to be the best linear estimation method for a given regression model. A good portion of this book deals with what can happen when one or more of the assumptions do not hold true, and what you can do to remedy such a situation. The classical assumptions are:

1. The dependent variable is linearly related to the coefficients, and the model contains the right independent variables (the model is specified correctly).
2. None of the independent variables have a perfect linear relationship with any of the other independent variables.
3. None of the independent variables are correlated with the error term.
4. The error term observations are independent of each other, so they are not correlated with each other.
5. The mean of the error term is zero.
6. The error term has a constant variance.
7. The error term is normally distributed (optional).

Assumption 1 has two requirements. The first one—that the dependent variable be linearly related to the coefficients—means that the B's all enter the regression equation in linear fashion, as occurs in Equation (2-1): $Y = B_0 + B_1X_1 + B_2X_2 + B_3X_3 + \cdots + B_kX_k + e$. In this equation, the independent variables also enter the regression equation in a linear fashion, but that isn't necessary to satisfy this assumption. Consider Equation (2-4).

$$Y = B_0 + B_1X_1 + B_2X_2^2 + e \qquad \textbf{(2-4)}$$

Here X_2 is squared, so the relationship between X_2 and Y is not linear. The relationship between Y and all the B's, however, is still linear and as long as the other assumptions hold true, ordinary least squares will still be the best estimation method.

The second requirement of assumption 1 is that the model contain the right independent variables. If extraneous (irrelevant) independent variables are included in the equation, or if important independent variables are omitted, ordinary least squares won't work very well. (We expand on this point in Chapter 4.)

Assumption 2 requires that none of the independent variables have a perfect linear relationship with any of the other independent variables. If they do, ordinary least squares cannot estimate separate slope coefficients for them. Think about it: Two independent variables that convey the *same* information are really the *same* variable. To see this, consider a model where the dependent variable is the amount you spend each month, and the independent variables are your income and the number of hours you work. If you are paid \$10.00 an hour, and your wage rate stays the same throughout the sample period, then the two independent variables are perfectly linearly related.

$$\text{income} = 10 \cdot (\text{number of hours}) \qquad (2\text{-}5)$$

The slope estimates produced by ordinary least squares give the average change in the dependent variable that we can expect for a one-unit change in an independent variable, keeping the other independent variables constant. If two or more of the independent variables are linearly related, then they will always move together. When this happens, it is impossible for ordinary least squares to estimate a slope keeping other variables constant, because at least one of the other variables doesn't stay constant. Ordinary least squares can't estimate a slope for income in the example here because the other independent variable (number of hours worked) is always moving along with income at the same time. That is, number of hours worked can't be held constant. The slope for hours worked can't be estimated either, for the same reason.

Even if two independent variables are not *perfectly* linearly related, there can still be a problem. If two (or more) independent variables are highly correlated in a linear fashion, **multicollinearity** exists. Ordinary least squares will then have a difficult time estimating separate slope estimates for the variables. We examine multicollinearity in more depth in Chapter 6.

Assumption 3 requires that none of the independent variables be correlated with the error term. Let's say that an independent variable X_1 is correlated with the error term in its regression model. Then the OLS method won't be able to estimate the slope of X_1 separately from movements in the error term. X_1 will be given credit for explaining movement in the dependent variable Y that it does not deserve; X_1 is getting credit for movement in Y that cannot be explained by the model and belongs to the error term. In such a case, the OLS slope estimate $\hat{B}_1$ will not be as good as it could be.

A violation of Assumption 3 is often a signal that the model has not been set up correctly. Perhaps a single-equation model is not adequate to describe the situation, and a model with two or more equations that interact at the same time is needed. Such multi-equation models are presented in Chapter 10.

Assumption 4 requires the error term observations to be independent and therefore not correlated with each other. The observed errors should be random; you should not be able to predict them. If they are correlated, this means that one observation's error has something to do with another observation's error. This would enable you to use one observation's error to predict a different one, but this would mean they are not random. When the observed errors follow a pattern so that they are correlated, this is called **autocorrelation** or **serial correlation**. Autocorrelation is a common problem in time-series regressions; we cover it in more detail in Chapter 7.

Assumption 5 requires that the mean of the error term be zero. The error term itself cannot be observed, but we know what the residuals (error term observations) are after we run the regression. If the mean of the residuals is anything but zero, the model could be better. To see why this is so, let's say the residuals have a mean of 10. This says that on average, the predicted value of the dependent variable is off by 10. The model is predicting values that are too low. The presence of an intercept in the model prevents this from happening. Since ordinary least squares finds its estimates by minimizing the sum of squared errors, it will choose an estimate for the intercept that forces the mean of the residuals to be zero. Again, suppose the residuals have a mean of 10, which makes the predicted dependent variable on average too low by 10. Ordinary least squares will automatically choose an intercept estimate that is higher by a value of 10, so that all the predicted values will be larger by 10, and the model will perform better. The predicted values of $\hat{Y}$ will then be closer to the actual values of Y. Also, the mean of the residuals will now be zero. In general, ordinary least squares will itself cause this assumption to hold true, *if* the other assumptions are true and the model contains a constant (which it should).

Assumption 6 requires the error term to have a constant variance. The error term observations must seem to come from the same probability distribution, one with a constant variance. This means the error term observations are such that the spread or dispersion around the mean appears to be roughly the same. A spread around the mean that increases or decreases according to a pattern is a flag that this assumption is violated. Figure 2-1 shows a set of error term observations that violate assumption 6. When the observations are arranged in order of the independent variable X_1, the spread of the observed errors follows a pattern; the spread around the mean becomes wider. This indicates the presence of **heteroskedasticity**, which means the error term in the regression model does not have a constant variance.

Heteroskedasticity is a common problem when running regressions with cross-section data. As an example, consider a regression utilizing cross-section household data where the dependent variable is consumption, and one of the independent variables is income. As income increases, so does consumption. In addition, wealthier households have more leeway in their budgets to alter their consumption habits. Because of this, as income increases, the *variance* of consumption also increases. This makes it harder for the model to predict the consumption habits of the wealthy and causes the error term observations to have a larger variance for those with higher incomes. This means heteroskedasticity is present. In Chapter 8 we describe heteroskedasticity and the problems it causes for OLS estimation in more detail.

Figure 2-1

Heteroskedasticity Violates Assumption 6.

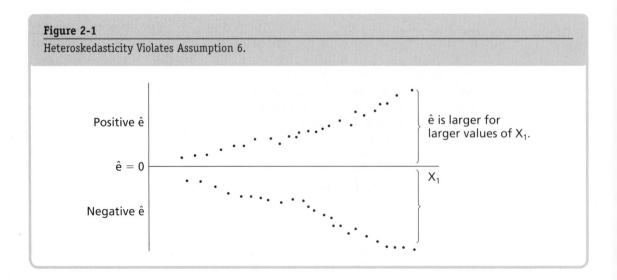

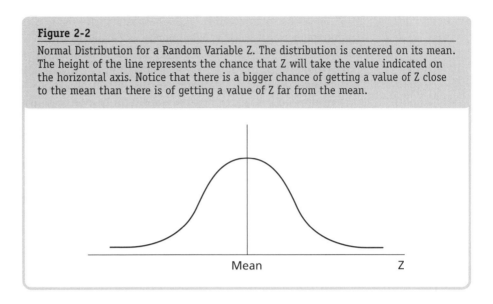

Figure 2-2

Normal Distribution for a Random Variable Z. The distribution is centered on its mean. The height of the line represents the chance that Z will take the value indicated on the horizontal axis. Notice that there is a bigger chance of getting a value of Z close to the mean than there is of getting a value of Z far from the mean.

Assumption 7 requires the error term to be normally distributed. The normal distribution is a specific type of probability distribution that is commonly used in statistics. It is symmetrical, and there is a greater chance of getting a value that is close to the mean than there is of getting a value that is far away from the mean. Figure 2-2 shows a normal distribution.

Assumption 7 is considered optional, since it is not absolutely required to make ordinary least squares the best linear estimation method. However, assumption 7 is important for conducting statistical tests on regression results; these tests are the subject of Chapter 3. Fortunately, the larger the sample size, the more likely assumption 7 will hold true. The Central Limit Theorem tells us that the mean of independently and identically distributed random variables will be normally distributed as the sample size becomes larger. If assumption 4 (error term observations are independent of each other) is true, then the independence requirement of the Central Limit Theorem is met. If assumptions 5 and 6 are true, so that all observed errors come from a distribution with a mean of zero and a constant variance, then they are identically distributed. Therefore, if assumptions 4–6 all hold true and the sample size is large enough, then by the Central Limit Theorem, the error term will be normally distributed. There is no firm rule that tells us how large the sample size has to be, but many researchers feel uncomfortable using a sample size less than 30. In the next section we discuss the desirable characteristics displayed by ordinary least squares when the first six assumptions hold true.

2-3   CHARACTERISTICS OF ORDINARY LEAST SQUARES

Sampling Distribution of OLS Slope Estimates

It is very important to realize that the $\hat{B}$'s produced by ordinary least squares are random variables. The $\hat{B}$'s will differ each time a new sample is used for the same model.

Each set of $\hat{B}$'s for a model is OLS's best estimate of the true values, calculated from the information that is in the data sample. To be able to talk about the accuracy or precision of the estimates, we need to examine the probability distribution of the $\hat{B}$'s. The probability distribution of the $\hat{B}$'s is called a **sampling distribution** because we get different values for $\hat{B}$'s from different samples of the population.

Assumption 7 requires that the error term be normally distributed, and as mentioned, the Central Limit Theorem helps make assumption 7 hold true. If the error term is normally distributed, the $\hat{B}$'s produced by ordinary least squares will also be normally distributed. Because of this, it is usually assumed that the $\hat{B}$'s are normally distributed. For any regression model, if you collect different samples of data, and use ordinary least squares to estimate the model over and over using a different sample each time, the probability distribution of each slope estimate will likely resemble Figure 2-2, especially if the number of samples used is large. Most of the time, you will have only one sample. The estimate you get for a slope estimate $\hat{B}$ might be too high or too low, but as the shape of the normal distribution in Figure 2-2 shows, you will have a better chance of getting a $\hat{B}$ close to the mean of the distribution than one far away from it. (Just think of $\hat{B}$ as the random variable instead of Z in Figure 2-2.)

To clarify this point, let's switch for a moment to a model utilizing cross-section data—5000 people tracking their monthly DVD purchases instead of just one. If we run a regression for each person, we will end up with 5000 estimates for each B—that is, 5000 $\hat{B}_0$ values, 5000 $\hat{B}_1$ values, and so on. Plotting the 5000 $\hat{B}_1$ values would give us an idea of what the $\hat{B}_1$ sampling distribution looks like. If the classical assumptions hold when the 5000 estimates for B_1 are plotted, the distribution of the estimates will be centered on the true value. We could also do this for other B's in the regression. This crucial idea—that the distribution of a large number of estimates will be centered on the true value—will be important in the next chapter.

Now we return to Quinn's data. Suppose Quinn tracks all the variables for our multiple DVD model for 12 more months so that we have another sample. Table 2-C shows the data in this second sample. Using ordinary least squares to estimate the multiple DVD model with this new sample gives us different results. The two sets of estimates are compared in Table 2-D.

As you can see, the estimates in Table 2-D are not the same for the two samples; this is because the estimates are random variables. The slope estimates for the two samples are close for INCOME and PRICE, but they are farther apart for RAINFALL. We have no way of knowing how close these estimates are to their true values because those values are not known. Fortunately, econometricians have figured out some basic characteristics of OLS estimates, which we discuss next.

Properties of Estimators

An **estimator** is a method for finding estimates. An estimator uses the sample data to come up with its best guess of the true value B. This guess, $\hat{B}$, is called an estimate. Ordinary least squares is an estimator because it is a procedure for calculating estimates for the B's in a model.

Three properties are often used to compare different estimators: bias, efficiency, and consistency. An estimator is **unbiased** if its expected value or mean equals its true value. This means that the sampling distribution of the estimator is centered on the true

Table 2-C

Quinn's Second Data Sample

Month	DVDEXP	INCOME	PRICE	RAINFALL
September	52.69	480	24.49	4.3
October	72.61	320	18.98	2.7
November	62.58	400	20.99	2.7
December	37.54	240	21.99	3.3
January	53.39	640	23.48	3.6
February	53.70	440	16.99	2.2
March	61.92	320	23.48	2.9
April	85.16	480	21.49	6.7
May	125.29	416	15.98	6.6
June	117.73	1280	21.24	3.8
July	120.77	1280	18.96	2.8
August	79.05	960	29.95	3.1

Table 2-D

Comparison of Multiple DVD Model Results*

Dependent Variable: DVDEXP

Variable	Original Sample Estimates	New Sample Estimates
Constant	89.09	78.24
INCOME	0.064	0.062
PRICE	−3.18	−3.29
RAINFALL	6.05	8.61

Observations: 12

*From Table 2-B.

value. Figure 2-3 shows the probability distribution of an unbiased estimator next to the probability distribution of a biased one. The fact that an estimator is unbiased does not guarantee that its estimate will be close to the true value. However, suppose there are two estimators that have sampling distributions with the same variance, but only

Figure 2-3

Probability Distributions of Unbiased and Biased Estimators. (a) An unbiased estimator produces estimates centered on the true value. (b) A biased estimator produces estimates that are not centered on the true value.

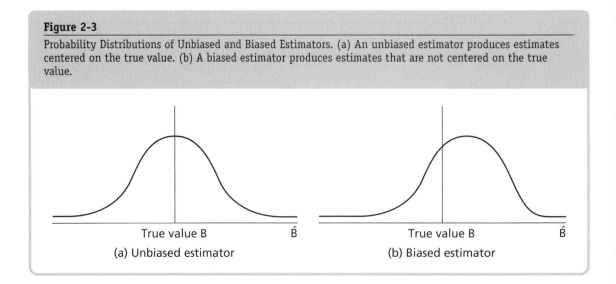

(a) Unbiased estimator

(b) Biased estimator

one of the estimators is unbiased. The unbiased estimator is more likely to give an estimate close to the true value.

Although the true value cannot be known, econometric theorists can derive proofs of whether an estimator will give biased estimates or not. Also, econometricians can examine the properties of an estimator using a Monte Carlo study. A **Monte Carlo study** uses made-up data to examine the properties of different estimators. In effect, when doing a Monte Carlo study, an artificial (fake) data set for a population is made up on a computer, and a random sample is taken from this data set. Regression models are then estimated using one or more estimators. This process is repeated over and over, finding estimates from many different samples. Since the data for the entire population is known (because it is made-up data), the true values are also known. Monte Carlo studies enable researchers to compare their estimates to the true values to see how well each estimator works. By following this process, by taking many samples and estimating the model many times and comparing the estimates to their true values, a researcher can get a good idea of whether the estimator is biased or unbiased.

Efficiency is another property used to compare estimators; given two unbiased estimators, the estimator with the lower variance is considered more efficient. Figure 2-4 shows the probability distributions of two estimators with different variances.

The narrow probability distribution has a smaller variance than the wider probability distribution. The narrower probability distribution with the smaller variance rises taller close to the mean. This means there is a greater chance of getting an estimate close to the mean with the narrow probability distribution. If the estimator that generated this probability distribution is unbiased, then the mean is also the true value. Therefore, the lower-variance estimator is more efficient.

A third property often used is **consistency**; an estimator is consistent if its estimates approach the true value when sample size becomes very large. This is the same as saying that as the sample size grows, the distribution becomes centered on the true value,

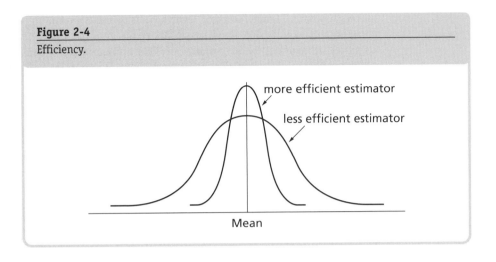

Figure 2-4

Efficiency.

more efficient estimator

less efficient estimator

Mean

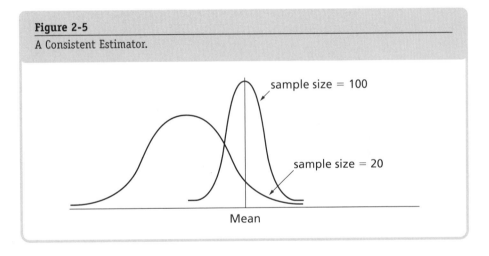

Figure 2-5

A Consistent Estimator.

sample size = 100

sample size = 20

Mean

and the variance of a consistent estimator will get smaller and smaller. The idea of consistency sounds similar to that of an unbiased estimator, but consistency is a weaker property. There could be an estimator that is consistent but still biased. Figure 2-5 shows probability distributions for a consistent estimator for increasing sample sizes.

Gauss-Markov Theorem

When the first six assumptions all hold true, ordinary least squares performs the way we want. We know this is true from the **Gauss-Markov theorem,** which states that when assumptions 1–6 all hold true, ordinary least squares is **BLUE** (**B**est **L**inear **U**nbiased **E**stimator). This means that of all the linear, unbiased methods we could use to estimate a regression model, if assumptions 1 through 6 are all true, ordinary least squares will work best. OLS is the most efficient of all linear unbiased estimators.

(Assumption 7, that the error term has a normal distribution, is not necessary.) It's important to note that the Gauss-Markov theorem does *not* mean that any one OLS slope estimate will be *accurate*—only that ordinary least squares is the best estimator under this one circumstance—that the first six assumptions hold true.

Estimating Variances for the Error Term and Slope Estimate

The error term and slope estimates are both random variables, which means they should have normal probability distributions. We need to be able to estimate the variance of the probability distributions for both the error term and the slope estimates. Since ordinary least squares is unbiased, if we have an estimate of the $\hat{B}$ variance, then we have an idea of how likely it is that we will get a $\hat{B}$ that is close to its true value. Along with an estimate of the error term variance, this helps us assess the performance of the model and the accuracy of its estimates. Estimating the variance for a $\hat{B}$ distribution will also be important in Chapter 3 when we calculate other statistics.

The error variance is usually represented by σ^2 (the Greek letter sigma squared). The equation for estimating the error variance for a simple regression model (one independent variable) shows why the sigma is squared.

$$\hat{\sigma}^2 = \frac{\text{sum of } \hat{e}^2 \text{ for all observations}}{n-2} \qquad (2\text{-}6)$$

The sigma-hat is squared because the variance $\hat{\sigma}^2$ comes from squared terms, the sum of all the squared observed errors. We use the hat (^) because this is the *estimated* variance of the error term; its true value, which we cannot know, is σ^2. To calculate a variance, we sum the squared deviation of each value from its mean. Here, the mean of $\hat{e}$ is zero, so we don't include it in the numerator in Equation (2-6). The $n - 2$ in the denominator adjusts for the degrees of freedom (our model has one independent variable, so the degrees of freedom are $n - k - 1 = n - 1 - 1 = n - 2$). This adjustment makes the variance estimate unbiased.

Once a value for $\hat{\sigma}^2$ is found, we can use it to estimate the variance for the slope estimate. Equation (2-7) shows how to find an estimate for a slope estimate ($\hat{B}_1$) variance when there is one independent variable in the regression.[3]

$$\text{V}\hat{\text{A}}\text{R}(\hat{B}_1) = \frac{\hat{\sigma}^2}{\text{sum of } (X - \overline{X})^2, \text{ added over all observations}} \qquad (2\text{-}7)$$

where X is the single independent variable.[4] Remember that the smaller $\text{V}\hat{\text{A}}\text{R}(\hat{B}_1)$ is, the better, because a small variance increases the likelihood of getting an estimate $\hat{B}_1$ close to the true value B_1. Look at Equation (2-7) closely. A small $\hat{\sigma}^2$ indicates that the errors are smaller, the model fits the data better, and $\text{V}\hat{\text{A}}\text{R}(\hat{B}_1)$ will be smaller. We will tend to get a better estimate $\hat{B}_1$ if $\hat{\sigma}^2$ is small.

---

[3] If more than one independent variable is necessary, then Equation (2-7) is more complicated because it must account for any correlation between the independent variables.

[4] The estimate of the variance for $\hat{B}_0$, the intercept estimate, is $\text{V}\hat{\text{A}}\text{R}(\hat{B}_1) = \hat{\sigma}^2\left(\frac{\text{sum of } X^2}{n \cdot \text{sum of } (X - \overline{X})^2}\right)$ where "sum of" indicates that what follows is summed for all observations.

If the sample size is larger, the bottom of Equation (2-7) will tend to be larger since there will be more $(X - \bar{X})^2$ terms to add up. This tells us that a larger sample size makes $\text{VÂR}(\hat{B}_1)$ smaller and makes it more likely that the slope estimate will be close to its true value.

Now consider the $(X - \bar{X})^2$ term. If the X-values are close to the mean, the $(X - \bar{X})^2$ terms will be small, making the bottom of the fraction in Equation (2-7) small so that $\text{VÂR}(\hat{B}_1)$ is larger. If the X-values are far from their mean, then the $(X - \bar{X})^2$ terms will be bigger, making the bottom of the fraction big, so that $\text{VÂR}(\hat{B}_1)$ is smaller. This means that the slope estimates tend to be better when the independent variable X moves around a lot. This makes sense. The regression is measuring how the dependent variable Y moves when X moves, so it will be easier to measure that if X is moving a lot. As an extreme example, if X always takes the same value for every observation, we cannot estimate the regression; it won't work: Since X doesn't change, ordinary least squares can't measure how Y moves when X moves.

SUMMARY

1. Most regression models need more than one independent variable. A regression model with more than one independent variable is a **multiple or multivariate regression model**.

2. Each slope coefficient B represents the average change we can expect in the dependent variable when its independent variable changes by one unit, keeping the other independent variables constant.

3. In general, it is not a good idea to rely on predicted values from regressions where the independent variables take values far from the values that are represented in the data sample. This kind of **extrapolation**, projecting beyond the range of the sample, can lead to mistakes.

4. **Degrees of freedom** measure the amount of information available to estimate a regression model; the degrees of freedom are equal to the sample size minus the number of coefficients that need to be estimated in the model, or $n - k - 1$ (n is the sample size, k is the number of independent variables in the model, and the 1 is for the intercept).

5. Ordinary least squares is the best method for estimating a linear regression model under certain conditions. These conditions are referred to as the **classical assumptions**, and are stated as follows:

   1. *The dependent variable is linearly related to the coefficients, and the model contains the right independent variables.*
   2. *None of the independent variables have a perfect linear relationship with any of the other independent variables.*
   3. *None of the independent variables are correlated with the error term.*
   4. *The error term observations are independent of each other, so they are uncorrelated with each other.*
   5. *The mean of the error term is zero.*
   6. *The error term has a constant variance.*
   7. *The error term is normally distributed (optional).*

6. Two (or more) independent variables that are highly correlated in a linear fashion indicate **multicollinearity**.

7. **Autocorrelation** or **serial correlation** occurs when the observed errors follow a pattern so that they are correlated.

8. **Heteroskedasticity** occurs when the error term in the regression model does not have a constant variance.

9. Always keep in mind that the $\hat{B}$'s produced by ordinary least squares are random variables. The $\hat{B}$'s will come out differently each time a different sample is used for the same model. The probability distribution of the $\hat{B}$'s is useful in assessing the accuracy or precision of the estimates. The probability distribution of the $\hat{B}$'s is called a **sampling distribution** because different values are found for $\hat{B}$ from different samples of the population.

10. Three properties are used to assess estimators. An estimator is **unbiased** if its expected value or mean is equal to its true value. This means that the sampling distribution of the estimator is centered on the true value. If two estimators are unbiased, the lower-variance estimator is considered more **efficient**. An estimator is **consistent** if its estimates approach their true values when sample size becomes very large.

11. The **Gauss-Markov theorem** states that when assumptions 1–6 all hold true, ordinary least squares is **BLUE** (**B**est **L**inear **U**nbiased **E**stimator). (Assumption 7 is optional.)

12. The smaller $\hat{VAR}(\hat{B}_1)$ is, the better, because the estimate $\hat{B}_1$ is more likely to be close to its true value B_1. [See Equation (2-7).] $\hat{VAR}(\hat{B}_1)$ will be smaller if:
    - The estimate of the error variance $\hat{\sigma}^2$ is small. [See Equation (2-6).]
    - The sample size is bigger.
    - X moves around a lot.

EXERCISES

1. Try to explain these terms without looking them up.
   - multiple or multivariate regression model
   - specification
   - extrapolation
   - degrees of freedom
   - multicollinearity
   - autocorrelation or serial correlation
   - heteroskedasticity
   - sampling distribution
   - estimator
   - unbiased
   - Monte Carlo study
   - efficiency
   - consistency
   - Gauss-Markov theorem
   - BLUE

2. Use an econometrics program along with the data presented in Table 2-A to estimate Quinn's DVD model expressed by Equation (2-2):

$$DVDEXP = B_0 + B_1INCOME + B_2PRICE + B_3RAINFALL + e$$

   a. Do your results match the results given in the text?
      Now use the data in Table 2-C to estimate the model.
   b. Do your results match the results given in the text?
   c. Why don't your results for part a match those for part b?

3. a. Without looking in the text, list and explain all seven classical assumptions.
   b. Why are the classical assumptions important?

4. a. How do the degrees of freedom affect the quality of regression results?
   b. Explain the relationship between the degrees of freedom, the number of independent variables, and the sample size that researchers must think about when they collect data for regressions.

5. Use the data in Table 2-A and econometric software to estimate these two regression models:

$$DVDEXP = B_0 + B_1PRICE + e$$

$$DVDEXP = B_0 + B_1RAINFALL + e$$

Explain why the slope estimates in these regressions differ from the results for the multiple regression model in Table 2-B. How does the interpretation of a slope estimate for a simple regression model differ from a multiple regression model?

6. a. Use the results in Table 2-B to find the predicted value for Quinn's DVD expenditures for a month where
    • her monthly income is $400
    • average DVD price is $20.00
    • it rains 2.0 inches
   b. Table 2-A contains the data utilized to estimate the results used for part a of this question. There is no observation in Table 2-A where INCOME is 400, PRICE is 20, and RAINFALL is 2.0. Does this mean that the predicted value you found for the data given here is especially untrustworthy? Why or why not?

7. Suppose that there is a flood where Quinn lives, and RAINFALL is 13.0 inches one month. That same month, INCOME is 600 and PRICE is 22.00.
   a. Use the results in Table 2-B to predict how much Quinn will spend on DVDs that month.
   b. Do you think this prediction will be close to the actual amount she spent? Why or why not?

8. Use the slope estimates in Table 2-B to answer these questions.
   a. Quinn's income goes up by $100 in a month where PRICE increases by $4.00 and the rainfall increases by 3 inches (compared to the previous month). What is the expected change in Quinn's DVD expenditures?
   b. If PRICE goes up by $2.00, how much would Quinn's income have to increase to keep her expected or predicted DVD expenditures the same?

c. If Quinn's predicted DVD expenditures increase by $30 but RAINFALL and PRICE stay the same, how much does her income increase?

9. As discussed in the chapter, each slope coefficient in a multiple regression measures the isolated effect of a one-unit change in its independent variable while the other independent variables are kept constant. Show that this is true by using the following steps:

    a. Find the predicted value for DVDEXP using the results in Table 2-B and the data for February shown in Table 2-A.

    b. Find the predicted values for DVDEXP if PRICE goes up a dollar to $27.49, but INCOME and RAINFALL stay the same as in part a.

    c. Subtract part a's answer from part b's. What do you notice about the difference between these two answers?

10. Consider Equation (2-7), which estimates the slope estimate variance:

$$\text{VÂR}(\hat{B}_1) = \frac{\hat{\sigma}^2}{\text{sum of } (X - \overline{X})^2, \text{ added over all observations}}$$

    a. How does the deviation of X from its mean affect the precision of $\hat{B}_1$?

    b. How does the sample size affect the precision of $\hat{B}_1$?

    c. How can the answers to parts a and b help you design a model?

11. Using the data in Table 2-A, find the sum of squared residuals for both the single and multiple regression model. Estimate

$$\text{DVDEXP} = B_0 + B_1\text{PRICE} + e$$

and

$$\text{DVDEXP} = B_0 + B_1\text{INCOME} + B_2\text{PRICE} + B_3\text{RAINFALL} + e$$

    (*Note*: Some software programs give the sum of squared residuals automatically; if your software doesn't do this, use it to give the residuals, then square each residual and add them across all observations.)

    a. Which regression has the smaller sum of squared residuals?

    b. Will your answer to part a be the same if different data samples are used? Explain.

    c. Will your answer to part a change if you compare single and multiple regressions for a different subject, one that has nothing to do with DVDs? Explain.

12. The table below gives cross-section data for 30 students who buy DVDs from 30 different places.

Observation	DVDEXP	INCOME	PRICE	RAINFALL
1	9.70	600	22.99	6.0
2	19.90	720	24.95	2.2
3	49.24	1120	19.99	1.0
4	9.26	455	24.50	2.7

Observation	DVDEXP	INCOME	PRICE	RAINFALL
5	30.94	974	23.95	0.8
6	38.39	880	18.99	0.2
7	33.10	422	20.00	1.3
8	26.76	1120	26.98	5.2
9	47.30	580	16.98	3.2
10	43.87	982	21.00	2.0
11	44.07	754	15.98	3.8
12	49.44	699	17.99	4.1
13	27.75	824	24.95	2.0
14	20.76	745	24.95	1.7
15	47.27	934	17.97	0.8
16	9.58	432	26.95	5.9
17	29.50	1023	19.80	3.3
18	14.30	623	26.95	4.1
19	22.73	798	24.97	3.8
20	24.61	687	22.85	2.2
21	26.47	987	22.95	1.6
22	18.09	863	25.95	3.0
23	42.44	642	19.50	4.1
24	15.30	475	22.80	5.2
25	38.19	685	19.95	3.6
26	32.66	865	21.90	1.2
27	50.93	983	18.00	2.5
28	27.24	465	20.10	2.2
29	30.24	783	22.30	4.1
30	30.67	854	22.30	2.8

    a. Use these cross-section data to estimate the DVD expenditures model.

    b. The slope estimate for RAINFALL is closer to zero here than what we found in the text. Although your answers to part a are just estimates, can you explain why the true value of the slope for RAINFALL might be closer to zero using cross-section data rather than Quinn's time-series data?

13. a. Are all unbiased estimators efficient?

    b. Are all unbiased estimators consistent?

    c. Are all consistent estimators unbiased?

14. How do you know if an estimator is unbiased, when the coefficient's true value is not known?

15. A commercial on late-night cable TV offers a new estimator for only $19.99, if you call now. The spokesman (who used to star in a science fiction series) claims that this estimator is more efficient than ordinary least squares, and that there is a 30-day money-back guarantee if you are not satisfied. However, toward the end of the commercial, small lettering at the bottom of the screen states "this estimator is not guaranteed to be unbiased." Is it worth $19.99 to find out the secret equation for this estimator? Explain.

3

Commonly Used Statistics for Regression Analysis

This chapter will explain:

- The difference between a sample and a population, and why it is important to use a random sample.

- The steps used in hypothesis testing, and how to conduct hypothesis testing.

- Statistical significance or error level, and the different types of errors that can occur in hypothesis testing.

- The difference between statistical significance and practical importance.

- The measures of a regression's performance, and how these measures are used.

Suppose we run a regression using annual income as the dependent variable, with age, height, and years of education as independent variables. We want to know if our regression results can be trusted. If we get a slope coefficient estimate of $-1,000$ for the height variable, does this mean that taller people tend to make less money? How do we know that the $-1,000$ estimate is not just a coincidence? What is the chance that, in reality, there is no relationship at all between height and income? This is the same as asking, "Even though we have $-1,000$ as the slope estimate, what is the chance that the true value of the slope is zero?" What is the chance that none of our independent variables have a relationship with income? The answers to these questions and many more await you in this action-packed chapter.

3-1 HYPOTHESIS TESTING: DO MY ESTIMATES MATTER?

Random Samples

To predict the outcome of an election, you could ask all eligible voters how they plan to vote. This approach would work well for a small group of friends who are going to vote on what movie to see, but for most political elections, this approach would be very time-consuming and expensive. Instead, you could ask some of the possible voters how they will vote and then base your prediction on their responses. In this example, the possible voters who are actually asked how they will vote are called the sample; all the possible voters are referred to as the population. In general, a **sample** consists of members of a group who are chosen to represent the whole group. The **population** includes all members of the group. (The group doesn't have to consist of people; it can be firms, countries, etc.)

It is important that the members of a sample be chosen at random. Using a random sample, however, does not guarantee the sample will represent the population. The advantage of random samples is that basic ideas from statistical theory can be used to make precise statements about predictions or estimates. If the sample is not random, it is more likely to represent something different from what we think it represents. For example, if you use your friends as your sample, your prediction for the election will not reflect the views of the population of all voters; it will reflect the views of the type of people you choose as friends. This could lead you to predict the election incorrectly. In general, it is important that the observations in the sample be chosen at random regardless of whether they are voters or anything else.

You may have seen the famous photograph of Harry Truman holding up a copy of the *Chicago Tribune* with the headline "Dewey Defeats Truman." You have never heard of President Dewey, however, because Truman actually defeated Thomas Dewey in the 1948 presidential election, winning 49.6% of the popular vote compared to 45.1% for Dewey. Truman captured 310 electoral votes, so the 1948 election was not nearly as close as the 2000 presidential election. Nevertheless, the major preelection polls had predicted a Dewey victory.[1] The editors of the *Chicago Tribune*, to meet their deadline, assumed these polls would turn out to be right and made the decision to print the headline before the actual election results were available.

Why did the polls predict the wrong outcome? One reason is that those conducting the poll failed to use a random sample. The sample was biased. Voters with only grade-school educations were underrepresented in the sample.[2] In other words, the percentage of those with only grade-school educations in the sample was too small; in the population as a whole, the percentage of voters with only grade-school educations was larger. **Selection bias** occurs when a particular group of observations is underrepresented in a sample. Voters with only grade-school educations must have favored Truman over Dewey. The preelection polls underestimated Truman's support, which led to the mistaken conclusion that Dewey would be elected. One possible cause of the selection bias was that some of the polls were conducted by telephone. In 1948, some people with lower incomes still did not have telephones. These lower-income individuals were also more likely to have only grade-school educations.

It is important to use random samples in regression analysis. If you are hired by an oil company to conduct regression analysis concerning the profitability of gas stations in the United States, make sure you are using a random sample of U.S. gas stations. If you are interested only in one firm's gas stations, make sure you are using a random sample of that company's gas stations. Otherwise, you could make a mistake like the "*Dewey Defeats Truman*" headline.

---

[1] For the statistics cited here and for more information, see Irwin Ross, *The Loneliest Campaign* (Westport, Conn.: Greenwood Press, 1968), pp. 245–252.

[2] *Ibid.*

Hypothesis Testing

The rest of this chapter discusses hypothesis testing, which can be applied to statistics calculated from random samples. The general steps of hypothesis testing are as follows:

1. Clearly state the hypothesis to be tested, both in words and in a null and alternative hypotheses format.
2. State the level of statistical significance (or error level) for the test. Once this is stated, you will be able to use a decision rule to tell how the hypothesis test turned out.
3. Run a regression to get the coefficient estimates and statistics necessary for the hypothesis test.
4. Use the decision rule along with the regression results to decide whether to reject the null hypothesis.

These steps are explained in the next sections.

The Null and Alternative Hypotheses

Hypothesis testing allows us to make conclusions about regression estimates and about the ideas we are investigating. Suppose an electronics store hires you as a consultant. The owner of the store wants to know how its prices, sales, and advertising affect revenue, so that she can plan her marketing strategy. You design the following multiple regression model, using cross-section data from competing electronics stores, for the month being studied.

$$\text{REVENUE} = B_0 + B_1 \text{ PRICE} + B_2 \text{ SALE ITEMS} + B_3 \text{ ADVERTISING} + e \textbf{ (3-1)}$$

where

$$\text{REVENUE} = \text{store revenues (in dollars), for each store}$$
$$\text{PRICE} = \text{dollar price of a standard set of typical items, for each store}$$
$$\text{SALE ITEMS} = \text{number of items marked as sale or special items, for each store}$$
$$\text{ADVERTISING} = \text{amount spent on advertising (in dollars), for each store}$$

After running a regression and conducting a hypothesis test, we might be able to make a statement like "There is only a 1% chance that the true value of B_2 is equal to zero." This in turn allows us to say something about the premise or theory we are investigating. For example, we could say, "Since there is only a 1% chance that B_2 is zero, it is likely that a change in the number of sale items will affect store revenues." The sample data, along with the regression process, allow us to find estimates for the slope coefficients, but these are just estimates, not true values.

The first step in conducting a hypothesis test is to clearly state the hypothesis. To be objective (and follow scientific methods), you must state the hypothesis before you run the regression and examine your results, not after. Your hypothesis should be stated both in words and in symbols that show the meaning those words have for the regression model. Stated in words, your hypothesis might be that advertising affects store revenues. This hypothesis can be restated using the regression model just specified. If advertising affects revenue, then B_3 should not equal zero, and we state this as the alternative hypothesis, H_A. This gives us our null hypothesis H_0 (the zero stands for null), that advertising does not affect store revenues. Now let's state these hypotheses in symbols:

$$H_0: B_3 = 0$$

$$H_A: B_3 \neq 0$$

Keep in mind that B_3 represents the true unknown value of the slope coefficient, *not* the estimate $\hat{B}_3$ that we get from the regression results.

When conducting hypothesis testing, we either reject or do not reject the null hypothesis. Purists never say "We accept the null hypothesis." It might seem that not rejecting the null hypothesis is the same as accepting it. In statistics, however, there is a difference. When a null hypothesis is rejected, we can make a powerful statement concerning the chance we are wrong and the null hypothesis is actually true. We can say something like "There is only a 1% chance that B_3 is actually zero and that no relationship exists between advertising and profits." If the null hypothesis cannot be rejected, we *cannot* say the null hypothesis is true with a 99% probability. When we cannot reject the null hypothesis, we don't have enough evidence to prove that it may be false. Neither do we have enough statistical evidence to prove that the null hypothesis is true. Here is an easy way to think about this: If you can reject the null hypothesis, it is likely that it is false. If you cannot reject the null hypothesis, think of the test as inconclusive. In order to prove something, we state its opposite as the null hypothesis and then see if the null hypothesis can be rejected. Null and alternative hypotheses like the ones above can be stated for every coefficient in a regression, including the intercept. (Remember, however, hypothesis testing for the intercept is rarely useful; see Sections 1-3 and 2-1.)

As we noted, the null hypothesis states the *opposite* of what we want to prove. Here, the hypothesis we want to prove is that advertising matters; it is related to revenue. This belief is expressed as $B_3 \neq 0$, the alternative hypothesis. The opposite is that advertising does not matter and is not related to revenue. If advertising does not matter, then the true value of the slope coefficient B_3 should be zero; this is the null hypothesis. A regression that shows that the null hypothesis $B_3 = 0$ is unlikely lends support to the original hypothesis that advertising matters when examining revenue.

One- and Two-Sided Tests

The set of null and alternative hypotheses shown above ($H_0: B_3 = 0$ and $H_A: B_3 \neq 0$) is a two-sided test. We call it a **two-sided test** because the null hypothesis is rejected if it seems likely that the true value of B_3 is on either "side" of the null hypothesis. If the estimate $\hat{B}_3$ is significantly different from zero on either side, positive or negative, the null hypothesis is rejected.

There are also one-sided tests. Suppose we change the original hypothesis from "advertising affects store revenues" to "advertising increases store revenues." Now our null and alternative hypotheses are

$$H_0: B_3 \leq 0 \quad \text{Advertising does not increase store revenues.}$$

$$H_A: B_3 > 0 \quad \text{Advertising increases store revenues.}$$

This is a **one-sided test** because the alternative hypothesis is on only one side of the null hypothesis. The null hypothesis will be rejected only if $\hat{B}_3$ is greater than zero (and this must be statistically significant). If $\hat{B}_3$ is less than zero, we do not reject the null hypothesis. Note that, as with the two-sided test, the null hypothesis states the opposite of what we expect to prove.

Now suppose the hypothesis we want to test is that advertising decreases store revenues. (This is an unlikely outcome, unless the advertising campaign is somehow offensive to potential customers. Note that revenues are different from profits. Revenues do not include the cost of the advertising, just the amount of money taken in by the store.) Then the null and alternative hypotheses are

H_0: $B_3 \geq 0$ Advertising does not decrease store revenues.

H_A: $B_3 < 0$ Advertising decreases store revenues.

This is also a one-sided test, since the null hypothesis will be rejected only if $\hat{B}_3$ is significantly less than zero.

Levels of Significance

The $\hat{B}$ values that we find in regressions are only estimates of the true slopes and intercept. There is always a chance that our conclusion about a null hypothesis involving a slope estimate will be wrong. Two types of errors can occur. When a null hypothesis is rejected on the basis of a slope estimate, we cannot be sure that the null hypothesis is really false. A **Type I error** occurs when the null hypothesis is actually true, but it is rejected. This means the truth is being rejected. A **Type II error** occurs when the null hypothesis is false, but it is not rejected. This means a false statement is not rejected.

A jury's decision to find a defendant guilty or not guilty is a classic situation for Type I and Type II errors. Here are the null and alternative hypotheses:

H_0: Defendant is innocent.

H_A: Defendant is guilty.

Table 3-A shows the four possibilities that can happen with a criminal trial, if the jury reaches a verdict.

Convicting an innocent person is a Type I error. Letting a guilty individual go free is a Type II error. If our judicial system is to follow the principle that one is innocent until proven guilty, it must be designed to minimize the probability of Type I errors. Our rules of law emphasize preventing an innocent individual from being convicted. We place less emphasis on preventing a guilty defendant from going free. Because our justice system minimizes the chance of Type I errors, Type II errors are more likely.

Hypothesis testing in econometrics works the same way as in the judicial system example, following the "innocent until proven guilty" premise. So that others will be convinced of your results, it is crucial that when you conclude that a null hypothesis can be rejected, there is only a small chance you are wrong. You want to avoid making a Type I error. As with our justice system, this means that when you conduct

Table 3-A

Type I and Type II Errors in a Jury Trial

	"Not Guilty" Verdict (Null hypothesis is *not* rejected.)	**"Guilty" Verdict** (Null hypothesis is rejected.)
Defendant is innocent. (Null hypothesis is true.)	Jury is correct—no error.	Type I error
Defendant is guilty. (Null hypothesis is false.)	Type II error	Jury is correct—no error.

hypothesis testing, you need to emphasize avoiding Type I errors rather than avoiding Type II errors.

In classical hypothesis testing, the probability of a Type I error is specified ahead of time. Suppose we set the chance of Type I error at 1%. If we end up rejecting the null hypothesis, then we know there is only a 1% chance that we are wrong and the null hypothesis is actually true. Figure 3-1 shows this situation using a normal probability distribution for H_0: B = 0 and H_A: B $\neq$ 0.

Figure 3-1 shows the distributions of slope estimates for two regressions that were run many times using different samples. If the null hypothesis is true, as in Figure 3-1a, there is only a 1% chance that we would get an estimate $\hat{B}$ so far from the true value of B = 0 that it would lie in one of the two darkened regions shown. (Since it is a two-sided test at a 1% error level, the rejection region is an area of $\frac{1}{2}$% in each tail of the distribution.) The estimate $\hat{B}$ is so far away from B = 0 that we reject the null hypothesis. It seems unlikely that B = 0. If we are wrong and the 1% chance has come true that B really does equal zero, we have made a Type I error. Considering that the estimate $\hat{B}$ is far from zero, it is more likely that the true situation is as shown in Figure 3-1b, where the null hypothesis is false (the true B does not equal 0). In Figure 3-1b, the estimate $\hat{B}$ is far enough away from zero that the null hypothesis is rejected, as it should be since it is false.

Suppose you planned to meet another student in your class to work on an econometrics project, but he never showed up. The next day you get a phone call explaining what happened: "Sorry I missed you yesterday. I was really looking forward to working on our project, but on the way over aliens abducted me. They took me to their home planet and conducted a series of mind-altering experiments on me. Fortunately, I was able to learn their language, so I challenged them to a game of poker and won my freedom. Their spaceship traveled faster than the speed of light, so all of this only took a day." Consider the following null and alternative hypotheses:

H_0: Everything he said is true.

H_A: He's lying.

Can you prove he is lying? Maybe not, but the probability that he is telling the truth is very small. It is so hard to believe he is telling the truth that you reject the null

Figure 3-1

Type I error.

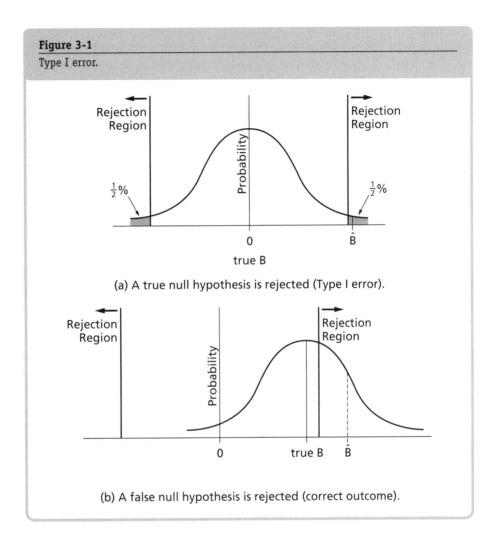

(a) A true null hypothesis is rejected (Type I error).

(b) A false null hypothesis is rejected (correct outcome).

hypothesis that everything he said is true. The chance that you are wrong and that he is telling the truth is very small. Hypothesis testing is set up the same way—the null hypothesis is rejected *only if* the chance that the null hypothesis is true is very small.

The second step in hypothesis testing, after stating the null and alternative hypotheses, is to state the significance level, or error level. The significance level is the probability of a Type I error that you are willing to accept when you test your hypothesis. In regression analysis, the error level is typically set at 5% or 1%. Rejecting the null hypothesis at a 1% significance level is more convincing than rejecting it at a 5% error level, but this is also less likely to happen. Occasionally, a 10% error level is used, which of course is even less convincing. Remember, a 10% error level means you stand a 10% chance of rejecting a true null hypothesis. Often this is considered too great a chance of Type I error.

3-2   CONDUCTING A t-TEST

The t-test is the most common test used in econometrics. This test helps us assess the chances of a slope's true value being zero. If this chance is small and the slope's true value is most likely something other than zero, then we can put more trust in our slope estimate. The t-test allows us to conduct a separate hypothesis test on each slope estimate. That is, we can test each slope estimate to see if its true slope is zero. We state the alternative hypothesis as either a one-sided or two-sided test, depending on our hypothesis concerning each slope coefficient and its independent variable. The t-test can also be applied to the intercept estimate, but as we noted earlier, this is rarely useful. Here is the general formula for the t-test:

$$t = \frac{\hat{B} - B_{null}}{SE(\hat{B})} \qquad (3\text{-}2)$$

where

$\hat{B}$ = estimate of a slope coefficient

B_{null} = value specified in the null hypothesis (usually zero)

$SE(\hat{B})$ = estimated standard error of the slope estimate, $\hat{B}$

If the slope estimate is calculated over and over with different data sets, it will take different values (see Section 2-3). The estimated standard error $SE(\hat{B})$ measures whether the different slope estimates vary a little (stay close to the same number) or a lot (they change a lot). A larger SE means the slope estimate moves around a lot; a smaller SE means the slope estimate moves less. The estimated standard error is the square root of the estimated variance [the estimated variance is given in Equation (2-7)].

Regardless of whether the test is one- or two-sided, B_{null} is usually zero. With a one-sided test (say H_0: B ≥ 0 and H_A: B < 0), zero still separates the null hypothesis from the alternative hypothesis—B_{null} is still zero in the t-statistic calculation. The only time B_{null} is not zero is if the null hypothesis is set to a value besides zero. For example, if H_0: B ≥ 5 and H_A: B < 5, B_{null} is 5. The same is true for a two-sided test. If H_0: B = 7 and H_A: B ≠ 7, then B_{null} is 7.

Since B_{null} is usually zero, Equation (3-2) is typically stated as

$$t = \frac{\hat{B}}{SE(\hat{B})} \qquad (3\text{-}3)$$

Examine this formula carefully. The t-statistic is the slope estimate $\hat{B}$ divided by the estimate of the standard error $SE(\hat{B})$. Dividing the slope estimate by $SE(\hat{B})$ adjusts the slope estimate by the size of the estimated standard error. Think about $\hat{B}$ first. The farther $\hat{B}$ is from zero, the larger its t-statistic, and the likelihood of rejecting the null hypothesis increases. This means that if we keep $SE(\hat{B})$ the same, we are more likely to reject the null hypothesis that the true B is zero. The same reasoning holds for a negative $\hat{B}$. The more negative $\hat{B}$, the more negative the t-statistic, and the likelihood again increases that the null hypothesis will be rejected. The absolute value of the t-statistic is what is important here. A t-statistic far from zero, in either the positive or negative direction, increases the chance that the null hypothesis will be rejected.

Now think about the $SE(\hat{B})$ part of the t-statistic. For a set value of $\hat{B}$, the smaller the estimated standard error, the larger the t-statistic, and the more likely the null hypothesis will be rejected. A small standard error means that the slope estimates do not tend to change much when the slope is estimated repeatedly. We can have more confidence in the slope estimate when $SE(\hat{B})$ is small. If the estimated standard error is large for a particular value of $\hat{B}$, then the slope estimates will vary a lot. With a larger $SE(\hat{B})$, we cannot place a lot of confidence in our $\hat{B}$ value. The t-statistic takes a lower value, and the likelihood that we will reject the null hypothesis decreases.

Critical Values and Decision Rules

We use critical values and decision rules to help us decide whether we should reject the null hypothesis. For a t-test, the critical t value t_c shows where the rejection region starts. In general, a **critical value** is the value of a test statistic that marks the beginning of the rejection region. The critical value for a t-test is found in a t-table by choosing the significance level you want to use. You will need the degrees of freedom, $n - k - 1$, when you look up the critical value. A **decision rule** tells you how to use a test statistic to decide whether to reject the null hypothesis. Here is the decision rule for a two-sided t-test: Reject the null hypothesis if the actual t-statistic from the regression results is farther from zero than the critical value.

$$\text{Reject the null hypothesis if } |t| > t_c \qquad \textbf{(3-4)}$$

The $|t|$ symbol tells you to take the absolute value of the t-statistic calculated from your regression results; you can ignore a negative sign on the t-statistic.

For a one-sided test, you must consider the type of null and alternative hypotheses you are using before you apply the decision rule. If the null and alternative hypotheses are H_0: $B \geq 0$ and H_A: $B < 0$, consider rejecting the null hypothesis only if your estimate, $\hat{B}$, is negative. (Also, if your estimate of B is negative, then you can use Decision Rule (3-4)). If $\hat{B}$ is positive, do not reject the null hypothesis. Now let's set up the opposite situation—that is, H_0: $B \leq 0$ and H_A: $B > 0$. In this test you consider rejecting the null hypothesis if the estimate of B is positive; you can also use Decision Rule (3-4). If $\hat{B}$ is negative, do not reject the null hypothesis.

Let's use the electronics store model, Equation (3-1), to show how we conduct t-tests.

$$\text{REVENUE} = B_0 + B_1 \text{ PRICE} + B_2 \text{ SALE ITEMS} + B_3 \text{ ADVERTISING} + e \textbf{ (3-1)}$$

Our first step is to state the hypotheses; we state a hypothesis for each independent variable. If one store has higher prices, customers can go to a different store, so it is reasonable to think that the slope coefficient for PRICE should be negative. This hypothesis implies a one-sided test. (Notice that we set up the null hypothesis as the *opposite* of what we expect to find.)

H_0: $B_1 \geq 0$ Higher prices do not decrease store revenues.

H_A: $B_1 < 0$ Higher prices decrease store revenues.

The number of sale items at a store can either increase or decrease revenue. If a larger number of sale items brings customers into the store or gets them to buy items they wouldn't normally buy, then more sale items increases revenue. However, if these are items that customers would have bought anyway, the lower prices are going to decrease revenue. The hypothesis here is that SALE ITEMS affects revenue in some way, either upward or downward. This hypothesis requires a two-sided test:

H_0: $B_2 = 0$ Number of sale items does not increase or decrease revenues.

H_A: $B_2 \neq 0$ Number of sale items does increase or decrease revenues.

Our third hypothesis is that advertising increases revenues. This requires a one-sided test. As with our previous two hypothesis tests, we make this statement the alternative hypothesis. The null hypothesis states the opposite, that advertising does *not* increase revenues.

$$H_0: B_3 \leq 0$$

$$H_A: B_3 > 0$$

The second step in a hypothesis test is to state the error level that we will use in the test; let's use a 5% error level. In the third step, we run the regression. Our results are shown in Table 3-B.

In our final step we use the decision rule to decide whether to reject the null hypothesis. (Most econometrics software programs calculate the t-statistics for you. For illustrative purposes, we show the calculation of a t-statistic below.) We then compare these t-statistics to their critical values to decide whether we can reject each null hypothesis. Looking at the t-table, the critical value for a two-sided test at 5% significance with 120 degrees of freedom is 1.98. (This regression has 120 degrees of freedom, n − k − 1 = 120.) For a one-sided test, the critical value is 1.66.

Table 3-B

Regression Results for Electronics Store Model

Dependent Variable: Revenue

Variable	Coefficient	Standard Error	t-Statistic	p-Value
Constant*	300,520.25	286,321.07	1.05	0.30
PRICE	−83,543.88	34,422.69	−2.43	0.017
SALE ITEMS	530.87	695.86	0.76	0.45
ADVERTISING	1.14	0.50	2.28	0.024

Observations: 124

$R^2 = 0.62$

Adjusted $R^2 = 0.61$

F-statistic $= 65.26$

*The term *constant* refers to the intercept.

calc
t-value > crit Reject
is sig at that level

The t-statistic for PRICE is

$$t = \frac{\hat{B}_1}{SE(\hat{B}_1)} = \frac{-83,543.88}{34,422.69} = -2.43$$

The hypotheses for PRICE are H_0: $B_1 \geq 0$ and H_A: $B_1 < 0$. Since the slope esti-mate is negative (as implied by the alternative hypothesis), we use Decision Rule (3-4), $|t| > t_c$. Using the calculated t-statistic and the one-sided critical value, we get $|-2.43|$ > 1.66. Figure 3-2 depicts this situation. (*Note:* Figure 3-2 *assumes* that the null hypothesis is true and therefore the distribution is centered on t = 0.) The PRICE slope estimate $\hat{B}_1 = -83,543.88$ is so far from zero that the t-statistic $|-2.43|$ exceeds its critical value of 1.66. (Remember, the absolute value of the t-statistic is what is impor-tant here.) It's unlikely we would get a slope estimate (and t-statistic) this far from zero if the true value of B_1 really is zero. Therefore, we can reject the null hypothesis that $B_1 = 0$. There is at most a 5% chance that the true value of B_1 is zero or positive. We conclude that a store that increases its prices will tend to lose revenue; likewise, decreasing a store's prices will tend to increase its revenue.

For a one-sided test, the 5% chance of Type I error is located on one side (or tail) of the probability distribution. For a two-sided test, the chance of Type I error is split between the two tails of the probability distribution.

The hypothesis for SALE ITEMS requires a two-sided test. The t-statistic from the regression results is 0.76, and the critical value for a two-sided test at a 5% significance level and 120 degrees of freedom is 1.98. As shown in Figure 3-3, since 0.76 is less than 1.98, the decision rule tells us the null hypothesis should not be rejected.

For $\hat{B}_3$, the slope estimate for ADVERTISING, a one-sided test is appropriate. The t-statistic is 2.28 (see Table 3-B). The slope estimate $\hat{B}_3$ takes a positive value, consistent with our alternative hypothesis; this means we can use Decision Rule (3-4). The criti-

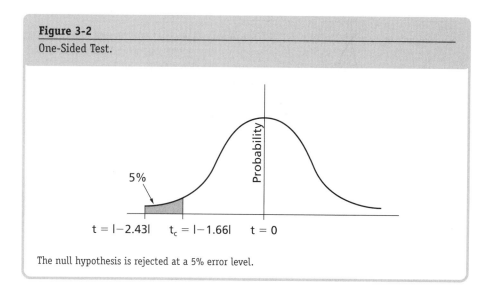

Figure 3-2

One-Sided Test.

5%

Probability

$t = |-2.43|$ $t_c = |-1.66|$ $t = 0$

The null hypothesis is rejected at a 5% error level.

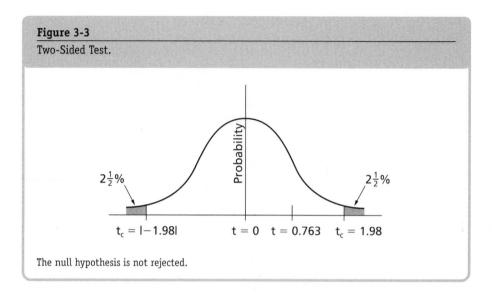

Figure 3-3

Two-Sided Test.

$t_c = |-1.98|$ $t = 0$ $t = 0.763$ $t_c = 1.98$

The null hypothesis is not rejected.

cal value is 1.66, the same as for the hypothesis test of B_1 (the slope estimate for PRICE). The t-statistic (2.28) is greater than its critical value (1.66). The null hypothesis $B_3 \leq 0$ is rejected at the 5% significance level; it is likely that the true value of B_3 is positive.

Let's look at one more test, in which the null hypothesis involves a number other than zero. Suppose we want to see whether a dollar spent on advertising will bring in another dollar in revenue or not. Here are our null and alternative hypotheses:

$$H_0: B_3 = 1$$

$$H_A: B_3 \neq 1$$

A true null hypothesis in this two-sided test means that advertising doesn't increase or decrease profits; every dollar spent on advertising just covers itself by generating another dollar in revenue. The value in the null hypothesis, 1, must be subtracted from the slope estimate when we calculate the t-statistic. Besides that, this test is the same as any other two-sided t-test. We start the test with Equation (3-2).

$$t = \frac{\hat{B} - B_{null}}{SE(\hat{B})} = \frac{1.14 - 1}{0.50} = \frac{0.14}{0.50} = 0.28 \qquad \text{(3-2)}$$

The critical value for a two-sided test at a 5% significance level with 120 degrees of freedom is 1.98, the same critical value we used for the SALE ITEMS t-test. Since the calculated t-statistic (0.28) is less than the critical value (1.98), we cannot reject the null hypothesis that $B_3 = 1$. It is entirely possible that every dollar spent on advertising increases revenues by a dollar. t-tests of this nature, where the null hypothesis is $B = 1$, are sometimes used for models where the slope measures an elasticity, to see if the elasticity could be 1. We discuss these types of models in Chapter 5.

p-Value

The last column of Table 3-B contains a statistic called the p-value. For a given hypothesis test, the p-value states the smallest significance level for which the null hypothesis can be rejected. Here is another way to say this: The **p-value** tells you the probability of Type I error, if you reject the null hypothesis. Most econometrics software automatically calculates a p-value for a two-sided test of H_0: B = 0 and H_A: B $\neq$ 0 for each estimate. In our two-sided test for SALE ITEMS, $\hat{B}_2$, the p-value is 0.45. This means that the null hypothesis can be rejected at a significance level of 0.45; there is a 45% chance that if the null hypothesis is rejected, the null hypothesis is true. The chance of Type I error here is large enough that the null hypothesis should not be rejected. We came to this same conclusion when we tested B_2 using classical hypothesis testing with a 5% significance level. Sometimes researchers simply report the p-value for the test instead of stating a significance level beforehand.

The hypothesis for ADVERTISING requires a one-sided test, but the p-value 0.024 in Table 3-B is for a two-sided test. For a one-sided test, the p-value is half of the two-sided test value. Here, the p-value for a one-sided test is 0.012. For H_0: $B_3 \leq 0$ and H_A: $B_3 > 0$, the null hypothesis can be rejected with a 5% chance of Type I error. This is consistent with our conclusion using the decision rule: The null hypothesis $B_3 \leq 0$ is rejected at a 5% significance level. (If the appropriate one-sided p-value is greater than 0.05, the chance of a Type I error is greater than 5%, and the null hypothesis cannot be rejected at this significance level.)

Confidence Intervals

A confidence interval is a range that contains B, the true value of the slope coefficient, with a specified probability. In the statement "The true value of the slope, B, lies between 10.5 and 18 with 95% probability," the researcher is 95% confident that B lies within this interval. This also means there is a 5% chance that B lies outside this interval. To calculate the confidence interval, we use the slope estimate, the standard error of the slope estimate, and a critical value for a two-sided test.

$$\hat{B} - [t_c \cdot SE(\hat{B})] < B < \hat{B} + [t_c \cdot SE(\hat{B})] \qquad \textbf{(3-5)}$$

The probability that the true value of the slope will fall within the interval depends on the t_c that we choose. To be 95% sure that the true value falls within the interval, we would use a t_c for a two-sided 5% significance level. For a 99% confidence level, we would use a t_c for a two-sided 1% significance level. Raising the confidence level makes the interval larger, since the chance of the true value falling outside the interval is smaller.

Let's use the results for SALE ITEMS in the electronics store model to compute a confidence interval. The critical value t_c is for a two-sided t-test with a 5% significance level and 120 degrees of freedom. (We used this same critical value for the two-sided hypothesis test of B_2.) Consulting Table 3-B gives us the lower and upper ends of the 95% confidence interval:

$$\hat{B}_2 - t_c \cdot SE(\hat{B}_2) = 530.87 - (1.98 \cdot 695.86) = -846.93 \qquad \text{Lower end of interval}$$
$$\hat{B}_2 + t_c \cdot SE(\hat{B}_2) = 530.86 + (1.98 \cdot 695.86) = 1908.66 \qquad \text{Upper end of interval}$$

This confidence interval tells us there is a 95% chance that the true value of the SALE ITEMS slope coefficient, B_2, lies between -846.93 and 1908.66. The chance that the true value of B_2 lies *outside* the interval is 5%. Also note that because the interval includes zero, we cannot say that there is only a 5% chance that the true B_2 is zero. This is the same as saying that we cannot reject the null hypothesis H_0: $B_2 = 0$ in a two-sided test. If a 95% confidence interval does not contain zero, then there is only a 5% chance the true value of B_2 is zero. (This is the same as saying the null hypothesis is rejected at 5% significance.) Confidence intervals can be used instead of classical hypothesis testing; the two methods are equivalent. Both classical hypothesis testing and confidence intervals will give you the same answer.

Statistical Significance Can Be Trivial

An independent variable that is statistically significant is not necessarily important. Suppose a statistically inclined truck driver wants to figure out what factors affect her truck's gas mileage. The driver sets up a regression model with miles per gallon for each trip (MPG) as the dependent variable. Her independent variables are outside temperature, average speed, average tire pressure, and the number of Garth Brooks songs played on the country music station during each trip. Our truck driver, because she is knowledgeable about regression, is also a skeptic. She wonders if variables can be significant by coincidence, so she has added the Garth Brooks variable to her model just to see what happens. Table 3-C shows her results.

In theory, outside temperature could affect the miles per gallon achieved. Perhaps the truck's engine doesn't work as well in very cold temperatures. If this is true, the slope coefficient for outside temperature should be positive and statistically significant. Of all the t-statistics shown in Table 3-C the t-statistic for TEMPERATURE is farthest

Table 3-C

Regression Results for Trucker's Model

Dependent Variable: MPG

Variable	Coefficient	Standard Error	t-Statistic	p-Value
Constant	12.74	17.58	0.72	0.47
TEMPERATURE	0.002	0.00005	40.00	0.00
GARTH	−0.038	0.014	−2.14	0.038
SPEED	−0.22	0.071	−3.10	0.00
TIRE PRESSURE	0.52	0.21	2.48	0.02

Observations: 50
$R^2 = 0.87$
Adjusted $R^2 = 0.85$
F-statistic = 77.33

from zero. The econometrics software lists the p-value as 0.00. Taken literally, this would mean that there is no chance that the true slope coefficient of TEMPERATURE is zero. We know, however, that this cannot be the case; there is always some probability of Type I error, even if it's very small. The software has rounded off the p-value— that is, the p-value is less than 0.005, so the program rounded the value down to 0.00.

However, statistical significance alone does not mean an independent variable is important. Even though the t-statistic for TEMPERATURE is farthest from zero, it is not the most important variable. The coefficient estimate is 0.002. Keeping other variables constant, this means that if TEMPERATURE rises by 1 degree, on average MPG will increase by only 0.002. A 10-degree rise in outside temperature generates only a 0.02 increase in miles per gallon. The slope coefficient of 0.002 may be statistically significantly different from zero, but that does not mean that TEMPERATURE is important for miles per gallon.

Common sense must be applied when interpreting regression results. Notice that GARTH is also statistically significant. The results indicate that when Garth Brooks songs are played on the radio, MPG gets worse. This doesn't make sense. This result is probably just a coincidence. The p-value reported for the GARTH slope t-test is 0.038. There is a 3.8% chance that the true value of the slope for GARTH is zero. Perhaps the 3.8% chance has occurred in this particular sample of data, giving us a Type I error. After seeing the results in Table 3-C, the driver is tempted to make up a theory to explain why GARTH is significant. After seeing the results, the driver wonders if maybe she drives faster when the radio plays Garth Brooks songs. If so, it would explain why more Garth Brooks songs are associated with lower miles per gallon. She could see if GARTH and SPEED are correlated or move together. However, she should be wary about inventing convoluted new theories after the fact. The truck driver is an experienced professional, so it doesn't make a lot of sense that she would change her speed depending on the songs being played on the radio. Besides, she doesn't always play the radio and she listens to several stations that don't play country music.[3] It is probably just luck that it came out this way. If we wanted to test this new Garth Brooks theory, we could ask the driver to collect more data so that we could rerun the regression to see if the GARTH coefficient estimate comes out both significant and negative again. If we get a statistically significant result over and over, then maybe our driver really does increase her speed during Garth Brooks songs!

SPEED and TIRE PRESSURE are both statistically significant at a 5% error level.[4] The coefficient estimate is 0.52 for TIRE PRESSURE and -0.22 for SPEED. At first glance, TIRE PRESSURE appears to be more important than SPEED. This is not necessarily true. The -0.22 slope estimate for SPEED indicates the average decrease in MPG for a 1 mile per hour change in speed, keeping the other independent variables constant. This is a very small change. The 0.52 slope estimate for TIRE PRESSURE gives the average increase in miles per gallon for a 1-pound increase in average tire pressure, keeping the other independent variables constant. These two units of measure

---

[3] If she didn't listen to the country music station the whole time, the driver could have acquired data for GARTH directly from the radio station.

[4] The driver never overinflates the tires; so in the data set, the higher the tire pressure, the closer it is to the best level.

are not comparable, and therefore we cannot conclude from these two slope estimates that TIRE PRESSURE is more important than SPEED.

3-3 F-TEST OF ALL INDEPENDENT VARIABLES

To test joint null hypotheses—that is, hypotheses that have more than one slope coefficient—we use the **F-test**. t-tests can be used only on null hypotheses involving one slope coefficient, as we noted earlier. F-tests can be designed to test different types of joint hypotheses. All econometrics software packages calculate one specific type of F-test for ordinary least squares regressions. This specific F-test asks, are any of the slope coefficients statistically different from zero? Here are the null and alternative hypotheses that such software uses to calculate the F-test:

$$H_0: B_1 = B_2 = B_3 = \cdots = B_k = 0$$

$$H_A: \text{At least one of these B's is not zero.} \tag{3-6}$$

where k is the number of independent variables in the regression.

If the null hypothesis is true, then none of the slope coefficients are statistically different from zero. We know this cannot be true unless *all* of the independent variables are worthless in explaining the dependent variable. If the regression is to have any value in explaining why the dependent variable takes the values that it does, we should be able to reject the null hypothesis given in Equation (3-6). However, the fact that the F-test allows us to reject the null hypothesis does not guarantee that the model is good at explaining the dependent variable. Sometimes an F-test rejects the null hypothesis shown in Equation (3-6) even when none of the individual t-statistics are statistically significant.[5] Here is how the F-statistic for the null hypothesis shown in (3-6) is calculated:

$$F = \frac{\text{ESS}/k}{\text{RSS}/(n - k - 1)} \tag{3-7}$$

The decision rule for the F-test is similar to that of the t-test. If an F-statistic calculated using Equation (3-7) is larger than its critical value, we reject the null hypothesis. The critical value is found from an F-distribution table. (See Table C or D in the Appendix.) As with the t-test, a significance level (usually 1% or 5%) must be chosen for the F-test. The critical value for the F-test has two numbers—for two different degrees of freedom—associated with it. (The t-statistic had one number for the degrees of freedom.) The two different degrees of freedom in the F-statistic are as follows:

1. k = number of independent variables in the regression [called the degrees of freedom in the numerator, since k appears in the top half of the F-statistic formula in (3-7)].

---

[5] This can happen if the independent variables are correlated (move in a related fashion). This phenomenon comes up again in Chapter 6, which discusses multicollinearity.

2. $n - k - 1$ = the regular degrees of freedom for the regression [called the degrees of freedom in the denominator, since $n - k - 1$ appears in the bottom half of the F-statistic formula in (3-7)].

When you look up the critical value for an F-test, remember that the degrees of freedom in the numerator are written along the top of the table, and the degrees of freedom in the denominator are along the side. You must use both to find the correct critical value for this test. The critical value is often written in the form $F_{k, n-k-1}$ where actual numbers are used to show the degrees of freedom in the numerator and denominator ($F_{4,60}$ for example).

Almost all econometrics software calculates the F-statistic for the null hypothesis shown in Equation (3-6). The F-statistic for the electronics store model is 65.26 (Table 3-B). Since there are 3 degrees of freedom in the numerator and 120 degrees of freedom in the denominator, Table D in the Appendix shows a critical value for $F_{3,120}$ of 3.95 at a 1% significance level. Since the F-statistic from the regression results, 65.26, is greater than its critical value of 3.95, the null hypothesis is rejected at a 1% significance level. It is very unlikely that the null hypothesis is true; at least one of the independent variables in the model appears to be statistically relevant. You can use F-tests to look at other joint null hypotheses besides $B_1 = B_2 = B_3 = \cdots = B_k = 0$ (that all slope coefficients are zero). These other applications of the F-test are presented in Section 5-3.

3-4 GOODNESS OF FIT: HOW WELL DOES IT WORK?

We can use t-tests to examine hypotheses concerning individual coefficients in the results, but we also want a measure of how well the regression model fits the data as a whole. The F-test of all independent variables discussed above is only of limited use. Since the null hypothesis is that *all* of the slope coefficients are zero, it is often easily rejected, even at a 1% significance level. Therefore, rejecting this particular null hypothesis does not mean the regression fits the data well. We need an overall measure of the regression's goodness of fit: How well does the regression work in explaining how the dependent variable moves?

Keep in mind, though, that goodness of fit does not prove causality. Excellent goodness of fit does not *prove* that the independent variables *cause* the dependent variable. However good a regression is, the best it can do is show that movement in the independent variables is associated with movement in the dependent variable (see Section 1-2).

R^2

The most common measure of goodness of fit is R^2. Sometimes called the coefficient of determination, most of the time this statistic is simply called "R-squared." R^2 is the ratio of the explained sum of squares to the total sum of squares:[6]

$$R^2 = \frac{ESS}{TSS} \tag{3-8}$$

---

[6] Section 1-3 introduces the total and explained sums of squares.

R^2 measures the portion of the movement in the dependent variable that can be explained by the regression model. The larger the R^2, the better the model's goodness of fit. The explained sum of squares can never be larger than the total sum of squares, and both are always positive. Because of this,

$$0 \le R^2 \le 1 \tag{3-9}$$

If R^2 is close to 1, then the regression explains most of the movement in the dependent variable. However, if R^2 equals 1, or is very close to 1 (say 0.9999), be suspicious! An R^2 of 1 is too good to be true—something is wrong. Perhaps there are mistakes in the data.[7] After being surprised by regression results with a very high R^2, two researchers discovered that an observation for one of the independent variables, which should have been a two-digit number, was incorrectly entered as 999,999,999. This single incorrect value, in a sample size of over 500, caused R^2 to increase dramatically in a misleading manner.[8] On the other hand, an R^2 close to zero means the regression is poor at explaining movement in the dependent variable.

There is no absolute standard for R^2, one that says, for example, "An R^2 larger than 0.75 (or any other number) means the model is good." Typically, R^2 is higher in time-series regressions than in cross-section regressions. The area of study is important also. If changes in the dependent variable are hard to explain, then 0.40 might be a great R^2, but if the dependent variable is easily predicted, an R^2 of 0.80 may indicate a poor fit.

Adjusted R^2

As a goodness-of-fit measure, R^2 has a serious problem. If a new independent variable is added to a regression, R^2 will increase, even if the new independent variable is a random number that has nothing to do with the dependent variable. Reconsider Equation (3-8) for a moment: $R^2 = ESS/TSS$. The denominator here, total sum of squares, measures movement in the dependent variable. Therefore, it doesn't change when an independent variable is added to the model. However, the numerator, explained sum of squares, does change when an independent variable is added; it increases. Just by pure luck, *any* set of numbers used as an independent variable will increase the explained sum of squares by at least a small amount. This doesn't mean that the new variable does us any good, though. Adding independent variables to a model burns up degrees of freedom: $n - k - 1$ gets smaller and smaller as k, the number of independent variables, gets larger. Fewer degrees of freedom means the software has less information to work with, making it harder for the estimates to be precise (the standard errors of the estimates will tend to be larger).

Adjusted R^2, symbolized by $\bar{R}^2$, solves the problem. **Adjusted R^2, $\bar{R}^2$,** changes the regular R^2 by taking the degrees of freedom into account. The fewer the degrees of free-

---

[7] Another cause of misleading high R^2 values is discussed in Section 4-3.

[8] The data were from an old magnetic mainframe computer tape, where 999,999,999 was used to indicate a missing value.

dom, the smaller the adjusted R^2, assuming everything else stays constant. When a new independent variable is added to a regression, it must add enough explanatory power to justify losing a degree of freedom, or the value of $\bar{R}^2$ will fall. In other words, when we add an independent variable, in order for to $\bar{R}^2$ to increase, there must be an increase in the explained sum of squares to compensate for losing a degree of freedom. Otherwise, $\bar{R}^2$ falls. This makes the adjusted R^2 a better measure of goodness of fit than the unadjusted R^2, because we can't "pump up" the adjusted R^2 by adding independent variables willy-nilly. The following equation converts regular R^2 to adjusted R^2 but most econometric programs report both R^2 and $\bar{R}^2$ automatically.

$$\bar{R}^2 = 1 - \left[(1 - R^2) \cdot \left(\frac{n-1}{n-k-1} \right) \right] \qquad \text{(3-10)}$$

When the number of independent variables is small, the difference between R^2 and $\bar{R}^2$ is small. As the number of independent variables increases, the difference becomes larger.

Here is a useful rule that tells you how $\bar{R}^2$ changes if an independent variable is omitted from a regression. Look at the t-statistic for the variable's coefficient estimate. If this t-statistic is less than 1, and the corresponding independent variable is dropped from the regression, $\bar{R}^2$ will rise. If it is greater than 1, and the corresponding independent variable is dropped from the regression, $\bar{R}^2$ will fall. From these rules, $\bar{R}^2$ will be maximized if you include only independent variables with t-statistics greater than 1.[9]

It is tempting—but poor procedure—to conduct econometric research by simply maximizing $\bar{R}^2$. Resist this temptation. Simply maximizing $\bar{R}^2$ is not the goal. It is more important to use common sense than to blindly follow rules to maximize $\bar{R}^2$. If econometrics were conducted strictly "by the rules," robots and computers would have long since replaced us. In the trucker's model, we saw how an independent variable could show statistical significance and still be a coincidence. If the truck driver conducting the research follows the rule for maximizing $\bar{R}^2$, she might leave in GARTH as an independent variable, even though it is silly. If the model is used with other data, or to forecast MPG in the future, including GARTH might very well weaken her model's performance.

Another key point—$\bar{R}^2$ can only be used to compare the goodness of fit between regressions in which the dependent variable and sample used in the regression are the same. (The independent variables can be different.) If the dependent variable measures the severity of earthquakes, an adjusted $\bar{R}^2$ of 0.50 would be impressive, because the severity of earthquakes is very difficult to predict. However, an adjusted $\bar{R}^2$ of 0.50 for time-series regression where interest rate is the dependent variable would be very poor indeed.

---

[9] P. J. Dhrymes, "On the Game of Maximizing Adjusted R^2," *Australian Economic Papers*, Vol. 9, December 1970, pp. 177–85.

SUMMARY

1. A sample should be chosen at random to make it more likely it will represent the population.

2. The steps of hypothesis testing are as follows:
    *   Clearly state the hypothesis to be tested, both in words and as null and alternative hypotheses.
    *   State the level of statistical significance for the test.
    *   Run a regression to get the coefficient estimates and statistics necessary for the hypothesis test.
    *   Use the decision rule along with the regression results to decide whether to reject the null hypothesis.

3. The null hypothesis is set up so that it is the opposite of the hypothesis to be tested. The alternative hypothesis represents the hypothesis to be tested.

4. If the alternative hypothesis features a "greater than" or "less than" symbol ($>$ or $<$), a one-sided test is appropriate. If the alternative hypothesis features a "not equals" symbol ($\neq$), a two-sided test is appropriate.

5. Two types of errors can occur in hypothesis testing. A **Type I error** occurs when the null hypothesis is true, but it is rejected. This means the truth is being rejected. A **Type II error** occurs when the null hypothesis is false, but it is not rejected. This means a false statement is not rejected.

6. The significance level, or error level, associated with a hypothesis test refers to the probability of Type I error. For example, if the null hypothesis can be rejected at a 5% error level, there is a 5% chance of Type I error.

7. The t-test is used to check whether a slope coefficient is statistically significantly different from zero, given a specified error level, such as 5%. A t-statistic is calculated using the formula:

$$t = \frac{\hat{B} - B_{null}}{SE(\hat{B})}$$

If this calculated t-statistic exceeds its critical value (found in a t-table), the null hypothesis is rejected.

8. An independent variable that is statistically significant is not necessarily important. A slope coefficient for an independent variable can be significantly different from zero; that does not by itself mean the independent variable has an important impact on the dependent variable.

9. An F-test is used to check the hypothesis that all slope coefficients in a regression are zero, given a specified error level. If the F-statistic exceeds its critical value (found in a table for the F-distribution), the null hypothesis is rejected. The critical value for the F-test has two numbers for two different degrees of freedom associated with it. The degrees of freedom in the numerator are the number of slope coefficients estimated in the regression, k. The degrees of freedom in the denominator are the "regular" degrees of freedom for the regression, $n - k - 1$. These degrees of freedom must be used to find the critical value for the F-test.

10. R^2 and **adjusted R^2** ($\bar{R}^2$) measure a regression's goodness of fit (how well the regression works in explaining the dependent variable). R^2 is the ratio of the

explained sum of squares to the total sum of squares. R^2 has a serious problem as a goodness-of-fit measure. If an additional independent variable is added to the regression, R^2 will increase, even if the new independent variable is a random number that has nothing to do with the dependent variable. When new independent variables are added to a regression, the degrees of freedom become smaller. Adjusted R^2 accounts for this by accounting for degrees of freedom.

EXERCISES

1. Try to explain these terms without looking them up.
   - sample
   - population
   - selection bias
   - decision rule
   - one-sided test
   - two-sided test
   - Type I error
   - Type II error
   - critical value
   - F-test
   - R^2
   - $\overline{R}^2$

2. a. What is the difference between a Type I and a Type II error?
   b. Which of these two types of errors is considered when conducting a t-test?

3. a. Consider the following statement: "B_2 is statistically significant at the 1% error level." Explain what this means so that someone unfamiliar with statistics can understand it.
   b. What if the statement is, "B_2 is statistically significant at the 5% error level"?
   c. From the researcher's point of view, which statement are you more likely to be able to prove? Which statement is more convincing? Briefly explain.

4. For the same estimate, which confidence interval will be larger, a confidence interval using a 1% chance of error or a 5% chance of error? Why?

5. Construct confidence intervals (rounded to two decimal places) for the slope coefficient estimates given for SPEED and TIRE PRESSURE in Table 3-C, at a 95% confidence level (this is the same as a 5% error level).

6. Theory should dictate whether a one-sided test or a two-sided test is appropriate for any particular situation. For example, if consumption is the dependent variable and income is an independent variable, then economic theory says the coefficient should be positive. In this case, it's appropriate to use a one-sided test. Suppose the coefficient estimate does come out positive. Now which type of test is more likely to reject the null hypothesis, a one-sided test or a two-sided test?

7. a. State null and alternative hypotheses for the slope coefficients in Quinn's multiple DVD model.

$$DVDEXP = B_0 + B_1 INCOME + B_2 PRICE + B_3 RAINFALL + e \quad (2\text{-}2)$$

    b. Explain how you can convert a p-value reported in standard regression results so that you can use it in a one-sided test.

8. Say whether each statement is true or false. If the statement is false, explain why.
   a. $\hat{B}_1$ is statistically significant at a 1% error level, so the null hypothesis is false.
   b. $\hat{B}_1$ is statistically significant at a 25% error level, so it is most likely that the null hypothesis is true.
   c. $\hat{B}_1$ is not statistically significant at a 5% error level, so the null hypothesis is not rejected, and there is a 5% chance the null hypothesis is false.
   d. It is impossible for a Type I error and a Type II error to occur at the same time.

9. When is it appropriate to use adjusted R^2 to compare two regressions?

10. a. What rule describes the relationship between adjusted R^2 and a t-statistic?
    b. What do you do if the two statistics give you contradictory results? In other words, what does it mean if the t-statistic indicates the coefficient for an independent variable is statistically insignificant, but the adjusted R^2 says the goodness of fit is better with the variable?

11. Suppose that an F-test rejects the null hypothesis that all the slope coefficients equal zero.
    a. Does this provide evidence that the regression gives a reasonable goodness of fit?
    b. If so, why? If not, what does the rejection of the null hypothesis tell us?

12. a. What does it mean to say, "statistical significance can be trivial"?
    b. Give an example of a regression with an independent variable that appears to have a statistically significant coefficient, yet it is still trivial. (Don't use an example given in the text.)

13. Suppose you want to find R^2 for the DVD results presented in Chapter 1. How could you use your answer from Question 14 of Chapter 1 to find R^2? Explain.

14. a. Here are the results for Quinn's multiple DVD model, estimated using the first sample 1 (Table 2-A). Find the missing values in the table (marked with a ?).

Quinn's Multiple DVD's Model: Regression Results for First Sample

Dependent Variable: DVDEXP

Variable	Coefficient	Standard Error	t-Statistic	Significant at a 5% error level?
Constant	89.09	41.01	?	?
INCOME	0.064	0.019	?	?
PRICE	−3.18	1.47	?	?
RAINFALL	6.05	4.37	?	?

Observations: 12

$R^2 = 0.79$

Adjusted $R^2 = ?$

F-statistic = 9.93

b. What do your answers in the last column tell you? Explain it in a way that someone who isn't studying econometrics can understand.

c. Compare the R^2 and adjusted R^2 you found in part a. Why aren't they closer together?

15. a. The following table gives the results of Quinn's multiple DVD model when it is estimated with the second sample (Table 2-C). Find the missing values in the table (marked with a ?).

Quinn's Multiple DVD's Model: Regression Results for Second Sample

Dependent Variable: DVDEXP

Variable	Coefficient	Standard Error	t-Statistic	Significant at a 5% error level?
Constant	78.24	31.63	?	?
INCOME	0.062	0.013	?	?
PRICE	−3.29	1.27	?	?
RAINFALL	8.61	3.17	?	?

Observations: 12

$R^2 = 0.81$

Adjusted R^2 = ?

F-statistic = 11.12

b. What can you conclude from looking at the answers you found for the last column?

c. Why do these results come out differently from those for the previous question? Is this a problem? Explain.

16. Suppose that for a sample size n = 20, a regression has $R^2 = 0.70$. Calculate the adjusted R^2 if

a. k = 4

b. k = 9

c. k = 14

d. What do your answers to parts a–c tell you about how adjusted R^2 works? Explain.

e. In reality, would R^2 stay the same as more independent variables are added? Does this change your answer to part d?

17. Suppose that for a regression with four independent variables, $R^2 = 0.70$. Calculate the adjusted R^2 if

a. n = 10

b. n = 20

c. n = 100

d. What do your answers to parts a–c tell you about the relationship between n and adjusted R^2? Explain.

e. Will R^2 stay at 0.70 if the sample size is increased? Is that a problem for the point you made in part d?

4

Basics in Conducting Econometric Research

In this chapter, you will learn about:

- How to choose a topic.
- How to choose good dependent and independent variables.
- How to adjust a time-series variable for inflation.
- How to adjust a cross-section variable to avoid estimation problems.
- What happens when important independent variables are omitted and unnecessary ones are added.
- Where to search the Internet for data.
- How to write an econometrics paper.

You have to do econometrics to learn it. It is critical that you do some type of econometrics research project in order to put the econometrics you are learning to use. In this chapter we guide you through a project. Section 4-1 is about choosing a topic to research. Section 4-2 examines how to conduct a search of the literature, to see what research has already been done on your topic. Next, Section 4-3 presents factors to consider when choosing variables for your model. Section 4-3 also explains what happens if you include an extra independent variable that does not belong in the model or if you omit a relevant one. Section 4-4 discusses the importance of objectivity in econometric research. Section 4-5 gives suggestions on where to find data for estimating your model. The last section, Section 4-6, describes a typical format used to write up your research.

4-1 CHOOSING A TOPIC

One of the most important factors in choosing a good topic is finding one that sounds interesting and fun to you. A topic that genuinely interests you is much more enjoyable to work on. Think about something you already know about, perhaps from a job or an interest you have. See if you can think of a question about it that could be answered using an econometric model. For example, if you like films, you might want to know what factors influence box office receipts. You could put together a regression model in which the dependent variable is the box office receipts for different films released during the past year. The independent variables could measure factors that, in theory, would be relevant to box office receipts, such as the amount of money spent on promoting and advertising the film, the film-making budget, and so on. (You can probably think of others.)

Econometrics is also applied to situations that are not strictly economic. For example, econometrics can be used to study sports. You could build a regression model to study what factors make a winning baseball team. The dependent variable could be percentage of games won in the past season by each team, and the independent variables could be performance statistics that measure each team's hitting, pitching, fielding, and so on. In fact, so many people are engaged in the study of baseball using statistics and econometrics that the activity has its own name, *sabermetrics*.[1]

Once you come up with an idea for a study, you need to make sure it is practical. Some ideas will be difficult to carry out because the data you need are either not available or very difficult to obtain. Conducting an extensive survey to get the data you need may take too long, and the data you end up with may not be accurate. Baseball players' salaries are publicly available, so you could include the amount each team pays in salaries as an independent variable in the baseball study mentioned above.[2] However, if you want to study the profits of dry cleaners, you might have a hard time, since dry cleaners' profits are private and not readily available. You could survey dry cleaning businesses to put together a sample, but some owners might not want to participate, and there would be no guarantee that those who do participate will be truthful. It would be tough to get around this problem, making the study difficult to complete.

If you are having trouble coming up with a good topic, think about issues you have studied in other classes, such as international trade, macroeconomics, economic development, labor, or other subjects that interest you. You may want to look at the data sources listed in Section 4-5 to see all the different types of data that are available, and that may inspire an idea for a project. Econometrics research can be fun, especially if you choose a topic that interests you.

4-2 THE LITERATURE REVIEW: WHAT'S BEEN DONE ALREADY

Once you have identified an area of interest for your study, you will need to see what research has been done in that area. Your model should be based on theory, so you may need to read appropriate sources to learn about accepted theory for your topic. For example, if you decide to build a regression model that tests how real wages affect immigration, you might consult a labor economics textbook. In addition, there are papers written by economists in academic journals that present theory applied to different situations. These papers often contain econometric models. You can search for

---

[1] For more information, http://www.baseball1.com/c-sabr.html provides links to sabermetric sites.
[2] Baseball salaries are available at http://asp.usatoday.com/sports/baseball/salaries. Click on the team you want and then click on salaries.

papers in the area of interest by using an on-line service called EconLit. Many university libraries provide access to this service. EconLit tells you what papers have been written about your topic and which journals have published these papers. When using the service, define your topic as precisely as you can. Otherwise, you will end up with a long list of papers, many of which will not be of interest to you.

As soon as you have a list of papers from EconLit that look promising, find the journals containing the papers in the library or through interlibrary loan, if your library doesn't have a particular journal. Some journals now post their papers on-line. A list of economics journals with links to their home pages can be found by going to http://www.econlit.org, and then clicking on "Journal List" on the left-hand side of the page. However, not all journals provide on-line access to their papers. Your library may provide another on-line service, called JSTOR (Journal Storage). JSTOR provides on-line back issues of some of the most prestigious economics journals, such as the *Journal of Political Economy* and the *American Economic Review*. If you're looking for a paper that is more than two years old, JSTOR may be a good place to locate it. Many libraries also have ABI/Inform, which is useful for finding articles in business periodicals and newspapers.

Some research papers examine the newest developments in theory. Others discuss econometric models; you can see the dependent and independent variables used and where the data come from, along with the results of the model. Be forewarned, though, that many of these papers are complicated. Even if you don't understand all the mathematics presented in a paper, you may still be able to learn something useful by noting what data and variables are used in the models. Reading the abstract, introduction, and conclusion may help you understand the main point of the paper even if you don't understand all the methods used in it.

Summarize each article you find that is relevant to your project. Keep track of the bibliographical information for each paper (title, author, name of the journal, volume and number or month and year of the issue, and page numbers). You will need this information if you cite the work in your paper, which you should do if the paper is useful in doing your research or if the paper would be useful to someone reading your work. If you use a statistic or fact from a paper that is not common knowledge, cite the paper so that someone reading your work can find the original source of the information. Provide the page number where the information is found so that your reader can easily access the material.

4-3 DETERMINING THE DEPENDENT AND INDEPENDENT VARIABLES

The main consideration in choosing the dependent and independent variables for a model is theory. The dependent and independent variables should make sense before you run any regressions. Theory also helps you determine the proper form of the regression. (There are other types of regressions besides the linear ones presented so far; some of these will be discussed in later chapters.)

Consider your dependent variable carefully. What are you trying to explain or measure? In Chapter 2 we featured a model in which the dependent variable was the amount spent on DVDs. We could have used other dependent variables, such as the number of

DVDs bought each month. Of course, changing the dependent variable in this manner changes the meaning of the regression. If the dependent variable is the number bought, instead of the amount spent, the slope estimates will relate a change in an independent variable to the average change in Q (quantity bought), rather than the change in P · Q (price multiplied by quantity, the amount spent). Since the price of DVDs varies depending on the movie, this difference changes the regression dramatically. Whether you use the number of DVDs bought or the amount spent on them as your dependent variable depends on what aspect of the situation you are studying.

Use theory *and* common sense to choose the independent variables. If your topic concerns economics, ask yourself what basic economic theory has to say about the situation. Is your model consistent with the relevant theory? Do the independent variables you have chosen make sense for the dependent variable in the model? Your answers to these questions should be a confident "yes" before you invest time in searching for data. Also, think about whether you are leaving out an important independent variable that should be included. This is where understanding the accepted theory behind your topic can help you avoid mistakes early on.

Don't throw everything you can think of into the model; this is as big a mistake as leaving out relevant variables. If the dependent variable in your model is the quantity sold of one brand of soft drink, theory indicates that the price of the soft drink should be an independent variable, along with prices of substitute or complementary goods. This doesn't mean that you should include the price of every substitute or complementary good you can think of; include only those that appear to have a strong relationship with the soft drink measured by the dependent variable. People drink soft drinks with many different foods, so it is unlikely that any one food will be a better complement to the soft drink than another. For example, if the price of pretzels changed, it probably won't have a serious effect on the amount of drink sold. Therefore, you wouldn't include the price of complementary goods in this particular regression.

If you use every possible independent variable that you can think of, you increase the chance of Type I error occurring somewhere in your regression. The more independent variables there are in your model, the more likely a Type I error will occur for at least one of the slope coefficients.

Let's say the drink you are studying is a cola. A good candidate for an independent variable is the price of a similar soft drink—another cola available in the same market—because it's a close substitute for the drink you are studying. Strictly speaking, beer could be considered a substitute for your cola, but this is a stretch. Beer really isn't a good candidate for an independent variable. An increase in the price of beer is unlikely to increase sales of your cola by a noticeable amount. Neither is a decrease in the price of beer likely to hurt the cola's sales. We discuss the consequences of omitting relevant independent variables and adding irrelevant ones in more detail later in this chapter.

Change Is Good: Variables Should Vary

Regression models work better if their variables change or move a lot within the sample data. Regression models are estimated by measuring how the dependent variable moves when an independent variable moves, keeping the remaining variables constant.

If the dependent variable hardly moves over the sample, or if an independent variable doesn't move much, you may not get a good estimate of how those two variables are related. In the cola example, if your sample is so small that amount of cola sold doesn't change much throughout the sample, you won't have enough information available in the data for the regression process to come up with good estimates. Without much movement in your dependent variable, the ordinary least squares method will have to make a big deal out of any small change in amount of cola sold. This could lead to inaccurate slope estimates. A larger sample with a lot of variation in the amount of cola sold is better. Such a sample contains more information, which gives the OLS method more to work with as you estimate relationships between the independent variables and the dependent variable.

It is also a good idea for each independent variable to vary considerably throughout the sample. Consider what happens if an independent variable never changes. The estimation procedure has no way of measuring how the quantity of cola sold changes when its price changes, if the price never changes! One way to deal with this potential problem is to use as large a sample size as possible; this makes substantial change more likely for all the variables in the model. Keep this concept in mind as you construct your model; avoid designing a model with a dependent or independent variable that is unlikely to vary much. Think about Quinn's multiple DVD model, in which monthly rainfall was an independent variable. If Quinn lives in the desert, we would not use this as an independent variable. In the desert, there is often no rainfall for months on end, and even when it does rain, the change in rainfall from one month to another is usually very small.[3] It is highly unlikely that desert rainfall would affect Quinn's DVD expenditures, and the effect would not be measurable. This variable would not vary enough to matter.

Tautology: A Perfect but Useless Regression

A **tautology** is a statement or equation that is true by definition. A regression that is a tautology always fits the data perfectly every time, regardless of what sample is used. A tautology is always true, so there is no point in using a regression to test it. From macroeconomics, gross domestic product (GDP) is defined as

$$GDP = C + G + I + (X - M) \qquad (4\text{-}1)$$

where

$$C = \text{consumption}$$
$$G = \text{government expenditures}$$
$$I = \text{investment}$$
$$X - M = \text{exports} - \text{imports}$$

Suppose we decide to estimate the following regression model:

$$GDP = B_0 + B_1C + B_2G + B_3I + B_4(X - M) + e \qquad (4\text{-}2)$$

---

[3] If interested, see http://www.desertmuseum.org/programs/flw_mohave.html.

This regression attempts to test whether changes in GDP are associated with changes in C, G, I, or (X − M). We already know the answer without running the regression. GDP is calculated by adding up C, G, I, and (X − M), so this regression will always work, by definition. Each slope coefficient has a true value of 1. If any one independent variable increases by a dollar, GDP automatically increases by a dollar. Also, the true value of the intercept B_0 is zero, since the GDP will be zero if C, G, I, and X − M are all zero. If the data are measured accurately, this regression will always have a perfect fit, an R^2 equal to 1. The slope estimates will all equal 1, and the intercept estimate will equal zero. There is no reason to run this regression; it tells us nothing, because we already know how the estimates will come out. You should avoid tautologies when designing a regression model.

Adjusting Time-Series Variables for Inflation

Time-series variables that are measured in money, such as income, gross domestic product, tax revenues, and price, will have larger values over time due to inflation. This affects regression results in a misleading way. An independent variable may seem to have a statistically significant coefficient, the independent and dependent variables may seem to be related, but what is really happening is they are both increasing just because of inflation. Consider the price of two goods that have little or nothing to do with each other, such as oil and books. If we run a regression with the price of oil as the dependent variable and the price of books as the independent variable, we might get a statistically significant, positive slope estimate for the price of books. However, it would be naïve to think that we have made an important discovery. The truth is, both are increasing over time because of inflation, not because books and oil have some sort of fundamental relationship.

Most of the time we want to eliminate the effects of inflation from our models. We must adjust each variable affected by inflation to account for the inflation. We want real values for our variables, without inflation making the values larger. An appropriate price index is used to do this. One of the most common price indexes that is used for this purpose is the Consumer Price Index. The Consumer Price Index (CPI), calculated by the Bureau of Labor Statistics, measures the cost of a common "basket of goods" over time. It is set equal to 100 for the years 1982–1984; these years are the basis for comparison. Equation (4-3) adjusts a nominal value (unadjusted) to an inflation-free value.

$$\frac{\text{nominal (raw) value}}{(\text{price index}/100)} = \text{real value (adjusted for inflation)} \qquad \textbf{(4-3)}$$

The price index is divided by 100 because the index is automatically defined as 100 in the base period. (As mentioned, the base period for the Consumer Price Index is 1982–1984, but it could be different for other indices.)

Equation (4-3) is very helpful. It can be used to adjust a variable's values for inflation and also to answer such questions as, Which is worth more, $50,000 in 1990 or $60,000 in 2000? Table 4-A gives four values for an individual's income and shows

Table 4-A

Nominal and Real Income

Year	Nominal (Unadjusted) Income ($)	Consumer Price Index*	Real (Adjusted) Income [Equation (4-3)]
1970	10,000.00	38.84	$\frac{10,000.00}{(38.84/100)} = \frac{10,000.00}{0.3884} = 25,746.65$
1980	20,000.00	82.38	$\frac{20,000.00}{(82.38/100)} = \frac{20,000.00}{0.8238} = 24,277.74$
1990	40,000.00	130.66	$\frac{40,000.00}{(130.66/100)} = \frac{40,000.00}{1.3066} = 30,613.81$
2000	60,000.00	172.19	$\frac{60,000.00}{(172.19/100)} = \frac{60,000.00}{1.7219} = 34,845.23$

*The Consumer Price Index can be found at http://www.economagic.com.

how to use Equation (4-3) to adjust these numbers for inflation. The resulting values, in the last column of the table, are said to be in 1983 dollars since the price index used has a value of 100 in 1982–1984; that is, they show what the income would have been worth in 1982–1984.

Notice that from 1970 to 1980, this individual's nominal income increased by $10,000, but his real income actually decreased slightly, from $25,746.65 to $24,277.74. Using only nominal income values from 1970 to 2000 in a time-series regression is likely to give us misleading results. The ordinary least squares method would calculate estimates using income values that are increasing over time, when in fact, real income decreased from 1970 to 1980. Also, the increase in real income from 1980 to 2000 is much smaller than the nominal values would lead us to believe. You can use Equation (4-3) to adjust *all* the observations of a time-series variable for inflation, so that your regression results reflect real changes in the variable, without inflation.

Adjusting Cross-Section Variables for Population Size

Often, when running a cross-section regression, the size of the observations or the units in a sample will differ, and this can cause heteroskedasticity (see Section 2-2). For example, in a cross-section data sample of the 50 U.S. states, California and New York have the biggest populations, and Wyoming has the smallest. To make sure that the population of a state does not unduly affect the results, express appropriate variables as *per capita* (per person) or in percentages where the denominator is state population. For example, if state tax revenues are to be included in a cross-section model, don't define the variable as the total tax revenues in each state, because California and New York have more tax revenues simply because they have more people. A better approach would be to define this variable as the state tax revenues per person. As another example, suppose the number of retirees is to be part of the model. Once again, California and New York have a lot of retirees compared to many other states, simply because California and New York have more people. Instead, define the variable as the percentage of people in the state who are retired. We discuss this approach to avoiding heteroskedasticity in more detail in Chapter 8.

Variable Definitions and Slope Estimates

The units in which a variable is defined affect both its value and the interpretation of its slope estimate. Suppose we run a simple cross-section regression where

$$CARS = \text{new cars sold per year over the Internet, in each state}$$

$$POP = \text{state population}$$

Consider the results shown in Equation (4-4), where the independent variable is statistically significant at a 1% error level:

$$CARS = 375 + 0.003 \cdot POP \tag{4-4}$$

The slope coefficient 0.003 means that for every additional person in the state, the number of new cars sold over the Internet in that state will go up by an average of 0.003. This 0.003 figure is so small that it's hard to understand what these results are telling us. Now consider another definition for state population:

$$POP2 = \text{state population, in thousands of people}$$

Estimating the regression again using POP2 gives us these results:

$$CARS = 375 + 3.0 \cdot POP2 \tag{4-5}$$

This 3.0 slope coefficient means that on average for each 1000-person increase in state population, there will be an average increase of 3 new cars sold over the Internet in that state. This is much easier for us to understand than the 0.003 slope estimate we found earlier. The intercept, t-statistics, R^2, adjusted R^2, and F-statistic will all be the same whether POP2 or POP is used. In general, regardless of the model, the only thing that changes when you redefine an independent variable in this manner is its slope coefficient.

The slope estimate of 3 in Equation (4-5) can be found without estimating the regression. From the first regression, Equation (4-4), we know that on average for each additional person 0.003 new cars are sold over the Internet. In the second regression, one unit of POP2 is 1000 people. Therefore, by simple arithmetic, a 1-unit increase in POP (1 person) increases the number of new cars sold on the Internet by 0.003, so a 1-unit increase in POP2 (1000 people) increases new cars sold by 3 ($0.003 \cdot 1000 = 3$).

Next suppose we keep POP as the independent variable but change the units of the dependent variable.

CARS2

= new cars sold per year over the Internet in each state, in hundreds of cars

Using CARS2 as our dependent variable gives us these results:

$$CARS2 = 3.75 + 0.00003 \cdot POP \tag{4-6}$$

Notice that the intercept estimate has changed. Once again, you don't have to actually estimate the regression to get these results. Since a 1-unit change in CARS2 is 100 cars, we can find both the slope and intercept estimates by dividing the original estimates in Equation (4-4) by 100. Also, the results shown in this new regression, Equation (4-6), will have the same t-statistics, F-statistic, R^2, and adjusted R^2 as the other regressions in this example. However, using CARS2 as our dependent variable makes the slope estimate so small that it's hard to interpret. Equation (4-5) is easier to interpret. The lesson here is, think carefully about units when you are defining variables.

When Independent Variables Are Omitted

Omitting an important independent variable from a regression causes bias in the remaining estimates. To see this, let's examine a regression with two independent variables.

$$Y = B_0 + B_1X_1 + B_2X_2 + e \tag{4-7}$$

What happens when X_2 is omitted from this regression? (Perhaps the researcher didn't realize it was relevant or the data were unavailable.)

$$Y = B_0 + B_1X_1 + u \qquad \text{where } u = e + B_2X_2 \tag{4-8}$$

The explanatory power of X_2, which should be captured by B_2X_2, will be missing. It is now part of the error term, as shown in Equation (4-8). The error term u consists of the regular error term e plus B_2X_2. If the missing independent variable is correlated with the other independent variable X_1 in the model, it causes bias in the slope estimate of X_1. Remember one of the seven classical assumptions: Each independent variable in the regression must be uncorrelated with the error term. If a relevant independent variable is missing *and* it is correlated with an independent variable in the regression, this classical assumption will be violated. The independent variable in the regression will be correlated with the error term (since the error term secretly contains the missing variable), and this will bias the slope estimate.

The exact amount of bias cannot be measured, because we don't know the true value of any slope estimate. We can, however, estimate the direction of the bias.

$$\text{direction of bias} = B_{\text{omitted}} \cdot r_{\text{included, omitted}} \tag{4-9}$$

Equation (4-9) is not an equation that we use to calculate a number. It tells us whether the direction or sign of the bias is likely to be positive or negative. A positive bias means the estimated slope tends to be greater than the true value; a negative bias means the estimated slope tends to be lower than the true value. In Equation (4-9), B_{omitted} represents the sign of the slope for the omitted variable, and $r_{\text{included, omitted}}$ is the correlation coefficient between the omitted variable and an independent variable in the regression, the one for which you want to find the direction of bias.

Let's use Quinn's DVD model from Chapter 2 to see how Equation (4-9) estimates the direction of bias for a slope estimate.

$$DVDEXP = B_0 + B_1 INCOME + B_2 PRICE + B_3 RAINFALL + e \quad \textbf{(2-2)}$$

Suppose we neglect to include RAINFALL, so that we estimate

$$DVDEXP = B_0 + B_1 INCOME + B_2 PRICE + u \quad \textbf{(4-10)}$$

where $u = e + B_3 RAINFALL$

We can use Equation (4-9) to predict the direction of bias for either B_1 or B_2. We try it for B_1. As we discussed in Chapter 2, Quinn spends more on DVDs when it rains, so B_3 [which becomes $B_{omitted}$ in Equation (4-9)] is positive. Quinn also tends to work more hours in bad weather, so $r_{included, omitted}$ is also positive. (In fact, using the data from Table 2-B to calculate a correlation coefficient between RAINFALL and INCOME gives a positive value of 0.38.) The expected direction of bias for the estimate of B_1 is

$$direction\ of\ bias = B_{omitted} \cdot r_{included, omitted} = (+) \cdot (+) = (+)$$

The $(+)$ means the estimate of B_1 will tend to be higher than the true value. Table 4-B shows results of this regression without RAINFALL, using the data from Table 2-A.

In our original regression, which included RAINFALL (Table 2-B), the slope estimate for INCOME was 0.064, but here it is 0.073. The 0.064 value is not the true value; we can never know the true value of the slope coefficient. However, this shows that the slope estimate for INCOME is larger when RAINFALL is left out of the regression than when it is included. This is consistent with our idea that the slope estimate for INCOME will have a positive bias when RAINFALL is omitted. You will be asked to consider the potential bias of $\hat{B}_2$, the slope estimate for PRICE when RAINFALL is omitted from the regression, in an exercise at the end of this chapter.

Table 4-B

Regression Results for DVD Model without RAINFALL

Dependent Variable: DVDEXP

Variable	Coefficient	Standard Error	t-Statistic	p-Value
Constant	116.67	37.61	3.10	0.013
INCOME	0.073	0.019	3.95	0.003
PRICE	−3.65	1.51	−2.43	0.038

Observations: 12

$R^2 = 0.74$

Adjusted $R^2 = 0.68$

F-statistic = 12.65

When Extra Independent Variables Are Added

An extra independent variable will not cause the other slope estimates in the regression to be biased. By extra, it is meant that the independent variable is unnecessary or irrelevant to the model. If an irrelevant independent variable is included in a regression, the true value of its coefficient should be zero, so it shouldn't affect the rest of the regression. However, the presence of an irrelevant independent variable does increase the variance of the other estimated coefficients in the model. This means the estimated standard errors of the coefficients in the model will tend to be bigger, and the t-statistics will tend to be closer to zero. Adjusted R^2 will decrease because the extra variable uses up a degree of freedom without providing any substantial explanatory power.

Suppose we add a number drawn at random as an independent variable to Quinn's DVD regression (for each observation, a different random number is chosen). This independent variable, RANDOM, is the ultimate in irrelevant independent variables—it has no meaning and can be related to Quinn's DVD expenditures only by pure coincidence.

$$DVDEXP = B_0 + B_1 INCOME + B_2 PRICE + B_3 RAINFALL + B_4 RANDOM + e \tag{4-11}$$

Table 4-C gives the results, using the data from Table 2-A, with RANDOM added to the regression.

The slope estimate for RANDOM is very close to zero, just as we expected. It is not statistically different from zero, as can be seen by the 0.845 p-value. When the remaining coefficients are compared to the original results (Table 2-B), they are different, but the differences are small. It makes sense that the estimates are not exactly

Table 4-C

Regression Results for DVD Model with RANDOM Added

Dependent Variable: DVDEXP

Variable	Coefficient	Standard Error	t-Statistic	p-Value
Constant	87.39	44.50	1.96	0.090
INCOME	0.062	0.022	2.84	0.025
PRICE	-3.23	1.59	-2.03	0.082
RAINFALL	6.34	4.88	1.30	0.235
RANDOM	0.0000430	0.00021	0.20	0.845

Observations: 12

$R^2 = 0.79$

Adjusted $R^2 = 0.67$

F-statistic = 6.56

the same, because they are estimates, and by random luck, RANDOM will have some slight correlation with the other independent variables. The adjusted R^2 in our original regression is 0.71.[4] In this new regression the adjusted R^2 of 0.67 is smaller because RANDOM has been added. Table 2-B doesn't give t-statistics, but the t-statistic for the coefficient on INCOME decreases from 3.40 to 2.84 when RANDOM is included, the t-statistic for the PRICE coefficient changes from -2.16 to -2.03, and the t-statistic for the RAINFALL coefficient changes from 1.38 to 1.30. (The t-statistic for the intercept falls from 2.17 to 1.96.) As expected, the adjusted R^2 fell and the t-statistics became closer to zero when the irrelevant variable, RANDOM, was included.

4-4 OBJECTIVITY IN ECONOMETRICS

A good econometrician is objective. Always use proper econometric procedure to see if the data provides evidence that either supports or rejects the hypothesis being tested. Your personal opinions or feelings about the topic under study should not affect how you report your results. If you try different versions of the model, adding or omitting an independent variable, report all these results in your paper. If two different versions of the model lead to different conclusions about the hypothesis you are investigating, discuss this in your paper. Conflicting results are still giving you information, and you should pass that information on to those who read your work. The point of doing econometric work is to learn about the topic and hypothesis being investigated. "Rigging" the study to come out a certain way by running different versions of the regression and ignoring ones that don't support your hypothesis is dishonest. Neither you nor your readers will gain knowledge by disregarding some of the evidence.

Remember, theory is your main consideration when you choose independent variables. Suppose that your dependent variable is the quantity of cola sold, and one of the independent variables is the price of the cola, but its slope estimate turns out to be statistically insignificant. It is important that you leave this variable in the model and report the result in your paper, *especially* because it is surprising. This result could mean several things. Perhaps people spend such a small amount of their income on cola that demand is very inelastic, so that the slope estimate for the price of cola would be close to zero. Perhaps the change in cola price is so small that there is no measurable reaction in the quantity sold, when changes in the other independent variables are taken into account by the regression process. A more general explanation is that there can be Type II error. That is, you are not rejecting a null hypothesis when it is false. Here, the false null hypothesis is that the B for cola prices is zero. In writing about your results, always keep in mind that Type I and Type II errors do occur. One regression by itself cannot prove anything; it can only give evidence that supports (or does not support) a hypothesis.

Our discussion here does not mean that in doing econometrics, you should just run one regression and write up the results. The ability of a model to give similar results when small changes are made in it is called **robustness.** Good models are robust models. This

---

[4] This 0.71 value is not included in Table 2-B because the meaning of adjusted R^2 had not been covered at that point in the text.

means you need to see if your results are affected by small changes in the model's specification. You want to know if changing the model slightly produces a large change in the value of a slope estimate, causes a slope estimate to lose or gain statistical significance, or creates a substantial change in the goodness of fit. If possible, find out whether a different data sample gives the same results. If adding or subtracting an independent variable gives you similar results and does not change your conclusions, that makes your conclusions stronger. If the results are different, then the supporting evidence is not as strong, or maybe the hypothesis holds only under certain conditions. Either way, you are adding to your knowledge (and your readers' knowledge) about the topic. A model that is not entirely robust doesn't mean that your research is poor—only that the information about your topic and hypothesis isn't as conclusive as you might like.

It is important that your results be **replicable**; this means that others should be able to take your same data, run the same regressions, and get the same results. If not, something is wrong. If the data you are using are publicly available, it is relatively easy for someone else to run the same regressions. In the academic world, researchers must make data from their published papers available to anyone who requests it. Also, others interested in your topic might change the model, adding or subtracting independent variables so they can see if your model is robust. If you check for robustness yourself, and report what you find in your paper, other researchers will appreciate your thoroughness and attention to detail.

4-5 FINDING AND USING DATA

Now that a lot of data are available on the Internet, it's easier than ever to do an econometrics project. In the "old days," researchers often spent days hunting around libraries looking for data sources and using copy machines to copy tables of data from books. Then came the tedious task of entering the data by hand onto a computer. Now search engines such as Google make finding data on the Internet a snap by comparison. Once you find the data you want, you can even download it into a spreadsheet without having to type in each number. This saves a tremendous amount of time, as you can imagine. Some websites even allow you to download data in spreadsheet format from the beginning. Almost all econometrics software can convert data in a spreadsheet to whatever type of file the software uses for data. The availability of data on the Internet allows you to focus on your topic and the econometric involved, instead of having to spend time entering data.

Consider putting your data into a spreadsheet even if this seems unnecessary at first and even if you can put the data directly into the econometrics software. Most spreadsheet programs allow you to organize and check the data more easily than econometrics software does. Always double-check your data after you set it up in the spreadsheet. Compare your data values to the values on the website or original source to make sure nothing went wrong when you moved the data to the spreadsheet. If you are using a very large or complex data sample—say customer information for a company with more than 1000 observations—you may need to use a database rather than a spreadsheet. Databases are harder to use than spreadsheets but may be necessary to organize a large sample properly.

Table 4-D

Useful Websites for Finding Data

Name	Address	Comment
Resources for Economists on the Internet	http://rfe.wustl.edu	Has links to data sources and other pages useful for economics.
Economagic	http://www.economagic.com	Features a wide variety of economic data.
WebEc	http://netec.wustl.edu/WebEc/WebEc.html	Includes links to data sites. Click on "economics data" on the left-hand side of the page for data links.
EconData	http://Econdata.net	Contains links to data sites. Specializes in sites with regional data.
U.S. Bureau of Labor Statistics	http://www.bls.gov	Gives the Consumer Price Index, unemployment data, wage data, and a lot more.
Mansfield University Business and Economics Numeric Data	http://www.mnsfld.edu/depts/lib/ecostats.html	Contains numerous links to sites with different kinds of data.
FedStats	http://www.fedstats.gov	Accesses data collected by various agencies of the U.S. government.
U.S. Census Bureau	http://www.census.gov	Gives census data that can be downloaded into a spreadsheet.
Economic Report of the President	http://w3.access.gpo.gov/eop	Contains macroeconomic data available for download in a spreadsheet format.
Yahoo Finance Historical Prices	http://chart.yahoo.com/d	Gives historical daily prices for most stocks.
FRED, an Economic Time-Series Database	http://research.stlouisfed.org/fred	Provides GDP, interest rates, and lots of other macroeconomic data. The Federal Reserve Bank of St. Louis maintains this website.
Financial Data Finder	http://fisher.osu.edu/fin/osudata.htm	Contains downloadable financial data.
FreeLunch	http://www.freelunch.com	Gives data that can be downloaded in Excel spreadsheets if you register. (Registration is free.)

Table 4-D gives only a small number of the useful websites for data; there are many more.[5]

---

[5] Often useful data can be found on websites whose main focus is not economics. For example, life expectancy and health care data can be found on the World Health Organization's website, http://www.who.int.

Outliers

An **outlier** is an observation that lies far from the other observations. An outlier takes a value that is not even close to the range for the other values. Suppose one of your variables is income and everyone's income in your sample is between 0 and $425,000, except for one person's income, which is listed as $100,000,000. The $100,000,000 value is an outlier. Outliers are important because they can dramatically change how a regression turns out. That one large value in your sample for income could make the estimates and levels of statistical significance completely different from a sample without this observation. An exercise at the end of this chapter allows you to see this for yourself. To see if your sample has outliers, plot the values for each variable on a graph. This can be done in most econometrics programs or by using a spreadsheet.

Outliers need to be found for another important reason—they can indicate a mistake in the data. In the income example above, you would need to find out whether that person really made $100,000,000 or whether it's a mistake. Extra zeros are all too easy to add; maybe this observation should really be $100,000. Double-check such outliers by going back to the original source. Sometimes it's obvious that an outlier is a mistake. If one of the observations for income is $-32,000$, you know this is a mistake because income should not be a negative number. If the outlier really is a mistake, and the correct value is unavailable, then that observation must be eliminated from your sample. (That person, firm, state, year, or other entity must be removed from the sample.)

The most important fact about outliers is that *you cannot eliminate an observation from a data set just because it is an outlier*. What if someone in your sample really did make $100,000,000? Then that observation contains legitimate information for your regression; it would be fraudulent to eliminate it and pretend that the $100,000,000 was a mistake.

4-6 WRITING ABOUT YOUR RESEARCH

Clarity and precision are key when you write about your research. Sentences should be short and easy to read. Present each thought or idea accurately and concisely so that its meaning is crystal clear. Try not to use really long sentences that drag on and on and combine so many ideas or details at once that it makes it harder for the reader to follow it, like this sentence is doing right at this very moment.

Be sure to leave yourself enough time. Write your paper carefully, proofread it, and make changes. Plan ahead. It would be a shame if all the attention and effort you put into your work is not appreciated because you ran out of time and wrote a sloppy paper. Consider the following situation: The model has been carefully constructed based on theory. Appropriate data for all the variables have been found. The regressions have been estimated and their results analyzed carefully and objectively. It's also 3:00 in the morning and the paper is due at 9:00 A.M. This is not good. This researcher won't be able to write up her work in a clear manner that reveals the quality of her work to the reader.

A research paper containing econometric results might have the following sections:

1. *Introduction.* Discuss the question or issue that you examined. Explain why it is interesting or relevant.

2. *Literature Review.* Summarize what others have learned about your research topic. Be sure to properly cite any work you mention.

3. *The Model.* Explain the theory that is relevant to your study. Make the connection between your regression model and the relevant theory very clear. Don't forget to carefully and precisely define each variable.

4. *The Data.* Explain where your data come from. Give sufficient information so that readers can find the same data to see if they can replicate your results. Researchers commonly provide a table of descriptive statistics for all the variables used in the paper. The table should include the mean and standard deviation along with minimum and maximum values for each variable. This gives readers an idea of what the data are like. Table 4-E is a typical table of descriptive statistics.

5. *The Results.* Here you present the econometric results. Be sure to mention the estimation procedure used, whether it is ordinary least squares or not (there are other methods; some we examine in later chapters). Include coefficient estimates, statistics for hypothesis testing, such as t-statistics and the F-statistic, and goodness-of-fit measures such as R^2 and adjusted R^2. Discuss the robustness of your model and the different versions of the model that you estimated. You don't want to overwhelm the reader with too many tables of regression results, so make an appendix of less important tables. Leave the most important tables in the results section of the paper, but make sure you say something in this section about the appendix, so readers will know what it includes. If you refer to specific tables in the appendix, make sure they have labels, such as Table A-1, Table A-2, or some other system that makes it clear which table is being referred to.

6. *Conclusions.* In this section of the paper, you want to explain what readers can learn from the research you have presented. What is the main lesson or conclusion? Try to explain your conclusions in a way that would be interesting to someone who doesn't care about the econometric details. Make this section of the paper short and to the point.

Table 4-E

Descriptive Statistics for Cross-Section DVD Model*

Variable	Minimum	Maximum	Mean	Standard Deviation
DVDEXP	9.26	50.93	30.35	12.66
INCOME	422	1120	765.80	203.02
PRICE	15.98	26.98	21.98	3.13
RAINFALL	0.20	6.00	2.89	1.54

n = 30 for all variables

*Data presented in Chapter 2 exercises.

7. *Appendix*. As noted above, tables of econometric results, showing robustness or lack of robustness, can be placed here. Make sure the tables are well organized and are given clear titles, so readers will be able to understand what they are looking at.

8. *References*. Any books, papers, articles, or other work that is cited in the paper should be included in the reference section. Give complete bibliographical information to make it easier for your readers to find these resources. The data sources should also be included here. Also give addresses for any websites that you used to gather data.

SUMMARY

1. Choose a research topic that is practical. Make sure that data are available and that you can acquire the data needed. The work will be more enjoyable if you choose a topic that interests you. A review of the existing literature will tell you what others have learned about the topic.

2. Theory is the main consideration in selecting the dependent and independent variables for your model. The dependent and independent variables should make sense before you run any regressions.

3. For the model to work well, the variables must change or move within the sample.

4. A **tautology** is a statement or equation that is true by definition. A regression that is a tautology always fits the data perfectly every time, regardless of what sample is used. A tautology is always true, so there is no point to using a regression to test it.

5. Time-series variables that are affected by inflation should be adjusted by a price index so that inflation doesn't affect the regression results. When running a cross-section regression, the size of the cross-section observations or units in the sample can differ, and this can cause heteroskedasticity. This problem can often be avoided if the variables are expressed on a per person or percentage basis.

6. An important independent variable that is missing from a regression causes the remaining estimates in the regression to be biased. If an irrelevant independent variable is added to a model, it doesn't cause bias; it causes the variances of other slope estimates to increase. This makes the t-statistics closer to zero. An irrelevant variable also decreases the adjusted R^2.

7. A good econometrician is objective. If you try different versions of the model (adding or omitting an independent variable), report these results in your paper. If two versions of the model lead to different conclusions about the hypothesis being investigated, discuss this result. Conflicting results give information, and you should pass that information on to your readers. Also, econometric results should be **replicable**; that is, others should be able to take your data, run the same regressions, and get the same results. A model is robust if small changes can be made to it and it still produces similar results. Robustness makes the results more convincing.

8. An **outlier** is an observation that lies far from the other observations. An outlier takes a value that is not even close to the range for the remaining values. Outliers are important because they can dramatically change regression results. Outliers

need to be double-checked against the original data because they can indicate a mistake in the data. However, the most important fact about outliers is that an observation cannot be eliminated from a sample just because it is an outlier.

9. Clarity and precision are key in writing about your research. Use short, easy-to-read sentences. Leave enough time to write the paper carefully, proofread it, and make needed changes.

EXERCISES

1. Try to explain these terms without looking them up.
   * tautology
   * Consumer Price Index
   * robustness
   * replicable result
   * outlier

2. a. Set up a regression model for the movie box office receipts mentioned in Section 4-1. Write definitions of the dependent and independent variables you will use, including additional independent variables not mentioned in the text.
   b. Do your independent variables make sense according to theory?
   c. Hypothesize whether each slope coefficient will be positive or negative.
   d. Do you think the data for all your variables are easily obtained?

3. Discuss the validity of these statements.
   a. If a relevant independent variable is left out of a model, the slope estimates for the model will be biased.
   b. If an irrelevant independent variable is included in a model, the remaining slope estimates are still unbiased.
   c. Therefore, it is better to include an irrelevant variable than to exclude a relevant one.

4. The following table gives annual U.S. federal income tax collections, along with the Consumer Price Index for each year. (Tax data are from http://www.economagic .com, and nominal GDP data are from the U.S. Department of Commerce, Bureau of Economic Analysis, http://www.bea.doc.gov.)

Year	Nominal Tax Collections (in millions of dollars)	CPI
1990	548,198	130.66
1991	546,810	136.17
1992	564,555	140.31
1993	593,752	144.48
1994	625,483	148.23
1995	685,528	152.38

Year	Nominal Tax Collections (in millions of dollars)	CPI
1996	754,877	156.86
1997	847,761	160.53
1998	940,402	163.01
1999	1,031,712	166.59

a. Calculate the real value of the tax collections for the years shown. (If you know how to use a spreadsheet, you can use a formula to calculate the answers more easily than if you calculate each year with a calculator.)

b. Starting with 1991, find the percent change in tax collections from the past year to the current one, for both nominal and real values. What do you notice about the two sets of numbers?

c. What would happen if you used the nominal values in a regression instead of the real values that you found in part a?

5. The following regression model is designed to study the number of people who leave a nursing home each year. Explain what is wrong with this model.

$$EXIT = B_0 + B_1 DEATHS + B_2 NUR + B_3 RELATIVES + B_4 HOSPITAL + e$$

where

EXIT = number of individuals who leave a nursing home each year

DEATHS = number of deaths at the nursing home each year

NUR = number of individuals who leave to go to a different nursing home each year

RELATIVES = number of individuals who leave to live with relatives each year

HOSPITAL = number of individuals who leave each year because they have entered a hospital

6. Consider the following cross-section regression results. Both the slope and intercept estimate are statistically significant at a 1% error level.

$$HOUSE\_EXP = 7000 + 0.17 \, INCOME$$

where

HOUSE_EXP = annual housing expenditures for each household, in dollars

INCOME = annual income for each household, in dollars

For parts a–d, write out what the results will be using the variable definitions given.

a. HOUSE_EXP = annual housing expenditures for each household, in thousands of dollars

INCOME = annual income for each household, in dollars

b. HOUSE_EXP = annual housing expenditures for each household, in dollars

INCOME = annual income for each household, in thousands of dollars

c. HOUSE_EXP = annual housing expenditures for each household, in thousands of dollars

INCOME = annual income for each household, in thousands of dollars

d. HOUSE_EXP = annual housing expenditures for each household, in tens of thousands of dollars

INCOME = annual income for each household, in tens of thousands of dollars

e. Which version is easiest to interpret?

f. What independent variables would you add to this model?

7. Reconsider Equation (4-10). Do you expect the estimate of B_2 to be biased since RAINFALL is omitted from the regression? If so, what direction do you expect the bias will take? If not, why don't you expect bias?

8. Reconsider the following cross-section DVD model, which was used in exercise 12 at the end of Chapter 2.

$$DVDEXP = B_0 + B_1INCOME + B_2PRICE + B_3RAINFALL + e$$

Question 12 in Chapter 2 notes that the 30 people used for the sample all live in different places. What would happen if they all lived in the same place?

9. A local police department has hired you to study what factors contribute to automobile accidents along a busy highway.

a. You could define the dependent variable as number of accidents per hour or number of accidents per day. Which do you think is better? Explain.

b. One independent variable the department wants you to investigate is the average speed of motorists on the highway. The police department has this information available for each hour of the day. Should you use data from all different hours of the day, or just during rush hours when traffic is heaviest? Explain.

10. If RANDOM, used in Equation (4-11), really is random, then why does it cause the other slope estimates in the model to come out differently? In other words, if RANDOM is truly random, shouldn't the slope estimates for INCOME, PRICE, and RAINFALL be the same in Table 4-C as they are in Table 2-B (where RANDOM isn't used)?

11. Suppose Quinn's budgeting discipline wavers and she spends $1000 on DVDs in a month where she only makes $500. Add the following observation to the data in Table 2-A so that there are now 13 observations.

Month	DVDEXP	INCOME	PRICE	RAINFALL
	1000.00	500.00	21.00	3.00

a. Is this observation an outlier? How can you tell?

b. Estimate Equation (2-2) using the data in Table 2-A.

$$DVDEXP = B_0 + B_1INCOME + B_2PRICE + B_3RAINFALL + e$$

Then, estimate the regression again, adding the 13th observation to the end of the sample. How do the results compare?

c. Should this observation be omitted from the sample?

Questions 12–15 guide you through designing and estimating a regression model. (Your answer to Question 4 in Chapter 1 may help you get started.)

12. Design a regression model concerning something that interests you. What is your dependent variable? What independent variables do you think should be included? Try to choose a topic that allows you to find the data you need.

13. Use the Internet to find data for the variables in your model. List the Internet addresses where you found the data.

14. Use the data you found in Question 13 to make a table of descriptive statistics for all the variables you are using in your model.

15. Use the data you found in Question 13 to estimate the model you designed in Question 12.

    a. Make a table that presents the regression results.
    b. What conclusions can you make from your results?
    c. What potential problems do you see with this regression? (No research is perfect; casting a critical eye over your research will make you a better econometrician.)

5

Additional Modeling Techniques

This chapter will show you how to:

- Take a variable that is not a number and express it numerically so that it can be used in a regression.

- Design and use tests to investigate unique hypotheses that involve more than one coefficient.

- Determine whether two data sets can be combined for use in one regression.

- Estimate a nonlinear relationship between variables using linear regression analysis.

You may have already thought of instances in which it would seem difficult to apply regression analysis. Econometrics is adaptable enough to handle all types of situations. In this chapter, we will examine techniques that you can use in a variety of interesting cases. First, we will take a characteristic that is not a number and include it in a regression by using a dummy variable. Next, you may encounter situations in which two independent variables affect each other's performance. Using an interaction variable improves such models. In Section 5-3, we expand the F-test (discussed in Chapter 3) to test different hypotheses in different models. Sections 5-4 and 5-5 will present other models that work when the relationship between the independent and dependent variables is not a straight line.

5-1 DUMMY VARIABLES AREN'T STUPID: WHEN A VARIABLE IS NOT A NUMBER

A variable that represents a number is called a **quantitative variable**. Income, unemployment rate, and a person's age are all quantitative variables since they are numbers. You may need to include factors in your model that are not numbers, such as a person's gender. Variables of this type are called **qualitative variables** because they reflect a property or feature that is not numerical. Regression software cannot work with a variable that is equal to "male" or "female," so something called a dummy variable is used to give it a numerical value.

Intercept Dummies

Dummy variables are often defined in this manner:

$$X_1 = 1 \quad \text{if person is male}$$
$$X_1 = 0 \quad \text{otherwise}$$

Usually, one of the possible values for the dummy variable is zero. This dummy variable can change the intercept for males in the sample as can be seen from the following example. (Note that defining "$X_1 = 1$ if female, 0 otherwise" would work fine also.)

Professional Wrestling Needs Dummies

Advertisers need to know who will be watching before committing money for TV commercials. Here, we want to see who spends time watching professional wrestling. It is likely that men and women have different viewing habits for this sport, so a dummy variable for gender is needed.

$$\text{HOURS} = B_0 + B_1\text{MALE} + B_2\text{INCOME} + B_3\text{AGE} + e \qquad \textbf{(5-1)}$$

where

$\qquad$ HOURS = hours spent watching professional wrestling on television, per month
$\qquad$ MALE = 1 if person is male, 0 otherwise
$\qquad$ INCOME = individual's annual income
$\qquad$ AGE = individual's age

Suppose a survey gives us the data shown in Table 5-A. Table 5-B shows the results from using this data to estimate the professional wrestling model.

Both MALE and INCOME are statistically significant at a 5% error level, and both have coefficients with the signs we would expect. The coefficient for AGE is statistically insignificant. Although its coefficient is positive, the high p-value of 0.27 indicates a 27% chance that the true value of the coefficient is actually zero. These results tell us that we can't be confident that older people tend to watch more wrestling. We can say, though, that people with higher incomes typically watch less wrestling. The INCOME coefficient is negative and significant at a 5% error level. Although at first glance the coefficient value of -0.000065 seems small, it really is not when you consider how INCOME and HOURS are measured. Income is annual income in dollars, so the -0.000065 value represents the average decrease in viewing hours for a trivial $1 increase in annual salary, keeping other variables constant. If someone's income increases by $5000, on average, keeping other variables constant, our results indicate that he or she will watch 0.3255 fewer hours of wrestling a month, or about 20 minutes less.[1] [$5000 \times -0.000065 = -0.33$ (indicating fewer hours of television); -0.33 hours $\times$ 60 minutes in an hour $= -19.8$ minutes]

---

[1] This may mean that people who do not watch much wrestling tend to make more money. (Unfortunately, this doesn't mean that if you cut back on watching wrestling by 20 minutes a month, your annual income will go up by $5000!) This question of whether the relationship between an independent and dependent variable is the other way around is called the question of causality. Testing for causality will be discussed in Chapter 10.

Table 5-A

Data for Professional Wrestling Model

Person	HOURS	MALE	INCOME	AGE
1	0	0	$58,600	41
2	0.5	0	15,000	19
3	1	1	76,700	54
4	2.5	0	20,500	22
5	0	0	72,100	48
6	1	1	84,200	52
7	10	1	12,700	24
8	1.75	0	42,250	60
9	4	1	32,750	28
10	0	0	142,300	58
11	1	1	98,250	35
12	13	1	24,200	67
13	1.75	1	18,800	30
14	4	1	31,000	21
15	0.25	0	22,000	32
16	1	0	30,200	33
17	16	1	27,260	39
18	2	1	42,250	56
19	6	1	27,850	31
20	0.25	0	37,500	57

MALE has a positive coefficient, 4.47, indicating that on average men watch wrestling 4.47 more hours a month than women, keeping INCOME and AGE constant. MALE is an intercept dummy variable, so the significant coefficient means that men and women have different intercepts. To see this, consider the results written like this:

$$\text{HOURS} = 0.86 + 4.47\,\text{MALE} - 0.000065\,\text{INCOME} + 0.073\,\text{AGE} \quad \text{(5-2)}$$

Table 5-B

Regression Results for Professional Wrestling Model

Dependent variable: HOURS

Variable	Coefficient	Standard Error	t-Statistic	p-Value
Constant	0.86	2.63	0.33	0.75
MALE	4.47	1.66	2.70	0.02
INCOME	−0.000065	0.000029	−2.25	0.039
AGE	0.073	0.064	1.14	0.27

Observations: 20

$R^2 = 0.45$

Adjusted $R^2 = 0.35$

Residual Sum of Squares = 216.15

F-statistic = 4.44

If the viewer is female, MALE is zero. Substituting zero for MALE into Equation (5-2) gives

[Women only]   HOURS = 0.86 − 0.000065 INCOME + 0.073 AGE   **(5-3)**

where the intercept is still 0.86. Now let's set MALE to 1 for a man. Substituting 1 for MALE into our original equation (5-1) gives

[Men only]   HOURS = 0.86 + 4.47 − 0.000065 INCOME + 0.073 AGE **(5-4)**

Adding the first two numbers in Equation (5-4) gives:

[Men only]   HOURS = 5.33 − 0.000065 INCOME + 0.073 AGE   **(5-5)**

Equation (5-3) gives the results for women, and Equation (5-5) is for men. The intercept is bigger for men; it is 5.33. It has increased by the value of the MALE coefficient, 4.47. Figure 5-1 shows the two different intercepts. To keep it simple, AGE is not included in the figure. Note that the slopes for the two lines in Figure 5-1 are the same. If the coefficient for MALE had been negative, the intercept for men would be smaller than the intercept for women.

The Dummy Variable Trap: Always Leave an Escape Route

Use one too many dummy variables in your model and you will find yourself in a dummy variable trap. To see how this happens, add another dummy variable to our professional wrestling model.

EXTRADUMMY = 1   if person is female, 0 otherwise

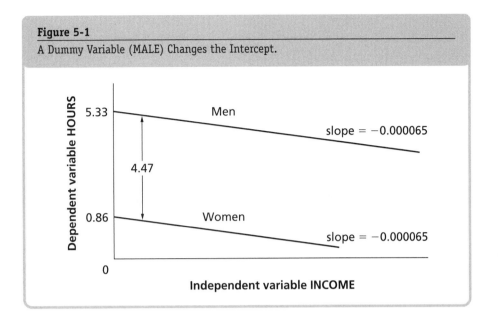

Figure 5-1

A Dummy Variable (MALE) Changes the Intercept.

This gives us

$$HOURS = B_0 + B_1MALE + B_2INCOME + B_3AGE + B_4EXTRADUMMY + e$$

(5-6)

This model will not work; estimating it results in a software error message. For a man, MALE is 1, so EXTRADUMMY must be 0. For a woman, MALE is 0, so EXTRADUMMY has to be 1. These two dummy variables give the *same* information. When the value of one variable is known, it tells us the value of the other. This is the dummy variable trap. Ordinary least squares cannot estimate slope coefficients for both MALE and EXTRADUMMY because they are perfectly linearly related.[2] To escape the dummy variable trap, always leave out one of the possible dummy variables. Here, the two possible categories, male and female, give us two possible dummy variables. We must exclude one of them. In general, include one less dummy variable than the number of possible categories. Here is an example that illustrates this for a case with four categories.

Seasonal Retail Sales Model

$$SALES = B_0 + B_1UNEMPLOY + B_2SUMMER + B_3FALL + B_4WINTER + e$$

(5-7)

[2] This is a case of extreme, or perfect, multicollinearity. (Multicollinearity is mentioned in Section 2-2 and will be discussed in more detail in the next chapter.)

where

SALES = real U.S. quarterly retail sales, in millions of 1983 dollars
UNEMPLOY = average unemployment rate (%), for each quarter
SUMMER = 1 during summertime, 0 otherwise
FALL = 1 during fall, 0 otherwise
WINTER = 1 during winter, 0 otherwise

Note that this model does not include a dummy variable for spring. Spring is omitted to avoid the dummy variable trap. Spring is our "escape route."

It might be tempting to simplify the model by replacing SPRING, FALL, and WINTER with a new variable, SEASON, where

SEASON = 0 during spring, 1 during summer, 2 during fall, and 3 during winter

However, using SEASON is not appropriate. This variable places the seasons in calendar order. The fact that winter comes between fall and spring on the calendar does not necessarily mean that the size of winter's seasonal effect on sales lies between the size of fall and spring's seasonal effects. Using SEASON makes the results come out differently than they should. Tables 5-C and 5-D present data and results for the seasonal retail sales model.

All three dummy variables are statistically significant. Since there is no dummy variable for spring, we can think of spring as the base season. The coefficients for SUMMER, FALL, and WINTER are then interpreted in terms of the base season. The coefficient for FALL means that, on average (keeping unemployment constant), fall's retail sales will be 9605.7 million dollars higher than spring's retail sales. We interpret the other dummy variable coefficients in the same way, by comparing them to spring. In general, coefficients for dummy variables are interpreted relative to the base category.

Slope Dummies

Dummy variables can also be used to allow the slope to change, rather than the intercept. Reconsider the professional wrestling model.

$$HOURS = B_0 + B_1 MALE + B_2 INCOME + B_3 AGE + e \qquad (5\text{-}1)$$

The relationship between income and hours of wrestling watched could be different for men than for women. Therefore, to estimate the model accurately, B_2 must be different for men than for women. This can be accomplished by adding a slope dummy variable of the form MALExINCOME (MALE multiplied by INCOME). For this example, the intercept dummy MALE and its coefficient B_1 are omitted. The model is now

$$HOURS = B_0 + B_2 INCOME + B_3 AGE + B_4 MALExINCOME + e \qquad (5\text{-}8)$$

(MALExAGE would also be a legitimate slope dummy variable.) Using the same data as before (Table 5-A), we get the results in Table 5-E.

The slope dummy is not statistically significant. These results do not support the idea that the relationship (or slope) between INCOME and HOURS depends on gender. In

Table 5-C

Data for Seasonal Retail Sales Model

Years: Quarter	SALES	UNEMPLOY	SUMMER	FALL	WINTER
1995:1	116,305.6	5.5	0	0	0
1995:2	130,413.5	5.7	1	0	0
1995:3	129,957.5	5.7	0	1	0
1995:4	138,739.6	5.6	0	0	1
1996:1	121,368.0	5.6	0	0	0
1996:2	134,401.8	5.5	1	0	0
1996:3	132,840.1	5.3	0	1	0
1996:4	142,583.9	5.3	0	0	1
1997:1	124,161.9	5.3	0	0	0
1997:2	135,639.0	5.0	1	0	0
1997:3	136,656.9	4.8	0	1	0
1997:4	145,135.8	4.7	0	0	1
1998:1	126,146.0	4.7	0	0	0
1998:2	142,509.7	4.4	1	0	0
1998:3	139,946.4	4.5	0	1	0
1998:4	152,278.8	4.4	0	0	1
1999:1	134,790.9	4.3	0	0	0
1999:2	150,354.6	4.3	1	0	0
1999:3	150,933.6	4.2	0	1	0
1999:4	162,547.2	4.1	0	0	1
2000:1	146,567.5	4.1	0	0	0
2000:2	158,447.0	4.0	1	0	0

These data are available at the text website or http://www.economagic.com. (SALES are nominal sales adjusted by the consumer price index.) Alternatively, for nominal sales see U.S. Census Bureau: Monthly Retail Trade Survey, at http://www.census.gov/mrts/www/mrts.html. CPI data are found at http://stats.bls.gov (Bureau of Labor Statistics). For UNEMPLOY, see http://www.stls.frb.org/fred/index.html by the St. Louis Fed.

Table 5-D

Results for Seasonal Retail Sales Model

Dependent variable: SALES

Variable	Coefficient	Standard Error	t-Statistic	p-Value
Constant	198,409.6	7,259.5	27.331	0.001
UNEMPLOY	−14,275.2	1,440.0	−9.913	0.001
SUMMER	12,310.1	2,273.0	5.416	0.001
FALL	9,605.7	2,379.3	4.037	0.001
WINTER	18,653.8	2,383.2	7.827	0.001

Observations: 22
$R^2 = 0.91$
Adjusted $R^2 = 0.89$
Residual Sum of Squares = 262,000,000
F-statistic = 43.69

Table 5-E

Regression Results for Professional Wrestling Model with a Slope Dummy

Dependent variable: HOURS

Variable	Coefficient	Standard Error	t-Statistic	p-Value
Constant	3.19	2.86	1.11	0.28
INCOME	−0.000084	0.000036	−2.33	0.03
AGE	0.077	0.075	1.03	0.32
MALExINCOME	0.000036	0.0000350	1.02	0.32

Observations: 20
$R^2 = 0.26$
Adjusted $R^2 = 0.16$
Residual Sum of Squares = 259.20
F-statistic = 1.82

this case, it is better to stick with the intercept dummy. To see how the slope dummy works, the slope dummy coefficient estimate 0.000036 is used below, although it is statistically insignificant. The discussion below shows how you could interpret a slope dummy coefficient that is statistically significant.

The results can be written as

$$\text{HOURS} = 3.19 - 0.000084 \text{ INCOME} + 0.077 \text{ AGE}$$
$$+ 0.000036 \text{ MALExINCOME} \qquad \text{(5-9)}$$

For a woman, MALE is zero, so the dummy variable, the last term above, becomes zero.

[Women only] $\text{HOURS} = 3.19 - 0.000084 \text{ INCOME} + 0.077 \text{ AGE}$ (5-10)

The slope representing the relationship between INCOME and HOURS stays the same, -0.000084. For a man, MALE is 1; substituting 1 in for MALE gives us

[Men only] $\text{HOURS} = 3.19 - 0.000084 \text{ INCOME} + 0.077 \text{ AGE}$
$$+ 0.000036 \text{ INCOME} \qquad \text{(5-11)}$$

Adding the two income terms together gives us

[Men only] $\text{HOURS} = 3.19 - 0.000048 \text{ INCOME} + 0.077 \text{ AGE}$ (5-12)

Comparing the equation for women (5-10) to that for men (5-12), we see that the income coefficient for men is closer to zero, and the intercept stays the same. Figure 5-2 shows how the two equations differ. Both slopes are negative, so we know that higher-income men and women tend to watch less wrestling than lower-income men and women. The steeper slope for women means that as income increases, the difference between hours watched by men and women increases. Here is another way to think

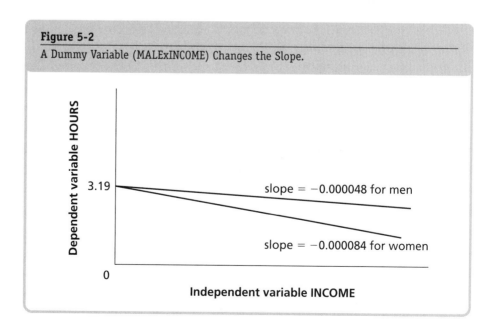

Figure 5-2

A Dummy Variable (MALExINCOME) Changes the Slope.

Dependent variable HOURS

3.19

slope = −0.000048 for men

slope = −0.000084 for women

0

Independent variable INCOME

about it: At lower incomes, women watch a little less wrestling than men, but at higher incomes, women watch a lot less wrestling than men.

We can also use intercept and slope dummy variables in the same model:

$$\text{HOURS} = B_0 + B_1\text{MALE} + B_2\text{INCOME} + B_3\text{AGE} + B_4\text{MALExINCOME} + e$$

$$(5\text{-}13)$$

Both the intercept and slopes can be different. A graph of these results would be two completely different lines, one for men and one for women. Instead of using a model with both slope and intercept dummies, we could use two separate regressions, especially if the sample size is not small. If the sample size was bigger, we could split the data into two data sets, one for men and one for women. Then we could run two separate regressions, if we believed that both the intercepts and slopes are different.

5-2 INTERACTION VARIABLES CAN'T LEAVE EACH OTHER ALONE

The effect of one independent variable can be influenced by another independent variable. To demonstrate interaction variables, let's use a model that predicts income based on age and education.

$$\text{INCOME} = B_0 + B_1\text{AGE} + B_2\text{EDUCATION} + B_3\text{AGExEDUCATION} + e$$

$$(5\text{-}14)$$

where

$$\text{INCOME} = \text{individual's annual income}$$
$$\text{AGE} = \text{individual's age}$$
$$\text{EDUCATION} = \text{individual's years of education (equals 12 for a high school graduate)}$$
$$\text{AGExEDUCATION} = \text{AGE multiplied by EDUCATION, for each individual}$$

AGExEDUCATION is an interaction variable; it differs from a slope dummy variable, because neither AGE nor EDUCATION is a dummy variable. We are using AGEx EDUCATION because AGE may affect INCOME differently for those with different levels of education. It seems plausible that AGE will matter more for people with higher levels of education, since the financial returns from education don't end with higher starting salaries. For example, higher levels of education often open up opportunities for promotions later on. Including AGExEDUCATION in our model accounts for this interaction effect. (You will have the opportunity to add an interaction variable to the professional wrestling model in an exercise at the end of the chapter.)

Table 5-F reports the regression results for the income model given by Equation (5-14). The interaction variable, AGExEDUCATION, is statistically significant at a 5% error level. The presence of AGExEDUCATION adds a new element to our interpretation of the slope estimates. If AGE increases by one year, keeping EDUCATION constant, AGExEDUCATION also increases. So the expected increase in INCOME is not simply $\hat{B}_1$, the slope estimate for AGE.

Table 5-F

Regression Results: Income Model with an Interaction Variable

Dependent variable: INCOME

Variable	Coefficient	Standard Error	t-Statistic	p-Value
Constant	−38,138	4353.62	8.76	0.00
AGE	289	54.43	5.31	0.00
EDUCATION	3,259	520.61	6.26	0.00
AGExEDUCATION	51	23.94	23.94	0.03

Observations: 20

$R^2 = 0.47$

Adjusted $R^2 = 0.32$

Residual Sum of Squares $= 211.75$

F-statistic $= 3.26$

The expected increase in INCOME if AGE increases by one year is:

$$\hat{B}_1 + \hat{B}_3 EDUCATION$$

The first term, $\hat{B}_1$, gives us the increase in INCOME when AGE increases by one, ignoring the interaction effect of AGE and EDUCATION. The second term, $\hat{B}_3$ EDUCATION, gives us the extra "punch"—or change in income—that occurs *because* of the interaction effect. When AGE increases, the size of the interaction effect depends on the level of EDUCATION. Therefore, EDUCATION must be included in the second term; the second term cannot be $\hat{B}_3$ by itself.[3] When someone with a high school education (EDUCATION = 12) gets a year older, the expected increase in his or her income is $289 + 51 \cdot EDUCATION = 289 + 51 \cdot 12 = \$901$ a year.

If EDUCATION is different by 1 and AGE stays the same, then the expected increase in INCOME is

$$\hat{B}_2 + \hat{B}_3 AGE$$

Let's compare two 40-year-olds; one has a Bachelor's degree and the other has a Bachelor's degree and a year of graduate school. The individual with a year of graduate school can expect to make more on average. The difference in INCOME is $3259 + 51 \cdot AGE = 3259 + 51 \cdot 40 = 5299$.

Since an interaction variable consists of two other independent variables from the same model, there can be a problem with multicollinearity. Recall from Section 2-2 that multicollinearity occurs when two (or more) independent variables are highly correlated in a linear fashion. (We discuss multicollinearity in more detail in Chapter 6.)

---

[3] Readers who are familiar with calculus can check that these terms are found by taking the derivative of Equation (5-14) with respect to AGE.

5-3 DESIGNING YOUR OWN F-TEST

The F-statistic usually presented with regression results is one specific type of F-test (see Chapter 3). In general, F-tests are used to test joint hypotheses—that is, hypotheses that involve more than one coefficient at a time. You can design your own F-tests to test many types of joint hypotheses. Step one is to state the joint null hypothesis that you wish to test. (Remember to set up the null hypothesis so that it is the opposite of what you expect to find. That way if you find what you expect, the null hypothesis will be false.) For example, the typical F-test states that all the coefficients in a regression (except for the intercept) are equal to zero.

$$H_0 = B_1 = B_2 = B_3 = \cdots = B_k = 0$$

Typically, you hope to reject this null hypothesis to find in favor of your alternative hypothesis. The alternative hypothesis is that at least one of these B's is significantly different from zero. All F-tests are two-sided tests.

In the second step, you run the regression model and find the residual sum of squares you will use in the F-statistic formula, Equation (5-15). This original regression is called the **unrestricted model** because no changes or restrictions have been forced on the regression. In an unrestricted model, coefficient estimates can take any value they would normally take, and the null hypothesis can turn out to be false.

In step 3, you alter the regression model to force the null hypothesis to be true, whether it really is true or not. This altered model is called the **restricted model** because you have changed or restricted the values that some of the coefficients can take. You then estimate the restricted model to find its residual sum of squares.

In step 4, you calculate an F-statistic using this formula:

$$F_{q, n-k-1} = \frac{\dfrac{RSS_{restricted} - RSS_{unrestricted}}{q}}{\dfrac{RSS_{unrestricted}}{n - k - 1}} \qquad (5\text{-}15)$$

where q is the number of restrictions present in the null hypothesis. Often, the null hypothesis is a group of coefficients that are each set equal to zero. In this case, the number of restrictions is the number of coefficients set equal to zero. In general, the number of restrictions equals the number of coefficients whose values are restrained by the null hypothesis. If the null hypothesis prevents the coefficient from taking whatever value it would naturally take, it is a restriction. The degrees of freedom in the unrestricted model are $n - k - 1$.

The F-statistic formula works by comparing the residual sums of squares of the restricted and unrestricted models. $RSS_{restricted}$ will always be larger than $RSS_{unrestricted}$. Some of the coefficients of the restricted model are being constrained, so it is impossible for the restricted model to fit the data as well as the unrestricted model. This makes $RSS_{restricted}$ larger than $RSS_{unrestricted}$. Consequently, the F-statistic will always be positive.

Suppose we test the null hypothesis $B_3 = B_4 = 0$ for a typical ordinary least squares regression. If the null hypothesis is true, the unrestricted model is likely to give estimates for B_3 and B_4 that are close to zero and insignificant. By removing X_3 and X_4 from the restricted model, B_3 and B_4 are forced to be zero. The restricted and unrestricted models will perform in a similar manner: $RSS_{unrestricted}$ will be close in value to that of $RSS_{restricted}$. Looking at Equation (5-15), if $RSS_{restricted}$ and $RSS_{unrestricted}$ are close in value, the F-statistic will tend to be small and statistically insignificant. The null hypothesis will not be rejected.

Now suppose that the null hypothesis is still $B_3 = B_4 = 0$, but the null hypothesis is actually false, so that at least one of the coefficients is not equal to zero. The unrestricted model will give unbiased estimates of B_3 and B_4 if the classical assumptions hold. In the restricted model, B_3 and B_4 are automatically forced to be zero, since X_3 and X_4 are not in the model. The restricted model will not fit the data as well as the unrestricted model did, since at least one of B_3 and B_4 is not really zero. This causes the difference between $RSS_{restricted}$ and $RSS_{unrestricted}$ to be a lot larger than if B_3 and B_4 actually are equal to zero. Looking at Equation (5-15), the F-statistic will tend to be larger and statistically significant. The null hypothesis can be rejected. The next example demonstrates the F-test.

F-Test Your Way to Riches

Here, dummy variables for different seasons are used to look for a pattern in the Dow Jones Industrial Average (DJIA). For example, perhaps stock prices tend to be lower in the winter and higher in the summer. We could use such a pattern, if it continues, to make money. Those of you who are familiar with the efficient market hypothesis know that most economists are skeptical that such a pattern exists.[4] Quarterly data are used for this model.

$$DJIA = B_0 + B_1GDP + B_2UNEMPLOY$$
$$+ B_3SUMMER + B_4FALL + B_5WINTER + e \qquad \textbf{(5-16)}$$

where

DJIA = Dow Jones Industrial Average, averaged quarterly
GDP = real Gross Domestic Product, in billions of 1996 dollars, per quarter
UNEMPLOY = average unemployment rate (%), each quarter
SUMMER = 1 during summer, 0 otherwise
FALL = 1 during fall, 0 otherwise
WINTER = 1 during winter, 0 otherwise

The data is given in Table 5-G, the results in Table 5-H.

---

[4] For a discussion of the efficient market hypothesis, see Roger Miller, Daniel Benjamin, and Douglass North, "Pure Competition on Wall Street" in *The Economics of Public Issues* 11th ed. (New York: Addison-Wesley, 1998), pp. 75–80.

Table 5-G

Data for Seasonal DJIA Model

Years: Quarter	DJIA	GDP	UNEMPLOY	SUMMER	FALL	WINTER
1995:1	3,962.987	7,488.7	5.5	0	0	0
1995:2	4,377.663	7,503.3	5.7	1	0	0
1995:3	4,690.263	7,561.4	5.7	0	1	0
1995:4	4,944.123	7,621.9	5.6	0	0	1
1996:1	5,436.780	7,676.4	5.6	0	0	0
1996:2	5,622.693	7,802.9	5.5	1	0	0
1996:3	5,661.923	7,841.9	5.3	0	1	0
1996:4	6,250.147	7,931.3	5.3	0	0	1
1997:1	6,841.877	8,016.4	5.3	0	0	0
1997:2	7,166.487	8,131.9	5.0	1	0	0
1997:3	7,935.223	8,216.6	4.8	0	1	0
1997:4	7,821.000	8,272.9	4.7	0	0	1
1998:1	8,280.477	8,404.9	4.7	0	0	0
1998:2	8,996.823	8,465.6	4.4	1	0	0
1998:3	8,495.150	8,537.6	4.5	0	1	0
1998:4	8,729.633	8,654.5	4.4	0	0	1
1999:1	9,474.143	8,730.0	4.3	0	0	0
1999:2	10,667.130	8,783.2	4.3	1	0	0
1999:3	10,900.570	8,905.8	4.2	0	1	0
1999:4	10,817.680	9,084.1	4.1	0	0	1
2000:1	10,768.860	9,191.8	4.1	0	0	0
2000:2	10,762.240	9,308.8	4.0	1	0	0

All data are available at the text website or http://www.economagic.com. Alternatively, for GDP, see http://www.bea.doc.gov/bea/dn1 .html by U.S. Department of Commerce, Bureau of Economic Analysis. For UNEMPLOY, see http://www.stls.frb.org/fred/index.html by the St. Louis Fed. DJIA is available at http://indexes.dowjones.com/home.html by Dow Jones and Co.

Table 5-H

Results for Seasonal DJIA Model—Unrestricted Model

Dependent variable: DJIA

Variable	Coefficient	Standard Error	t-Statistic	p-Value
Constant	−8,134.68	11,062.60	−0.74	0.47
GDP	2.66	0.86	3.10	0.01
UNEMPLOY	−1,297.72	819.38	−1.58	0.13
SUMMER	125.15	271.22	0.46	0.65
FALL	157.23	287.50	0.55	0.59
WINTER	−37.77	285.22	−0.13	0.90

Observations: 22

$R^2 = 0.97$

Adjusted $R^2 = 0.96$

Residual Sum of Squares = 3,511,568

F-statistic = 99.62

Unfortunately, none of the seasonal dummy variables are statistically significant, ruining our "get rich quick scheme." If we expand the sample to include data from the beginning of 1948, giving us 210 observations, unemployment becomes statistically significant at a 1% error level with a negative coefficient, as expected, but the three seasonal dummies remain insignificant. An F-statistic can be calculated to test the joint null hypothesis that none of the seasons matter.

$$H_0: B_3 = B_4 = B_5 = 0$$

H_A: At least one of B_3, B_4, or B_5 is not equal to zero.

Our estimates in Table 5-H for B_3, B_4, and B_5 were allowed to take whatever value made the regression line fit the data best. This gives us the unrestricted model. To form the restricted model, we force B_3, B_4, and B_5 to be zero by eliminating SUMMER, FALL, and WINTER from the regression equation.

$$DJIA = B_0 + B_1 GDP + B_2 UNEMPLOY + e \qquad (5\text{-}17)$$

The results for this restricted model are given in Table 5-I. Now we can calculate the F-statistic for testing the null hypothesis $H_0: B_3 = B_4 = B_5 = 0$ using the residual sums of squares from both the unrestricted and restricted models (Tables 5-H and 5-I). (Recall that the F-statistic given in Table 5-H tests the joint null hypothesis

Table 5-I

Results for Seasonal DJIA Model—Restricted Model Dependent Variable: DJIA

Variable	Coefficient	Standard Error	t-Statistic	p-Value
Constant	−7,384.99	10,183.57	−0.725	0.477
GDP	2.61	0.79	3.293	0.004
UNEMPLOY	−1,347.68	756.05	−1.783	0.091

Observations: 22

$R^2 = 0.97$

Adjusted $R^2 = 0.96$

Residual Sum of Squares = 3,652,782

F-statistic = 283.95

H_0: $B_1 = B_2 = B_3 = B_4 = B_5 = 0$. The econometrics software does not calculate the F-statistic wanted here.)

$$F_{q,\,n-k-1} = \frac{\dfrac{RSS_{restricted} - RSS_{unrestricted}}{q}}{\dfrac{RSS_{unrestricted}}{n-k-1}} = F_{3,\,16} = \frac{\dfrac{3,652,782 - 3,511,568}{3}}{\dfrac{3,511,568}{22-6}}$$

$$= \frac{47,071.333}{219,473} = 0.214$$

The number of restrictions, q, is 3 for the three dummy variable coefficients that are set to zero. The critical value for $F_{3,\,16}$ at 5% significance is 3.24. (See the Appendix, Table C.) The calculated value, 0.214, is much less than the critical value, 3.24, so the null hypothesis cannot be rejected. The evidence does not support a seasonal pattern in the Dow Jones Industrial Average. This is the result we expected, since the dummy coefficients are insignificant according to their individual t-statistics. You can also use the F-test to test a joint null hypothesis that sets two or more slope coefficients equal to each other, such as H_0: $B_3 = B_4$. An exercise at the end of the chapter features a joint null hypothesis of this type.

Chow Test: Testing for Identical Twin Regressions

The F-test can also be used to see if coefficients estimated using different data but the same model are equal. This type of F-test is called the **Chow test**.[5] The Chow test is useful to see if we can combine time-series data from before and after an important

---

[5] Gregory C. Chow, "Tests of Equality Between Sets of Coefficients in Two Linear Regressions," *Econometrica*, Vol. 28, No. 3, July 1960, pp. 591–605.

event. For example, the Chow test can tell us whether two data sets from before and after World War II can be combined. You can also use the Chow test to decide if data for two different locations or groups can be combined—for example, whether data from the United States and Canada can be combined for a model concerning interest rates or whether data for men and women can be combined for a model about income.

The Chow test is based on the formula for the F-test; only now the unrestricted model has two regressions in it.

$$Y = B_0 + B_1X_1 + B_2X_2 + \cdots + B_kX_k + e$$

for the first data set with n_1 observations in it.

(5-18a)

$$Y = B_0 + B_1X_1 + B_2X_2 + \cdots + B_kX_k + e$$

for the second data set with n_2 observations in it.

(5-18b)

The null hypothesis is that the coefficients are equal across the two sets of regression results. That is, B_0 in the first regression equals B_0 in the second regression, B_1 in the first regression equals B_1 in the second regression, and so on. If the null hypothesis is rejected, the two sets of data must be kept separate and the two regressions run independently of each other. If the null hypothesis is not rejected, the two data sets can be combined and only one regression is necessary. (If the Chow test says it is allowable, combining the data is often preferable, because the sample size will be larger.)

As in all F-tests, to form the restricted model, we assume the null hypothesis is true. For the Chow test, this means the coefficients from Equations (5-18a) and (5-18b) are equal and the data can be combined for one regression. The restricted model is:

$$Y = B_0 + B_1X_1 + B_2X_2 + \cdots + B_kX_k + e,$$

for a combined data set with $n_1 + n_2$ observations in it.

(5-19)

Below on the left is the original F-statistic formula, and on the right is the equivalent formula for the Chow test.

$$F_{q,\, n-k-1} = \frac{\dfrac{RSS_{restricted} - RSS_{unrestricted}}{q}}{\dfrac{RSS_{unrestricted}}{n - k - 1}}$$

Original F-statistic formula

(5-20)

$$= F_{k+1,\,(n_1+n_2)-2(k+1)} = \frac{\dfrac{RSS_{restricted} - (RSS_1 + RSS_2)}{k + 1}}{\dfrac{RSS_1 + RSS_2}{(n_1 + n_2) - 2(k + 1)}}$$

Chow test formula

Notice that $RSS_{restricted}$ is the same for both the Chow test and previous F-tests; it is the residual sum of squares for the regression given by Equation (5-19). $RSS_{unrestricted}$

is the residual sum of squares from the regressions (5-18a) and (5-18b) added together. $RSS_{unrestricted}$ is represented by $RSS_1 + RSS_2$ in Equation (5-20). The number of restrictions, q, is now $k + 1$. The restricted model has one restriction for each coefficient (including the intercept). The degrees of freedom in the denominator are now $(n_1 + n_2) - 2(k + 1)$ for the unrestricted model, instead of $n - k - 1$. The degrees of freedom for the unrestricted model are calculated by taking the sample size for Equations (5-18a) and (5-18b) added together, $n_1 + n_2$, and subtracting off $2(k + 1)$, the total number of coefficients estimated in the two regressions of the unrestricted model.

Gasoline Revenue and OPEC

In 1973, the Organization of Petroleum Exporting Countries (OPEC) decreased their oil production, causing dramatically higher prices for gasoline. From January 1973 to January 1975, gasoline prices increased approximately 45%, and by the end of the decade gasoline prices had more than doubled.[6] We can use a Chow test to see if gasoline station revenue data from before 1973 can be combined with later data. The model is:

$$GASREV = B_0 + B_1PRICE + B_2UNEMPLOY$$

$$+ B_3SUMMER + B_4FALL + B_5WINTER + e \qquad \text{(5-21)}$$

where

GASREV = real retail gasoline sales revenues, in millions of 1983 dollars, quarterly[7]

PRICE = a price index for gasoline, averaged over each quarter

UNEMPLOY = average unemployment rate, for each quarter

SUMMER = 1 during summertime, 0 otherwise

FALL = 1 during fall, 0 otherwise

WINTER = 1 during winter, 0 otherwise

Tables 5-J and 5-K give the results for the two regressions that comprise the unrestricted model. The first regression stops at the end of 1972, before OPEC reduced oil production, and the second regression starts with 1973 and continues to the second quarter of 2000.

The restricted model shown in Table 5-L is the same as above, except that all the data are used in one regression. It is the restricted model because the coefficients are restricted to be the same before, during, and after 1973.

---

[6] See Consumer Price Index for Gasoline, U.S. Bureau of Labor Statistics, available at http://www.economagic .com.

[7] GASREV is retail gasoline revenues adjusted by the general consumer price index. Data are available at the text website. Also, the nominal retail gas revenues data, CPI, PRICE, and UNEMPLOY, are available at http://www.economagic.com. Alternatively, use nominal retail gas sales by U.S. Census Bureau: Monthly Retail Trade Survey, at http://www.census.gov/mrts/www/mrts.html. General CPI data and PRICE (the gasoline price index) are at http://www.stats.bls.gov by the Bureau of Labor Statistics. (For the gasoline price index, click on "Data" then "Selective Access" and progress through the screens that follow, choosing series SETB01.) For UNEMPLOY, see http://www.stls.frb.org/fred/index.html by the St. Louis Fed.

Table 5-J

Results for Gasoline Revenue Model—Unrestricted Model
(Regression 1, 1967–1972, Quarterly Data)

Dependent variable: GASREV

Variable	Coefficient	Standard Error	t-Statistic	p-Value
Constant	−11,271.760	4,165.634	−2.706	0.015
PRICE	998.941	165.779	6.026	0.001
UNEMPLOY	206.575	120.585	1.713	0.104
SUMMER	1,544.889	246.197	6.275	0.001
FALL	1,727.664	251.536	6.868	0.001
WINTER	1,092.065	255.935	4.267	0.001

Observations: 24

$R^2 = 0.92$

Adjusted $R^2 = 0.89$

Residual Sum of Squares = 3,264,647

F-statistic = 38.92

Table 5-K

Results for Gasoline Sales Model—Unrestricted Model
(Regression 2, 1973–2000 Quarterly Data)

Dependent variable: GASREV

Variable	Coefficient	Standard Error	t-Statistic	p-Value
Constant	17,594.690	681.660	25.812	0.001
PRICE	77.334	4.767	16.223	0.001
UNEMPLOY	−111.451	79.040	−1.410	0.162
SUMMER	2,065.952	319.496	6.466	0.001
FALL	2,513.808	322.429	7.796	0.001
WINTER	1,550.121	322.364	4.809	0.001

Observations: 110

$R^2 = 0.77$

Adjusted $R^2 = 0.76$

Residual Sum of Squares = 148,000,000

F-statistic = 70.21

Table 5-L

Results for Gasoline Sales Model—Restricted Model (1967–2000 Quarterly Data)

Dependent variable: GASREV

Variable	Coefficient	Standard Error	t-Statistic	p-Value
Constant	14,500.870	510.142	28.425	0.001
PRICE	95.499	3.880	24.616	0.001
UNEMPLOY	113.364	76.798	1.476	0.142
SUMMER	1,942.189	316.232	6.142	0.001
FALL	2,373.913	318.560	7.452	0.001
WINTER	1,497.568	318.544	4.701	0.001

Observations: 134

$R^2 = 0.861$

Adjusted $R^2 = 0.855$

Residual Sum of Squares = 217,000,000

F-statistic = 158.353

The Chow test uses the residual sums of squares from the unrestricted and restricted models.

$$F_{k+1,(n_1+n_2)-2(k+1)} = \frac{\dfrac{RSS_{restricted} - (RSS_1 + RSS_2)}{k+1}}{\dfrac{RSS_1 + RSS_2}{(n_1 + n_2) - 2(k+1)}}$$

$$= F_{6,\,122} = \frac{\dfrac{217,000,000 - 3,264,647 - 148,000,000}{5+1}}{\dfrac{3,264,647 + 148,000,000}{(24 + 110) - 2(5 + 1)}}$$

$$= \frac{\dfrac{65,735,353}{6}}{\dfrac{151,264,647}{122}} = 8.84$$

At a 1% error level, the critical value of $F_{6,\,122}$ is approximately 2.96. The calculated F-statistic of 8.84 exceeds the critical value, so the null hypothesis can be rejected at a 1% error level. This means that data from before 1973 cannot be combined with the later data. The relationship between the independent and dependent variables changed when OPEC reduced oil production in 1973.

5-4 POLYNOMIAL MODELS: CURVES CAN BE LINEAR REGRESSIONS

Most cost and production functions are curves with changing slopes, not straight lines with constant slopes. The **polynomial model** enables us to estimate curves. In the polynomial model, independent variables can be squared, cubed, or raised to any exponential power. The coefficients still appear in the regression in a linear fashion, allowing the regression to be estimated as usual (see Section 2-2). Some examples of polynomial models are

$$Y = B_0 + B_1 X_1 + B_2 (X_1)^2 + B_3 X_3 + e \qquad \text{(5-22)}$$

$$Y = B_0 + B_1 X_1 + B_2 (X_1)^2 + B_3 (X_1)^3 + e \qquad \text{(5-23)}$$

At first glance, the independent variables in each of these polynomial models seem to be highly correlated, since the same independent variables appear more than once, in different forms. (A similar problem was discussed in Section 5-2, where we added an interaction term to the professional wrestling model.) Multicollinearity may not exist here, however, because the variables are not *linearly* correlated. For example, in Equation (5-23), X_1, $(X_1)^2$, and $(X_1)^3$ share a nonlinear correlation.

Sports Car Production Costs

Suppose an exotic sports car company wants to estimate its average cost function. Here is its polynomial model for estimating the average cost function:

$$\text{AVECOST} = B_0 + B_1 \text{CARS} + B_2 (\text{CARS})^2 + e \qquad \text{(5-24)}$$

where
  AVECOST = average cost per car, in dollars
     CARS = number of cars produced per week

Table 5-M gives data for the average cost at different levels of weekly production. Table 5-N gives the results for this model.

We can use these results to estimate the average cost for different levels of production, which gives us the average cost curve shown in Figure 5-3. Such information is useful in planning future production schedules.

5-5 LOG MODELS: ESTIMATING ELASTICITIES

In a log model, the natural logarithm is used to transform one or more of the variables. Log models express nonlinear relationships between the dependent and independent variables. As with the polynomial model, even though the relationship is nonlinear, the coefficient enters the regression in a linear manner. We'll examine two commonly used log models, the double-log and semi-log models.

Table 5-M

Data for Polynomial Sports Car Model

Observation	CARS	AVECOST
1	50	42,250
2	100	40,825
3	150	36,540
4	200	37,135
5	250	29,500
6	300	32,250
7	350	25,230
8	400	31,842
9	450	21,568
10	500	18,225
11	550	28,759
12	600	36,102
13	650	33,215
14	700	31,460
15	750	42,512
16	800	42,890
17	850	51,230
18	900	55,985
19	950	65,320
20	1,000	74,586

The Double-Log Model

The **double-log model** consists of taking the natural logarithm of the dependent and independent variables.

$$\ln(Y) = B_0 + B_1 \ln(X_1) + B_2 \ln(X_2) + \cdots + B_k \ln(X_k) + e \qquad \textbf{(5-25)}$$

Table 5-N

Results for Polynomial Sports Car Model

Dependent variable: AVECOST

Variable	Coefficient	Standard Error	t-Statistic	p-Value
Constant	51,671.10	2,870.231	18.002	0.001
CARS	-121.662	12.590	-9.664	0.001
$(CARS)^2$	0.142	0.0116	12.224	0.001

Observations: 20
$R^2 = 0.933$
Adjusted $R^2 = 0.925$
Residual Sum of Squares $= 253,000,000$
F-statistic $= 117.929$

Figure 5-3

Estimated Average Cost Curve for Polynomial Sports Car Model. The $\star$ symbols are data points from Table 5-M.

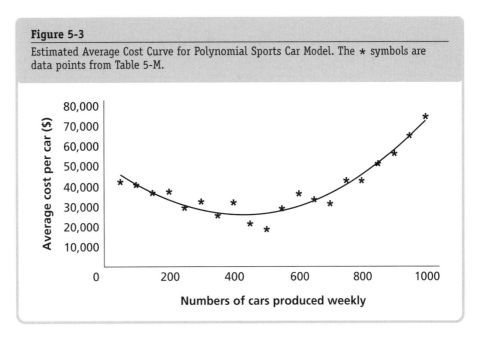

Except for the intercept, the coefficients of a double-log model are elasticities. Elasticity is the percentage movement in one variable that results when another variable changes 1%. The estimate of B_1 estimates the average percentage change in Y for a 1% change in X_1, keeping the other variables constant. The most commonly used elasticity is price elasticity of demand, which measures the percentage change in quantity demanded for a 1% change in the good's price. Elasticities of all types can be estimated with double-log models. Double-log models are appropriate when the theoretical relationship between the independent and dependent variables has a constant elasticity, but not a constant slope.

Estimating the Price Elasticity of Demand for Compact Discs

Suppose a large record store adds a new section of European techno music discs. In order to estimate the price elasticity of demand for these discs, the store conducts an experiment. Each day for 20 days, the store lowers the price for these CDs and tracks how many are sold. The store has a large number of techno music CDs in stock, so the amount sold is the quantity demanded. Table 5-O gives data for such an experiment.

Table 5-O

Data for Estimating Techno CD Double-Log Model

Day	Quantity Demanded	Price ($)
1	1	25
2	1	24
3	2	23
4	4	22
5	7	21
6	8	20
7	8	19.5
8	9	18.5
9	10	18
10	10	17.5
11	13	17
12	18	16
13	20	15
14	23	14
15	24	13
16	27	12
17	30	11
18	33	10
19	35	9
20	37	8

The appropriate double-log model for estimating the price elasticity of demand is

$$\ln(\text{QUANTITY}) = B_0 + B_1 \ln(\text{PRICE}) + e \qquad \textbf{(5-26)}$$

Many economics textbooks depict demand curves as linear (so that the slope is constant), but the elasticity changes along the curve. Demand curves need not be linear. This model gives a demand curve that is nonlinear and has a constant elasticity. Results from this double-log model are given in Table 5-P.

The estimate of the price elasticity of demand is 2.937. (Although the slope coefficient estimate is -2.937, the price elasticity of demand is stated as a positive number.) For every 1% decrease in price, the quantity demanded will typically increase by 2.937%.

The Semi-Log Model

The **semi-log model** is an adaptation of the double-log model where only some of the variables are transformed by the natural logarithm. The semi-log model can take different forms, such as

$$Y = B_0 + B_1 \ln(X_1) + B_2 \ln(X_2) + e \qquad \textbf{(5-27)}$$

$$Y = B_0 + B_1 X_1 + B_2 \ln(X_2) + e \qquad \textbf{(5-28)}$$

$$\ln(Y) = B_0 + B_1 X_1 + B_2 X_2 + e \qquad \textbf{(5-29)}$$

Independent variables that are, in theory, linearly related to the term on the left-hand side of the equation [Y or $\ln(Y)$] are entered into the regression without a logarithmic transformation. If the theoretical relationship is nonlinear, then a logarithmic transformation may be appropriate. Equations (5-27) and (5-28) model situations where the effect of X on Y becomes smaller as X becomes larger. For example, Equation (5-28) could be used if Y is consumption, and X_2 is income. As income increases, consumption increases, but consumption increases more slowly when income reaches a certain level. The effect is represented properly in the regression by taking the logarithm

Table 5-P

Results for Techno CD Double-Log Model

Dependent variable: ln(QUANTITY)

Variable	Coefficient	Standard Error	t-Statistic	p-Value
Constant	10.474	1.020	10.270	0.001
ln(PRICE)	-2.937	0.366	-8.015	0.001

Observations: 20

$R^2 = 0.781$

Adjusted $R^2 = 0.769$

Residual Sum of Squares $= 5.137$

F-statistic $= 64.248$

of X_2. This relationship between income and consumption is known in microeconomics as the Engel curve.

Models of the form shown in Equation (5-29) are often used to estimate economic growth for different countries or regions. Theory tells us that economic growth occurs in a nonlinear, exponential fashion. In Equation (5-29), B_1 and B_2 each represent the average percentage increase in the dependent variable for a one-unit (not 1%) increase in the corresponding independent variable. The logarithmic transformation of zero is undefined. Dummy variables, as well as other variables that take a zero value, must be used without logarithmic transformations.[8]

SUMMARY

1. Dummy variables take variables that are not numbers and express them as numerical variables so that they can be used in regression analysis. Example: MALE = 1 if person is male, 0 otherwise. This type of dummy variable changes the intercept of the regression when the dummy is equal to 1.

2. The dummy variable trap occurs when the model has one too many dummies. To escape the dummy variable trap, always leave out one possible dummy variable. In general, the number of dummy variables is one less than the number of possible categories.

3. Dummy variables can be used to allow the slope, rather than the intercept, to change. To form a dummy variable that changes the slope, multiply an intercept dummy by a regular independent variable. Example: MALExINCOME is a slope dummy.

4. The effect of one independent variable can be influenced by another independent variable. To capture this effect, create an interaction variable by multiplying the two independent variables together.

5. Different F-tests can be designed to test many types of joint hypotheses. (A joint hypothesis is a null hypothesis that involves more than one coefficient at a time.) In general, conduct the test by following these steps:
   - First, determine the joint null hypothesis that you wish to test.
   - Run the regression model and find the residual sum of squares to be used in the F-statistic formula, Equation (5-15). This regression is called the unrestricted model because no changes or restrictions have been forced on the regression.
   - Alter the regression model to force the null hypothesis to be true, whether it really is true or not. This altered model is called the restricted model because the values that some of the coefficients can take have been changed or restricted. Estimate the restricted model to find its residual sum of squares.
   - Calculate an F-statistic using Equation (5-15). Compare this value to the critical value found on a F-distribution table to conclude the hypothesis test.

[8] If theory requires the dummy variable to have a logarithmic transformation, make sure you define the dummy so that it does not take a zero value.

6. The Chow test is a type of F-test that checks whether different data sets can be combined for use in one regression [Equation (5-20)]. The Chow test is useful for checking whether time-series data from before and after an important event can be combined. The Chow test can also be used to see if data for two different locations or groups can be combined.

7. Polynomial models enable us to estimate curves and are used to estimate cost and production functions. In polynomial models, independent variables can be squared, cubed, or raised to any exponential power. Each coefficient still appears in the regression in a linear fashion, allowing the regression to be estimated as usual.

8. In a log model, the natural logarithm is used to transform one or more of the variables. Log models express nonlinear relationships between the dependent and independent variables. The double-log model consists of taking the natural logarithm of the dependent and independent variables. Except for the intercept, the coefficients of the double-log model are elasticities. The semi-log model is an adaptation of the double-log model where only certain variables are transformed by the natural logarithm. Some semi-log models are used to study situations in which the effect of X on Y becomes smaller as X becomes larger [Equations (5-27) and (5-28)]. Other semi-log models are used to estimate economic growth models [Equation (5-29)].

EXERCISES

1. Try to explain these terms without looking them up.
   - quantitative variable
   - qualitative variable
   - dummy variable
   - interaction variable
   - unrestricted model
   - restricted model
   - Chow test
   - polynomial model
   - double-log model
   - semi-log model

2. Is an interaction variable the same as a slope dummy variable? Why or why not?

3. a. Consider the cross-section regression

$$INCOME = B_0 + B_1 EDUCATION + B_2 MALE + e$$

where EDUCATION is the person's years of schooling and MALE is equal to 1 if the individual is male; 0 otherwise. Show how the intercept changes for males compared to females.

   b. Now say the regression is

$$INCOME = B_0 + B_1 EDUCATION + B_4 (EDUCATION \times MALE) + e$$

Show how the slope coefficient for EDUCATION differs for males compared to females.

4. A large brokerage firm hires financial advisors to work with clients, but they are not paid commission. When someone new is hired, their salary varies depending on different factors. The following regression is used to estimate the relationship between salaries paid and a few key factors:

$$SALARY = B_0 + B_1 EXPERIENCE + B_2 GPA + B_3 CFP + B_4 NOCFP + e$$

where
$\quad\quad\quad$ SALARY = annual salary for each newly hired advisor
$\quad$ EXPERIENCE = years of experience before joining firm
$\quad\quad\quad\quad\quad$ GPA = grade point average in college
$\quad\quad\quad\quad\quad$ CFP = 1 if individual is a certified financial planner, 0 otherwise
$\quad\quad\quad$ NOCFP = 1 if individual is not a certified financial planner, 0 otherwise

Explain what is wrong with this regression.

5. Consider the following time-series models, which attempt to explain employment for construction workers.

$\quad$ i. $EMPLOYMENT_1 = B_0 + B_1 GDP + B_2 SUMMER +$
$\quad\quad B_3 WINTER + B_4 FALL + B_5 SPRING + e$

$\quad$ ii. $EMPLOYMENT_2 = B_0 + B_1 GDP + B_2 SUMMER +$
$\quad\quad B_3 WINTER + B_4 FALL + e$

$\quad$ iii. $EMPLOYMENT_3 = B_1 GNP + B_2 SUMMER + B_3 WINTER +$
$\quad\quad B_4 FALL + e$

where
EMPLOYMENT = number of construction workers employed in the economy
$\quad\quad\quad\quad$ GDP = real gross domestic product for that quarter

Dummy variables:
SUMMER = 1 during summer, 0 otherwise
$\quad\;\;$ FALL = 1 during fall, 0 otherwise
WINTER = 1 during winter, 0 otherwise
SPRING = 1 during spring, 0 otherwise

a. Which of these models is most appropriate? Why did you reject the other two?
b. How you would test the hypothesis that in general, the seasons of the year do not affect EMPLOYMENT?

6. Consider the following two regressions on two separate samples: male students and female students. The sample size for each group is 500. Assume all the students are in the same academic program.

$$Male\ students:\quad GPA = B_0 + B_1 STUDY + e$$

$$Female\ students:\quad GPA = B_2 + B_3 STUDY + e$$

where

GPA = grade point average of student

STUDY = average hours a week the student spends studying

a. What does it mean if $B_0 = B_2$ and $B_1 = B_3$?

b. How you can test the joint null hypothesis H_0: $B_0 = B_2$ and $B_1 = B_3$?

7. Ordinary least squares is based on the idea that the independent variables have a linear relationship with the dependent variable. If a polynomial model is used, the independent variables are assumed to have a nonlinear relationship with the dependent variable. Polynomial models are often estimated using ordinary least squares. Is it cheating to use ordinary least squares to estimate a nonlinear model?

8. Consider the following polynomial regression results where you are not told what variables X and Y stand for, but you do know that the slope coefficients are statistically significant at a 1% error level and that the regression fits the data well.

$$Y = 2000 + 2.0X - 0.5X^2$$

Does the 2.0 slope coefficient estimate for X tell you that X and Y are positively related? Describe the relationship between X and Y.

9. Using the data from the professional wrestling model (Table 5-A), estimate this polynomial model:

$$HOURS = B_0 + B_1 GENDER + B_2 INCOME + B_3 (INCOME)^2 + B_4 AGE + e$$

a. What do the results tell you about the relationship between INCOME and HOURS?

b. Is the answer to part a absolutely clear? Why or why not?

10. A person's age and income are often positively related. In the professional wrestling model, a person's age may influence the relationship between income and hours of wrestling watched. Add an interaction variable, AGExINCOME, to this model and estimate the model using the data in Table 5-A. Discuss your results.

11. Use the data from Table 5-O to estimate

$$QUANTITY = B_0 + B_1 PRICE + e$$

How does the interpretation of the results compare with the interpretation of the results in Table 5-P, where the double-log model is used?

12. Using the data for the retail sales model (Table 5-C), test the joint null hypothesis that the season of the year does not affect retail sales.

13. The following cross-section model uses personal consumption expenditures as the dependent variable. Annual income and wealth serve as independent variables. (All variables are in dollars.)

$$CONSUMPTION = B_0 + B_1 INCOME + B_2 WEALTH + e$$

The table below provides the necessary data. (These data can also be downloaded from the text website.)

Observation	Consumption	Income	Wealth
1	28,815	29,000	700
2	55,653	38,000	42,000
3	68,835	46,000	38,000
4	73,523	64,000	80,000
5	18,607	27,000	6,000
6	163,191	125,000	437,000
7	39,358	41,000	46,000
8	22,786	16,000	500
9	31,565	32,000	55,000
10	67,555	52,000	83,000
11	21,888	32,000	8,000
12	52,511	30,000	57,000
13	36,422	35,000	500
14	63,983	48,000	78,000
15	46,894	36,000	40,000
16	84,273	38,000	73,000
17	58,266	56,000	87,000
18	51,955	42,000	77,000
19	53,246	44,000	70,000
20	46,505	50,000	102,000
21	72,928	68,000	50,000
22	45,279	23,000	70,000
23	67,379	72,000	10,000
24	26,138	20,000	3,000
25	121,638	87,000	375,000

Observation	Consumption	Income	Wealth
26	38,800	25,000	50,000
27	10,757	24,000	2,000
28	33,349	18,000	300
29	49,131	5,000	800
30	19,191	12,000	20,000

a. Suppose you want to test the hypothesis that income and wealth affect consumption in *exactly* the same way. State the null and alternative hypotheses for the test.

b. Write out the regressions you will have to run to test the null and alternative hypotheses stated in part a.

c. Use the data given to conduct the relevant hypothesis test at a 1% error level. Show how you calculated the hypothesis test. Can you reject the null hypothesis you wrote in part a?

14. Use the data from Exercise 13 to estimate this double-log model:

$$\ln(CONSUMPTION) = B_0 + B_1 \ln(INCOME) + B_2 \ln(WEALTH) + e$$

a. Are the slope coefficients significant at a 5% error level?

b. Explain what each slope estimate means.

15. Consider the following semi-log model:

$$CONSUMPTION = B_0 + B_1 \ln(INCOME) + B_2 \ln(WEALTH) + e$$

a. Explain how the meaning of this model differs from the linear and double-log models used in the previous two exercises.

b. Use the data from the last two exercises to estimate this semi-log model. Are the slope coefficients significant at a 5% error level?

c. How do you decide which model should be used, the linear, double-log, or semi-log model?

6

Multicollinearity: When Independent Variables Have Relationships

In this chapter, you will learn:

- The concept of multicollinearity: A problem with ordinary least squares estimation when two independent variables are closely linearly related.
- The symptoms that signal when multicollinearity is present.
- How to measure multicollinearity.
- How to deal with multicollinearity.

Chapters 6–8 deal with violations of the classical ordinary least squares assumptions. The classical assumptions are rules for how a healthy regression model should work. When the assumptions hold true, the regression model has desirable properties, and the OLS procedure is BLUE (Best Linear Unbiased Estimator). When one assumption is violated, something goes wrong, as if the regression has an illness. Different "illnesses" occur when different assumptions are violated. Each illness exhibits symptoms that, like a real disease, can help us identify what is wrong. Like medical researchers (except not as well paid), top econometricians work late into the night searching for cures that allow these models to live healthy, productive lives. And, just as in the medical profession, some treatments cure only symptoms, some cure the actual disease, and an inappropriate treatment can actually make things worse.

6-1 THE ILLNESS

Ordinary least squares assumes that no independent variable is a linear function of another independent variable. Remember that each slope estimate in an OLS regression gives the average change in Y for a one-unit change in X, *holding all other independent variables constant*. If one independent variable is a linear function of another, then when one changes value so does the other. It is impossible for the OLS procedure to estimate a slope for either independent variable. Consider the following time-series model for a student working part-time who gets paid by the hour:

$$\text{SPENDING} = B_0 + B_1\text{INCOME} + B_2\text{HOURS} + e \qquad \text{(6-1)}$$

where

SPENDING = amount of money the student spends each month
INCOME = amount of money the student earns each month, before taxes
HOURS = number of hours the student works each month

If the student always gets paid the same hourly wage, say \$10, then INCOME is a linear function of HOURS.

$$\text{INCOME} = \$10 \cdot \text{HOURS} \tag{6-2}$$

INCOME and HOURS always move together. Every time HOURS increases by 1, INCOME increases by 10. The OLS procedure will not be able to find values for the estimates $\hat{B}_1$ or $\hat{B}_2$. The value of $\hat{B}_1$ should be the estimated average increase in SPENDING when INCOME increases by \$1, keeping HOURS constant, but the only way INCOME can increase is if HOURS increases. HOURS can't be constant when INCOME changes, and INCOME can't be constant when HOURS changes. If we attempt to estimate the regression given by Equation (6-1), and the student's wage is always the same, the econometrics software will display an error message. It is impossible to compute the estimates $\hat{B}_1$ or $\hat{B}_2$. This is **perfect multicollinearity**; these two independent variables have a perfect linear relationship.

What if the student gets a raise? Then Equation (6-2) changes. If the wage changes, INCOME and HOURS will not exhibit perfect multicollinearity. INCOME and HOURS still tend to move together. They may even be highly correlated, but the linear relationship is no longer perfect, so we have **multicollinearity** but not perfect multicollinearity. If the wage changes often enough, the OLS procedure will be able to compute values for the estimates $\hat{B}_1$ and $\hat{B}_2$, but there is still trouble. Since income is determined by wages and hours, INCOME and HOURS will contain much of the same information. This makes it hard for the OLS procedure to distinguish between the slope coefficients B_1 and B_2. This is the essence of multicollinearity. Although the software can find values for the slope estimates, there will be problems with the estimates (as we discuss in the next section).

Most of the multicollinearity that we encounter is not perfect multicollinearity. Experienced researchers understand that if wages are held constant, INCOME and HOURS have a perfect linear relationship and should not be used as independent variables in the same model. There can be a theoretical connection between independent variables that implies multicollinearity. It makes sense theoretically that INCOME and HOURS could have multicollinearity, especially if the individual is paid by the hour. Since income is the number of hours multiplied by the hourly wage rate, in theory there could be a multicollinearity problem, even if the wage rate is not always the same. Ultimately, however, multicollinearity is a characteristic displayed by the data. This means that for a given model, one sample may give results that exhibit multicollinearity, but a different sample may not.

Here is a fictional example that will be used throughout the chapter to discuss multicollinearity. Mia is studying for a set of 15 exams. Mia does her best studying at the library, but sometimes she studies at home. She kept track of her study habits carefully, so that we can run the following regression:

$$\text{SCORE} = B_0 + B_1\text{STUDY} + B_2\text{LIBRARY} + e \tag{6-3}$$

where

      SCORE = score for each exam
      STUDY = hours spent studying for each exam
   LIBRARY = hours spent in the library

Mia does not have a lot of experience formulating models, so it didn't occur to her when she collected the data that STUDY and LIBRARY would have a potential multicollinearity problem. When Mia is at the library, she might look for a pulp fiction novel to read later, but she spends most of her time studying. For any one exam, if she spends more time at the library, it is very likely she is spending more time studying. In theory, there could be a multicollinearity problem with STUDY and LIBRARY. We won't know for sure until we examine the data and look for symptoms in the regression results.

6-2 THE SYMPTOMS

Multicollinearity generates the following characteristics or symptoms:

1. **Estimates will still be unbiased.** Fortunately, even if there is serious multicollinearity, the estimates of B will still be unbiased, as long as the other classical OLS assumptions hold true.

2. **Standard errors of the estimates increase.** Independent variables that exhibit multicollinearity contain similar information; this is why such variables tend to move together. The OLS procedure has a difficult time estimating separate slope coefficients for variables that move in a similar manner, so the slope estimates will not be very precise. This means that the standard errors for the slope estimates will be large. Larger standard errors indicate that the sampling distribution for the slope estimate has become wider; the chance that the estimates will be farther away from the true values thus increases. If multicollinearity is severe, the slope estimate may end up having the opposite sign of the true value (it is positive when the true value is negative or negative when the true value is positive). The slope estimates are unbiased as stated above, but this just means that if we run the regression many times using different data, the slope estimates from the different regressions will tend to average out toward the true value.

3. **t-Statistics are small.** The formula for the t-statistic is

$$t = \frac{\hat{B} - B_{null}}{SE(\hat{B})}$$

where B_{null} is usually zero (see Chapter 3). The standard error of the estimate appears in the denominator. Since multicollinearity increases the standard error of the estimate, the t-statistics will be smaller than they would be if there were no multicollinearity.

4. **Goodness of fit is not diminished.** The t-statistics for two or more independent variables may be low if they have multicollinearity. Together, the variables may still do a good job of explaining movement in the dependent variable. The R^2, adjusted R^2, and F-statistic can still be high, even with multicollinearity. This means that a

regression with multicollinearity can still be good for forecasting. When a regression has a high F-statistic and adjusted R^2 but low t-statistics, there is likely to be a multicollinearity problem.

5. **Estimates vary widely if the specification of the model is changed.** It is difficult for the OLS procedure to differentiate between two slope coefficients when their variables are highly correlated. In order to come up with separate estimates for the two different slope estimates, OLS will use any small difference in the way the variables move to distinguish them. If two brothers look almost alike, you will use any little difference you can find to tell them apart, including small differences that normally would not catch your attention. This is similar to how ordinary least squares works when there is multicollinearity. Because of this, any change in the model causes estimates to come out very differently—for example, the sign of the estimate may change from positive to negative, or vice versa.

6. **Slope estimates for independent variables without multicollinearity are not seriously affected.** Suppose a regression has three independent variables and two of them are highly correlated, so there is multicollinearity. If the third independent variable has a small or no correlation with the other two, its slope estimate and standard error will not be seriously affected by the multicollinearity problem.

Now, let's return to our exam score model. Table 6-A gives Mia's data.

Using this data, we estimate Equation (6-3), $SCORE = B_0 + B_1 STUDY + B_2 LIBRARY + e$, and get the results given in Table 6-B.

The results in Table 6-B show classic symptoms of multicollinearity. The adjusted-R^2 is 0.65 and the 14.20 F-statistic, significant at a 1% error level, is large.[1] These statistics indicate that the regression model explains a good portion of the movement in SCORE. However, neither independent variable has a statistically significant coefficient. The model's explanatory power cannot be attributed either to STUDY alone, or to LIBRARY alone. The explanatory power must be coming from STUDY and LIBRARY working together, which as you now know indicates multicollinearity. The presence of multicollinearity also makes it difficult for the OLS procedure to estimate the slope coefficients B_1 for STUDY and B_2 for LIBRARY. Although the estimates are unbiased, they are not very precise, so we cannot place much faith in their estimates, 0.35 and 1.59. The low t-statistics indicate this lack of precision. What we need now are ways to measure the magnitude of the multicollinearity.

6-3 MEASURING MULTICOLLINEARITY

There is no real test for multicollinearity, because any regression with more than one independent variable is likely to have at least some multicollinearity. We need to get an idea of *how much* multicollinearity is present, so we will discuss the most popular ways to measure this. Most regressions display some degree of multicollinearity, so it's important that you avoid multicollinearity paranoia. Economics majors are particularly at risk when it comes to multicollinearity paranoia. Economics tells us that many factors

---

[1] The critical value is 6.93 (see Table D in the Appendix). The degrees of freedom in the numerator equal 2, since the model has two independent variables. The degrees of freedom in the denominator equal $n - k - 1 = 15 - 2 - 1 = 12$.

Table 6-A

Mia's Data for Her Study Habits and Exam Performance

Exam Number	SCORE	STUDY	LIBRARY
1	78	6	4
2	88	13	12
3	73	7	2
4	81	8	8
5	84	12	10
6	77	9	4
7	86	12	13
8	43	2	0
9	80	9	8
10	58	6	2
11	68	5	3
12	93	24	20
13	82	8	9
14	92	16	18
15	86	14	10

in different markets and different parts of the economy affect each other, so it often seems that all of a regression's independent variables are related. That doesn't mean that your regressions necessarily have serious multicollinearity problems, though. What you need is a way to measure the amount of multicollinearity present.

Correlation Coefficients

One simple way to measure multicollinearity is to look at the **correlation coefficient** for two independent variables. The correlation coefficient measures the extent to which two variables move together.[2] (We usually call this measure r, not to be confused with

---

[2] The correlation coefficient between any two variables (call them C and D) is

$$r = \frac{\text{sum of } [(C - \bar{C})(D - \bar{D})]}{\sqrt{[\text{sum of } (C - \bar{C})^2] \cdot [\text{sum of } (D - \bar{D}^2]}}$$

where "sum of" means that the term that follows is calculated and summed for each observation in the data.

Table 6-B

Regression Results for Mia's Exam Score Model

Dependent variable: SCORE

Variable	Coefficient	Standard Error	t-Statistic	p-Value
Constant	61.39	4.78	12.83	0.00
STUDY	0.35	1.03	0.34	0.74
LIBRARY	1.59	0.94	1.70	0.12

Observations: 15

$R^2 = 0.70$

Adjusted $R^2 = 0.65$

F-statistic = 14.20

R^2, which measures goodness of fit for a regression.) Most econometrics software has a command that calculates the correlation coefficient between two variables. If your regression has more than two independent variables, you would compute a correlation coefficient for any two variables that concern you. Notice that r can take a value from -1 to $+1$. If r is less than zero, the two variables are negatively correlated (inversely related). That is, when one variable goes up, the other tends to go down, and vice versa. If r is -1, the two variables are *perfectly* negatively correlated; they always move in opposite directions. If r is 0, the variables are not correlated—a change in one does not give you any information about the movement of the other variable. The two variables appear to have nothing to do with each other. If r is positive, the variables are positively correlated; they tend to move in the same direction: When one variable increases, the other also tends to increase, and vice versa. If r is 1, the variables are *perfectly* positively correlated. They *always* move in the same direction.

A correlation coefficient close to zero indicates that the two variables being examined do not tend to move together, so you probably don't have a serious multicollinearity problem. The closer r is to $+1$ or -1, the more likely there is a serious multicollinearity problem. Usually in economics multicollinearity is generated by variables with a positive correlation coefficient; however, a negative correlation coefficient close to -1 also indicates severe multicollinearity. The correlation coefficient for STUDY and LIBRARY (calculated from the data in Table 6-A) is 0.93, which is close to 1. This confirms our suspicion that substantial multicollinearity is present in the results from Mia's exam score model. We don't have an absolute rule that tells us what the correlation coefficient has to be before we consider multicollinearity a problem. Some researchers use 0.80 as a very rough guide. According to this informal standard, you should be concerned if the correlation coefficient between two independent variables is 0.80 or greater. However, always remember that r is *not* a perfect measure of multicollinearity. If three or four independent variables are correlated, there could be substantial multicollinearity present, even if none of the correlation coefficients are very high.

Regress One Independent Variable on Another

Another way to measure multicollinearity is to regress one of the independent variables on another, as if one of them is the dependent variable. In the exam score model, the two independent variables STUDY and LIBRARY exhibit multicollinearity. To get additional information about the extent of the problem, we can run a regression using STUDY as the dependent variable and LIBRARY as the only independent variable. (*Note*: It does not matter which of the two independent variables we use as the dependent variable.) A significant F-statistic confirms the presence of a multicollinearity problem.[3]

$$\text{STUDY} = B_0 + B_1\text{LIBRARY} + e \qquad \qquad \textbf{(6-4)}$$

Using the same data as before, we get the results in Table 6-C. The F-statistic is significant at a 1% error level.[4] Also, the R^2 is high. Both of these results confirm that a substantial relationship exists between LIBRARY and STUDY, one that would cause multicollinearity in the original exam score model results.

Variance Inflation Factor

The **variance inflation factor** (**VIF**) measures multicollinearity by regressing one independent variable on *all* of the remaining independent variables. Let's look at a regression with three independent variables. To use the variance inflation factor to look for any possible multicollinearity, we run three regressions, one for each independent

Table 6-C

Regression Results for Measuring Multicollinearity in Mia's Exam Score Model

Dependent variable: STUDY

Variable	Coefficient	Standard Error	t-Statistic	p-Value
Constant	3.14	0.96	3.29	0.01
LIBRARY	0.84	0.10	8.82	0.00

Observations: 15

$R^2 = 0.86$

Adjusted $R^2 = 0.85$

F-statistic = 77.79

---

[3] There is only one independent variable in this regression, so we could also use the t-statistic for the slope estimate instead of the F-statistic. In this situation (one independent variable in the regression), the F-statistic is equal to the square of the slope coefficient's t-statistic. In Table 6-C, the slope coefficient's t-statistic is 8.82, and $(8.82)^2$ is 77.79, the same as the F-statistic.

[4] The critical value is 9.07 (see Table D in the Appendix).

variable. If our original regression is $Y = B_0 + B_1X_1 + B_2X_2 + B_3X_3 + e$, we would run the following three regressions:

1. X_1 as the dependent variable and X_2 and X_3 as independent variables
2. X_2 as the dependent variable and X_1 and X_3 as independent variables
3. X_3 as the dependent variable and X_1 and X_2 as independent variables[5]

For a regression with more than three independent variables, you would run more regressions, following this pattern.

Next, for each of these regressions, we calculate the variance inflation factor using this formula:

$$VIF = \frac{1}{1 - R^2} \qquad (6\text{-}5)$$

where R^2 is the *unadjusted* R^2 from a regression using an original independent variable (an X) as the dependent variable. Keep in mind that the R^2 in Equation (6-5) is *not* the R^2 from the original regression that we suspect has multicollinearity; this R^2 comes from regressing one independent variable on the remaining independent variables. The variance inflation factor gets its name from the fact that if the R^2 in Equation (6-5) is high, the variances of the slope estimates (and the standard errors) will also be high or inflated. If you had three independent variables in the original model, you would compute three VIFs with Equation (6-5), using the R^2 from each separate regression from the three listed earlier.

Because our example has only two independent variables, it would seem that two regressions are needed. One regression is to use STUDY as the dependent variable and LIBRARY as an independent variable.

We ran the first regression in Equation (6-4). Table 6-C gives the R^2 as 0.86. Plugging this value in the variance inflation factor formula gives

$$VIF = \frac{1}{1 - R^2} = \frac{1}{1 - 0.86} = \frac{1}{0.14} = 7.14$$

Some researchers believe that a variance inflation factor greater than 4 indicates a serious multicollinearity problem. It's useful to realize that if the R^2 from regressing one independent variable on the others is greater than 0.75, the VIF will be greater than 4. Using 0.75 as the R^2 in the VIF equation shows why this is true.

$$VIF = \frac{1}{1 - R^2} = \frac{1}{1 - 0.75} = \frac{1}{0.25} = 4.0$$

However, strictly following a rule such as this one can lead to multicollinearity paranoia. Even with a VIF greater than 4, you should still consider whether the multicollinearity is serious enough to require a change in your model. As we demonstrate in Section 6-4, sometimes the best thing to do is nothing.

---

[5] An intercept should be included in all three regressions.

We still have one regression to run, with LIBRARY as the dependent variable and STUDY as the independent variable. The R^2 for this regression is 0.86, which gives us a variance inflation factor of 7.14, exactly the same as above! This is not a coincidence. VIF values always come out equal if the original regression has only two independent variables.[6]

Three different measures of multicollinearity have confirmed that Mia's exam score model exhibits serious multicollinearity:

1. The correlation coefficient r between two independent variables is high.
2. Regressing one independent variable on the other gives a significant F-statistic.
3. The variance inflation factor is greater than 4.

Remember, our original regression results also gave us a big clue that substantial multicollinearity was present in the model. The t-statistics for the slope coefficients were statistically insignificant, but the R^2, adjusted R^2, and F-statistic all indicated a regression that fit the data well. This is a classic symptom of multicollinearity. Next, we discuss ways to treat the illness.

6-4 TREATING MULTICOLLINEARITY

Several approaches are used to handle multicollinearity. This section discusses four of the most popular methods: Leave the model alone, eliminate an independent variable, redesign the model, or increase the sample size.

Leave the Model Alone

Sometimes if you're lucky, you can simply do nothing! As mentioned earlier, multi-collinearity increases the standard errors of the estimates, which makes the t-statistics fall. If the t-statistics are high enough so that the coefficients are still statistically sig-nificant, this can be signaling the multicollinearity is not that serious. Even with severe multicollinearity, the t-statistics may still be significant if the explanatory power of the independent variables is strong enough. Regardless of the reason, if the t-statistics are significant, it may be best to leave the model alone. There is no reason to mess with something that works; the "medicine" you apply might do more harm than the multi-collinearity "disease" itself. However, in the exam score model, the t-statistics are not statistically significant, so we cannot afford the luxury of doing nothing.

Eliminate an Independent Variable

One simple remedy for multicollinearity is to eliminate an independent variable that is generating the problem. Sometimes when we initially formulate models, we're reluc-tant to leave out potentially relevant information, so we end up including redundant variables—that is, variables that convey the same information as other variables. This

---

[6] When a regression has only one variable on the right-hand side of the equals sign, and you switch the vari-ables, as we did with LIBRARY and STUDY, the R^2 will be the same. This of course gives you the same VIF values.

causes multicollinearity. Removing the redundant variable(s) rids the model of multi-collinearity. Use this method with care, however. Eliminating a relevant independent variable biases the results.

Consider a regression where the dependent variable is revenues for different wheat farms. Two of the independent variables are the number of acres of wheat harvested on each farm and the number of bushels of wheat grown. These variables are redundant; they provide nearly identical information. Including both of them creates multi-collinearity. One of these variables should be eliminated, *probably* the number of acres because the number of bushels of wheat grown more directly determines revenue. (It doesn't include damaged wheat that cannot be sold.)

We might try this approach with our exam score model. If we eliminate STUDY or LIBRARY from the regression, the multicollinearity disappears. However, this could be a mistake. Both variables contain similar information, but it is not clear that they are redundant. Perhaps the hours Mia actually studies at the library represent higher-quality study than when she studies elsewhere. Removing LIBRARY from the regression means this information will not be available in our model to help explain changes in Mia's exam scores. If we remove STUDY, we also remove information about Mia's study time outside of the library. It seems better to remove LIBRARY. Always base such decisions on theory and common sense and the meaning of the variables, not on the results of the regression. If the multicollinearity is substantial, the results will not look that different, regardless of which variable is removed. Table 6-D gives the results of the exam score model with LIBRARY removed.

The t-statistic for STUDY now shows statistical significance at a 1% error level. When LIBRARY was included in the model and there was multicollinearity, the t-statistic for STUDY was insignificant. If we include LIBRARY and omit STUDY, the coefficient for LIBRARY is significant at 1%. This is additional confirmation that serious multicollinearity was present in our original model. Keep in mind, though, that if the variables do not really measure the same thing, removing a variable eliminates valuable information from the model.

Table 6-D

Regression Results for Mia's Exam Score Model without LIBRARY

Dependent variable: SCORES

Variable	Coefficient	Standard Error	t-Statistic	p-Value
Constant	58.19	4.70	12.37	0.00
STUDY	1.96	0.42	4.72	0.00

Observations: 15

$R^2 = 0.63$

Adjusted $R^2 = 0.60$

F-statistic $= 22.30$

Redesign the Model

Multicollinearity sometimes alerts us to the fact that we haven't specified a model correctly; then we need to think about the model again. For example, this time-series model concerning new car sales is likely to have severe multicollinearity:

$$CARS = B_0 + B_1 INCOME + B_2 PRICE + e \qquad \text{(6-6)}$$

where

$\qquad$ CARS = number of new cars sold each year per 10,000 people

$\qquad$ INCOME = annual income per household, in dollars

$\qquad$ PRICE = average new-car price each year

INCOME and PRICE will be highly correlated, causing a big multicollinearity problem. Both variables will increase over time because of inflation. Redesigning the model to account for inflation cures the multicollinearity. To do this, we replace INCOME and PRICE by measures of income and auto prices that are adjusted for inflation.

Increase the Sample Size

The best remedy has been saved for last. An old but sometimes annoying econometric saying is that "The best cure for multicollinearity is, Add more data to the sample." This idea can be annoying because sometimes it is impossible to find more data. Adding data to the sample gives the OLS procedure more information to work with. This in turn allows the procedure to distinguish between the ways different independent variables move, which makes the coefficient estimates more precise. If this happens, the multicollinearity will be eliminated.

Let's improve our exam score model by adding more data. Mia asks another student, Vincent, to give her his test scores, the number of hours he has studied, and the number of hours he spends at the library. Vincent has taken the same exams as Mia; this allows us to use the same variables: SCORES, STUDY, and LIBRARY. The expanded data set is presented in Table 6-E.

Vincent is less devoted to his studies than Mia. When he visits the library, he also chats with friends and talks on his cell phone—in other words, Vincent isn't always studying when he's at the library. Compare Vincent's data for STUDY and LIBRARY in Table 6-E. As you can see, the hours that Vincent studies are much fewer than the hours he spends in the library. Because he doesn't spend as much time studying as Mia, his scores are not as good. For Vincent, STUDY and LIBRARY are not as correlated as they are for Mia. Adding Vincent's data to the sample should help alleviate the multicollinearity problem. Adding Vincent's data to Mia's gives us a data set with 30 observations. This is a pooled time-series cross-section data set because it includes data from different periods of time *and* data from the same time period across different individuals, firms, or locations. To see the cross-section aspect of this data set, notice that Mia and Vincent both have a SCORE, STUDY, and LIBRARY value for exam 1, given at the same time. Pooled time-series cross-section regressions are discussed in more detail in Chapter 9.

Table 6-E

Expanded Data Set for Exam Score Model

	Observation	Exam Number	SCORE	STUDY	LIBRARY
	1	1	78	6	4
	2	2	88	13	12
	3	3	73	7	2
	4	4	81	8	8
	5	5	84	12	10
	6	6	77	9	4
Mia's Data (Observations 1–15)	7	7	86	12	13
	8	8	43	2	0
	9	9	80	9	8
	10	10	58	6	2
	11	11	68	5	3
	12	12	93	24	20
	13	13	82	8	9
	14	14	92	16	18
	15	15	86	14	10
	16	1	48	4	0
	17	2	73	7	12
	18	3	54	2	6
Vincent's Data (Observations 16–30)	19	4	67	5	4
	20	5	71	6	3
	21	6	60	4	2
	22	7	46	1	2
	23	8	80	15	5
	24	9	62	3	8

(*continued*)

Table 6-E

(Continued)

Observation	Exam Number	SCORE	STUDY	LIBRARY
25	10	75	7	5
26	11	37	3	0
27	12	77	6	12
28	13	69	5	4
29	14	75	8	6
30	15	65	6	3

Vincent's Data
(Observations
16–30)

We rerun the regression model, including Vincent's data and adding a dummy variable for Vincent:

$$\text{SCORE} = B_0 + B_1\text{STUDY} + B_2\text{LIBRARY} + B_3\text{VINCENT} + e \qquad \textbf{(6-7)}$$

where

SCORE, STUDY, and LIBRARY have the same meanings as in Equation (6-3)
VINCENT = 1 if observation is for Vincent; 0 otherwise

Table 6-F gives the results of this model using the expanded data set.

Table 6-F

Regression Results for Exam Score Model Using Data from both Mia and Vincent

Dependent variable: SCORES

Variable	Coefficient	Standard Error	t-Statistic	p-Value
Constant	55.71	4.00	13.92	0.00
STUDY	1.34	0.51	2.66	0.01
LIBRARY	1.06	0.46	2.30	0.03
VINCENT	−4.21	3.33	−1.27	0.22

Observations: 30
$R^2 = 0.73$
Adjusted $R^2 = 0.70$
F-statistic = 23.42

The multicollinearity appears to be gone. Both STUDY and LIBRARY have significant coefficients at a 5% error level, and both coefficients are positive, as we would expect. The dummy variable VINCENT is insignificant. Removing VINCENT from the regression does not significantly change the rest of the results.

Let's look at the measures of multicollinearity to make sure the problem is truly resolved. The correlation coefficient r for STUDY and LIBRARY is now 0.77; it was 0.93 when only Mia's data was used. STUDY and LIBRARY still tend to move in the same direction, but the correlation is substantially less now that Vincent's data is included.

Using our second measure of multicollinearity—regressing one of the correlated independent variables on another—we need to see if the F-statistic is significant. With STUDY as the dependent variable and LIBRARY as the independent variable, we get the results given and in Table 6-G.

The F-statistic is significant at a 1% error level, still indicating some multicollinearity.[7] This F-statistic (41.83) is much lower than when only Mia's data was used (77.79). This is consistent with the drop in the correlation coefficient r noted earlier. We still have some multicollinearity, but not as much as before.

Using Equation (6-5) to calculate the variance inflation factor, we get

$$VIF = \frac{1}{1 - R^2} = \frac{1}{1 - 0.60} = \frac{1}{0.40} = 2.50$$

The VIF of 2.50 is substantially below the 7.14 value we got when only Mia's data was used.

Adding data to our model lessened the multicollinearity considerably. Although STUDY and LIBRARY still exhibit some multicollinearity, both are statistically significant at a 5% error level (see Table 6-F). Unless we can add even more data, we should now leave our regression alone, rather than try to reduce the multicollinearity further.

Table 6-G

Regression Results for Measuring Multicollinearity When Using Both Mia's and Vincent's Data

Dependent variable: STUDY

Variable	Coefficient	Standard Error	t-Statistic	p-Value
Constant	2.88	0.96	3.02	0.01
LIBRARY	0.75	0.12	6.47	0.00

Observations: 30

$R^2 = 0.60$

Adjusted $R^2 = 0.59$

F-statistic = 41.83

---

[7] Table D in the Appendix gives the critical value as 7.64.

SUMMARY

1. Perfect multicollinearity occurs when two independent variables have a perfect linear relationship. Perfect multicollinearity creates problems for ordinary least squares, because ordinary least squares requires that no independent variable be a linear function of another independent variable.
2. The symptoms of multicollinearity are as follows:
   - Estimates are still unbiased.
   - Standard errors of the estimates increase.
   - t-Statistics are smaller than they would be if there was no multicollinearity.
   - Goodness of fit is not diminished.
   - Estimates vary widely if the specification of the model changes.
   - Slope estimates for independent variables that do not have multicollinearity are not seriously affected.
3. There is no real test for multicollinearity, because any regression with more than one independent variable is likely to have at least some multicollinearity. Since most regressions display some degree of multicollinearity, it is important to avoid multicollinearity paranoia. We need to get an idea of how much multicollinearity is present. The following methods are used to measure multicollinearity:
   - Correlation coefficients
   - Regressing one independent variable on another
   - Variance inflation factor
4. Several approaches can be used to handle multicollinearity.
   - Leave the model alone.
   - Eliminate an independent variable.
   - Redesign the model.
   - Increase the sample size.

EXERCISES

1. Try to explain these terms without looking them up.
   - perfect multicollinearity
   - multicollinearity
   - correlation coefficient
   - variance inflation factor
2. Without looking at the text or your notes, explain why multicollinearity is a problem for ordinary least squares estimation.
3. Rank the following models, listing the model most likely to have a serious multicollinearity problem first, and the model least likely to have a multicollinearity problem last.
   a. Dependent variable: Consumption
      Independent variables: Wealth; Income
   b. Dependent variable: Revenue from hot dog sales
      Independent variables: Number of buns used; Number of hot dogs used; Price

   c. Dependent variable: Box office receipts per film
      Independent variables: Money spent on advertising; Average rating by famous film critics; Dummy variable is 1 if an actor in the film has previously won an Oscar, 0 otherwise

4. When looking at regression results, what symptoms signal multicollinearity?

5. Say you want to estimate a cross-section model about baseball. The dependent variable is the total home attendance for the year. Two of the independent variables are the percentage of games won by the team and the average number of runs scored by the team.
   a. One of your classmates claims that this model will exhibit multicollinearity because the percentage of games won by the team and the number of runs scored are correlated. Is this correct? Explain.
   b. What other independent variables do you think belong in the model?

6. Consider the adage from Section 6-4: "The best cure for multicollinearity is, Add more data to the sample."
   a. Would adding data decrease the multicollinearity in Chapter 5's professional wrestling model? Explain. (See Exercise 12.)
   b. Why is the best cure for multicollinearity often the hardest cure? Explain.

7. A regression's goodness of fit is not diminished by multicollinearity. Are there situations in which ignoring multicollinearity may be the best approach? If so, describe such a situation. If not, why not ignore it?

8. Four approaches for treating multicollinearity are examined in this chapter. Without looking in the chapter or your notes, list the four approaches and briefly explain when each approach is appropriate.

9. What is multicollinearity paranoia? How can you guard against it?

10. A variance inflation factor of 4.0 or larger [Equation (6-5)] is considered by some to be evidence of a multicollinearity problem. We demonstrated in the text that an R^2 of 0.75 or larger will generate a VIF of 4.0 or larger. If you remember this fact, is there any reason to compute the VIF? Why or why not?

11. In Table 6-C, where STUDY is the dependent variable and LIBRARY the independent variable, the B estimate is 0.85, but the correlation coefficient r between STUDY and LIBRARY is 0.93. Shouldn't these numbers be the same? In general, what is the difference between the correlation coefficient r and a B estimate?

12. The professional wrestling model in Chapter 5 uses age and income as independent variables. The regression is

$$HOURS = B_0 + B_1 MALE + B_2 INCOME + B_3 AGE + e \qquad (5\text{-}1)$$

where
  HOURS = hours spent watching professional wrestling on television, per month
  MALE = 1 if person is male, 0 otherwise
  INCOME = individual's annual income
  AGE = individual's age

Often, people make more money as they gain experience in the workplace. What different methods can you use to see if there is a multicollinearity problem with

AGE and INCOME? Use these different methods to gather evidence as to whether there is a multicollinearity problem.

13. Exercise 13 in Chapter 5 contains a data set for estimating this model:

$$\text{CONSUMPTION} = B_0 + B_1\text{INCOME} + B_2\text{WEALTH} + e$$

a. Apply the various methods presented in this chapter to see if there is a multicollinearity problem, using the data given in Exercise 13 in Chapter 5.

b. Considering the results you found in part a, do you think multicollinearity is a serious problem here?

c. In theory, should INCOME and WEALTH be correlated?

d. Do your answers to parts b and c agree with each other, or are they contradictory? Explain.

7

Autocorrelation: A Problem with Time-Series Regressions

In this chapter, you will focus on:

- The concept of autocorrelation: Errors in a regression model should not follow a pattern.

- Different types of autocorrelation.

- Symptoms of autocorrelation.

- How to test for autocorrelation.

- Designing models so that there is no autocorrelation in the first place.

- How to force autocorrelation out if necessary.

Suppose that every morning you watch a weather report featuring your favorite meteorologist on the local morning news. You use his forecasts to decide what clothes to wear. You notice that in the winter months, once you get outside, you are always cold. After a while, you realize that the temperature predicted by the meteorologist is always higher than the actual temperature. Then, during the spring, you realize the temperature he predicts is always lower than the actual temperature. Something is wrong with the meteorologist's method. Since his winter forecasts are always too high, why doesn't he start lowering his predictions? When spring rolls around, then his predictions are always too low. Why doesn't he realize this and raise his spring forecasts? This is the essence of autocorrelation: The errors follow a pattern, showing that something is wrong with the regression model.

One of the classical assumptions of the ordinary least squares procedure is that the observations of the error term are independent of each other. Each error term observation must not be correlated with the error term observation that is next to it. If this assumption is violated and the error term observations *are* correlated, autocorrelation is present. Autocorrelation is a common problem in time-series regressions. Like other violations of the classical assumptions, we can view autocorrelation as a regression "illness." When autocorrelation is present, the error term observations follow a pattern. Such patterns tell us that something is wrong.

In Section 7-1, we examine why autocorrelation is a problem for ordinary least squares. In Section 7-2, you will learn how to recognize the symptoms of autocorrelation. Next we present a test for autocorrelation. The final two sections of the chapter describe two possible solutions to the problem. Section 7-4 discusses how you can prevent the illness, by eliminating the underlying cause of the autocorrelation. Section 7-5 shows you how to treat the symptoms by eliminating the observed effects of autocorrelation, even if you cannot cure the illness itself.

7-1 THE ILLNESS

Autocorrelation (also called **serial correlation**) occurs when the error term observations in a regression are correlated. The theoretical error term e is a random variable that is part of the regression model, even before it is estimated (see Section 1-2). This error term represents a random "shock" to the model, or something that is missing from the model. However, we can never see the actual error term e. Therefore, we use the error term observations or residuals (ê) to check for autocorrelation. If they follow a pattern, this pattern is evidence of autocorrelation.

Remember that the error term observations (residuals) are $Y - \hat{Y} = \hat{e}$. We see the error term observations only after we estimate the model, and they differ with each data set used to estimate the same regression. In this way, the difference between e and ê parallels the difference between B and $\hat{B}$. (The true value of the slope B can never be observed; we find the slope estimate $\hat{B}$ only after we estimate a regression. The value for the slope estimate $\hat{B}$ differs when different data are used to estimate the same regression.)

We will use a simple model examining the relationship between Microsoft's marketing and advertising expenditures and its revenues to illustrate autocorrelation. The regression is:

$$REVENUES = B_0 + B_1 MARKETING + B_2 SECONDQ + B_3 THIRDQ \\ + B_4 FOURTHQ + e \tag{7-1}$$

where

REVENUES = Microsoft's real quarterly revenues, in millions of dollars[1]

MARKETING = Microsoft's real quarterly expenditures on marketing and advertising, in millions of dollars

SECONDQ = 1 when REVENUES and MARKETING are from the second quarter, 0 otherwise

THIRDQ = 1 when REVENUES and MARKETING are from the third quarter, 0 otherwise

FOURTHQ = 1 when REVENUES and MARKETING are from the fourth quarter, 0 otherwise

Table 7-A gives the data from the first quarter of 1987 through the third quarter of 2000. We will present the regression results using this data in a later section. Now, however, let's look at the error term observations from those regression results (Figure 7-1).

The top square plotted in Figure 7-1 is the observed error for the first quarter in 1987; the bottom square is the observed error for the third quarter in 2000. Error term

---

[1] "Real" means the values are adjusted for inflation.

Table 7-A

Data for Microsoft Revenue Model

Year	Quarter	REVENUES	MARKETING	SECONDQ	THIRDQ	FOURTHQ
1987	1	60.02	13.44	0	0	0
	2	71.62	16.80	1	0	0
	3	85.66	18.36	0	1	0
	4	86.68	22.54	0	0	1
1988	1	88.74	23.26	0	0	0
	2	132.73	31.48	1	0	0
	3	136.02	32.75	0	1	0
	4	141.27	40.72	0	0	1
1989	1	145.48	37.81	0	0	0
	2	169.81	46.90	1	0	0
	3	158.02	40.91	0	1	0
	4	175.58	45.29	0	0	1
1990	1	183.55	49.99	0	0	0
	2	232.73	56.44	1	0	0
	3	237.14	58.53	0	1	0
	4	252.80	64.32	0	0	1
1991	1	273.74	72.70	0	0	0
	2	339.97	95.87	1	0	0
	3	357.80	94.39	0	1	0
	4	383.44	96.59	0	0	1
1992	1	421.15	115.38	0	0	0
	2	490.70	138.05	1	0	0
	3	486.87	130.59	0	1	0
	4	578.58	155.74	0	0	1

(continued)

Table 7-A

(Continued)

Year	Quarter	REVENUES	MARKETING	SECONDQ	THIRDQ	FOURTHQ
1993	1	575.82	165.62	0	0	0
	2	655.34	199.72	1	0	0
	3	669.35	195.49	0	1	0
	4	718.96	190.72	0	0	1
1994	1	678.94	174.51	0	0	0
	2	776.25	188.98	1	0	0
	3	846.69	201.43	0	1	0
	4	876.14	200.49	0	0	1
1995	1	841.80	212.11	0	0	0
	2	996.06	265.44	1	0	0
	3	1064.33	285.22	0	1	0
	4	1082.03	263.02	0	0	1
1996	1	1345.16	331.61	0	0	0
	2	1461.03	353.92	1	0	0
	3	1468.54	363.48	0	1	0
	4	1493.38	343.85	0	0	1
1997	1	1507.21	324.63	0	0	0
	2	1752.81	398.88	1	0	0
	3	2092.23	397.31	0	1	0
	4	2079.69	380.88	0	0	1
1998	1	2059.30	416.92	0	0	0
	2	2329.72	468.15	1	0	0
	3	2438.19	429.62	0	1	0
	4	2532.22	420.21	0	0	1

(*continued*)

Table 7-A

(Continued)

Year	Quarter	REVENUES	MARKETING	SECONDQ	THIRDQ	FOURTHQ
1999	1	2547.39	417.98	0	0	0
	2	3125.75	477.74	1	0	0
	3	2747.66	507.67	0	1	0
	4	3425.52	534.87	0	0	1
2000	1	3168.30	531.38	0	0	0
	2	3559.01	598.02	1	0	0
	3	3267.48	601.96	0	1	0

Data are available at the text website or http://www.microsoft.com/msft/download/historypivot.xls. These data were then adjusted for inflation using the urban CPI available at http://www.economagic.com or http://stats.bls.gov.

observations to the left of the center line are less than zero and the observed errors to the right of the line are greater than zero. Here a positive observed error is usually followed by another positive observed error. Likewise, a negative observed error is usually followed by a negative observed error. The sign of the preceding observed error thus predicts the sign of almost all of the observed errors shown in Figure 7-1. These observed errors follow an easily recognized pattern. They are not random. This signals that our model has an autocorrelation problem.

The presence of autocorrelation does not mean that the values of one independent variable are correlated over time. Also, it does not mean that independent variables are correlated with each other, as occurs with multicollinearity. For each observation, the error term represents the distance between the actual value of the dependent variable and the predicted value. Think of the error term as the model's "mistake." These mistakes must not follow a pattern. If there is such a pattern, then there must be some way to improve the model so that the regression does a better job of predicting the dependent variable. A model that exhibits autocorrelation can perform better than it is.

The most common type of autocorrelation, **first-order autocorrelation**, is present when an observed error tends to be influenced by the observed error that immediately precedes it in the previous time period. We call this first-order autocorrelation because only one time period separates the two correlated error term observations. This can be stated as

$$e_t = \rho e_{t-1} + u_t \tag{7-2}$$

where e_t is the error from a regression in the current time period and e_{t-1} is the error from the preceding time period. The Greek letter rho, ρ (pronounced "row"), is the autocorrelation coefficient. It shows the relationship between e_t and e_{t-1} in a manner

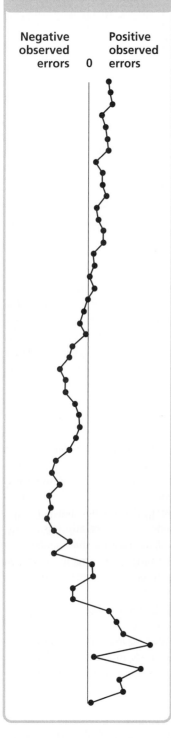

Figure 7-1

Error Term Observations from Microsoft Revenues Model.

| Negative observed errors | 0 | Positive observed errors |

similar to how a slope coefficient works in a regression. If ρ is 0.5, then on average each error will *tend* to be half the value of the preceding error. Any particular error e_t will not be exactly half of e_{t-1}, the preceding error, because of the presence of u_t, which is the error term for Equation (7-2). u_t is different from e_t or e_{t-1} because it follows the classical OLS assumptions. This means that u_t is random and is not correlated with previous or subsequent values of u_t such as u_{t-1} or u_{t+1}. Figure 7-1 shows first-order autocorrelation, since the sign of each error term observation tends to be the same as the sign in the preceding time period.

The value of ρ must fall between -1 and $+1$. If ρ becomes larger than $+1$, following Equation (7-2), each error will tend to be larger than the one before it. As the errors get larger and larger, the regression becomes unstable; the software can no longer estimate the regression properly. When this happens, some econometricians say the regression "explodes." If ρ is less than -1, the errors are alternating between positive and negative, and they are getting farther and farther from zero over time until, once again, the regression explodes. If ρ were to exactly equal $+1$ or -1, the effect of one error on the next would not die out over time. For these reasons, ρ must be greater than -1 and less than $+1$.

If ρ is zero, then one error has nothing to do with the next error, so there is no autocorrelation. The errors we see will not follow a pattern over time.

If ρ is positive, the errors tend to have the same sign from one period to the next. If e_{t-1} is positive, then e_t tends to be positive; if e_{t-1} is negative, e_t tends to be negative. A positive ρ indicates **positive autocorrelation**, also called **positive serial correlation**. The error term observations in Figure 7-1 exhibit positive first-order autocorrelation.

If ρ is negative, the errors tend to alternate signs, indicating **negative autocorrelation** or **negative serial correlation**. In this situation, a positive observed error term is usually followed by a negative one, which is usually followed by a positive one, and so on. Figure 7-2 shows what negative autocorrelation looks like. Negative autocorrelation is less common than positive autocorrelation.

As we move from one period to the next in Figure 7-2, from top to bottom on the figure, the error term observations tend to alternate signs, going from positive to negative and back to positive again.

There are other types of autocorrelation besides first-order autocorrelation. If seasonal data are being used, the error e_t could depend on the error from the same season a year ago, e_{t-4}. Instead of $e_t = \rho e_{t-1} + u_t$ describing the situation, as with first-order autocorrelation, $e_t = \rho e_{t-4} + u_t$ now describes the autocorrelation. This situation might occur if the dependent variable is the number of swimmers who use the outdoor community pool each quarter of the year. The error for summer might be correlated with the error from the previous summer, four seasons ago. This is more likely to occur if the regression doesn't include an independent variable to account for the fact that more people use the pool in the summer (a dummy variable for summer).

Figure 7-2

Negative Autocorrelation.

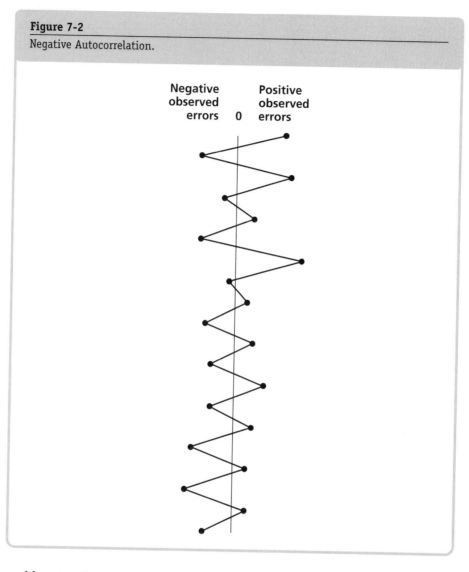

More complex types of autocorrelation also occur. The error for the current period e_t might depend on both the error from the last period, e_{t-1}, and the error from two periods ago, e_{t-2}. The effect of previous errors on e_t can go back even further, causing e_t to be influenced by a whole string of previous errors. (We discuss these types of autocorrelation in Chapter 11, which focuses on time-series models.)

Autocorrelation is a problem because its presence means that useful information is missing from the model. Such information might explain the movement in the dependent variable more accurately. Like the weatherman at the beginning of this chapter, a model that exhibits autocorrelation could be doing better. The presence of autocorrelation means that a model is making a similar mistake over and over as it attempts to explain movement in the dependent variable Y. Once you know that autocorrelation is present, often you can use this knowledge to improve your model.

7-2 THE SYMPTOMS

Now let's examine the effect of autocorrelation on regression results. Using the Microsoft revenue model [Equation (7-1)] and the data from Table 7-A, we get the results in Table 7-B.

According to these OLS results, MARKETING is statistically significant at a 1% error level, and the coefficient estimate has the positive sign we would expect.[2] However, autocorrelation could be affecting this result, making it appear significant when it is not. The three dummy variables are all statistically insignificant. Apparently, the market for software doesn't have a strong seasonal component. The F-test supports this conclusion (see Section 5.3). Running the regression without the three dummy variables does not substantially change the result for MARKETING or the other statistics shown in Table 7-B.

The Gauss-Markov theorem (discussed in Chapter 2) says that ordinary least squares will have a set of desirable qualities when the classical assumptions hold. If autocorrelation is present, one of these classical assumptions does not hold. This means that some of the desirable qualities or properties described by the Gauss-Markov theorem will not be true anymore. In economics, most of the time we encounter positive

Table 7-B

Results for Microsoft Revenue Model

Dependent variable: REVENUE

Variable	Coefficient	Standard Error	t-Statistic	p-Value
Constant	−225.88	75.32	−3.00	0.00
MARKETING	5.77	0.18	32.10	0.00
SECONDQ	−11.47	87.60	−0.13	0.90
THIRDQ	64.45	89.39	0.72	0.47
FOURTHQ	28.20	87.79	0.32	0.75

Observations: 55

$R^2 = 0.95$

Adjusted $R^2 = 0.95$

Residual Sum of Squares = 2,685,801

F-statistic = 258.77

Durbin-Watson statistic = 0.44

---

[2] The t-statistic for MARKETING has a p-value listed as 0.00. Recall from Section 3-2, Table 3-C that when this occurs, the p-value has been rounded off. In this case, the p-value is less than 0.005, and the p-value has been rounded down to 0.00.

autocorrelation, not negative autocorrelation.[3] When ordinary least squares is used to estimate a model with positive autocorrelation, these three symptoms show up:

1. *Autocorrelation by itself leaves the coefficient estimates unbiased.* When autocorrelation is present, the OLS procedure still produces unbiased estimates. The expected value of an estimate $\hat{B}$ is still the true value of B. (This means that if you run the regression more than once using different data and then average all the $\hat{B}$'s, you should come out with the true value.) However, autocorrelation often occurs because an independent variable is missing from the model. A relevant independent variable that is missing from the model can bias the coefficient estimates of the remaining variables, even without autocorrelation. The estimates for the Microsoft revenue model may be biased, if the autocorrelation is due to a missing independent variable. There must be other important factors besides marketing and advertising expenditures that affect Microsoft's revenues. It is likely that there are independent variables missing from this model. Autocorrelation alone does not cause the estimates to be biased, but when the autocorrelation comes from a missing independent variable, the estimates will be biased.

2. *Autocorrelation increases the variance of the coefficient estimates.* The $\hat{B}$'s vary more from their true value than they would if there were no autocorrelation. The autocorrelation causes the $\hat{B}$ sampling distribution to become wider. Since there is no bias, the expected value of $\hat{B}$ is the true value. However, because autocorrelation increases the variance of the coefficient estimates, any one estimate is likely to be farther from the true value than if autocorrelation is not present. This makes the true values of the standard errors larger than they would be without autocorrelation. However, the *estimates* of the standard errors are *smaller* (symptom 3).

3. *The estimated standard errors given by ordinary least squares will be smaller than the true values.* Since these estimated standard errors end up being in the bottom half of the formula used to calculate the t-statistic, the t-statistics for the regression will be larger than they should be. When autocorrelation is present, the t-statistics will be larger than their true values. Left untreated, autocorrelation is dangerous for the researcher. Anyone examining the work can easily criticize it, pointing out that coefficients that seem to be significant may be insignificant, since the t-statistics are higher than their true values. The F-statistic, R^2, and adjusted R^2 may not be accurate either. These symptoms can be fatal for any model, making the results at best unclear and at worst meaningless.

7-3 TESTING FOR THE ILLNESS: THE DURBIN-WATSON STATISTIC

Early detection is key to curing many diseases. We can easily recognize the autocorrelation present in the Microsoft revenue model simply by looking at the pattern in Figure 7-1. Most of the time, however, autocorrelation is not as severe as this, so it is harder

---

[3] If the autocorrelation is negative, the coefficient estimates will still be unbiased, but the effect on the slope estimate variance and the estimated standard errors is not as clear.

to recognize. Even if you think autocorrelation is present just from looking, you should back this up with objective statistical evidence. You need a test for first-order autocorrelation. The **Durbin-Watson statistic** provides such a test.[4] The Durbin-Watson statistic tests for first-order autocorrelation only. Also, it does not work properly if a dependent variable from a preceding time period is used as an independent variable in the model.[5] Most econometric software programs calculate the Durbin-Watson statistic automatically. To see how the Durbin-Watson statistic is calculated, let's break it down by numerator and denominator. To find the numerator, follow these steps:

1. Starting with the *second* error term observation, find the difference between the current error term observation $\hat{e}_2$ and the preceding time period's error term observation, $\hat{e}_1$: $(\hat{e}_2 - \hat{e}_1)$.
2. Square the number found in step 1: $(\hat{e}_2 - \hat{e}_1)^2$.
3. Repeat this process, advancing the time period by one each time you get back to step 1. Add the numbers from step 2 for all the time periods. The number of values you add will be one less than the total number of time periods, since you started with the second observed error term.
4. The sum you found in step 3 is the numerator in the Durbin-Watson statistic:

$$(\hat{e}_2 - \hat{e}_1)^2 + (\hat{e}_3 - \hat{e}_2)^2 + (\hat{e}_4 - \hat{e}_3)^2 + \cdots + (\hat{e}_n - \hat{e}_{n-1})^2$$

To find the denominator, follow these steps:

1. Take each error term observation and square it: $\hat{e}_1^2, \hat{e}_2^2, \hat{e}_3^2, \ldots$.
2. Add all the values you found in step 1:

$$\hat{e}_1^2 + \hat{e}_2^2 + \hat{e}_3^2 + \cdots + \hat{e}_n^2$$

The Durbin-Watson statistic is

$$\text{D.W.} = \frac{(\hat{e}_2 - \hat{e}_1)^2 + (\hat{e}_3 - \hat{e}_2)^2 + (\hat{e}_4 - \hat{e}_3)^2 + \cdots + (\hat{e}_n - \hat{e}_{n-1})^2}{\hat{e}_1^2 + \hat{e}_2^2 + \hat{e}_3^2 + \cdots + \hat{e}_n^2} \quad \textbf{(7-3)}$$

Notice that the number of values summed in the numerator of Equation (7-3) is one less than the number of values summed in the denominator.[6] This is how it is supposed

---

[4] J. Durbin and G. Watson, "Testing for Serial Correlation in Least-Squares Regression," *Biometrika*, Vol. 38, 1951, pp. 159–77.
[5] A dependent variable from a preceding time period is called a lagged dependent variable. For a test that works in this case, see J. Durbin, "Testing for Serial Correlation in Least-Squares Regression When Some of the Regressors Are Lagged Dependent Variables," *Econometrica*, Vol. 38, 1970, pp. 410–421.
[6] Using summation signs (see Section 1-4), the Durbin-Watson statistic is

$$\text{D.W.} = \frac{\sum_{t=2}^{t=n} (\hat{e}_t - \hat{e}_{t-1})^2}{\sum_{t=1}^{t=n} \hat{e}_t^2}$$

to work; the numerator starts with the second observed error term and the denominator starts with the first observed error term. The Durbin-Watson statistic works this way because if we start the numerator with the first observed error term instead of the second one, we would not have an initial value to subtract off.

Step 1 for the numerator takes the difference between an error term observation and the error term observation from the time period before it. This means that the order of the error term observations is important in calculating the Durbin-Watson statistic. In a time-series model, the observations are always ordered by time, but in a cross-section model, the order of observations is arbitrary. For example, a cross-sectional model using the fifty states could be arranged alphabetically. Alphabetical order has nothing to do with the characteristics of the states themselves. If we reorder the data in the cross-section so that the biggest state comes first and the smallest state last, we get a different Durbin-Watson statistic. This makes the Durbin-Watson statistic meaningless for most cross-section regressions. Fortunately, autocorrelation is not a typical problem for cross-section models, since the order of the data is arbitrary. However, autocorrelation can occur in models that use both cross-section and time-series data. (We discuss these types of models in Chapter 9.)

Changing the order of observations in a time-series regression does not eliminate autocorrelation. It just prevents the Durbin-Watson statistic from detecting it. The coefficient estimates, t-statistics, F-statistic, and adjusted R^2 remain the same; only the Durbin-Watson statistic changes. The autocorrelation still exists, but now it is hidden because the data are no longer in the right order. Always arrange time-series data in chronological order.

The Durbin-Watson statistic is related to the autocorrelation coefficient ρ. Approximately, the Durbin-Watson statistic equals $2 - 2\rho$. Some useful information can be derived from this relationship. If there is no autocorrelation, then ρ is 0. This makes the Durbin-Watson statistic equal to 2. The worst possible case of first-order positive autocorrelation occurs when ρ is very close to $+1$. If ρ is equal to 1, the Durbin-Watson statistic will be $2 - 2\rho = 2 - (2 \cdot 1) = 0$. This means the closer the Durbin-Watson statistic is to zero, the more likely serious positive autocorrelation exists. For first-order negative autocorrelation, the worst possible case occurs when ρ is close to -1. If ρ is equal to -1, the Durbin-Watson statistic will be $2 - 2\rho = 2 - [2 \cdot (-1)] = 4$. This means that when the Durbin-Watson statistic is closer to 4, the chances of first-order negative autocorrelation increase. In summary, the Durbin-Watson statistic varies from 0 to 4: Values closer to 0 indicate positive autocorrelation; values close to 2 indicate no autocorrelation; and values closer to 4 indicate negative autocorrelation.

Most hypothesis tests use a critical value to separate the regions where the null hypothesis is rejected or not rejected. The Durbin-Watson statistic has three regions: reject the null hypothesis, do not reject the null hypothesis, and an inconclusive region. If the Durbin-Watson statistic falls in the inconclusive region, then the test is unable to reach a decision. Since there are three regions instead of the usual two, the Durbin-Watson test requires two critical values. (t-Tests and F-tests need only one critical value.) These two critical values are referred to as d_U ("d-upper") and d_L ("d-lower") and are given in Tables E and F in the Appendix. Use the number of independent variables in your regression to find the correct column for d_U and d_L in the table, and the sample size n to find the correct row.

The procedure for the test differs depending on whether you are checking for positive or negative autocorrelation. When testing for positive first-order autocorrelation, use the Durbin-Watson statistic to test:

$$H_0: \rho \leq 0$$

$$H_A: \rho > 0$$

This is a one-sided test—the null hypothesis of no autocorrelation versus the alternative hypothesis of positive autocorrelation.[7]

By examining the pattern of the error term observations in Figure 7-1, we already know the Microsoft revenue model exhibits positive autocorrelation. Sometimes autocorrelation is not obvious and cannot be detected without performing the Durbin-Watson test. When the Durbin-Watson statistic is less than 2, there could be positive autocorrelation. The Durbin-Watson statistic for the Microsoft revenue model is 0.44. (See Table 7-B.) Table E in the Appendix gives Durbin-Watson d_L and d_U critical values at 5% significance for one-sided tests. There are four independent variables in the Microsoft regression, and the sample size is 55. The two critical values needed for the test are $d_L = 1.41$ and $d_U = 1.73$.[8] The decision rules for the Durbin-Watson test for positive autocorrelation are as follows:

- If the Durbin-Watson statistic is less than d_L, reject the null hypothesis of no autocorrelation; assume positive autocorrelation.
- If the Durbin-Watson statistic is greater than d_U, do not reject the null hypothesis of no autocorrelation; assume no autocorrelation.
- If the Durbin-Watson statistic lies between d_L and d_U (or exactly equal to either d_L or d_U), the test is inconclusive.

If the Durbin-Watson statistic is less than d_L, the Durbin-Watson statistic is so far below 2 and so close to 0 that it is unlikely we would get such a low Durbin-Watson statistic when there is no positive autocorrelation. We reject the null hypothesis; there probably is positive autocorrelation. If the Durbin-Watson statistic is greater than d_U, the Durbin-Watson statistic is so close to 2 that positive autocorrelation may not be present in the model. In this case, we do not reject the null hypothesis.

The Durbin-Watson statistic for the Microsoft Revenue model is below d_L ($0.44 < 1.41$), so we reject the null hypothesis of no autocorrelation at a 5% significance level. We can assume that there is positive autocorrelation. The results of the model must be interpreted cautiously—*if* they are even to be taken seriously at all, considering the problems discussed in the preceding section. In particular, because of the autocorrelation, it is not safe to say that the coefficient for MARKETING is statistically significant even though the t-test in Table 7-B reports it is significant at 1%. This t-statistic is a mistake caused by the autocorrelation. It is too high. We will discuss steps that can be taken to correct the autocorrelation problem in Sections 7-4 and 7-5.

---

[7] Technically, the one-sided test shown here is really the null hypothesis of either no autocorrelation or negative autocorrelation versus the alternative hypothesis of positive autocorrelation.

[8] These critical values are found by interpolation. For a 5% significance level, with k = 4, $d_L = 138$ for n = 50 and $d_L = 144$ for n = 60. (Appendix Table E.) For n = 55, we assume d_L = the average of 138 and 144, or 141. d_U is found the same way.

The decision rules for a Durbin-Watson negative autocorrelation test are different from those for positive autocorrelation. Now the null and alternative hypotheses are

$$H_0: \rho \geq 0$$

$$H_A: \rho < 0$$

When the Durbin-Watson statistic comes out greater than 2, negative autocorrelation may be present. Here are the decision rules for a Durbin-Watson test of negative autocorrelation:

- If the Durbin-Watson statistic is greater than $4 - d_L$, reject the null hypothesis of no autocorrelation; assume negative autocorrelation.
- If the Durbin-Watson statistic is less than $4 - d_U$, do not reject the null hypothesis of no autocorrelation; assume no autocorrelation.
- If the Durbin-Watson statistic lies between $4 - d_L$ and $4 - d_U$ (or exactly equal to either $4 - d_L$ or $4 - d_U$), the test is inconclusive.

Since d_L will always be a smaller value than d_U, $4 - d_L$ will always be a higher value than $4 - d_U$. If the Durbin-Watson statistic is larger than $4 - d_L$, it is far enough from 2 and close enough to 4 that we can reject the null hypothesis of no autocorrelation. We must assume that negative autocorrelation is present. If the Durbin-Watson statistic is smaller than $4 - d_U$, it is close enough to 2 that we do not reject the null hypothesis. Then we assume there is no autocorrelation. If the Durbin-Watson statistic is between $4 - d_L$ and $4 - d_U$, the test is inconclusive.

Suppose a regression with a sample size of 70 and 3 independent variables has a Durbin-Watson statistic of 2.27. Table E in the Appendix gives us $d_L = 1.53$ and $d_U = 1.70$ for a 5% significance test. Then $4 - d_L = 4 - 1.53 = 2.47$, and $4 - d_U = 4 - 1.70 = 2.30$. Since $2.27 < 2.30$, the Durbin-Watson statistic is less than $4 - d_U$, so we do not reject the null hypothesis. We assume there is no autocorrelation. If the Durbin-Watson statistic had been between 2.30 and 2.47, the test would be inconclusive. If the Durbin-Watson statistic had been above 2.47, we would assume there is negative autocorrelation.

7-4 TREATING THE DISEASE

There are two general approaches to dealing with autocorrelation. One approach, discussed in Section 7-5, eliminates the symptoms of autocorrelation by using an estimation method other than ordinary least squares. The best approach—discussed here—is to prevent autocorrelation from occurring in the first place, rather than just ridding the model of symptoms. Autocorrelation can infect a regression if there are relevant independent variables missing from the model. For the Microsoft revenue model, other independent variables besides marketing and advertising expenditures must be relevant. For example, Microsoft spends money on research and development (R&D) of new products. These expenditures are also likely to affect revenues. Let's add a new independent variable RESEARCH to the model:

RESEARCH = Microsoft's real expenditures on R&D, in millions of dollars

It takes time for R&D expenditures to affect revenue both in theory and in practice. Therefore, we add RESEARCH to the model as a lagged variable; the value for RESEARCH will be the value from four quarters (1 year) before the current time period. This four-quarter lag is indicated by RESEARCH(-4) in Equation (7-4).

$$\text{REVENUES} = B_0 + B_1\text{MARKETING} + B_2\text{SECONDQ} + B_3\text{THIRDQ}$$
$$+ B_4\text{FOURTHQ} + B_5\text{RESEARCH}(-4) + e \tag{7-4}$$

The data for Microsoft's R&D expenditures are given in Table 7-C. Data for 1986 are needed, even though the sample for the other variables starts with 1987. The first quarter value for 1986 (3.66) is necessary to have the first observation of RESEARCH(-4)

Table 7-C

Data for Microsoft's R&D Expenditures

Year	First Quarter	Second Quarter	Third Quarter	Fourth Quarter
1986	3.66	4.59	4.55	6.34
1987	6.27	7.07	9.62	10.40
1988	12.92	13.61	15.11	17.45
1989	18.90	20.22	23.26	26.22
1990	31.24	31.70	35.72	39.27
1991	37.83	39.82	43.90	50.84
1992	53.37	61.52	63.88	71.88
1993	73.38	76.98	80.13	94.67
1994	91.34	101.60	104.74	113.61
1995	117.99	130.75	143.26	171.88
1996	179.35	194.85	214.15	256.15
1997	261.33	280.27	294.72	323.91
1998	372.45	398.12	373.93	450.70
1999	395.50	430.20	397.05	558.64
2000	490.78	530.47	571.92	

Data are available at the text website or http://www.microsoft.com/msft/download/historypivot.xls. These data were then adjusted for inflation by using the urban CPI available at http://www.economagic.com or stats.bls.gov.

when the regression starts in the first quarter of 1987. The regression's last observation is the third quarter of 2000; the value of RESEARCH(-4) for this observation is taken from the third quarter of 1999. It is 397.05. Most econometrics software programs have features that allow you to use lagged independent variables without any fuss. (More will be said about lagged independent variables in Chapter 11.)

Adding RESEARCH(-4) may reduce or eliminate the autocorrelation problem, if it is an appropriate independent variable for this model. Figure 7-3 shows the error term observations we get when we include RESEARCH(-4) in the model (using the data from Tables 7-A and 7-C).

It is not clear from looking at Figure 7-3 whether some positive autocorrelation is still present or whether it has been eliminated. Certainly, if some positive autocorrelation remains, it is not as pronounced as before. To see this, compare parts a and b (Figure 7-1 has been repeated as part b). The error term observations change signs (move across the center line) much more frequently in part a than they do in part b. In part a it is a lot harder to predict the sign of an observed error simply by noting whether the preceding term is positive or negative, so we cannot tell whether autocorrelation is present just by looking. The Durbin-Watson test may help.

Table 7-D presents the results for the Microsoft revenue model with RESEARCH(-4) included. If RESEARCH is lagged by a different number of quarters (instead of 4), the results are similar. The Durbin-Watson statistic here is 2.14, a lot closer to 2 than the Durbin-Watson statistic for the original model, 0.44 (see Table 7-B). The number of independent variables in the model has changed because we added RESEARCH, so we must use Table E in the Appendix again to find the appropriate d_L and d_U. Now $d_L =$ 1.38 and $d_U = 1.77$ at 5% significance with 5 independent variables and 55 observations.[9] The Durbin-Watson statistic is greater than d_U since $2.14 > 1.77$. This test result allows us to assume that positive autocorrelation is no longer present.[10]

There are probably other relevant independent variables missing from this model. It is unlikely that MARKETING and RESEARCH(-4) are the only important independent variables.[11] Also, a single-equation model may not describe Microsoft's revenue generating process very well. (Multiple-equation regression models are discussed in Chapter 10.) The important point here is that adding a missing relevant independent variable cured our autocorrelation problem.

When a relevant independent variable is left out, the explanatory power it brings to the model is assigned elsewhere by the OLS procedure. When RESEARCH(-4) was omitted, part of its explanatory power was assigned to the error term. This caused the

---

[9] Once again, these critical values are found by interpolating between the critical values for n = 50 and n = 60 (see last footnote).

[10] It may seem obvious there is no positive autocorrelation since the Durbin-Watson statistic is greater than 2. However, if you look at Table E in the Appendix for low sample sizes, there are some d_U values that are slightly greater than 2. This means that even if the Durbin-Watson statistic is greater than 2, it is still possible for a Durbin-Watson positive autocorrelation test to be inconclusive.

[11] MARKETING and RESEARCH have a high correlation coefficient, indicating multicollinearity. Since both variables are highly significant, as discussed in Section 6-4, it is reasonable to use both variables in this regression.

Figure 7-3

Error Term Observations from Microsoft Revenues Model with RESEARCH(-4) Included.

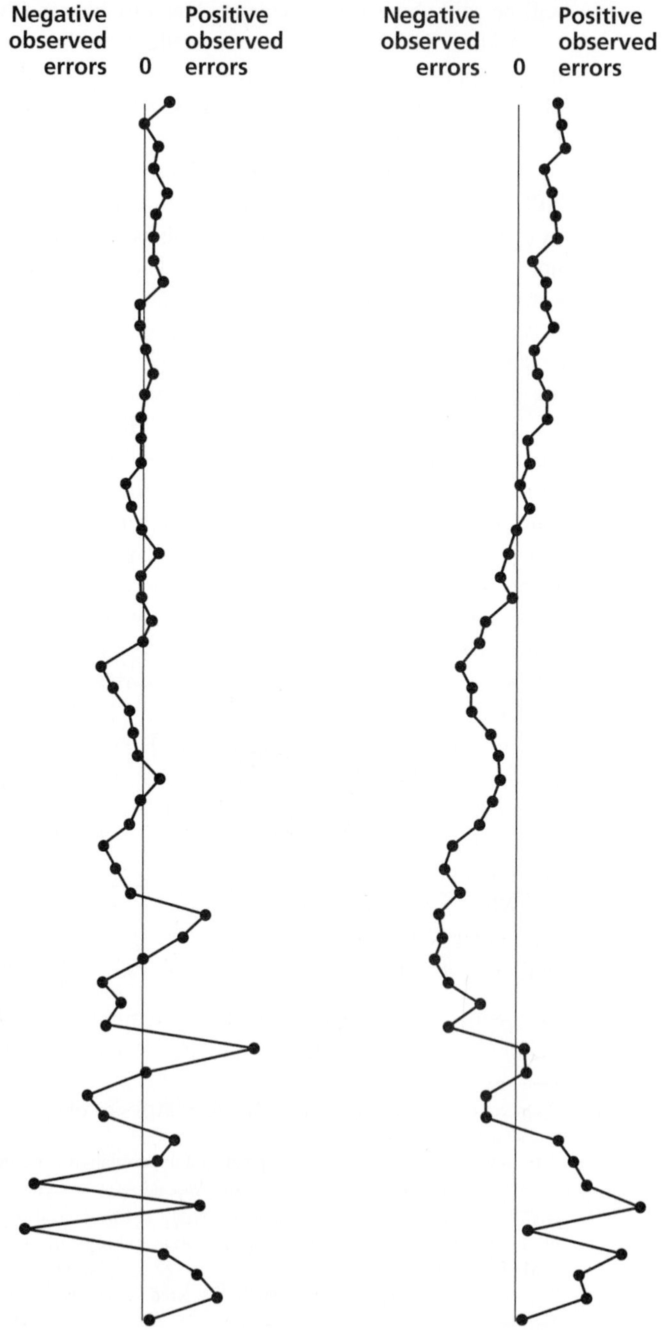

(a) With RESEARCH(-4)   (b) Without RESEARCH(-4)
                                       (original model)

Table 7-D

Results for Microsoft Revenue Model Including RESEARCH(-4)

Dependent variable: REVENUE

Variable	Coefficient	Standard Error	t-Statistic	p-Value
Constant	14.67	23.90	0.61	0.54
MARKETING	1.97	0.17	11.63	0.00
SECONDQ	-10.41	25.15	-0.41	0.68
THIRDQ	-22.69	25.92	-0.88	0.39
FOURTHQ	-43.35	25.38	-1.71	0.09
RESEARCH(-4)	5.21	0.22	23.62	0.00

Observations: 55

$R^2 = 0.99$

Adjusted $R^2 = 0.99$

Residual Sum of Squares = 216860.2

F-statistic = 2624.16

Durbin-Watson statistic = 2.14

error term to be correlated with RESEARCH(-4). If RESEARCH(-4) is correlated with itself over time, which is likely, this causes the error term to be correlated with itself over time, giving us autocorrelation. MARKETING will also be given some of the credit for explaining REVENUE that should have been credited to RESEARCH(-4). This will cause the coefficient estimate for MARKETING to be biased. The higher the correlation between MARKETING and the missing RESEARCH(-4), the more biased the coefficient estimate for MARKETING. As discussed in Section 7-2, autocorrelation by itself does not produce biased estimates. However, a missing independent variable does produce biased estimates, so regressions with autocorrelation caused by missing relevant independent variables will have biased estimates.

Autocorrelation can also be present in a model if the functional form of the regression is incorrect. Suppose we take the natural logs of REVENUE, MARKETING, and RESEARCH(-4) before we estimate the regression in the Microsoft revenues model.

$$\ln(\text{REVENUES}) = B_0 + B_1 \ln(\text{MARKETING}) + B_2\text{SECONDQ} + B_3\text{THIRDQ}$$
$$+ B_4\text{FOURTHQ} + B_5 \ln(\text{RESEARCH}(-4)+e \qquad \textbf{(7-5)}$$

When we estimate this model using the same data as before, the autocorrelation returns, even though we have included RESEARCH(-4). The Durbin-Watson statistic is 0.76, indicating positive autocorrelation at a 5% (and even a 1%) significance level. The linear model containing RESEARCH(-4) gives better results since it does not exhibit autocorrelation.

The best approach to the autocorrelation problem is to try to formulate the model correctly in the first place. Here, omitting the R&D variable from the model caused positive first-order autocorrelation. This is one reason why it is important to think about theory when formulating models. For regressions dealing with economics, economic theory can guide you in including relevant independent variables and in using the correct functional form for the model. Whatever your field, using theory to formulate the model correctly to begin with prevents a lot of trouble.

7-5 TREATING THE SYMPTOMS

There are situations in which autocorrelation cannot be eliminated by changing the model. Perhaps the omitted independent variables that would help are not available or cannot be measured. Rather than toss the model out we treat the symptoms. This is a second-best solution because we have not cured the disease. It is always preferable to use the right model so that there is no autocorrelation. But, when this can't be done, "brute force" methods are available to make the error term observations uncorrelated, so that the symptoms of autocorrelation do not occur. (The estimates will be efficient and the t-statistics will be correct, and so on.) The regression will appear normal—will not exhibit autocorrelation—but the underlying model is the one that produced the auto-correlation in the first place.

Consider a generic simple regression model:

$$Y_t = B_0 + B_1X_t + e_t \qquad \text{(7-6)}$$

The t subscripts indicate that this is a time-series regression and that for each observation the values of Y and X are both from the same time period.[12] If this model has first-order autocorrelation, then, as expressed by Equation (7-2), this period's error and the preceding one are related: $e_t = \rho e_{t-1} + u_t$. Remember, u_t represents an error term that follows OLS assumptions, so u_t is independent of its preceding value, u_{t-1}. We can force the autocorrelation out of the model if we can replace e_t by u_t, since u_t meets the OLS assumptions. Here is how this is done.

First we rearrange Equation (7-2) by subtracting ρe_{t-1} from each side to get

$$e_t - \rho e_{t-1} = u_t \qquad \text{(7-7)}$$

We want to find a way to eliminate the correlated errors (the e's) from the regression and replace them with random errors (the u's). If we can rearrange the regression so that $e_t - \rho e_{t-1}$ appears in the regression, then we can use Equation (7-7) to substitute the good error term (u's) for the bad ones (e's).

First, consider Equation (7-6). This regression is not just for time period t but for all the time periods included in the data. Instead of using $Y_t = B_0 + B_1X_t + e_t$, it is valid to move everything back one period. Then we have

$$Y_{t-1} = B_0 + B_1X_{t-1} + e_{t-1} \qquad \text{(7-8)}$$

---

[12] Throughout most of the book, the t subscripts have been omitted for simplicity, but here they are necessary.

Next, multiply both sides of (7-8) by the autocorrelation coefficient ρ:

$$\rho Y_{t-1} = \rho B_0 + \rho B_1 X_{t-1} + \rho e_{t-1} \qquad \text{(7-9)}$$

We are almost there. We want to get $e_t - \rho e_{t-1}$ into the regression so we can use (7-7) to replace $e_t - \rho e_{t-1}$ with u_t, forcing out the autocorrelation. Take the original regression (7-6) and subtract (7-9) from it, on both the left- and right-hand sides of the equation:

$$Y_t = B_0 + B_1 X_t + e_t$$

$$-\rho Y_{t-1} = -(\rho B_0 + \rho B_1 X_{t-1} + \rho e_{t-1})$$

$$Y_t - \rho Y_{t-1} = B_0 - \rho B_0 + (B_1 X_t - \rho B_1 X_{t-1}) + e_t - \rho e_{t-1}$$

The bottom line, the answer to this subtraction, can be rewritten as

$$Y_t - \rho Y_{t-1} = B_0(1 - \rho) + B_1(X_t - \rho X_{t-1}) + e_t - \rho e_{t-1} \qquad \text{(7-10)}$$

Now $e_t - \rho e_{t-1}$ appears in the regression, and we can eliminate the e terms that exhibit autocorrelation by substituting u_t in for $e_t - \rho e_{t-1}$ [Equation (7-7)]:

$$Y_t - \rho Y_{t-1} = B_0(1 - \rho) + B_1(X_t - \rho X_{t-1}) + u_t \qquad \text{(7-11)}$$

Equation (7-11) does not have autocorrelation. Think of $Y_t - \rho Y_{t-1}$ as one variable, the new dependent variable. $B_0(1 - \rho)$ is the new intercept and $X_t - \rho X_{t-1}$ is the new independent variable. This is called a **generalized difference equation** because we find it by taking the difference of the two equations. This process also works with more than one independent variable; we used only one here for simplicity. The generalized difference equation is a type of generalized least squares, a different estimation method from ordinary least squares.

We need an estimate for the autocorrelation coefficient ρ before we can estimate the regression in Equation (7-11). Both the Cochrane-Orcutt and AR(1) methods find an estimate of ρ and complete the regression estimation. The Cochrane-Orcutt method has been the most commonly used method, but now that econometrics software is more sophisticated, the AR(1) method is becoming more popular.

The Cochrane-Orcutt Method

This method estimates ρ several times until the estimates stop changing, or converge. The Cochrane-Orcutt method is often called an iterative process because it repeats certain steps over and over.[13] The steps are:

1. Estimate the regression using ordinary least squares.
2. Use the error term observations from step 1 to estimate $e_t = \rho e_{t-1} + u_t$, getting an estimate for ρ.

---

[13] D. Cochrane and G. H. Orcutt, "Application of Least-Squares Regressions to Relationships Containing Autocorrelated Error Terms," *Journal of the American Statistical Association*, Vol. 44, 1949, pp. 32–61.

3. Use the estimate for ρ along with the data for the dependent and independent variables to estimate the generalized difference equation, (7-11).
4. Using the error term observations from step 3, go back to step 2 and estimate ρ again. Repeat this process until the estimate of ρ stays about the same; then estimate the generalized difference equation one last time.

Your results will include an estimate for ρ, along with the coefficient estimates, t-statistics, and other statistics you expect. Most software programs that provide the Cochrane-Orcutt method also show you the intermediate estimates for ρ that were used during the process. The sample size will be one less than the number of observations available, since no observation precedes the first one to use as Y_{t-1} or X_{t-1} in Equation (7-11). The first observation is automatically omitted, because it provides Y_{t-1} and X_{t-1} for the second observation, which starts the regression. The coefficient estimate results given by the Cochrane-Orcutt process are usually very close to the results given by the AR(1) method. Now let's look at an example of AR(1) results.

The AR(1) Method

The AR(1) method uses a nonlinear technique to estimate the autocorrelation coefficient ρ and the B coefficient estimates all at once. The details of the method are complex and will not be covered here. AR(1) is considered a more powerful method, but for practical purposes, the differences between the AR(1) and Cochrane-Orcutt methods seem small.

Suppose Microsoft released data only for revenue and marketing, but not for R&D. Then we might resort to using Cochrane-Orcutt or AR(1) to deal with the autocorrelation problem, since RESEARCH(-4) cannot be used as an independent variable. Figure 7-4 shows the error term observations when the AR(1) process is applied to the original Microsoft revenue model, which exhibited positive first-order autocorrelation [RESEARCH(-4) is not included]. These error term observations are observations of u_t from Equation (7-11). They should follow the OLS assumptions and should not exhibit autocorrelation.

As shown in Figure 7-4a, the error term observations do not exhibit a clear pattern after we apply AR(1) to the regression. Table 7-E presents our results using the AR(1) method. (*Note*: The variable listed as AR(1) is not an independent variable at all. It is the AR(1) method's estimate of ρ, the autocorrelation coefficient.)

The variables listed in Table 7-E are actually generalized difference variables. This means that where Table 7-E lists the variable MARKETING, it really means the variable $MARKETING_t - \rho MARKETING_{t-1}$, matching the format given in Equation (7-11). The same is true with the dependent variable. That is, the dependent variable here is not REVENUE, it is $REVENUE_t - \rho\,REVENUE_{t-1}$. Each observation in the time series is now a term containing values from the current time period and the preceding period.

The estimate of ρ is 0.80, which lies between 0 and 1, as we expect for a ρ when positive autocorrelation is present. MARKETING is still statistically significant at a 1% significance level, so the original autocorrelation did not cause us to mistake an insignificant variable for a significant one. Note that the t-statistic for the MARKETING coefficient fell from 32.10 to 11.23 (see Table 7-B). This supports the idea that autocorrelation inflates t-statistics. The F-test shows that as a group the dummy vari-

Figure 7-4

Comparison of Error Term Observations Using AR(1) for Microsoft Revenue Model.

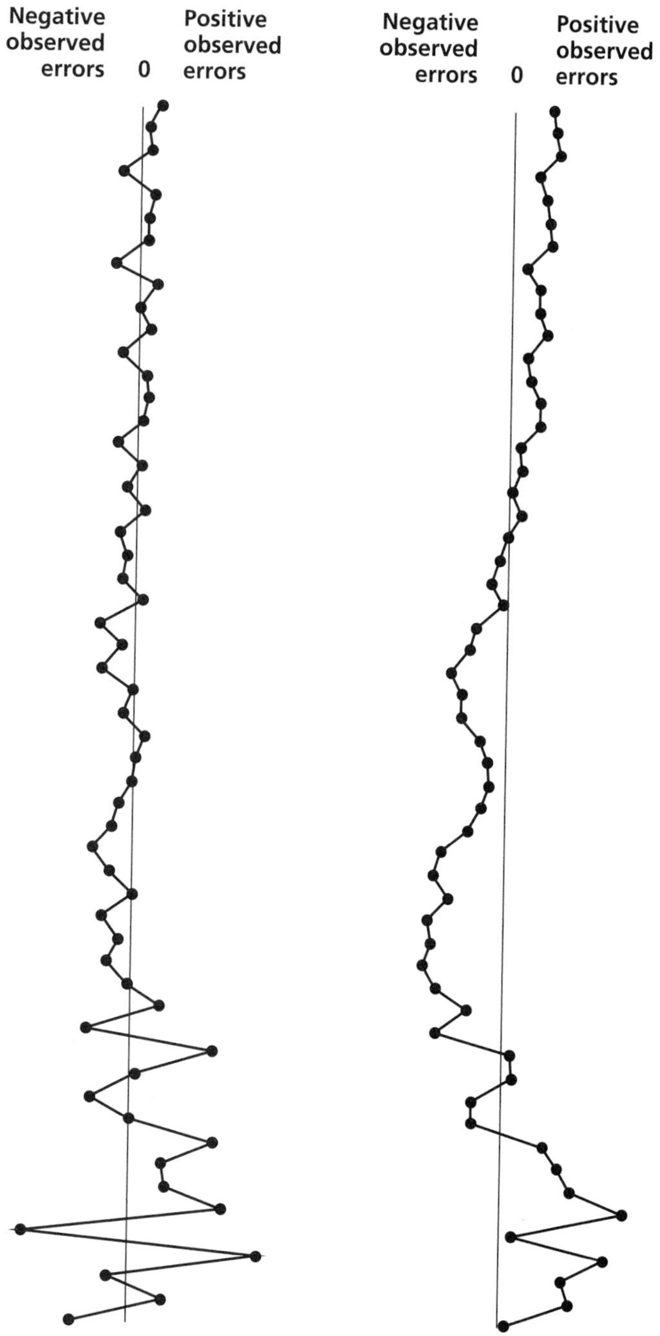

(a) AR(1) forces
autocorrelation out

(b) Autocorrelation in
original model

Table 7-E

Results for Microsoft Revenue Model Estimated by AR(1) Excluding RESEARCH(-4)

Dependent variable: REVENUE

Variable	Coefficient	Standard Error	t-Statistic	p-Value
Constant	-151.27	171.56	-0.88	0.38
MARKETING	5.45	0.49	11.23	0.00
SECONDQ	-10.50	37.83	-0.28	0.78
THIRDQ	65.99	45.01	1.47	0.15
FOURTHQ	17.22	39.07	0.44	0.66
AR(1) [estimate of ρ]	0.80	0.090	8.93	0.00

Observations: 54

$R^2 = 0.98$

Adjusted $R^2 = 0.98$

Residual Sum of Squares = 1,027,335

F-statistic = 542.99

Durbin-Watson statistic = 2.60

ables are not statistically significant at a 5% error level. Removing the dummy variables from the regression using the AR(1) method does not cause much change in the remaining coefficient estimates or statistics.

Both the Cochrane-Orcutt and AR(1) methods force first-order autocorrelation out of models, eliminating the symptoms or problems that accompany autocorrelation. It is always better to cure autocorrelation in your model by identifying what is causing the autocorrelation in the first place. Use the brute force methods of Cochrane-Orcutt and AR(1) only as a last resort. Otherwise, you may overlook an important variable that adds insight to your research.

SUMMARY

1. **Autocorrelation** (also called **serial correlation**) occurs when the errors follow a pattern; it is a violation of the classical assumption that the errors are independent of each other. Autocorrelation is a common problem in time-series regressions. It indicates that a relevant independent variable is missing from the model.
2. **First-order autocorrelation** is present when an error is influenced by the error from the preceding time period. The autocorrelation coefficient ρ (Greek letter rho, pronounced "row") shows the relationship between e_t and e_{t-1} in a manner

similar to how a slope coefficient works in a regression. The value of ρ must fall between -1 and $+1$.

3. **Positive autocorrelation** occurs when the error term tends to keep the same sign from one period to the next. **Negative autocorrelation** occurs when the sign of the error term tends to alternate back and forth between positive and negative. Positive autocorrelation is more common than negative autocorrelation in economics.

4. There are other types of autocorrelation besides first-order autocorrelation. For example, if seasonal data are used, the error e_t could depend on the error from the same season a year ago, e_{t-4}.

5. Autocorrelation:
   - leaves the coefficient estimates unbiased (unless a relevant independent variable is missing)
   - increases the variance of the coefficient estimates
   - makes the estimated standard errors given by ordinary least squares too small

   Autocorrelation is a serious problem because it makes the t-statistics larger than they should be. The misleadingly large t-statistics can make you think that a slope estimate is statistically significant when it is not.

6. The **Durbin-Watson statistic** can be used to test for first-order autocorrelation, if the dependent variable does not also appear as a lagged independent variable in the model. The Durbin-Watson ranges from 0 to 4. The closer the Durbin-Watson statistic is to 0, the more likely positive first-order autocorrelation is present. The closer it is to 2, the more likely there is no autocorrelation. The closer it is to 4, the more likely negative first-order autocorrelation is present.

7. Different approaches are used to treat autocorrelation. The best approach is to reformulate the model to eliminate the autocorrelation. Sometimes this is accomplished by adding a missing independent variable or by changing the functional form of the regression. However, there are situations in which autocorrelation cannot be eliminated by changing the model. In these cases, a generalized difference equation is used.

$$Y_t - \rho Y_{t-1} = B_0(1 - \rho) + B_1(X_t - \rho X_{t-1}) + u_t \qquad \text{(7-11)}$$

An estimate of ρ must be found to estimate a **generalized difference equation**. Either the **Cochrane-Orcutt method** or the **AR(1) method** can be used to estimate ρ and the generalized difference equation. The Cochrane-Orcutt method estimates ρ and then estimates Equation (7-11), repeating the process until the estimate of ρ stays about the same. The AR(1) method is a nonlinear method that estimates ρ and the other coefficients all at once. The coefficient estimate results given by the two methods are usually close to each other.

EXERCISES

1. Try to explain these terms without looking them up.
   - serial correlation
   - first-order autocorrelation

- positive autocorrelation
- negative autocorrelation
- Durbin-Watson statistic
- Generalized difference equation
- Cochrane-Orcutt method
- AR(1)

2. Autocorrelation causes problems for ordinary least squares regression. Explain the autocorrelation problem in a simple way as you would to a friend who doesn't know much about econometrics.

3. Autocorrelation, if left unchecked, can be particularly dangerous for a researcher who has found statistically significant results. Explain why this is so.

4. a. Besides autocorrelation, what is the biggest problem with the Microsoft revenues model as expressed by Equation (7-1)?

   b. Is your answer to part a somehow related to the autocorrelation problem? Explain.

5. Conduct a Durbin-Watson test at a 5% error level for each case given. Is the null hypothesis of no first-order autocorrelation rejected, not rejected, or is the test inconclusive? Use the appropriate one-sided test for each Durbin-Watson statistic given.

   a. D.W. = 1.27, N = 40, k = 2
   b. D.W. = 1.27, N = 25, k = 2
   c. D.W. = 2.45, N = 80, k = 5
   d. D.W. = 2.45, N = 80, k = 1

6. a. In Exercise 5, what does the difference between your answers to parts a and b tell you about how the Durbin-Watson test works?

   b. What does the difference between your answers to parts c and d in Exercise 5 tell you about how the Durbin-Watson test works?

7. The text indicates that when we add missing independent variables we are treating the illness of autocorrelation, but if we use a generalized difference equation we are just treating its symptoms. What does this mean? In other words, what is the distinction between adding missing variables to treat the illness and using a generalized difference equation to treat the symptoms?

8. The Cochrane-Orcutt method can be used to estimate a generalized least squares equation when autocorrelation is present. Without looking at the text or your notes, explain how the procedure works, including how the equation is estimated.

9. Using the data from Table 7-A, use ordinary least squares to estimate the Microsoft revenue model again for the first three years only (1987, 1988, 1989), so that the sample size is 12. Below are the same data for the 12 quarters of 1987–1989, but the order of the data is different. Run the regression again using the order shown here. Are the Durbin-Watson statistics the same?

Year	Quarter	REVENUES	MARKETING	SECONDQ	THIRDQ	FOURTHQ
1987	1	60.02	13.44	0	0	0
	4	86.68	22.54	0	0	1
	3	85.66	18.36	0	1	0
	2	71.62	16.80	1	0	0
1988	1	88.74	23.26	0	0	0
	4	141.27	40.72	0	0	1
	3	136.02	32.75	0	1	0
	2	132.73	31.48	1	0	0
1989	1	145.48	37.81	0	0	0
	4	175.58	45.29	0	0	1
	3	158.02	40.91	0	1	0
	2	169.81	46.90	1	0	0

10. What does the Durbin-Watson statistic mean for a cross-section regression? (*Hint:* Consider your answer to Exercise 9.)

11. Combine the data in Tables 2-A and 2-C to create one data set for the DVD expenditures model. (Make sure you keep the data in order, so that the data from Table 2-A represents the first year of data, and that the data in Table 2-C follows, representing the second year. Keep the months in order, also.) Use this combined data set to estimate the DVD expenditures model [see Equation (2-2)]. Conduct a Durbin-Watson test for first-order autocorrelation using a 5% error level.

12. Use the AR(1) method to correct for first-order autocorrelation in Exercise 11. Compare the AR(1) results to the original results you found in Exercise 11. What does your answer to the preceding exercise have to do with this comparison of results?

13. You may see a time-series regression that contains a trend variable, sometimes called T. The trend variable just increases one unit for every unit of time that passes in the data. To set up a trend variable for the Microsoft revenues model, we would use T = 1 for the first quarter, 2 for the second quarter, 3 for the third quarter, and so forth, until the last quarter of data where T = 55 (since n = 55). The trend variable is supposed to represent any linear trend over time that is not being captured by other variables in the model. However, this is cheating in a way, because although you may increase the explanatory power of your model by including the trend variable, you also know that the trend variable really just represents some unknown missing variables. A significant trend variable means that

a linear trend is associated with changes in the dependent variable, but this doesn't tell you what is driving the trend or what is missing from the model.

a. Estimate the following regression using the data in Table 7-A.

$$REVENUES = B_0 + B_1 MARKETING + B_2 SECONDQ + B_3 THIRDQ$$
$$+ B_4 FOURTHQ + B_5 T + e$$

where $T = 1$ for the first observation, 2 for the second observation, and so on, so that the last observation has $T = 55$.

b. Is the slope estimate for T statistically significant at a 5% error level? If so, does this add to our understanding of Microsoft revenues?

c. The original Durbin-Watson statistic (without T in the model) indicated autocorrelation (see Table 7-B). Does the inclusion of T in the model change the results of the Durbin-Watson test?

8

Heteroskedasticity: A Problem with Cross-Section Regressions

In this chapter, you will learn:

- The concept of heteroskedasticity—A problem that occurs when the error term does not have a constant variance.

- The symptoms of heteroskedasticity.

- How to test for heteroskedasticity.

- How to design models so there is no heteroskedasticity to begin with.

- How to eliminate heteroskedasticity by force, if necessary.

In the game of darts, a small miscalculation of 5% can cause a thrown dart to be off by less than an inch and miss the bull's-eye. In a space shuttle launch, a miscalculation of 5% could cause the shuttle to miss its target by thousands of miles, causing an international or even an interplanetary incident. The space shuttle has a much longer trip to make than the dart, so any small error in how the shuttle is aimed is magnified to a much greater extent than with the dart. The point here is that observations that deal with larger sizes can often generate larger errors than observations that deal with smaller sizes. This means that observations representing a bigger size, such as a larger state or corporation, can have error term observations that are larger in magnitude than those from observations representing smaller states or corporations. When this happens, the classical assumption of ordinary least squares that the error term variance must be constant does not hold. The errors from larger-sized observations come from a probability distribution with a different variance than the errors from smaller-sized observations. As you learned in Chapters 6 and 7, when the classical assumptions do not all hold, the regression will have a problem or illness.

8-1 THE ILLNESS

One of the OLS assumptions is that the error term observations must be **homoskedastic**: They must have a constant variance. This does not mean that each error term observation is the same size; it just means that each error term observation comes from the same probability distribution. When this assumption does not hold and the error term observations have different variances, **heteroskedasticity** is present.[1] Heteroskedastic errors come from different probability distributions that have different variances. Figure 8-1a shows a probability distribution for a homoskedastic (constant variance) error term; Figure 8-1b shows two distributions that together give a heteroskedastic error term, since the two distributions have different variances. If the error term is homoskedastic, the error term observations are drawn from the same probability distribution. If the error term is heteroskedastic, the error term observations come from more than one probability distribution. Note that one of the distributions in Figure 8-1b is wider than the other. The wider distribution has a greater variance than the more narrow distribution, since the values from the wider distribution fluctuate around zero more.

Heteroskedasticity occurs most often in cross-section data where there are large differences in size between the observations. Consider a study of state government tax revenues for 50 states.[2] California's population is 69 times that of Wyoming.[3] It makes

Figure 8-1

Constant Error Term Variance vs. Heteroskedasticity.

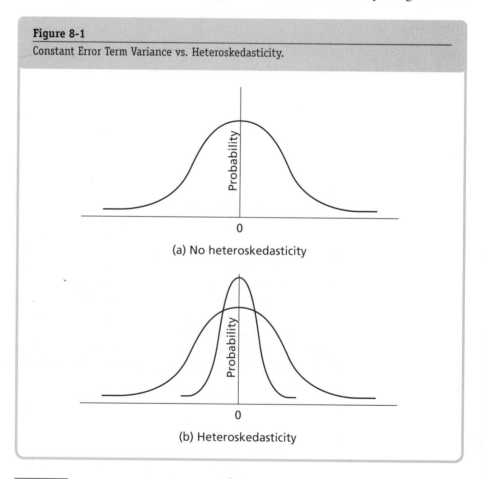

(a) No heteroskedasticity

(b) Heteroskedasticity

[1] Heteroskedasticity is also spelled "heteroscedasticity."
[2] This model is formally stated in an exercise at the end of the chapter.
[3] State populations are given in Table 8-A.

sense that with all those taxpayers, California's tax revenues will be more difficult to predict than Wyoming's. The error term observations for California might tend to have a larger absolute value than that of Wyoming. In its most simple form, heteroskedasticity can be generated by error term observations coming from two different distributions with different variances, such as the distributions shown in Figure 8-1b. Most heteroskedasticity is more complicated. The state tax revenue regression could have an error variance that is proportional to the population in the state.

A common form of heteroskedasticity occurs when the error-term variance follows the magnitude of a factor called Z. Z can be an independent variable from the model, or it can be a variable that is not part of the model at all. Usually Z is a measure of each observation's size. For a cross section of firms, Z might be the firm's assets or the number of employees. State population is a good choice for Z in the state tax revenue example. The larger Z is for a particular observation, the larger the error variance. Z is sometimes called the *proportionality factor*. Since it often measures observation size, it is also called the **size factor Z**.

We can summarize these ideas using symbols.

No Heteroskedasticity:
Error term variance $= \sigma^2$, where σ^2 is equal to a constant number   **(8-1)**

Heteroskedastic:
Error term variance for first observation $= \sigma_1^2$ **(8-2)**
Error term variance for second observation $= \sigma_2^2$
Error term variance for third observation $= \sigma_3^2$
and so on, until
Error term variance for last observation $= \sigma_n^2$
(Here the subscripts on each σ^2 indicate they can take different values from each other; σ^2 can be different for each observation.)

Heteroskedastic with Z: **(8-3)**
Error term variance for first observation $= \sigma^2 Z_1^2$
Error term variance for second observation $= \sigma^2 Z_2^2$
Error term variance for third observation $= \sigma^2 Z_3^2$
and so on, until
Error term variance for last observation $= \sigma^2 Z_n^2$
(Here σ^2 is always the same number for each observation. The error term variance can differ for each observation because Z can take a different value in each observation.)

σ is the Greek letter sigma; σ^2 symbolizes variance in econometrics and statistics. When there is no heteroskedasticity, (8-1), each error term observation comes from a probability distribution with the same variance. The variance is equal to a number such as 10, and it doesn't change. When there is heteroskedasticity, (8-2), the variance can take different values for different observations. Next (8-3) describes a particular type of heteroskedasticity in which the error-term variance is proportional to Z, which typically measures the size of each observation.

Heteroskedasticity often arises from specification error. Models that do not adequately account for different-sized observations will often exhibit heteroskedasticity.

We can avoid heteroskedasticity in our state tax revenue example if we specify the dependent variable as state tax revenues *per capita* (per person) rather than just state tax revenues. Some of the independent variables in the model would need to be per person also.

Remember that the OLS procedure finds its estimates by minimizing the sum of the squared errors. As it tries to minimize this sum, it pays more attention to observations with large errors. If an error term observation comes from a distribution with a larger variance, then the observed error itself will tend to be larger or farther from zero.[4] The observations with large errors tend to be the observations that are bigger in size to begin with, because of the heteroskedasticity. If heteroskedasticity is present in the state tax revenue example, the more populated states will tend to have larger error term observations. Heteroskedasticity causes ordinary least squares to exaggerate the importance of observations representing larger sizes. California, New York, and other heavily populated states will be given too much emphasis in the state tax revenue model when there is heteroskedasticity.

Plotting error term observations or residuals against a Z factor can reveal heteroskedasticity, if it is severe. Z is usually some appropriate measure of size for the data. In a cross section of states, Z might be population. Figure 8-2 shows what heteroskedasticity might look like for the state tax revenue example using population as the measure.

As Figure 8-2 shows, states with bigger populations also have larger error term observations. As you look at the right side of the figure, the error variance increases.

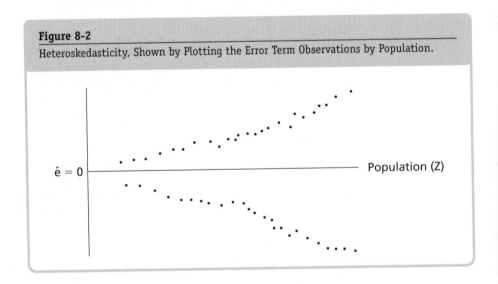

Figure 8-2

Heteroskedasticity, Shown by Plotting the Error Term Observations by Population.

$\hat{e} = 0$

Population (Z)

---

[4] This is true because the mean of the errors in any regression has to be zero. (See Section 2-2.) The variance measures how values for the variable are spread around the mean. The more they spread out around the mean, the bigger the variance will be. Since the mean is zero, errors from distributions with larger variances will tend to be farther from zero.

Notice how the error term observations swing farther away from zero as the population increases and you move to the right in the figure.

The following example will be used throughout the chapter to illustrate how to deal with heteroskedasticity. The Artist Formerly Known as Bob (who now uses the symbol (: to represent his name) completed a concert tour where he performed one show in each of the 50 states.[5] He has asked us to build a regression model to evaluate his concert revenues. Equation (8-4) gives the regression model.

$$\text{REVENUE} = B_0 + B_1\text{ADVERTISING} + B_2\text{STADIUM} + B_3\text{CD} + B_4\text{RADIO} + B_5\text{WEEKEND} + e \tag{8-4}$$

where

$$
\begin{aligned}
\text{REVENUE} &= \text{revenue from each concert, in dollars} \\
\text{ADVERTISING} &= \text{advertising costs for each concert, in dollars} \\
\text{STADIUM} &= \text{maximum capacity of each stadium for each concert} \\
\text{CD} &= \text{number of Bob's compact discs sold in concert area 6 months} \\
&\quad \text{prior to show} \\
\text{RADIO} &= \text{index of how often Bob's songs are played on the radio in each} \\
&\quad \text{concert area (RADIO ranges from 1 to 5, with 1 = his songs} \\
&\quad \text{are rarely played; 5 = Bob's songs are played so often that you} \\
&\quad \text{can't avoid hearing them)} \\
\text{WEEKEND} &= 1 \text{ if concert is held on a Friday or Saturday night, 0 otherwise}
\end{aligned}
$$

The ticket price is not included in this model, because it is always the same ($95). Table 8-A gives the hypothetical data from Bob's 50-state concert tour. (POPULATION is not in the regression but will be used later in the chapter.)

These data are used to estimate the regression given by Equation (8-4). The observations are in alphabetical order by state name. As long as the observations are in alphabetical order, a plot of error term observations will not be helpful in discussing heteroskedasticity. Since the population of states varies a great deal, making each observation a different size, there could be heteroskedasticity. The error term variance could be in proportion to each state's population; the size factor Z could be the population of the state. If the data in Table 8-A are reordered so that the least populated state (Wyoming) comes first and the most populated state (California) comes last, the slope coefficients and t-statistics will be the same, but the order of the error term observations will be different. Figure 8-3 shows the error term observations when the data are ordered by population, so that the least populated state comes first and the most populated state comes last.

Figure 8-3 indicates the possibility of heteroskedasticity, although it is not as clear as in Figure 8-2. Figure 8-3 is divided into three sections, where the error variance differs. Section I contains the 10 least populated states and has the smallest observed error variance. Section II includes states ranked 11 through 45 in population. Here the error variance is larger than in section I, but not as large as in section III. Section III, with the

---

[5] Note that more recently (: has returned to using his original name, Bob. Apparently, using a symbol for his name didn't work out any better for him than it did for a more famous (and creative) recording artist.

Table 8-A

Data from Concert Tour

State	REVENUE	ADVERTISING	STADIUM	CD	RADIO	WEEKEND	POPULATION
AL	1,396,500	87,397	21,000	4,370	1	0	4,369,862
AK	475,000	18,585	5,000	1,239	1	0	619,500
AZ	2,090,000	95,567	22,000	9,557	1	1	4,778,332
AR	1,520,000	51,027	16,000	7,654	2	0	2,551,373
CA	4,940,000	331,451	52,000	33,145	5	0	33,145,121
CO	1,795,500	81,123	21,000	8,112	2	0	4,056,133
CT	1,615,000	65,641	17,000	6,564	2	0	3,282,031
DE	665,000	22,606	7,000	1,507	1	0	753,538
FL	3,762,000	151,112	44,000	45,334	4	1	15,111,244
GA	1,872,450	77,882	27,000	7,788	2	0	7,788,240
HI	855,000	35,565	9,000	3,556	1	0	1,185,497
ID	1,140,000	37,551	12,000	1,252	1	0	1,251,700
IL	2,418,700	121,284	38,000	24,257	3	0	12,128,370
IN	2,375,000	118,858	25,000	5,943	2	1	5,942,901
IA	1,330,000	57,388	14,000	2,869	1	0	2,869,413
KS	1,425,000	53,081	15,000	5,308	1	0	2,654,052
KY	1,263,500	79,217	19,000	3,961	2	0	3,960,825
LA	1,672,000	87,441	22,000	2,186	2	0	4,372,035
ME	1,140,000	37,591	12,000	1,253	1	0	1,253,040
MD	2,185,000	103,433	23,000	18,101	2	1	5,171,634
MA	2,375,000	123,503	25,000	18,526	2	1	6,175,169
MI	2,945,000	98,638	31,000	9,864	3	1	9,863,775
MN	1,995,000	95,510	21,000	23,878	2	1	4,775,508
MS	1,425,000	55,372	15,000	4,153	1	1	2,768,619
MO	1,852,500	109,367	25,000	2,734	2	0	5,468,338

(continued)

Table 8-A

(Continued)

State	REVENUE	ADVERTISING	STADIUM	CD	RADIO	WEEKEND	POPULATION
MT	760,000	26,483	8,000	441	1	0	882,779
NE	1,235,000	49,981	13,000	1,666	1	0	1,666,028
NV	1,330,000	54,278	14,000	7,237	1	1	1,809,253
NH	855,000	36,034	9,000	1,201	1	0	1,201,134
NJ	2,755,000	81,434	29,000	12,215	3	1	8,143,412
NM	1,235,000	52,195	13,000	3,480	1	0	1,739,844
NY	5,415,000	181,966	57,000	36,393	5	1	18,196,601
NC	1,539,000	153,016	27,000	11,476	1	0	7,650,789
ND	475,000	19,010	5,000	634	1	0	633,666
OH	2,166,000	112,567	38,000	5,628	2	0	11,256,654
OK	1,453,500	67,161	17,000	3,358	2	0	3,358,044
OR	1,615,000	66,323	17,000	13,265	2	0	3,316,154
PA	2,736,000	119,940	36,000	11,994	3	0	11,994,016
RI	760,000	29,725	8,000	1,982	1	0	990,819
SC	1,407,900	77,715	19,000	7,771	1	0	3,885,736
SD	665,000	21,994	7,000	733	1	0	733,133
TN	1,662,500	109,671	25,000	5,484	1	0	5,483,535
TX	3,192,000	200,441	48,000	10,022	4	0	20,044,141
UT	1,425,000	42,597	15,000	2,130	2	1	2,129,836
VT	475,000	17,812	5,000	1,187	1	0	593,740
VA	2,074,800	137,458	26,000	13,746	2	0	6,872,912
WA	2,137,500	115,127	25,000	11,513	2	0	5,756,361
WV	1,330,000	54,208	14,000	1,807	1	0	1,806,928
WI	2,052,000	105,009	24,000	10,501	2	0	5,250,446
WY	380,000	14,388	4,000	959	1	0	479,602

Population data can be found at the text website or http://www.census.gov/population/estimates/state/st-99-1.txt.

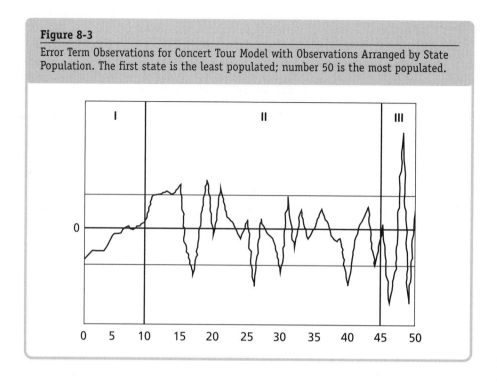

Figure 8-3

Error Term Observations for Concert Tour Model with Observations Arranged by State Population. The first state is the least populated; number 50 is the most populated.

5 most populated states, has the largest error variance. Although the sections are not divided equally, notice how the error term observations grow larger and move somewhat more wildly as the states with larger populations are plotted. This indicates there could be heteroskedasticity. We examine formal tests for heteroskedasticity in Section 8-3.

8-2 THE SYMPTOMS

Heteroskedasticity violates the OLS classical assumptions. Ordinary least squares cannot be BLUE (best linear unbiased estimator) when heteroskedasticity is present. The symptoms of heteroskedasticity look remarkably like those for autocorrelation even though the two problems are very different. Heteroskedasticity typically occurs in cross-section regressions and autocorrelation occurs in time-series regressions. Heteroskedasticity has the following symptoms:

1. Heteroskedasticity leaves the coefficient estimates unbiased. As with autocorrelation, when heteroskedasticity is present, the OLS process still produces unbiased estimates. The expected value of an estimate $\hat{B}$ is still the true value of B. This means that if you run the regression many times using different data and then average all the $\hat{B}$'s, you should get the true value. Also, as in autocorrelation, a missing independent variable can cause heteroskedasticity. If this is the problem, the remaining slope estimates will be biased, as they always are when a relevant independent variable is missing.

2. Heteroskedasticity increases the variance of the coefficient estimates. This symptom is different from the error-term distributions shown in Figure 8-1. Here the coefficient estimates, the $\hat{B}$'s, vary more from their true value than if there were no heteroskedasticity. The heteroskedasticity causes the $\hat{B}$ sampling distribution to become wider. Since there is no bias, the expected value of $\hat{B}$ is the true value. Because heteroskedasticity increases the variance of the coefficient estimates, any one coefficient estimate is likely to be farther from the true value than if heteroskedasticity was not present.

3. Heteroskedasticity causes the OLS procedure to underestimate the standard errors of the coefficients. This results in the t-statistics that are larger than they should be. The F-statistic will also be larger than its true value. As in autocorrelation, the presence of heteroskedasticity opens the researcher's work to criticism. The researcher may reject null hypotheses that should not be rejected, since the t-statistics are larger than their true values.

These problems occur because of a potential relationship between any of the independent variables and the error term. Heteroskedasticity often means that the errors tend to be larger when the size factor Z is larger. If an independent variable is correlated with Z, and the error term is correlated with Z, then the independent variable is correlated with the error term. This causes the coefficient estimates to vary more, increasing their standard error.

Bob's concert tour model may have a heteroskedasticity problem. Recall the regression equation:

$$\text{REVENUE} = B_0 + B_1\text{ADVERTISING} + B_2\text{STADIUM} + B_3\text{CD}$$
$$+ B_4\text{RADIO} + B_5\text{WEEKEND} + e \tag{8-4}$$

We estimate the regression using the data in Table 8-A. Table 8-B gives the OLS results.

All the slope coefficients appear to be statistically significant at a 5% error level or better, except for CD, which is insignificant. Unfortunately, for The Artist Formerly Known as Bob, if heteroskedasticity is present, the t-statistics are unreliable. It is possible that some of these coefficients that seem statistically significant are actually insignificant. We need to conduct formal statistical tests to see if Bob's concert tour model exhibits heteroskedasticity and, if so, how severe the problem is.

8-3 TESTING FOR THE ILLNESS: THE PARK TEST AND THE WHITE TEST

Although plotting the error term observations by size may give us a visual indication of whether there is heteroskedasticity, a statistical test is still necessary. Eyeballing a plot of observed error term observations reveals heteroskedasticity only in dramatic cases. There are many tests for heteroskedasticity because there are many types of heteroskedasticity. We describe two common tests, the **Park test** and the **White test**. Many econometrics programs have the White test built in, so it is easy to use. The Park test takes a little more effort. Since you must specify the size factor Z when you use the

Table 8-B

Results for Concert Tour Model

Dependent variable: REVENUE

Variable	Coefficient	Standard Error	t-Statistic	p-Value
Constant	73,215.34	70,909.63	1.03	0.31
ADVERTISING	3.15	1.33	2.37	0.02
STADIUM	34.66	7.89	4.39	0.00
CD	8.30	6.05	1.37	0.18
RADIO	300,425.69	70,633.17	4.25	0.00
WEEKEND	356,003.51	84,215.38	4.23	0.00

Observations: 50

$R^2 = 0.96$

Adjusted $R^2 = 0.95$

Residual Sum of Squares = 2.12×10^{12}

F-statistic = 201.97

Durbin-Watson statistic = 1.93

Park test, it cannot be built into a software program as easily as the White test. This may be inconvenient, but it also means that the Park test can be used to test for heteroskedasticity using a specific Z. The White test also tests for the size factor Z style of heteroskedasticity, but you do not actually specify Z or necessarily know which variable is appropriate for Z.

The Park Test

The challenge of the Park test is to determine which variable to use as Z, the size factor.[6] Although it may be a challenge, the Park test is useful because it tells whether you have successfully identified the correct Z. Here are the steps for the Park test:

1. Decide what variable should serve as Z (usually something that measures the relative size of the observations).
2. Run the original regression,

$$Y = B_0 + B_1X_1 + B_2X_2 + \cdots + B_kX_k + e \qquad (8\text{-}5)$$

where your original model has k independent variables. Be sure to save the error term observations (residuals) found by the software; you will use these values in

---

[6] R. Park, "Estimating with Heteroscedastic Error Terms," *Econometrica,* Vol. 34, 1966, p. 888.

the steps below. (Most econometrics programs either save the error term observations for you automatically or allow you to request that they be saved.)

3. Square the error term observations.
4. Take the natural logarithms of both Z and the squared error term observations, then run the following regression:

$$\ln(\hat{e}^2) = B_0 + B_1 \ln Z + u \qquad (8\text{-}6)$$

Here we are using the squared error term observations to form the dependent variable, the natural logarithm of $\hat{e}^2$. $\hat{e}$ indicates actual values for an observed error term as opposed to e which indicates a theoretical, unobserved error term in a regression model. There is one independent variable: the natural logarithm of the size factor Z. [Note that although the notation B_0 and B_1 appear in both Equations (8-5) and (8-6), the values of these coefficients will be different in the two equations.] u is a new error term that follows the OLS classical assumptions.

5. Conduct a t-test on B_1, coefficient for ln Z. If the slope coefficient is significantly different from zero at a 5% error level, assume there is heteroskedasticity. Otherwise, assume there is no heteroskedasticity related to the Z you chose. It is still possible that there is heteroskedasticity related to a different Z. You may want to try the Park test more than once, if there is more than one good measure of size that could be used as Z. Don't test every independent variable as a possible Z, because this might result in a Type I error; you might reject the null hypothesis of constant error variance and think heteroskedasticity is present when in fact it is not.

If there is no heteroskedasticity, then Z should not be related to the variance of the error term. In the Park test, $\hat{e}^2$ represents an estimate of the error term variance. If Z and $\hat{e}^2$ are unrelated, then the t-test should be insignificant. If there is heteroskedasticity where the error variance is proportional to Z, then $\hat{e}^2$ and Z will be related, and the t-test should come out significant.

Bob's concert tour model can be tested for heteroskedasticity using the Park test. Our first step is to choose Z. Population is a good choice for Z because it provides a measure of size for each state that would seem to be related to concert revenues. It makes sense that if only one concert is performed in each state, the more populated the state, the more people will attend the concert.

In the second step, we to run the original regression and save the error term observations. In step 3, we square the error term observations. In step 4, we first take the natural logarithm of both the squared error term observations and the population size factor, and then run the regression:

$$\ln(\hat{e}^2) = B_0 + B_1 \ln(\text{POPULATION}) + u \qquad (8\text{-}7)$$

Table 8-C gives the Park test results.

The coefficient for ln(POPULATION) is statistically significant at a 5% error level (p-value = 0.04). POPULATION does seem to be related to the error variance. We should assume there is heteroskedasticity, and also that POPULATION is the size factor Z on which the heteroskedasticity depends.

Table 8-C

Park Test for Concert Tour Model, Using POPULATION as Z

Dependent variable: $\ln(\hat{e}^2)$

Variable	Coefficient	Standard Error	t-Statistic	p-Value
Constant	13.36	4.67	2.86	0.01
ln(POPULATION)	0.64	0.31	2.07	0.04

Observations: 50

$R^2 = 0.08$

Adjusted $R^2 = 0.06$

Residual Sum of Squares = 234.99

F-statistic = 4.27

Durbin-Watson statistic = 1.44

The White Test

Another popular test for heteroskedasticity, the White test, is built into many econometric software packages.[7] The White test is more general than the Park test; it is not limited to one specific choice of Z. However, this also means that the White test can't help confirm that heteroskedasticity is related to a specific size factor Z that you have in mind. You will understand the results of the White test better if you know how the test works, even though many econometrics programs allow you to run the test automatically. Here are the steps of the White test:

1. Run the original regression, saving the error term observations for use in the next steps. (This is the same as step 2 of the Park test, but here we do not have to choose a Z ahead of time.)
2. Square the error term observations.
3. Use the squared error term observations as the dependent variable and, for the independent variables, include:
   a. Every independent variable from the original regression
   b. Every independent variable from the original regression squared
   c. Each independent variable from the original regression multiplied by another independent variable (Do this using all possible combinations of independent variables.)

   If the original regression has three independent variables, X_1, X_2, and X_3, the regression for the White test is

$$\hat{e}^2 = B_0 + B_1X_1 + B_2X_2 + B_3X_3 + B_4X_1^2 + B_5X_2^2 + B_6X_3^2 \\ + B_7X_1X_2 + B_8X_1X_3 + B_9X_2X_3 + u \tag{8-8}$$

---

[7] Halbert White, "A Heteroskedasticity-Consistent Covariance Matrix Estimator and a Direct Test for Heteroskedasticity," *Econometrica*, Vol. 48, 1980, pp. 817–838.

where

- B_1X_1, B_2X_2, and B_3X_3 are terms that include the original independent variables (called for in step 3a).
- $B_4X_1^2$, $B_5X_2^2$, and $B_6X_3^2$ are terms that include every independent variable from the original regression squared (step 3b).
- $B_7X_1X_2$, $B_8X_1X_3$, and $B_9X_2X_3$ are terms that include each independent variable multiplied by every other independent variable (as required by step 3c).
- u is an error term that meets the OLS assumption, just like in the Park test.

4. Test the statistical significance of the whole equation by using the test statistic nR^2. (The sample size n multiplied by the unadjusted R^2.) Find the critical value for the test by using a table for the chi-squared distribution (Appendix Table G). The degrees of freedom for the critical value equals the number of slope coefficients in Equation (8-8). For the example shown, the degrees of freedom for the critical value is 9. If nR^2 is larger than the critical value, the null hypothesis of constant error variance is rejected; we assume we have heteroskedasticity. The test is often done at a 5% significance level.

As noted earlier, the White test is a more general version of the Park test. Instead of testing for heteroskedasticity relative to one specific Z, the White test checks for several different types of heteroskedasticity all at once. If any of the terms described in step 3 have a strong enough relationship with the error variance, the White test concludes that there is heteroskedasticity. Looking at the results of Equation (8-8) gives clues about the appropriate Z, but the White test itself does not reveal Z. Note that the White test does not use logarithms like the Park test.

The White test involves estimating a lot more slope coefficients than the Park test [compare Equation (8-8) to Equation (8-6)]. This can make the degrees of freedom for estimating Equation (8-8) small, which weakens the White test. In some cases, you may not be able to run the White test because the degrees of freedom for Equation (8-8) are negative.[8] Under these circumstances, the Park test is a better choice.

We can perform a White test on Bob's concert tour model. Table 8-D gives these results.

The regression for the White test has a lot of terms in it, since the original regression contains five independent variables. The test statistic we are interested in for the White test is nR^2. Here nR^2 is $50 \times 0.79 = 39.5$. The degrees of freedom for the chi-squared critical value is 19, since there are 19 slope coefficients in the White test regression in Table 8-D. The critical value at 5% significance with 19 degrees of freedom is 30.1 (see the Appendix, Table G). Since 39.65, the calculated value from the regression results, is greater than the critical value of 30.1, the null hypothesis of constant error variance is rejected. The White test is telling us that heteroskedasticity is present. The Park test gave us the same conclusion. We should proceed assuming the concert tour model has a heteroskedasticity problem.

---

[8] Note that this refers to the degrees of freedom for the White test regression, not the degrees of freedom used to find the critical value from the chi-squared distribution (which is equal to the number of slope coefficients).

Table 8-D

White Test for Concert Tour Model[9]
Dependent variable: $\hat{e}^2$

Variable	Coefficient	Standard Error	t-Statistic	p-Value
Constant	1.89×10^{11}	4.95×10^{10}	3.82	0.00
ADVERTISING	5,149,460	2,482,203	2.08	0.05
STADIUM	−15,030,148	9,079,681	−1.66	0.11
CD	10,749,212	6,681,980	1.61	0.12
RADIO	-2.95×10^{11}	9.51×10^{10}	−3.11	0.00
WEEKEND	5.14×10^{10}	6.91×10^{10}	0.74	0.46
$(ADVERTISING)^2$	35.37	28.00	1.26	0.22
$(STADIUM)^2$	1,580.49	680.02	2.32	0.03
$(CD)^2$	274.18	293.80	0.93	0.36
$(RADIO)^2$	1.42×10^{11}	5.27×10^{10}	2.69	0.01
ADVERTISING · STADIUM	−599.86	276.15	−2.172	0.04
ADVERTISING · CD	−178.43	177.35	−1.01	0.32
ADVERTISING · RADIO	2,284,099	1,453,695	1.57	0.13
ADVERTISING · WEEKEND	2,436,290	1,576,309	1.55	0.13
STADIUM · CD	1,731.93	904.71	1.91	0.07
STADIUM · RADIO	−12,192,611	8,764,398	−1.39	0.17
STADIUM · WEEKEND	−21,643,059	9,259,410	−2.34	0.03
CD · RADIO	−19,563,691	7,208,794	−2.71	0.01
CD · WEEKEND	−1,179,236	5,923,193	−0.20	0.84
RADIO · WEEKEND	1.06×10^{11}	4.94×10^{10}	2.14	0.04

Observations: 50

$R^2 = 0.79$

Adjusted $R^2 = 0.66$

Residual Sum of Squares = 5.14×10^{22}

F-statistic = 6.04

Durbin-Watson statistic = 1.61

---

[9] Note that there is no WEEKEND^2 term. WEEKEND is a dummy variable that takes a value of either 0 or 1. Since $0^2 = 0$ and $1^2 = 1$, WEEKEND^2 = WEEKEND. WEEKEND^2 and WEEKEND cannot both be included in the regression because they are exactly the same; there would be perfect multicollinearity if both were included.

8-4 TREATING THE DISEASE

The best way to treat heteroskedasticity is to redesign the model so that the heteroskedasticity does not exist in the first place. Often, heteroskedasticity occurs because the different sizes of the observations are not accounted for. One way we can redesign the model is to divide some of the variables by the size factor Z, if such a Z is available. This standardizes the variables by adjusting them by the size of each observation. For a cross section of states, we would divide variables by state population; this gives us variables defined in *per capita* units (per person). Give careful thought to which variables should be divided by Z. Only variables that are affected by the value of Z should be divided by Z.

We can apply this treatment to Bob's concert tour model. The dependent variable, REVENUE, is likely to take on larger values in states with bigger populations. Dividing REVENUE by POPULATION adjusts the variable so that when a state has a higher value for the dependent variable, it indicates the state has higher revenue per person, not just higher total revenue because there are more people living there. Every independent variable that has a relationship with population can be divided by POPULATION. This should go a long way toward incorporating the effects of POPULATION into our model, and eliminating the heteroskedasticity. After redesigning our model in this manner, we get the regression in Equation (8-9).

$$\frac{\text{REVENUE}}{\text{POPULATION}} = B_0 + B_1 \frac{\text{ADVERTISING}}{\text{POPULATION}} + B_2 \frac{\text{STADIUM}}{\text{POPULATION}}$$
$$+ B_3 \frac{\text{CD}}{\text{POPULATION}} + B_4 \text{RADIO} + B_5 \text{WEEKEND} + e \tag{8-9}$$

Notice that RADIO and WEEKEND have not been divided by POPULATION. RADIO is an index that measures how often The Artist Formerly Known as Bob's songs are played on the radio. POPULATION does not influence the value that RADIO takes in each state. The same is true of WEEKEND; whether or not the concert takes place on a weekend has nothing to do with the state population. Table 8-E gives the results of the redesigned model, using the same data as before from Table 8-A.

Compare Tables 8-E and 8-B (page 168). The slope coefficients estimates have different values in the two models. This is because we changed the units of the dependent variable and some of the independent variables. In our redesigned model in Table 8-E, the dependent variable is now concert revenue per person in the state (not total concert revenue per state, as in Table 8-B). Likewise, ADVERTISING is now state advertising expenditures per person. ADVERTISING appeared to have a statistically significant coefficient in the original model that contained heteroskedasticity (Table 8-B). In the redesigned model (Table 8-E), the coefficient estimate for ADVERTISING/POPULATION is not statistically significant.

A Park test for the redesigned concert tour model indicates that heteroskedasticity still exists. A White test for this model gives an nR^2 test statistic of 24.20. The degrees of freedom for the White test is 19, the same in both models, because 19 slope coefficients are estimated in the White test regression. (Table 8-D gives the White test regression for the original concert tour model. The White test regression for the redesigned

Table 8-E

Results for Redesigned Concert Tour Model

Dependent variable: $\frac{\text{REVENUE}}{\text{POPULATION}}$

Variable	Coefficient	Standard Error	t-Statistic	p-Value
Constant	−0.23	0.034	−6.58	0.00
$\frac{\text{ADVERTISING}}{\text{POPULATION}}$	2.21	2.009	1.10	0.28
$\frac{\text{STADIUM}}{\text{POPULATION}}$	109.05	5.71	19.09	0.00
$\frac{\text{CD}}{\text{POPULATION}}$	7.93	5.22	1.52	0.14
RADIO	0.025	0.007	3.43	0.00
WEEKEND	0.043	0.012	3.49	0.00

Observations: 50

$R^2 = 0.98$

Adjusted $R^2 = 0.98$

Residual Sum of Squares = 0.045

F-statistic = 502.99

Durbin-Watson statistic = 1.75

model has the same number of slope coefficients, because the number of independent variables is the same.) The chi-squared critical value for a 5% significance level and 19 degrees of freedom is 30.1. Since the calculated nR^2 test statistic of 24.2 is less than the critical value of 30.1, we do not reject the null hypothesis of constant error variance. The White test does not find substantial evidence of heteroskedasticity in the redesigned model. Since the Park and White test give different outcomes in this case, we can conclude that the redesigned model still has some heteroskedasticity, but it is not nearly as serious as with the original concert model.

8-5 TREATING THE SYMPTOMS

There are two ways to suppress the heteroskedasticity problem without redesigning the model. The first approach, weighted least squares, seems like a cure for heteroskedasticity in theory, but in practice it makes the interpretation of the coefficient estimates difficult. However, weighted least squares is a popular approach to heteroskedasticity and can be useful, so you need to understand it. Another approach corrects the standard errors and t-statistics without fixing the heteroskedasticity at all.

Weighted Least Squares

The **weighted least squares (WLS)** approach assumes the heteroskedasticity present in a model is based upon a size factor Z. Consider a generic regression model with two independent variables in it:

$$Y = B_0 + B_1X_1 + B_2X_2 + e \qquad\qquad\text{(8-10)}$$

Suppose this model has heteroskedasticity of the type described by Equation (8-3) where the error term variance is equal to σ^2Z^2. The size of the errors will be proportional to Z in this case. We can force the heteroskedasticity from the model by dividing everything in the regression by Z. This standardizes the errors so they follow the OLS classical assumptions, making heteroskedasticity no longer a problem. This method of dividing by Z, called weighted least squares, is a specific form of generalized least squares (GLS). We can use generalized least squares to transform a regression that does not meet the classical assumptions into one that does. Dividing both sides of Equation (8-10) by Z gives

$$\frac{Y}{Z} = \frac{B_0}{Z} + B_1\frac{X_1}{Z} + B_2\frac{X_2}{Z} + \frac{e}{Z} \qquad\qquad\text{(8-11)}$$

Since the magnitude of e is positively related to the size of Z, it can be shown that e/Z = u, where u is an error term that meets the classical assumptions.

$$\frac{Y}{Z} = \frac{B_0}{Z} + B_1\frac{X_1}{Z} + B_2\frac{X_2}{Z} + u \qquad\qquad\text{(8-12)}$$

`Equation (8-12) is a weighted least squares regression, but there is something odd about it. There is no intercept in the regression. B_0 was the intercept, but now it is divided by the size factor Z, so that it represents a slope coefficient for an independent variable defined as 1/Z, the inverse of Z. Without an intercept, the regression line is forced through the origin, changing the slope estimates (see Section 1-2). Typically, an intercept is added to the regression. Let a_0 be the intercept.

$$\frac{Y}{Z} = a_0 + \frac{B_0}{Z} + B_1\frac{X_1}{Z} + B_2\frac{X_2}{Z} + u \qquad\qquad\text{(8-13)}$$

Equation (8-13) is a weighted least squares regression. Every variable, including the dependent variable Y, is divided by the size factor Z that determines the error variance. Another way to look at it is that each observation is weighted by 1/Z, the inverse of Z, so that the error variance is constant.

The problem with weighted least squares as shown by Equation (8-13) is that the slope coefficients are hard to interpret. The meaning of B_0 has changed. Originally the intercept, B_0 is now a slope coefficient for the independent variable 1/Z. The variable 1/Z was not even part of the original regression. If, according to theory, 1/Z is a legitimate independent variable, it should have been included in the regression in the first place. If 1/Z is not an appropriate independent variable, it should not be in the regression. The interpretation of B_1 and B_2 has also changed. In the original regression, Equation (8-10),

B_1 is the slope coefficient for X_1. Now B_1 is the slope coefficient of X_1/Z. If theory says that X_1, not X_1/Z, belongs in the model, then we want to estimate the slope coefficient that relates X_1 to Y, not X_1/Z. In this case, B_1 in the WLS model doesn't tell us what we want to know, since B_1 Equation (8-13) is the slope coefficient for X_1/Z, not X_1. On the other hand, if X_1/Z is supposed to be in the model according to theory, we should put it in the original regression rather than obtaining it indirectly by using weighted least squares. This same reasoning is also true for B_2.

Interpreting the coefficients becomes even more complicated if Z is included as an independent variable in the original model. Suppose the original OLS regression with heteroskedasticity is

$$Y = B_0 + B_1X_1 + B_2Z + e \qquad \text{(8-14)}$$

Applying weighted least squares to Equation (8-14) means that we divide each term by Z:

$$\frac{Y}{Z} = \frac{B_0}{Z} + B_1\frac{X_1}{Z} + B_2\frac{Z}{Z} + \frac{e}{Z} \qquad \text{(8-15)}$$

As before, e/Z is the same as u, where u is an error term with a constant variance.

$$\frac{Y}{Z} = \frac{B_0}{Z} + B_1\frac{X_1}{Z} + B_2 + u \qquad \text{(8-16)}$$

Since Z/Z is 1, B_2 ends up being by itself with no independent variable next to it. This means that B_2 becomes the intercept instead of B_0. B_0 is now the slope coefficient for $1/Z$, but $1/Z$ was not an independent variable in the original OLS regression (8-14). Z was an independent variable in the original regression, but in the WLS regression (8-16), Z does not appear directly as an independent variable; it only appears as $1/Z$. This makes it hard to interpret the WLS coefficients. None of the coefficients (B_0, B_1, or B_2) in Equation (8-16) can be easily interpreted as the slope coefficient for Z. Econometrics software will report B_0 as a slope coefficient when it is the intercept in the original OLS model. B_2 will be listed in the results as an intercept even though it is a slope coefficient in the original model. Weighted least squares is a popular technique, but interpreting the results can be confusing. Redesigning the model makes it easier to interpret the results.

Weighted least squares can be applied to Bob's concert tour model. POPULATION is a good choice for Z. The original regression, Equation (8-4), is reproduced here:

$$\text{REVENUE} = B_0 + B_1\text{ADVERTISING} + B_2\text{STADIUM} + B_3\text{CD}$$
$$+ B_4\text{RADIO} + B_5\text{WEEKEND} + e \qquad \text{(8-4)}$$

Since POPULATION is not an independent variable in (8-4), the weighted least squares appropriate here matches the form of Equation (8-13). The WLS regression looks like

$$\frac{\text{REVENUE}}{\text{POPULATION}} = a_0 + B_0 \frac{1}{\text{POPULATION}} + B_1 \frac{\text{ADVERTISING}}{\text{POPULATION}}$$

$$+ B_2 \frac{\text{STADIUM}}{\text{POPULATION}} + B_3 \frac{\text{CD}}{\text{POPULATION}} \qquad (8\text{-}17)$$

$$+ B_4 \frac{\text{RADIO}}{\text{POPULATION}} + B_5 \frac{\text{WEEKEND}}{\text{POPULATION}} + u$$

Table 8-F gives the WLS results for Bob's concert tour model. Notice that the software reports the dependent variable as REVENUE even though it is really REVENUE/POP-ULATION. The same is true for all the independent variables. In Table 8-F, ADVER-TISING is really ADVERTISING/POPULATION. STADIUM is really STADIUM/POPULATION, and so on.

The WLS results in Table 8-F appear somewhat similar to the OLS results that exhibit heteroskedasticity in Table 8-B (page 168). However, interpreting the results is not as straightforward. For example, consider the slope estimate for WEEKEND. In the OLS results (Table 8-B) the slope estimate for WEEKEND is 356,003. If the concert takes place on a weekend, on average concert revenues will be \$356,003 higher, hold-ing the other independent variables constant. The WLS results in Table 8-F give the slope estimate for WEEKEND as 695,840. WEEKEND in Table 8-F is really WEEKEND/POPULATION, but WEEKEND divided by POPULATION doesn't make sense. WEEKEND takes either a value of 1 when the concert is on a Friday or Saturday night and 0 for other nights. This means that WEEKEND/POPULATION has a value of 1 divided by the population if the concert is Friday or Saturday, and 0 otherwise. The slope estimate value of 695,840 does not mean the same thing as the 356,003 did in the OLS results. In fact, it is not clear what the 695,840 value means. This demonstrates the problem with interpreting weighted least squares results. Redesigning the model to eliminate heteroskedasticity is preferable.

Correcting Standard Errors and t-Statistics for Heteroskedasticity

In this method you eliminate one of the main symptoms or problems with het-eroskedasticity, but leave the heteroskedasticity intact in the model. The standard errors and the t-statistics will be inaccurate when ordinary least squares is used to estimate a regression that has heteroskedasticity. Halbert White, who invented the White test, also figured out how to calculate standard errors more accurately when heteroskedasticity is present.[10] His method for calculating the standard errors works best when the sample

---

[10] Halbert White, "A Heteroskedasticity-Consistent Covariance Matrix Estimator and a Direct Test for Het-eroskedasticity," *Econometrica,* Vol. 48, 1980, pp. 817–838. Another technique that can be used to calculate the standard errors when heteroskedasticity is present is given in W. K. Newey and K. D. West, "A Simple, Positive Semi-Definite Heteroskedasticity and Autocorrelation Consistent Covariance Matrix," *Economet-rica,* Vol. 55, 1987, pp. 703–708.

Table 8-F

Weighted Least Squares Results for Concert Tour Model

Dependent variable: REVENUE
Weighting series: POPULATION

Variable	Coefficient	Standard Error	t-Statistic	p-Value
Constant	−262,544.2	170,660.9	−1.54	0.13
ADVERTISING	4.95	1.06	4.66	0.00
STADIUM	24.58	10.35	2.38	0.02
CD	8.38	5.58	1.50	0.14
RADIO	393,140.5	121,455.4	3.24	0.00
WEEKEND	695,840.4	146,630.9	4.75	0.00

Observations: 50

$R^2 = 0.99$

Adjusted $R^2 = 0.99$

Residual Sum of Squares = 7.44×10^{12}

F-statistic = 220.77

Durbin-Watson statistic = 2.03

size is large, and it is included in some econometrics programs. With better estimates of the standard errors, the t-statistics will be more accurate. Usually the standard errors corrected for heteroskedasticity are larger than the uncorrected standard errors. The t-statistics will be smaller when calculated using the corrected standard errors, but they will be more accurate. The details of White's method are presented in advanced courses. The method involves a more complicated concept for heteroskedasticity than the size factor Z idea. Applying White's method to Bob's concert tour model gives the results in Table 8-G.

The coefficient estimates, R^2, adjusted R^2, and F-statistic are the same as those in Table 8-B (page 168). Only the standard errors and t-statistics are different. Now that the standard errors have been corrected for heteroskedasticity, the t-statistics are lower, except for the WEEKEND coefficient's t-statistic. The most importance difference is that the slope coefficient for ADVERTISING is now insignificant. Without correcting the standard errors for heteroskedasticity, we would mistakenly believe that the ADVERTISING coefficient is significant at a 5% error level (see Table 8-B). White's method for correcting standard errors for heteroskedasticity is useful, but it does not eliminate the problem. The slope estimates will still come from distributions that have greater variances than if there was no heteroskedasticity. You are less likely to get an estimate that is close to the true value. A redesigned model with no heteroskedasticity is still better.

Table 8-G

Results for Concert Tour Model with Standard Errors and t-Statistics Corrected for Heteroskedasticity (Using White's Method)

Dependent variable: REVENUE

Variable	Coefficient	Standard Error	t-Statistic	p-Value
Constant	73,215.34	95,545.02	0.77	0.45
ADVERTISING	3.15	1.95	1.61	0.11
STADIUM	34.66	10.02	3.46	0.00
CD	8.30	8.28	1.00	0.32
RADIO	300,425.69	80,135.47	3.75	0.00
WEEKEND	356,003.51	78,030.18	4.56	0.00

Observations: 50

$R^2 = 0.96$

Adjusted $R^2 = 0.95$

Residual Sum of Squares $= 2.12 \times 10^{12}$

F-statistic $= 201.97$

Durbin-Watson statistic $= 1.93$

SUMMARY

1. One of the OLS classical assumptions is that the error term must be **homoskedastic**: It must have a constant variance. This does not mean that each error term observation has the same size; it means that each error term observation comes from the same probability distribution. When **heteroskedasticity** is present, the error term observations come from different probability distributions that have different variances. Heteroskedasticity most often occurs in cross-section data where there are large differences in size among the observations.

2. A common form of heteroskedasticity occurs when the error variance follows the magnitude of a factor called **Z**. Z can be an independent variable from the model, or it can be a variable that is not part of the model at all. Usually Z is a measure of the size of each observation, such as state population.

3. Heteroskedasticity often comes from a specification error. If the model does not adequately account for the different sizes of the observations, this can cause heteroskedasticity.

4. Heteroskedasticity
   - leaves the coefficient estimates unbiased.
   - increases the variance of the coefficient estimates.
   - makes the estimated standard errors given by ordinary least squares too small. This is a serious problem because it makes the t-statistics too large.

The misleadingly large t-statistics can make the researcher think that a slope estimate is statistically significant when it is not.

5. Two common tests for heteroskedasticity are the Park test and the White test. The **Park test** checks for heteroskedasticity with respect to a size factor Z, where the researcher chooses the Z used. The **White test** is a more general test for heteroskedasticity, but it does not confirm that heteroskedasticity is related to a specific size factor Z.

6. The best way to treat heteroskedasticity is to redesign the model so that the heteroskedasticity does not exist in the first place. Often, heteroskedasticity occurs because the different sizes of the observations are not accounted for in the model. One way to redesign the model is to divide some of the variables by the size factor Z, if such a Z is available. This standardizes the variables by adjusting them by the size of each observation. For example, for a cross section of states, divide variables by state population, making the variables stated in units per person.

7. There are two ways to treat heteroskedasticity if redesigning the model is not an option. In **weighted least squares**, all the variables, dependent and independent, are divided by a size factor Z. Another approach is to leave the heteroskedasticity alone, and correct the estimated standard errors, so that the t-statistics will be correct even though heteroskedasticity is still present.

EXERCISES

1. Try to explain these terms without looking them up.
   - homoskedastic
   - heteroskedasticity
   - size factor Z
   - Park test
   - White test
   - weighted least squares

2. Why is heteroskedasticity normally associated with cross-section regressions, but not with time-series regressions?

3. a. Heteroskedasticity, when left untreated, can leave a researcher who has found statistically significant results open to criticism. Explain why.
   b. What other common econometric problem has the same setback as your answer to part a?

4. Heteroskedasticity causes problems for ordinary least squares regression. Explain the heteroskedasticity problem in a simple way as you would to a friend who doesn't know much about econometrics.

5. For each cross-section model described here, comment on whether the model is likely to have heteroskedasticity. If heteroskedasticity may be a problem, suggest a variable for the size factor Z. Your suggestion for Z does not necessarily have to be one of the variables in the model.
   a. Dependent variable: Family food expenditures
      Independent variables: Income, Consumer price index measuring the cost of food
   b. Dependent variable: Students' scores on an exam

Independent variables: Number of lectures student missed, Student's grade point average prior to beginning of class

c. Dependent variable: Number of defective lamps manufactured each day in a factory

Independent variable: Number of workers who call in sick that day and are replaced by temporary workers

d. Dependent variable: Number of eggs laid per hen in a week

Independent variables: Age of the hen, Hours of daylight (Hens produce fewer eggs in the winter when there are less hours of daylight, unless they are exposed to artificial light.)

6. How would you improve the models described in Exercise 5? What independent variables would you add, and/or what would you do differently?

7. List the steps in the Park test for heteroskedasticity. (See if you can do this without looking at the text.) Why do these steps lead to a test that works for heteroskedasticity?

8. One method of dealing with heteroskedasticity corrects the standard errors for the effects of heteroskedasticity and leaves the actual model alone. Discuss the advantages and disadvantages of this approach.

9. a. Without looking at the text, explain how weighted least squares works.

   b. What is the major problem with using weighted least squares?

10. a. How do these two approaches differ: weighted least squares and redesigning a model that exhibits heteroskedasticity?

    b. If heteroskedasticity is present, why is it better to redesign the model than to use weighted least squares?

11. The Park test checks for heteroskedasticity using a size factor Z chosen by the researcher. In this chapter, we conducted a Park test for the concert tour model using population as our size factor Z. We found evidence of heteroskedasticity. Conduct the test again, using the CD variable as Z instead of population.

12. The professional wrestling model in Chapter 5 uses cross-section data consisting of different individuals. Using the data in Table 5-A, conduct a White test to see if there is evidence of heteroskedasticity.

13. Data for the following cross-section model are given in Exercise 13 in Chapter 5.

$$\text{CONSUMPTION} = B_0 + B_1\text{INCOME} + B_2\text{WEALTH} + e$$

Use the data from Exercise 13 to decide if there is a heteroskedasticity problem. How do you know?

14. Section 8-1 mentions a tax revenue model, but does not present regression results for the model. Consider this cross-section tax revenue model:

$$\text{TAXREV} = B_0 + B_1\text{GSP} + B_2\text{UNEMPLOYMENT} + e$$

where

TAXREV = each state's tax revenues for 2000, in millions of dollars

GSP = gross state product for 2000 (similar to GDP except it measures the gross domestic product of each state), in millions of dollars

UNEMPLOYMENT = state unemployment rate (%) for 2000

Note that TAXREV and GSP are nominal values, not adjusted for inflation. Data for the model are given in the following table.

Data for Tax Revenue Model

State	TAXREV	GSP	UNEMPLOYMENT
AL	6,438.438	119,921	4.6
AK	1,423.287	27,747	6.6
AZ	8,100.737	156,303	3.9
AR	4,870.561	67,724	4.4
CA	83,807.960	1,344,623	4.9
CO	7,075.047	167,918	2.7
CT	10,171.240	159,288	2.3
DE	2,132.131	36,336	4.0
FL	24,817.260	472,105	3.6
GA	13,511.280	296,142	3.7
HI	3,334.743	42,364	4.3
ID	2,377.251	37,031	4.9
IL	22,788.800	467,284	4.4
IN	10,104.350	192,195	3.2
IA	5,185.394	89,600	2.6
KS	4,848.235	85,063	3.7
KY	7,694.610	118,508	4.1
LA	6,512.382	137,700	5.5
ME	2,661.080	35,981	3.5
MD	10,354.450	186,108	3.9
MA	16,152.870	284,934	2.6
MI	22,756.400	325,384	3.6
MN	13,338.530	184,766	3.3

(*continued*)

State	TAX REV	GSP	UNEMPLOYMENT
MS	4,711.594	67,315	5.7
MO	8,571.548	178,845	3.5
MT	1,410.760	21,777	4.9
NE	2,981.047	56,072	3.0
NV	3,717.255	74,745	4.1
NH	1,696.085	47,708	2.8
NJ	18,147.600	363,089	3.8
NM	3,743.178	54,364	4.9
NY	41,735.840	799,202	4.6
NC	15,315.390	281,741	3.6
ND	1,172.373	18,283	3.0
OH	19,676.370	372,640	4.1
OK	5,840.022	91,773	3.0
OR	5,945.675	118,637	4.9
PA	22,466.910	403,985	4.2
RI	2,034.909	36,453	4.1
SC	6,381.391	113,377	3.9
SD	927.245	23,192	2.3
TN	7,739.590	178,362	3.9
TX	27,424.140	742,274	4.2
UT	3,978.697	68,549	3.2
VT	1,483.155	18,411	2.9
VA	12,648.040	261,355	2.2
WA	12,567.380	219,937	5.2
WV	3,343.266	42,271	5.5
WI	12,575.190	173,478	3.5
WY	963.650	19,294	3.9

      a. Before you estimate the model and conduct any tests, do you think this model might have a heteroskedasticity problem? Why or why not?

      b. Estimate the model using the data provided.

      c. Conduct a White test. Do the results of this test support your answer to part a? Chi^2

      d. Are there other potential problems with this model?

15. a. Use the population data from Table 8-A and weighted least squares to estimate the model from Exercise 14. Using POPULATION as Z (even though POPULATION does not appear in the model).

      b. Write a new formulation for the model that could address the heteroskedasticity problem, using the POPULATION variable given in Table 8-A.

      c. Estimate the model you wrote in part b.

      d. Conduct a test (of your choice) to see if heteroskedasticity is present in the new model you estimated in part c.

      e. Which do you think is more useful, the results you found in part a or in part c?

9

Pooling Data Across Time and Space

After reading this chapter, you will know:

- How cross-section and time-series data can be combined to form one data set.

- Different methods of estimating regressions using combined cross-section time-series data sets.

- The difference between various estimation methods and when to use each one.

Pooled data combine cross-section and time-series data together. In this chapter, we examine special techniques for estimating regression models that used pooled data. Recall that cross-section models use observations at the same point in time but from different entities. The data can be from different countries, firms, people, or some other entity, as long as they are measured for the same time period. Time-series data are measured across different time periods, but for the same country, firm, person, or other entity. Pooled cross-section time-series data contain data for different cross-section entities and for different time periods. For example, a pooled data set concerning immigration might include the population of each state for each year from 1971 through 2000. There are different values for the population of each state, and within each state, there are different values for population over time. This gives 1500 (50×30) different values for the population variable, since there are 50 different state values for each year and 30 years of data. The time-series data show changes in population over time, and the cross-section data show differences in population across states. Pooling these two data sets enables us to study both in the same model. Pooled data contains information across both time and space.

If the data set contains observations from the same countries, firms, or people (or other entities) over time, then the pooled data are called **panel data**. If the different time periods contain data for different countries, firms, or people, then the pooled data are not panel data. Panel data are often more useful than nonpanel pooled data, because the countries, firms, or people are held constant over time with panel data. This allows us to compare what happens across time more easily.

In this chapter, we examine different ways to estimate regressions using pooled cross-section time-series data. In Section 9-1, we discuss the simplest ways to use pooled data and the problems that can result. More complicated (but often necessary) methods follow in Sections 9-2 through 9-4. Section 9-5 summarizes criteria that you should consider when you are deciding which estimation method to use.

9-1 MIXING THE DATA: DIFFERENCES BETWEEN TIME AND SPACE DISAPPEAR

Throughout this chapter, we use an example with data from different industries and different time periods to illustrate the various ways to estimate pooled cross-section time-series regressions. The industries are (1) iron and steel; (2) rubber and plastics; (3) stone, clay, and glass; and (4) textiles. These categories are cross-sectional in nature. The variables are

SHIP = value of goods shipped by an industry

   each year, in millions of dollars, adjusted for inflation

EMPLOY = number of employees in an industry,

   for each year, in thousands of employees

OVERTIME = average number of overtime hours

   worked per week, in an industry, for each year

Values for these variables have been collected for 1980 through 2000, for each of the four industries mentioned above; this gives us the time-series aspect of the data. For each year from 1980 to 2000, there are four SHIP values, one for each industry. Overall, there are 84 values for SHIP, EMPLOY, and OVERTIME. (4 industries multiplied by 21 years). Since the four industries are the same ones in every time period, these pooled data are panel data.

We also use a new naming system for the variables. Each variable name is followed by an underscore _, and then the name of the industry that the data came from. For example, SHIP_TEXTILE is the value of goods shipped for the textile industry for each year from 1980 through 2000.[1] EMPLOY_RUBBER is the number of rubber industry employees for each year, 1980–2000. Table 9-A gives 1980–2000 data for the four industries. In some regressions, the names SHIP, EMPLOY, and OVERTIME will be used to indicate that all the values of those variables are used, even though they come from different industries. For example, the variable SHIP is the values of SHIP_IRON, SHIP_RUBBER, SHIP_STONE, and SHIP_TEXTILE. As mentioned, SHIP has 84 observations because SHIP_IRON, SHIP_RUBBER, SHIP_STONE, and SHIP_TEXTILE each have 21 observations.

Table 9-A gives the data we will be using. Looking down the second column of the table, we see all the values for SHIP_IRON from 1980 through 2000. Each row represents one year. Going down the table from one row to the next is like traveling through time. Now consider the top row, the data for 1980. Looking across a row is like traveling across space. The first three columns of the row show values for three variables

---

[1] This convention for naming pooled variables is convenient for running pooled regressions in Eviews. See the Eviews help under "pool naming series."

in the iron and steel industry for 1980. In the next three columns we travel across space to a different industry—the rubber industry—but it is still 1980.

We could analyze this data by running four separate time-series regressions, one for each industry. We would use the data from the first three columns of the table for the first regression; the data from the second three columns for the second regression, and so on.

$$\text{SHIP\_IRON} = B_0 + B_1\text{EMPLOY\_IRON} + B_2\text{OVERTIME\_IRON} + e \quad \textbf{(9-1)}$$

$$\text{SHIP\_RUBBER} = B_3 + B_4\text{EMPLOY\_RUBBER}$$
$$+ B_5\text{OVERTIME\_RUBBER} + e \quad \textbf{(9-2)}$$

$$\text{SHIP\_STONE} = B_6 + B_7\text{EMPLOY\_STONE}$$
$$+ B_8\text{OVERTIME\_STONE} + e \quad \textbf{(9-3)}$$

$$\text{SHIP\_TEXTILE} = B_9 + B_{10}\text{EMPLOY\_TEXTILE}$$
$$+ B_{11}\text{OVERTIME\_TEXTILE} + e \quad \textbf{(9-4)}$$

In Equations (9-1) through (9-4), the coefficients have all been given different subscripts to show that they can have different values. The intercept in Equation (9-2) is B_3, not B_0 as it is in Equation (9-1). This tells us the intercepts can be different in each equation. The same is true with the slope coefficients. The slope coefficient for EMPLOY has a different subscript in each equation to show that its slope coefficient can be different for each regression. There is no reason to believe that the relationship between the number of people employed and the value of goods shipped will be the same in each industry. The coefficients can differ across space (across industries) since we have set up a different regression for each industry, but the coefficients remain the same across time. For example, we have assumed that the relationship between the number of employees and the value of goods shipped in the rubber industry remains the same throughout the 1980–2000 time period. Each regression has its own error term e that has nothing to do with the error terms from the other regressions.

Using the data in Table 9-A for the four regressions in Equations (9-1) to (9-4) gives each regression a sample size of 21 (there are 21 years of data for each industry, and each industry is considered separately). This may not be the best way to study the relationships between employment, overtime, and value of shipments for these industries. By estimating the regressions separately, we are assuming that the four industries have nothing to do with each other. Also we are assuming that an event that affects one of the industries does not affect any of the others. A general slowdown in the economy could affect all four of these industries. By using four separate equations to estimate the model, we miss out on information contained in the data set for one industry that affects another. For example, SHIP_STONE, EMPLOY_STONE, or OVERTIME_ STONE may contain information that would be of value in estimating the coefficients for one of the other industries. This means our estimates will be less accurate. However, if we combine the data for the four industries, our sample size increases, and we can use all the available information to estimate the coefficients.

You may be thinking of another possibility—running separate cross-section regressions for each year, instead of a separate time-series for each industry. This does not

Table 9-A

Pooled Cross-Section Time-Series Data for Industry Model

Year	IRON AND STEEL INDUSTRY			RUBBER AND PLASTIC INDUSTRY		
	SHIP_IRON	EMPLOY_IRON	OVERTIME_IRON	SHIP_RUBBER	EMPLOY_RUBBER	OVERTIME_RUBBER
1980	15,334.61	253.41	3.42	59,650.52	763.82	2.74
1981	14,240.31	220.81	3.04	60,685.18	772.25	3.03
1982	9,990.67	164.39	1.87	59,385.49	729.28	2.66
1983	9,375.50	139.55	2.80	63,122.49	742.83	3.54
1984	11,002.73	143.05	3.69	70,211.46	813.19	3.91
1985	10,029.13	131.44	3.37	70,272.70	818.22	3.58
1986	9,428.12	119.38	3.72	71,508.25	822.45	3.80
1987	9,353.58	114.26	4.37	76,245.54	842.08	4.10
1988	10,314.71	115.35	4.83	80,742.72	865.64	4.13
1989	10,157.57	110.74	3.95	81,663.89	887.95	3.77
1990	9,537.09	101.34	3.52	80,553.61	887.58	3.59
1991	8,601.11	92.33	3.06	77,687.57	861.88	3.58
1992	8,452.31	85.66	3.43	80,954.75	877.63	4.07
1993	8,892.53	82.35	4.12	84,991.29	908.99	4.38
1994	9,602.97	84.38	5.21	91,175.58	953.13	4.70
1995	9,997.81	86.02	4.36	95,639.72	979.92	4.13
1996	10,160.66	81.95	3.97	95,930.51	982.69	4.24
1997	10,478.04	80.85	4.41	97,559.34	996.10	4.53
1998	11,100.66	80.63	3.81	97,023.26	1004.91	4.41
1999	10,999.85	76.60	3.97	98,846.77	1005.68	4.48
2000	10,084.79	71.66	3.77	100,060.40	1004.78	4.24

Data are available at the text website or http://www.economagic.com or http://www.bls.gov/data/, from the U.S. Bureau of Labor Statistics. SHIP_IRON, SHIP_RUBBER, SHIP_STONE, and SHIP_TEXTILE are adjusted for inflation using the U.S. urban consumer price index, where the years 1982–1984 are set equal to 100.

Table 9-A

(Continued)

Year	STONE, GLASS, CLAY INDUSTRY			TEXTILE INDUSTRY		
	SHIP_STONE	EMPLOY_ STONE	OVERTIME_ STONE	SHIP_ TEXTILE	EMPLOY_ TEXTILE	OVERTIME_ TEXTILE
1980	53,966.63	648.00	3.77	57,343.72	847.68	3.18
1981	50,833.10	643.17	3.78	55,276.33	822.97	2.97
1982	45,093.26	538.75	3.49	49,239.38	749.43	2.18
1983	47,888.55	557.92	4.13	53,948.8	741.33	3.51
1984	51,116.00	593.08	4.74	54,230.07	746.13	3.23
1985	51,894.33	577.17	4.77	50,763.87	702.18	3.21
1986	54,059.76	615.83	4.84	52,174.87	702.93	4.05
1987	54,105.17	599.58	5.05	55,258.09	725.29	4.41
1988	53,395.81	610.25	5.16	54,649.00	728.25	3.95
1989	51,408.17	639.83	5.13	54,260.55	719.79	4.05
1990	48,774.54	629.33	4.83	50,156.00	691.44	3.56
1991	44,023.99	579.83	4.55	48,049.93	670.04	4.08
1992	44,557.07	548.67	4.86	50,423.80	674.12	4.28
1993	45,417.94	534.33	5.19	51,194.69	675.11	4.44
1994	48,055.32	556.92	5.73	52,640.92	676.38	4.68
1995	49,829.60	586.17	5.53	52,416.49	663.17	4.19
1996	52,561.05	607.17	5.87	51,159.07	626.54	4.28
1997	56,206.62	614.50	5.87	52,250.65	616.09	4.63
1998	59,011.09	592.25	6.28	49,460.05	597.58	4.47
1999	62,298.06	628.92	6.38	47,040.07	560.23	4.34
2000	60,494.19	599.92	6.16	44,531.36	541.31	4.27

work for the data in Table 9-A. Running separate cross-section regressions for these data would involve running 21 different regressions, one for each year. The first regression would use the first row of data from Table 9-A; this would be a cross section for 1980. The last regression would use the last row of data, covering the year 2000. The coefficients could change through time, since there is a different regression for each year, but they would remain the same across industries or space. Each regression's sample size is only 4, since for each year, we have data on four industries. This approach seems to make sense for a data set with many industries and only a few years, but it would still be misguided. Such an approach assumes that whatever happens in one year has nothing to do with the next year.

In the rest of this chapter, we examine estimation techniques that allow us to use all the information in our industry data to find the regression estimates. Instead of running separate time-series or separate cross-section regressions, we will combine the data across time and industry. The simplest way to do this is to assume that the intercept and slope coefficients are the same over time and for all the industries. Here is the regression:

$$SHIP = B_0 + B_1 EMPLOY + B_2 OVERTIME + e \qquad \text{(9-5)}$$

Recall that SHIP includes the values for SHIP_IRON, SHIP_RUBBER, SHIP_STONE, and SHIP_TEXTILE.[2] The fact that different industries are involved is simply ignored. The same is true for EMPLOY and OVERTIME. The sample size is 84; we will use all the values in Table 9-A to estimate the regression. This is the proper regression *if* the true value of the intercept stays the same for every industry and for every year. The estimate of B_1 found by regressing Equation (9-5) will be useful *only if* the relationship between the number of employees and the value of goods shipped is the same for every industry and every year in the sample. This is also true for B_2. Pooling the data together in this manner using Equation (9-5) ignores differences in time and space. This is the same as saying the coefficients stay the same over time and across industries. Table 9-B gives the results using data from Table 9-A to estimate Equation (9-5).

Both independent variables have positive coefficient estimates that are significant at a 1% error level. It makes sense that more employees and more overtime would be associated with a higher value of goods shipped. The 86.74 estimate for B_1 indicates that if 1000 employees are added, the value of goods shipped increases on average by 86.74 million dollars, keeping hours of overtime worked constant. (EMPLOY is defined in thousands of employees, and SHIP in millions of dollars, adjusted for inflation.) For our model to make sense, it must be true that if one industry has 1000 more employees than another industry (but the same hours of overtime) the effect on SHIP is the same as if an industry adds 1000 workers from one year to the next. This seems unlikely. It seems more probable that adding 1000 workers will affect SHIP differently in different industries. In many cases (including this example), the true value of the coefficients is not the same across both time and cross-sectional entities. Note that a Durbin-Watson statistic would not tell us anything here, since the regression uses both cross-section and time-series data. The Durbin-Watson statistic has meaning only for

---

[2] Eviews uses the convention SHIP?, the variable name followed by a question mark, omitting industry names, to indicate a variable that includes data for all the industries (or other cross-sectional entities).

Table 9-B

Results for Industry Model with Pooled Cross-Section Time-Series Data (Intercept and slope coefficients are forced to be constant across time and industries)

Dependent variable: SHIP

Variable	Coefficient	Standard Error	t-Statistic	p-Value
Constant	$-14{,}040.10$	3,234.08	-4.34	0.00
EMPLOY	86.74	2.18	39.87	0.00
OVERTIME	3,168.47	731.48	4.33	0.00

Observations: 84

$R^2 = 0.95$

Adjusted $R^2 = 0.95$

Residual Sum of Squares = 2,675,700,446

F-statistic = 826.39

time-series data. In the next three sections, we discuss other estimation techniques that you can use with pooled data.

9-2 SEEMINGLY UNRELATED REGRESSIONS ARE ACTUALLY RELATED

Seemingly Unrelated Regression can be a confusing name. Seemingly unrelated regression (SUR) is a set of regression equations that *seems* unrelated but is in reality related.[3] Seemingly unrelated regression equations don't appear to be related because they resemble Equations (9-1) through (9-4). In Equations (9-1) through (9-4) we made the bold (and mistaken) assumption that the industries had nothing to do with each other, so we could estimate each regression separately. Recall Equations (9-1) through (9-4).

$$SHIP\_IRON = B_0 + B_1 EMPLOY\_IRON + B_2 OVERTIME\_IRON + e \quad \textbf{(9-1)}$$

$$\begin{aligned} SHIP\_RUBBER = B_3 &+ B_4 EMPLOY\_RUBBER \\ &+ B_5 OVERTIME\_RUBBER + e \end{aligned} \quad \textbf{(9-2)}$$

$$\begin{aligned} SHIP\_STONE = B_6 &+ B_7 EMPLOY\_STONE \\ &+ B_8 OVERTIME\_STONE + e \end{aligned} \quad \textbf{(9-3)}$$

$$\begin{aligned} SHIP\_TEXTILE = B_9 &+ B_{10} EMPLOY\_TEXTILE \\ &+ B_{11} OVERTIME\_TEXTILE + e \end{aligned} \quad \textbf{(9-4)}$$

---

[3] A. Zellner, "An Efficient Method of Estimating Seemingly Unrelated Regression and Test for Aggregation Bias," *Journal of the American Statistical Association*, Vol. 57, 1962, pp. 348–368.

In seemingly unrelated regression the regressions actually do have something to do with each other. **Seeming unrelated regression** allows the error terms to be correlated across separate but related regressions. The e's in the four regressions above do not have to be independent from each other in any one time period. This way the SUR procedure can use the correlation between error terms to improve the estimates. If we run the regressions separately, we have to assume that error terms in different equations are not correlated. Any correlation between error terms in regressions is valuable information; it is trying to tell us something. It could be telling us that there is some change or event in that time period that affects more than one industry. The change is not captured by any of the independent variables, and that is why it shows up in the error term. The SUR procedure uses this information to improve the coefficient estimates.

Most econometrics programs have commands that run SUR automatically. Seemingly unrelated regression uses these steps:

1. Each equation is estimated separately using ordinary least squares.
2. Error term observations are saved from the regressions in step 1.
3. Error term observations are used to estimate the error variances and correlations between error terms for different regressions.[4]
4. Estimated error variances and correlations are utilized in a generalized least squares procedure to estimate the regressions.

Seemingly unrelated regression is unbiased for large sample sizes (it is consistent). There are two situations in which seemingly unrelated regression turns out the same as running separate OLS regressions: (1) if the correlation between error terms in the individual regressions is zero, or (2) if every value for each independent variable is the same across every equation. As an example of the second situation, if we add a measure of the U.S. money supply as an independent variable to all of the regressions in Equations (9-1) through (9-4), the values for this independent variable will be the same for all four regressions. The money supply takes the same value in any one year regardless of which industry is being studied. If all the independent variables are like this, if they take the same values across the different regressions, seemingly unrelated regression and ordinary least squares will give the same results.

We can use the SUR method and the data in Table 9-A to estimate Equations (9-1) through (9-4). The results are given in Tables 9-C through 9-F.[5] At first glance, these results seem to be separate regression results, but they are not. Estimates of error term correlations across the industries are used by the SUR procedure to improve the estimates. This is why, as stated earlier, seemingly unrelated regression actually consists

---

[4] If error term observations for the same regression are correlated, so that there is autocorrelation, a more complicated version of seemingly unrelated regression should be used. See David K. Guilkey and Peter Schmidt, "Estimation of Seemingly Unrelated Regressions with Vector Autoregressive Errors," *Journal of the American Statistical Association*, Vol. 68, 1973, pp. 642–647.

[5] The student version of Eviews offers an "analogue to seemingly unrelated regression." (See the Eviews help under pool estimation.) If this option is chosen along with the fixed effects option and separate slope estimates for each industry, the procedure produces results that are exactly the same as with seemingly unrelated regression. The results in Table 9-C through 9-F are typical SUR results, estimated with the full version of Eviews. The only difference between the two versions of Eviews is that the student version of seemingly unrelated regression does not report separate R^2 measures for each regression equation.

Table 9-C

SUR Results for Iron Industry Equation

Dependent variable: SHIP_IRON

Variable	Coefficient	Standard Error	t-Statistic	p-Value
Constant	5,367.24	1,427.20	3.76	0.00
EMPLOY_IRON	27.45	4.60	5.97	0.00
OVERTIME_IRON	477.13	294.98	1.62	0.11

Observations: 21
$R^2 = 0.66$
Adjusted $R^2 = 0.62$
Residual Sum of Squares $= 18,664,838.11$

Table 9-D

SUR Results for Iron Industry Equation

Dependent variable: SHIP_RUBBER

Variable	Coefficient	Standard Error	t-Statistic	p-Value
Constant	−51,962.17	2999.02	−17.33	0.00
EMPLOY_RUBBER	142.87	5.85	24.43	0.00
OVERTIME_RUBBER	1,704.48	961.36	1.77	0.08

Observations: 21
$R^2 = 0.99$
Adjusted $R^2 = 0.99$
Residual Sum of Squares $= 43,356,773$

Table 9-E

SUR Results for Iron Industry Equation

Dependent variable: SHIP_STONE

Variable	Coefficient	Standard Error	t-Statistic	p-Value
Constant	−4,479.77	11,191.40	−0.40	0.69
EMPLOY_STONE	69.05	18.20	3.80	0.00
OVERTIME_STONE	2,976.12	781.73	3.81	0.00

Observations: 21
$R^2 = 0.64$
Adjusted $R^2 = 0.60$
Residual Sum of Squares $= 1.85 \times 10^8$

Table 9-F

SUR Results for Iron Industry Equation

Dependent variable: SHIP_TEXT

Variable	Coefficient	Standard Error	t-Statistic	p-Value
Constant	3,596.00	4,882.37	0.74	0.46
EMPLOY_TEXT	52.05	4.66	11.18	0.00
OVERTIME_TEXT	3,140.84	544.43	5.77	0.00

Observations: 21

$R^2 = 0.835$

Adjusted $R^2 = 0.817$

Residual Sum of Squares = 31,122,367

of regressions that are related. In our example, the SUR results are similar to the OLS results for the four regressions (you can see this for yourself if you use the data in Table 9-A to run the four regressions separately using ordinary least squares). In many cases, however, seemingly unrelated regression substantially improves upon the estimates found by ordinary least squares.

9-3 THE FIXED EFFECTS MODEL: EVERYONE DESERVES A DIFFERENT INTERCEPT

The **fixed effects model** incorporates differences between firms, states, people, or other cross-sectional entity by allowing the intercept to change. The intercept is different for each firm or cross-sectional entity, but each intercept stays constant over time. The fixed effects model attributes any differences between cross-sectional entities to the intercept; it leaves the slope coefficients the same. This way, all the cross-section data can be used in one regression, along with the time-series data. The model resembles the pooled model in Section 9-1 where all the data are simply combined, but here each different entity in the cross section has its own intercept.

The fixed effects model works by using dummy variables for the intercepts. Each cross-sectional entity in the model (each firm, state, or person) has its own intercept dummy variable. This way each firm, state, or person has its own intercept. This approach would seem to land us in the dummy variable trap. Recall from Section 5-1 that the dummy variable trap occurs when we forget to leave out one of the possible dummy variables. This creates perfect multicollinearity. In a fixed effects model, we avoid the dummy variable trap by leaving out the regular B_0 intercept. This way, each dummy variable represents the intercept for that cross-section observation. If we include the regular B_0 intercept, we must omit one dummy variable. The coefficient estimates for the remaining dummy variables would represent changes in the intercept relative to the omitted dummy's entity. This is how coefficients for dummy variables are usually interpreted. However, it is much easier to omit the B_0 intercept in a fixed effects model, so that the coefficient of each dummy represents a different intercept for that entity. Let's see how this applies to our example.

First, we need dummy variables for each cross-sectional entity.

IRON = 1 if the observation is from the iron and steel industry; 0 otherwise

RUBBER = 1 if the observation is from the rubber industry; 0 otherwise

STONE = 1 if the observation is from the stone, clay, or glass industry; 0 otherwise

TEXTILE = 1 if the observation is from the textile industry; 0 otherwise

Now we can use a fixed effects model to pool the cross-section and time-series data. That way we can estimate just one regression with a sample size of 84, instead of 4 regressions, each with a sample size of 21. Recall that SHIP, EMPLOY, and OVER-TIME are made up of observations from all four industries.

$$\text{SHIP} = B_1\text{EMPLOY} + B_2\text{OVERTIME} + B_3\text{IRON} + B_4\text{RUBBER} + B_5\text{STONE} + B_6\text{TEXTILE} + e \quad (9\text{-}6)$$

There is no B_0 intercept in Equation (9-6). Instead, the regression includes all four possible dummy variables, each representing a different industry. The estimate of each dummy variable coefficient (B_3 through B_6) represents a different intercept for each industry. An observation from the iron industry makes IRON 1, and RUBBER, STONE, and TEXTILE all 0. Substituting 1 in for IRON and 0 in for RUBBER, STONE, and TEXTILE changes Equation (9-6) to

$$\text{SHIP} = B_1\text{EMPLOY} + B_2\text{OVERTIME} + B_3 + e \quad (9\text{-}7)$$

B_3, the coefficient for the dummy variable IRON, appears by itself in Equation (9-7), without an independent variable next to it, just as B_0 does when it serves as an intercept. This means that B_3 is acting as the intercept here. B_3 is the intercept whenever the observation comes from the iron industry. When an observation comes from the rubber industry, B_3 disappears from the equation since IRON is zero. RUBBER becomes 1, so B_4 will remain in the equation as the intercept. Each industry gets its own intercept. The different intercepts allow the model to capture differences between the industries. Fixed effects is really just a special type of ordinary least squares with dummy variables used with pooled cross-section time-series data. Some econometrics software includes a fixed effects option that runs fixed effects automatically, so that you do not have to add the dummy variables yourself.

The fixed effects model can also be run with a regular B_0 intercept if one dummy variable is omitted. For example, adding B_0 and omitting TEXTILE gives

$$\text{SHIP} = B_0 + B_1\text{EMPLOY} + B_2\text{OVERTIME} + B_3\text{IRON} + B_4\text{RUBBER} + B_5\text{STONE} + e \quad (9\text{-}8)$$

Here B_3 represents the change in the intercept when the iron industry is compared to the omitted entity, the textile industry.

Most researchers find it easier to interpret the regression results if all the dummy variables are included in the regression and B_0 is omitted. Recall Equation (9-6).

$$\text{SHIP} = B_1\text{EMPLOY} + B_2\text{OVERTIME} + B_3\text{IRON}$$
$$+ B_4\text{RUBBER} + B_5\text{STONE} + B_6\text{TEXTILE} + e \qquad \textbf{(9-6)}$$

Table 9-G gives fixed effects results using Equation 9-6.

Comparing Table 9-G to Tables 9-C through 9-F illustrates the potential advantage of fixed effects over seemingly unrelated regression. Fixed effects allows all the data to be used in one regression, so the sample size is much bigger. The sample size is 84 for fixed effects, but only 21 per regression with seemingly unrelated regression. The degrees of freedom for the fixed effects model is 78 ($84 - 6 = 78$). In the SUR model, the degrees of freedom is only 18 ($21 - 2 - 1 = 18$) for each equation. Only three coefficients (including the intercept) are estimated in each SUR equation, but six coefficients are estimated in the fixed effects model, because of the dummy variables. If the fixed effects model is appropriate, its estimates are likely to be more accurate because it gives us more degrees of freedom. However, a large number of cross-sectional entities will require a lot of dummy variables in the fixed effects regression, making the degrees of freedom substantially smaller than the sample size. Also note that when using fixed effects, the independent variables must vary over time. If an independent variable varies over the cross-sectional entities, but not over time, it causes a multicollinearity problem with the dummy variables. The fixed effects dummy variables pick up differences between the industries or cross-sectional entites that stay the same over time.

Table 9-G

Fixed Effects Results for the Industry Model

Dependent variable: SHIP

Variable	Coefficient	Standard Error	t-Statistic	p-Value
EMPLOY	92.19	5.38	17.15	0.00
OVERTIME	4,645.11	510.18	9.11	0.00
IRON	−17,760.74			
RUBBER	−18,691.64			
STONE	−26,686.29			
TEXTILE	−29,950.36			

Observations: 84

$R^2 = 0.99$

Adjusted $R^2 = 0.99$

Residual Sum of Squares = 790,590,705

F-statistic = 5,572.50

The R^2 for a fixed effects regression is often high, since the intercept dummy variables pick up differences between the cross-sectional entities. However, the dummy variables cannot explain why the differences between entities occur. The dummy variables are more of a "trick" to represent differences between industries; they do not support any particular explanation for why the industries might be different. The high R^2 for a fixed effects model can make it seem as if the model is providing more insight than it really is.

No standard errors or t-statistics are shown for the dummy variables in Table 9-G.[6] Since the coefficient for each dummy represents the intercept for a different industry, we want to ask, Are the intercepts for each industry actually the same? If they are, then we can use one intercept for all four industries, and we do not need to use the fixed effects model. We can go back to using Equation (9-5): SHIP = B_0 + B_1EMPLOY + B_2OVERTIME + e. If the intercepts are not all the same for the different industries, then the fixed effects model is preferable to the model in Equation (9-5). Recall that the fixed effects model for this example is

$$\text{SHIP} = B_1\text{EMPLOY} + B_2\text{OVERTIME} + B_3\text{IRON}$$
$$+ B_4\text{RUBBER} + B_5\text{STONE} + B_6\text{TEXTILE} + e \qquad \text{(9-6)}$$

Since we want to test whether all the intercepts for the different industries are the same or not, our test hypotheses are

$$H_0: B_3 = B_4 = B_5 = B_6$$

$$H_A: B_3, B_4, B_5, B_6 \text{ are not all equal.}$$

The F-test described in Section 5-3 can be used in this situation. Remember that this F-test must be calculated manually; it is not the same as the F-test that appears automatically in most regression results. The F-test formula uses numbers from both a restricted and an unrestricted regression. Recall from Chapter 5 that in a restricted regression the null hypothesis is forced to be true. In the current situation, the restricted regression is Equation (9-5) where the intercept is forced to be the same for all four industries. Equation (9-5) does not have the dummy variables and assumes a common intercept B_0. This is the same as saying that $B_3 = B_4 = B_5 = B_6$, as stated in the null hypothesis. The unrestricted regression is the fixed effects model in Equation (9-6), since it allows the intercepts (B_3, B_4, B_5, and B_6) to take a different value for each industry. The residual sum of squares is 2,675,700,466 (Table 9-B) for the restricted model and 790,590,705 (Table 9-G) for the unrestricted model. The number of restrictions, q, is 3. In the null hypothesis ($H_0: B_3 = B_4 = B_5 = B_6$), one of the coefficients, say B_3, can take any value, but then B_4, B_5, and B_6 must all take the same value as B_3. This gives us three restrictions. The degrees of freedom for the unrestricted model are not equal to n − k − 1 as they were in Section 5-3. The fixed effects model, which serves as the unrestricted model in this F-test, has n − k degrees of freedom since the model

---

[6] Eviews does not report standard errors or t-statistics for the dummy variables in a fixed effects model.

does not use B_0 as the intercept. (The -1 in $n - k - 1$ comes from the B_0, which is in most regressions.)

$$F_{q,n-k} = \frac{\dfrac{RSS_{restricted} - RSS_{unrestricted}}{q}}{\dfrac{RSS_{unrestricted}}{n - k}} = \frac{\dfrac{2,675,700,446 - 790,590,705}{3}}{\dfrac{790,590,705}{84 - 6}}$$

$$= \frac{\dfrac{1,885,109,741}{3}}{\dfrac{790,590,705}{78}} = \frac{628,369,914}{10,135,778} = 61.995$$

This F-statistic is significant at a 1% error level. (See Table D in the Appendix.) We can reject the null hypothesis that the intercept is the same for all four industries. For this example, the fixed effects model is superior to the model with just one common intercept.

The fixed effects model could be made more general by adding slope dummy variables along with the intercept dummy variables. This would allow each industry in our example to have different slope coefficients as well as different intercepts. However, a model that contains both intercept and slope dummy variables is almost the same as running separate regressions. But there is a difference. For the model with both slope and intercept dummy variables, the error variance must be the same for the whole sample, since only one regression is used. With separate regressions, the error variance can differ for each regression, so that the error variance can differ for each industry or cross-sectional entity.

9-4 THE RANDOM EFFECTS MODEL: THEY ALL MAKE THEIR OWN ERRORS

A **random effects model** incorporates differences between cross-sectional entities by allowing the intercept to change, as in the fixed effects model, but the amount of the change is random. A random effects model is appropriate if each industry or entity in the cross-section data is chosen at random to represent a larger population. The different intercepts for different cross-sectional entities are considered to be randomly drawn from a normal probability distribution. With the fixed effects model, the differences between the intercepts for different industries are considered constant, not random. The fixed effects model assumes the intercepts differ because the industries have fundamentally different characteristics. The random effects model assumes each industry in our example is drawn from a sample, and the differences between the intercepts occur because of random variation. The random effects model is often used when the cross-sectional entities are a random sample of some overall population. If the four industries in our example are randomly chosen to represent a larger population of industries, a random effects model makes sense. For a pooled cross-section time-series of the 50 states, a fixed effects model would make more sense than a random effects model, because the 50 states represent the entire U.S. population.

The random effects model pools all the data together, and at first glance looks like a regular OLS regression:

$$Y = B_0 + B_1X_1 + B_2X_2 + \cdots + B_kX_k + e \qquad (9\text{-}9)$$

Equation (9-9) has no intercept dummies as in the fixed effects model. This makes the degrees of freedom for random effects larger for the same study. The intercept B_0 used here is interpreted differently than in an OLS regression. Here B_0 represents the mean of the intercept. The actual intercept varies for each industry or cross-sectional entity. The difference in intercepts across industries or cross-sectional entities is captured by the error term e. e has two components. One component follows the OLS assumptions for an error term. The other component represents the difference between each industry's intercept and the intercept mean, B_0. This component is the same across time, but it differs for each industry. Because this component of the error term stays constant over time, the error term e in the random effects model will not follow OLS assumptions. Specifically, for any industry in our example, the error terms will be correlated across time. This means that ordinary least squares cannot be used as the estimation method.

Many econometrics software programs allow you to run random effects models automatically. The random effects procedure follows these steps:

1. OLS regression is used on the entire pooled cross-section time-series sample.
2. The error term observations from step 1 are used to estimate error variances and correlations between errors.
3. The estimates from step 2 are used to perform generalized least squares, giving estimates for the random effects model.
4. Some econometrics programs then use the results from step 3 to estimate how far each industry or cross-sectional entity's intercept is from the mean intercept, B_0.

Random effects can be applied to our industry model. The regression is

$$SHIP = B_0 + B_1EMPLOY + B_2OVERTIME + e \qquad (9\text{-}10)$$

This looks like the OLS regression in Equation (9-5) where all the industries have the same intercept. Here, however, each industry has its own intercept, but the intercept contains a random component. B_0 is the mean of the intercepts, and the difference between the mean and the actual value of the intercept is contained in the error term e. As stated, this means that the error term e will not follow OLS assumptions. Random effects is used following the steps outlined above to give the results in Table 9-H.

Comparing the results for random effects and fixed effects (Table 9-G) shows very little difference in the coefficient estimates for the two independent variables, EMPLOY and OVERTIME. In the fixed effects model, the estimate for EMPLOY's coefficient is 92.19. In the random effects model it is 91.54. Both estimates are statistically significant at a 1% error level. For OVERTIME, fixed effects gives a coefficient estimate of 4,645.11. It is 4,627.85 with random effects. Again, both estimates are statistically significant at a 1% error level. In this example, it does not seem to matter much whether a fixed effects or random effects model is used, but in other situations it can matter a lot.

Table 9-H

Random Effects Results for the Industry Model

Dependent variable: SHIP

Variable	Coefficient	Standard Error	t-Statistic	p-Value
Constant (Mean)	−22,831.07	5,664.77	−4.03	0.00
EMPLOY	91.54	5.04	18.18	0.00
OVERTIME	4,627.85	504.00	9.18	0.00
Difference from mean constant for each industry:				
IRON	5178.14			
RUBBER	4748.35			
STONE	−3361.66			
TEXTILE	−6564.83			

Observations: 84

$R^2 = 0.99$

Adjusted $R^2 = 0.99$

Residual Sum of Squares = 804,299,968

Some econometrics programs also give information so you can find estimates for each industry's intercept. Table 9-H gives an estimate that shows how each industry's intercept differs from the mean intercept, B_0.[7] The difference from the mean intercept for the iron industry is 5178.14. This means that an estimate for the iron industry intercept can be found using the mean intercept B_0 and this 5178.14 figure. This estimate is −22,831.07 + 5178.14 = −17,652.93. For the stone industry, the estimate of the intercept is −22,831.07 − 3361.66 = −26,192.73.

9-5   A COMPARISON OF SUR, FIXED EFFECTS, AND RANDOM EFFECTS

In this section we present a concise comparison of the different estimation methods for pooled cross-section time-series models. The information presented here is repeated from previous sections for convenience.

---

[7] Table 9-H resembles the standard student Eviews output for a random effects model, but the words in italics have been added for clarity. Be aware that on the student Eviews output for random effects, "C" (which usually stands for constant or intercept) is the mean of the intercept. The values on the lower half of the output table that appear to be intercept values for different cross-section categories are actually differences from the mean intercept; they are not the intercepts themselves. To make this clear, this part of Table 9-H is preceded by the author's comment *"Difference from mean constant for each industry."*

Pooled Model with a Common Intercept (Section 9-1)

1. One regression is used for the whole pooled sample, so the degrees of freedom are larger than with seemingly unrelated regression. Also, there are no intercept dummy variables, so there are more degrees of freedom than with fixed effects.
2. The intercept and slope coefficient estimates are forced to be the same for all cross-sectional entities.
3. The F-test described in Section 9-3 tells whether the intercept is the same for all cross-sectional entities. If the intercepts are not the same, consider using a different model such as the fixed effects model.

Seemingly Unrelated Regression (Section 9-2)

1. Seemingly unrelated regression allows a better use of information than ordinary least squares in running separate regressions for each cross-sectional entity.
2. Intercepts and slope estimates can differ for different cross-sectional entities.
3. The degrees of freedom may be small because separate regressions are used for each cross-sectional entity.

Fixed Effects Model (Section 9-3)

1. This model is most appropriate when differences between the intercepts for the cross-sectional entities are considered constant, not random.
2. Different intercepts for each cross-sectional entity are allowed, but the slope coefficients remain the same.
3. One regression is used for the whole pooled sample, so the fixed effects model has more degrees of freedom than seemingly unrelated regression.
4. If there are a lot of cross-sectional entities, the number of intercept dummies will be large, decreasing the degrees of freedom compared to the sample size.
5. The F-test in Section (9-3) tells whether the intercept is the same across all cross-sectional entities so that the dummy variables can be omitted and replaced with one intercept, or whether the fixed effects model should be used.

Random Effects Model (Section 9-4)

1. This model is most appropriate when the entities in the cross-section data are chosen at random to represent a larger population.
2. Like fixed effects, random effects allows the intercepts to differ for different cross-sectional entities, but the differences in the intercepts are considered random, not fixed. The slope coefficients are forced to be the same, like fixed effects.
3. This model will have more degrees of freedom than fixed effects for the same study, because random effects does not use intercept dummy variables.

SUMMARY

1. Pooled data combine cross-section and time-series data together. Using pooled data can be advantageous because the sample size increases compared to an ordinary cross-section or time-series regression. It allows the researcher to study changes across both time and cross-section observations.

2. One way to estimate a regression with pooled data is to simply combine all the data from different time periods and different cross-sectional entities. In this approach, the researcher assumes that the intercept and slope coefficients are the same over time and for all the cross-sectional entities. By running the regression this way, the researcher may be ignoring important differences that exist over time or between cross-sectional entities.

3. Despite the name, in seemingly unrelated regression the regressions actually do have something to do with each other. Seemingly unrelated regression allows the error terms to be correlated across equations, and uses this correlation to improve the estimates. This correlation is ignored if the regressions are estimated separately.

4. The fixed effects model incorporates differences between cross-sectional entities by allowing the intercepts to change. The intercept differs for each cross-sectional entity, but it stays constant over time. Fixed effects attributes any differences between cross-sectional entities to the intercept, and leaves the slope coefficients the same. This way, all the cross-section data can be used in one regression, along with the time-series data. Fixed effects works by using dummy variables for the intercepts.

5. When using a fixed effects model, each firm, state, or individual has its own dummy variable. This would seem to land us in the dummy variable trap. The dummy variable trap is avoided by leaving out the regular B_0 intercept.

6. An F-test can be used to test the null hypothesis that the dummy variable coefficients that represent each cross-sectional entity in a fixed effects model are the same. If the null hypothesis is rejected, the fixed effects model is preferable to running a regular regression without the fixed effects dummy variables.

7. A random effects model incorporates differences between cross-sectional entities by allowing the intercept to change, as in fixed effects, but the amount of the change is random. Random effects is appropriate if each category in the cross-section data is chosen at random to represent a larger population.

EXERCISES

1. Try to explain these terms without looking them up.
    - pooled data
    - panel data
    - seemingly unrelated regression (SUR)
    - fixed effects model
    - random effects model

2. Consider the model

    $$\text{WAGE} = B_1\text{AGE} + B_2\text{EDUCATION} + B_3\text{MALE} + B_4\text{FEMALE} + e$$

    Is this model caught in the dummy variable trap discussed in Chapter 5? Why or why not?

3. Seemingly unrelated regression means that the regressions seem unrelated, but in fact they are related.
   a. How are the regressions in seemingly unrelated regression related?
   b. Without looking in the text, explain how seemingly unrelated regression works.

4. a. For each model listed, explain whether the model tends to have greater or fewer degrees of freedom compared to the other models.
      i. pooled model with a common intercept
      ii. seemingly unrelated regression
      iii. fixed effects model
      iv. random effects model
   b. List a possible disadvantage for each model that tends to have more degrees of freedom. List a possible advantage for each model that tends to have fewer degrees of freedom.

5. When should a fixed effects model be used, and when should random effects be used?

6. Explain why a random effects model cannot be estimated using ordinary least squares.

7. If you have more than one year of cross-section data available, should you always combine it into one pooled data set? Why or why not?

8. Using the data in Table 9-A, run the regressions given in Equations (9-1) to (9-4) as separate ordinary least square regressions. Compare the slope estimates to those found using seemingly unrelated regression in Tables 9-C to 9-F.
   a. Are the slope coefficients the same?
   b. If so, explain why the estimates came out the same. If not, explain why they came out differently.

9. Suppose you want to study electricity consumption. You have annual cross-section electricity consumption data along with data for 5 independent variables, for 50 states, for 2 years. You also know that each state has a different intercept and that the intercepts don't change over time. Would it be a good idea to combine the two years of data into one data set and run the regression as a fixed effects model? Why or why not?

10. Use the data in Table 6-E for Mia and Vincent to estimate the test score model using fixed effects. Compare the results to those given in Table 6-F from

$$SCORE = B_0 + B_1 STUDY + B_2 LIBRARY + B_3 VINCENT + e \quad \text{(6-7)}$$

where VINCENT = 1 if observation is for Vincent; 0 otherwise
   a. How do the slope coefficients differ from the results in Table 6-F?
   b. Explain why they are the same or why they are different.

11. Compare the estimates for the intercept and the slope coefficient for Vincent given in Table 6-F with the estimates for the two intercepts for Vincent and Mia found when you estimated the fixed effects model in Exercise 10.
   a. What is the mathematical relationship between these estimates?
   b. Why does this relationship occur?

12. In Chapter 2, a DVD expenditures model is estimated twice, using two different sets of data. The regression is

$$DVDEXP = B_0 + B_1 INCOME + B_2 PRICE + B_3 RAINFALL + e \quad \text{(2-2)}$$

Each data set contains 12 monthly observations. The degrees of freedom can be increased if the two years of data are pooled. Using pooled data, can the DVD expenditures model be estimated the way it is written in Chapter 2 or should fixed effects be used, giving a different intercept for each year? Use the data in Tables 2-A and 2-C to conduct a test and answer this question.

13. In Exercise 12, data from two years are combined to form one data set. Regardless of whether or not a fixed effects model is used, which test tells you whether the data can be pooled? Use the data in Tables 2-A and 2-C to see if it was appropriate to pool the data in this case. (*Hint:* The necessary test was covered in a previous chapter.)

10

Simultaneous-Equation Systems: When One Equation Is Not Enough

This chapter will explain:

- When you need more than one equation in a regression model.

- The problems that occur when ordinary least squares is used to estimate a model with equations that are determined at the same time.

- How to estimate a model that contains equations that are determined at the same time.

Sometimes a situation can be described with a single sentence, and sometimes it takes a whole book. Econometric models are the same way. So far all our models have been described by a single equation, but sometimes one equation is not enough. Suppose you want to estimate how many pizzas a pizzeria sells each month. At first glance, the quantity of pizzas sold looks like a "natural" for the dependent variable, with the price of pizza as an independent variable; however, this does not give us the correct model. Theory requires two equations to describe this situation, one for supply and one for demand. Using two equations establishes the values for price and quantity at the same time.[1] Price and quantity are both dependent variables here, because they are both determined by other variables in the supply and demand equations. When a model needs more than one equation because two (or more) dependent variables are determined at the same time, it is called a **simultaneous-equation system.**

Ordinary least squares cannot be used to estimate a simultaneous-equation system. The OLS procedure estimates each equation separately, and does not take into account that the equations are part of a larger system. The estimates will be biased. In this chapter, we set up and estimate a regression model that needs more than one equation. We also test a single-equation regression to see if we need to use more than one regression equation in the model.

---

[1] In Chapters 1 and 2, we used only one equation for Quinn's DVD expenditures model, because her individual purchasing behavior would not substantially affect the quantity supplied or market price of DVDs.

10-1 A TWO-EQUATION MODEL FOR PIZZA

Let's set up a two-equation, supply and demand model for a pizzeria:

$$\text{Demand: } Q = B_0 + B_1 P + B_2 COMP + e \qquad (10\text{-}1)$$

$$\text{Supply: } Q = \alpha_0 + \alpha_1 P + \alpha_2 WAGE + \alpha_3 CHEESE + e \qquad (10\text{-}2)$$

where
- Q = quantity of pizzas sold by pizzeria each month
- P = average price of a pizza each month, adjusted for inflation
- $COMP$ = average pizza price each month at competing area restaurants, adjusted for inflation
- $WAGE$ = average hourly wage at the pizzeria each month, adjusted for inflation
- $CHEESE$ = index of the inflation-adjusted price of cheese used at the pizzeria each month

Note that we use Q for both supply and demand. Each month, the pizzeria's market is in equilibrium—that is, the quantity supplied by the pizzeria equals the quantity demanded by its customers. Q stands for both quantity demanded and quantity supplied, because they are the same in any one month. The Greek letter alpha (α) in Equation (10-2) indicates that the coefficients in Equation (10-2) take different values than those in Equation (10-1).

Economic theory dictates whether an independent variable belongs in the demand equation or the supply equation. COMP belongs in the demand equation because the pizza price at competing area restaurants affects the pizzeria's demand equation. WAGE and CHEESE reflect input costs for making pizza, so theory places them in the supply equation.

Usually the independent variables are given; the model does not determine them. When values for a variable come from outside the model—when the values are taken as given—the variable is called **exogenous** ("exo" means outside). COMP, WAGE, and CHEESE are all exogenous variables, since the pizzeria model does not try to explain why these variables take the values they do. We take the values of COMP, WAGE, and CHEESE as given.

The model, in theory, determines or explains the values of the dependent variable. When the model can (in theory) explain the values of a variable, the variable is called **endogenous** ("endo" means inside). Think of endogenous variables as coming from inside the model, since the model determines the values of these variables. Here, even though P appears on the right-hand side of the regression equations, it is not given from outside the model like a typical independent variable. Instead, price and quantity are determined simultaneously by the intersection of the supply and demand curves. Equations (10-1) and (10-2) together form a model that gives values for the price and quantity of pizza at the same time, based on other variables in the equations. Equations (10-1) and (10-2) form a model that can explain or predict P and Q; this makes *both* P and Q endogenous variables. P is endogenous even though it appears on the right-hand side of (10-1) and (10-2). If we place P on the left-hand side as the dependent variable with Q on the right-hand side, we get the *same* model, because P and Q are both endogenous variables. P and Q function as dependent variables at the same time, in both equations. If we reverse P and Q in (10-2), the result (10-3) still represents the same model.

$$\text{Demand: } Q = B_0 + B_1P + B_2COMP + e \qquad \text{(10-1)}$$

$$\text{Supply: } P = \alpha_0 + \alpha_1Q + \alpha_2WAGE + \alpha_3CHEESE + e \qquad \text{(10-3)}$$

The coefficients in (10-3) will take different values than those in (10-2). Expressing the model this way using Equations (10-1) and (10-3) makes it clear that both P and Q are endogenous variables. However, nothing is wrong with our original supply equation (10-2).

Suppose we add a new variable to the supply equation: $P(-1)$, where $P(-1)$ is the average price of pizza last month. In any month, we already know the value of $P(-1)$, since it is from the preceding month. $P(-1)$ is a lagged endogenous variable. The current pizza price P is determined by the system of equations, but because $P(-1)$ is from last month, it is known. Lagged endogenous variables and exogenous variables are called **predetermined variables** since, in any one time period, their values are already given; they are not being determined by the system of equations.

The model given by Equations (10-1) and (10-2) is a simultaneous-equation system written out so that one can see the economic theory behind the model. Equation (10-1) is for demand, and Equation (10-2) is for supply. Equations (10-1) and (10-3) also represent the same model. These equations are called **structural equations** because they show us the model's underlying theory.

We can also write the supply and demand model for pizza in a different format. Now only predetermined variables are on the right-hand side of the equations.

$$Q = \pi_0 + \pi_1COMP + \pi_2WAGE + \pi_3CHEESE + e \qquad \text{(10-4)}$$

$$P = \pi_4 + \pi_5COMP + \pi_6WAGE + \pi_7CHEESE + e \qquad \text{(10-5)}$$

Neither equation here is the demand equation, and neither equation is the supply equation. Instead, Equation (10-4) gives the quantity of pizzas sold as a function of every predetermined variable in the complete system of equations. Equation (10-5) gives the average price of pizza based upon the same set of predetermined variables. This way of writing a simultaneous system of equations (where only predetermined variables are on the right-hand side) is called the reduced form, so Equations (10-4) and (10-5) are called **reduced-form equations.** The Greek letter pi (π) is often used in reduced-form equations to indicate coefficients.

The reduced-form equation is not particularly useful for learning about the model. For example, the model's structural equation tells us a lot more about how customers react to price increases. Reduced-form equations are useful for forecasting *if* you don't care about the underlying model or why the dependent variables take the values they do. The advantage of reduced-form equations has to do with the fact that the endogenous variables (P and Q) don't appear on the right-hand side of the equations. Because of this, simultaneity is not a problem. Reduced-form equations like Equations (10-4) and (10-5) can be estimated with ordinary least squares. Structural equations, where dependent variables like P and Q appear on the right-hand side, cannot be estimated with ordinary least squares because the estimates will be biased.

10-2 THE IDENTIFICATION PROBLEM: HOW TO TELL SUPPLY FROM DEMAND

A structural equation in a simultaneous-equation system can be estimated only if the equation is identified. **Identification** means there is enough information in a simultaneous-equation system for the equation's coefficients to be estimated. A simultaneous equation system can have some equations that are identified and some that are not. A few examples will make this concept clearer. Suppose we try to estimate the pizzeria's supply and demand equations but we leave out all of the predetermined variables.

$$\text{Demand: } Q = B_0 + B_1 P + e \qquad\qquad \textbf{(10-6)}$$

$$\text{Supply: } Q = \alpha_0 + \alpha_1 P + e \qquad\qquad \textbf{(10-7)}$$

Both the demand and supply equations in this model contain the same variables, P and Q. B_1 should be negative because an increase in price is associated with a decrease in Q along the demand curve, keeping everything else constant. However, α_1 should be positive because an increase in price is associated with an increase in Q along the supply curve, keeping everything else constant. Because the variables in the two equations are exactly the same, there is no way that any estimation process can find distinct, different estimates for B_1 and α_1. Equations (10-6) and (10-7) are unidentified. Each month we have a price and quantity for the pizzeria that represents the intersection (the equilibrium point) for supply and demand that month. However, there is no other information in the model to tell us what the slopes of the demand and supply curves look like, so B_1 and α_1 cannot be estimated. This has nothing to do with sample size; the sample size could be very large and the equations would still be unidentified. The problem lies with the model itself. The model needs some exogenous or predetermined variables for the equations to be identified. Figure 10-1 depicts the situation.

Figure 10-1 shows what happens when both equations are unidentified. The price and quantity data give us the equilibrium point where the supply and demand curves intersect, but there is no way to estimate the slopes of the curves. When an equation is unidentified, we need to think about what factors make the equations different. We can then add these factors as independent variables to the appropriate equations. For example, the price that other restaurants charge for pizza affects demand, but not supply. Suppose we add COMP, the average pizza price charged by competitors, to the demand equation.

$$\text{Demand: } Q = B_0 + B_1 P + B_2 COMP + e \qquad\qquad \textbf{(10-8)}$$

$$\text{Supply: } Q = \alpha_0 + \alpha_1 P + e \qquad\qquad \textbf{(10-9)}$$

Inserting COMP in the demand equation gives an additional piece of information that identifies the supply equation. COMP appears in the demand equation, but it makes the supply equation identified. The demand equation is still unidentified. As COMP changes over time, the demand curve shifts. As the demand curve shifts around, the P and Q data we have allow us to see different points where the demand and supply curves intersect. Since changes in COMP do not cause the supply curve to move, α_1 in Equa-

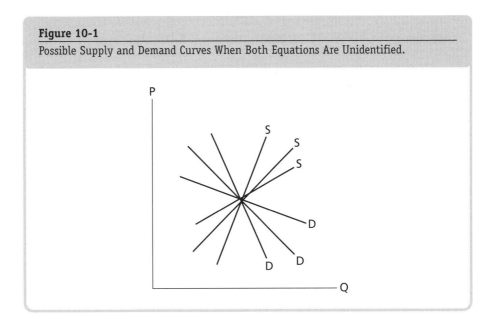

Figure 10-1

Possible Supply and Demand Curves When Both Equations Are Unidentified.

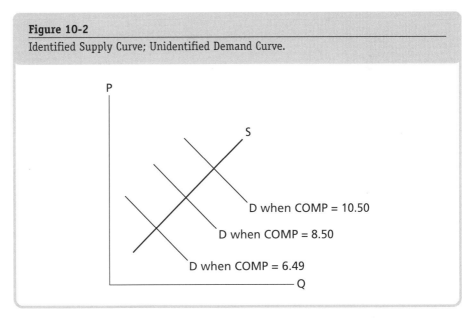

Figure 10-2

Identified Supply Curve; Unidentified Demand Curve.

tion (10-9) can be estimated and the supply curve can be identified as the demand curve shifts around. Figure 10-2 shows how using COMP in the demand curve identifies the supply curve.

In Figure 10-2, adding a predetermined variable to the demand equation identifies the supply equation. The demand curve can be identified if we add a different predetermined variable (besides COMP) to the supply equation. The original supply equation in (10-2) contained two predetermined variables.

$$\text{Demand: } Q = B_0 + B_1P + B_2COMP + e \qquad \textbf{(10-1)}$$

$$\text{Supply: } Q = \alpha_0 + \alpha_1P + \alpha_2WAGE + \alpha_3CHEESE + e \qquad \textbf{(10-2)}$$

If we use Equation (10-2) as the supply equation, the demand equation is identified. In fact, now the demand equation is **overidentified** because we have more predetermined variables than we need for identification. Only one predetermined variable is necessary in the supply equation to identify demand, but we have two, WAGE and CHEESE. Overidentification sounds like a problem, but it is not. Economic theory says that both WAGE and CHEESE belong in the supply equation. They help measure the costs of producing pizza and should be relevant for the supply equation.

The Order Condition

The **order condition** is satisfied when for every nonlagged endogenous variable appearing on the right-hand side of the equation, a predetermined variable in the system has been excluded from the equation. The order condition is a necessary condition for an equation to be identified, but it is not sufficient. This means that an equation can meet the order condition and still *not* be identified. All identified equations meet the order condition, but so do some unidentified equations. The order condition is useful because if an equation does not meet the order condition, we know that it is not identified.

To see how the order condition works, let's apply it to our previous examples. Reconsider Equations (10-6) and (10-7).

$$\text{Demand: } Q = B_0 + B_1P + e \qquad \textbf{(10-6)}$$

$$\text{Supply: } Q = \alpha_0 + \alpha_1P + e \qquad \textbf{(10-7)}$$

In Equation (10-6), one nonlagged endogenous variable, P, is on the right-hand side of the equation. For this demand equation to meet the order condition, there must be a predetermined variable in Equation (10-7) that is not in Equation (10-6). There is no such variable, so Equation (10-6) does not meet the order condition. This tells us that (10-6) is unidentified. The same is true for Equation (10-7). The supply equation shown by (10-7) has one nonlagged endogenous variable on the right-hand side, but there is no predetermined variable in the other equation, (10-6), that is excluded from Equation (10-7). Therefore, Equation (10-7) is also unidentified. This supports our earlier conclusion, that both Equations (10-6) and (10-7) are unidentified.

Now let's apply the order condition to the next system we considered, Equations (10-8) and (10-9).

$$\text{Demand: } Q = B_0 + B_1P + B_2COMP + e \qquad \textbf{(10-8)}$$

$$\text{Supply: } Q = \alpha_0 + \alpha_1P + e \qquad \textbf{(10-9)}$$

The demand equation has one nonlagged endogenous variable, P, on the right-hand side. There is no predetermined variable in the supply equation that is omitted from the demand equation. The demand equation does not satisfy the order condition and therefore is unidentified. The supply equation also has one nonlagged endogenous variable, P, on the right-hand side. Now, however, we spot a predetermined variable in the demand equation that is excluded from the supply equation: COMP. The supply equation meets the order condition, and therefore might be identified. As discussed earlier, the supply equation (10-9) actually is identified.

Let's try one more, our first example.

$$\text{Demand: } Q = B_0 + B_1P + B_2COMP + e \qquad \textbf{(10-1)}$$

$$\text{Supply: } Q = \alpha_0 + \alpha_1P + \alpha_2WAGE + \alpha_3CHEESE + e \qquad \textbf{(10-2)}$$

Once again the demand equation has one nonlagged endogenous variable, P, on the right-hand side. Two predetermined variables in the system are omitted from the demand equation, WAGE and CHEESE. The order condition is satisfied for the demand equation, and it turns out that the demand equation is identified. (The demand equation is overidentified but, as stated earlier, that is not a problem.) The supply equation has one nonlagged endogenous variable. For the supply equation to satisfy the order condition, we need a predetermined variable in the system that is omitted from the supply equation. COMP does the job. The order condition is met for the supply equation (10-2) and it turns out to be identified.

Keep in mind that the order condition is necessary for an equation to be identified, but it is not sufficient. There is no guarantee that an equation that meets the order condition will be identified. As discussed, if an equation does *not* meet the order condition, it is guaranteed to be unidentified. The rank condition is sufficient to guarantee that an equation is identified. The rank condition is mathematically difficult, and will not be covered here.[2]

10-3 ORDINARY LEAST SQUARES HAS ISSUES WITH SIMULTANEITY

Simultaneity occurs when one equation is used to describe a model that really needs two or more equations. A regression equation implies that in theory, the variables on the right-hand side of the equation affect the variable on the left-hand side, but not the other way around. Simultaneity occurs when the variable on the left-hand side affects a right-hand side variable. As stated, ordinary least squares gives biased estimates if there is simultaneity in the model. The bias occurs because one of the classical assumptions is violated. The assumption that all independent variables are uncorrelated with the error term will not hold true. The nonlagged endogenous variable on the right-hand side will be correlated with the error term. Figure 10-3 uses the pizzeria's demand and supply equations (10-1) and (10-3) to show the correlation.

Any movement in the dependent variable that is not explained by the independent variables is captured by the error term. The dependent variable will be correlated with

---

[2] Interested readers who are familiar with matrix algebra should see Takeshi Amemiya, *Advanced Econometrics* (Cambridge, Massachusetts: Harvard University Press, 1985), pp. 236–240.

Figure 10-3

Simultaneity Causes Correlation Between Independent Variable and Error Term.

1. Error term and Q are correlated.
2. P and Q are correlated and are determined simultaneously, since P and Q are both endogenous.
3. Q and e are correlated, and P and Q are simultaneous, so P and e must be correlated. A correlation between P and e violates a classical assumption of ordinary least squares.

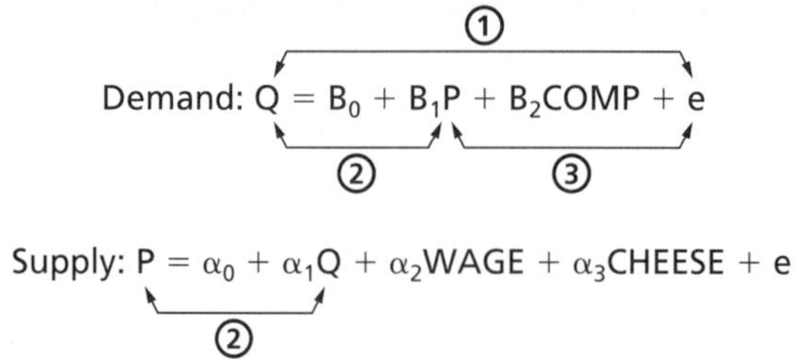

$$\text{Demand: } Q = B_0 + B_1P + B_2COMP + e$$

(1)   (2)   (3)

$$\text{Supply: } P = \alpha_0 + \alpha_1Q + \alpha_2WAGE + \alpha_3CHEESE + e$$

(2)

Figure 10-4

No Simultaneity, So No Correlation Between Independent Variable and Error Term.

1. Error term and Y are correlated.
2. X_1 and Y are correlated, but are not simultaneous. There is no strong correlation between X_1 and e.

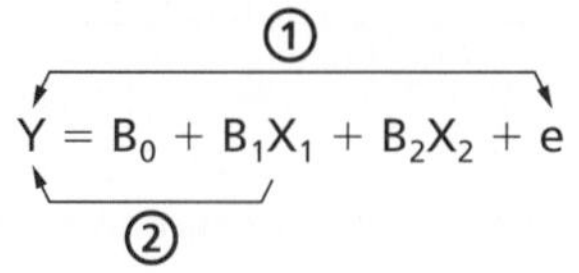

$$Y = B_0 + B_1X_1 + B_2X_2 + e$$

(1)   (2)

the error term, so Q and e are correlated (see arrow 1 in Figure 10-3). Supply and demand generate the values of P and Q at the same time, so P and Q are correlated (see arrow ②, in both equations). Since Q and e are correlated, and Q and P are correlated, then e and P must also be correlated (arrow ③). This violates a classical OLS assumption.

In contrast, the generic multiple regression model in Figure 10-4 does not have simultaneity. The independent variable X_1 is exogenous, but it is not determined simultaneously. This means that no other equation is necessary to complete the model.

In Figure 10-4, the error term is correlated with the dependent variable Y, as usual. Let's focus on X_1. Y and X_1 are correlated, but not simultaneously determined. Movements in X_1 are associated with movements in Y, but there is no "feedback" from Y to X_1. Arrow ② between X_1 and Y points in one direction only (toward Y), not in both directions as in Figure 10-3. X_1 and e should not exhibit any strong correlation. The classical assumptions should hold. When simultaneity is present, a chain of correlation causes a variable on the equation's right-hand side to be correlated with the error term, violating the classical assumptions (Figure 10-3). In Figure 10-4, there is no simultaneity, so the chain is broken. There is no reason to believe that any variable on the right-hand side of the equation in Figure 10-4 will be correlated with the error term.

OLS estimates are biased for regressions in which an independent variable is correlated with the error term. Ordinary least squares works by looking at how the dependent variable moves, attributing parts of this movement to different independent variables. In Equations (10-1) and (10-2), if Q increases whenever P falls, keeping COMP constant, the OLS procedure attributes the increase in Q to the change in P. Since P and the error term move together, and the error term is unobserved, ordinary least squares ignores the error term and thinks that P is fully responsible for the change in Q, even though the error term plays a part in the change. This means that ordinary least squares will overestimate the slope coefficient for P. A good method for estimating simultaneous-equation systems is presented later in the chapter. First, let's test a regression equation for simultaneity.

10-4 CHECKING FOR SIMULTANEITY WITH THE HAUSMAN TEST

The Hausman test that we examine in this section can be applied to a single-equation regression model to see if one of the variables on the right-hand side might be endogenous. If there is only one equation in the model, and there is a nonlagged endogenous variable on the right-hand side, there is a simultaneity problem and we must add more equations to our model. There are various forms of the Hausman test.[3] The Hausman test we use here checks for correlation between a variable from the equation's right-hand side and the error term in a multiple regression model. There are four steps to the test.

1. Take the right-hand side variable you want to test, and use it as the dependent variable with all the predetermined variables available (from every equation in the model) serving as independent variables. (This is the same as running a reduced-form regression.)
2. Save the error term observations (residuals) from step 1.
3. Add the error term observations (ê) as an independent variable to the original structural form equation that the variable being tested comes from. Use ordinary least squares to estimate the regression.
4. Use the t-statistic to see if the slope coefficient (from step 3) for the error term observations is statistically significant. If so, there is evidence of simultaneity.

---

[3] J. Hausman, "Specification Tests in Econometrics," *Econometrica*, Vol. 46, 1978, pp. 1251–1271. Also see D. E. Spencer and K. N. Berk, "A Limited Information Specification Test," *Econometrica*, Vol. 49, 1981, pp. 1079–1085.

If the original structural equation does not have a simultaneity problem, then the error term should have nothing to do with any of the right-hand side variables. The error term should take random values. If the error term is random, it should not have any explanatory power in the regression in step 3; the error term observations should be statistically insignificant. In this case, the original structural equation can be estimated with ordinary least squares.

If simultaneity is present, the error term observations will be correlated with one of the independent variables (as explained in the preceding section.) This correlation causes the slope coefficient for the error term observations in step 3 to come out statistically significant. Let's apply the Hausman test to the pizzeria example. The pizzeria's owner collected the data in Table 10-A. The supply and demand equations are as before:

$$\text{Demand: } Q = B_0 + B_1P + B_2COMP + e \qquad \textbf{(10-1)}$$

$$\text{Supply: } Q = \alpha_0 + \alpha_1P + \alpha_2WAGE + \alpha_3CHEESE + e \qquad \textbf{(10-2)}$$

Table 10-A

Data for Pizza Model

Month	Q	P	COMP	WAGE	CHEESE
1	1949	5.55	9.40	5.90	101.57
2	1932	7.44	6.22	6.00	112.10
3	2013	8.24	9.54	6.00	108.97
4	2114	8.54	11.10	6.25	105.47
5	1912	7.37	9.11	6.25	107.25
6	1919	7.35	6.69	6.30	101.58
7	2015	6.85	9.66	6.50	94.75
8	1914	6.94	9.17	6.50	100.91
9	1966	6.69	9.91	6.60	95.27
10	2027	7.63	10.76	6.80	94.57
11	1840	8.47	9.49	6.90	107.07
12	1735	8.22	7.84	7.00	109.18
13	1731	7.48	6.49	7.15	104.83

(continued)

In theory, P and Q are jointly determined by supply and demand, so P is endogenous even though it is on the right-hand side of the equation. Economic theory predicts simultaneity. To test for simultaneity in Equation (10-1), we run a Hausman test using the data in Table 10-A. [We could also run the test on Equation (10-2).] The first step is to use P as a dependent variable in a regression where the independent variables are the three predetermined variables in the system (COMP, WAGE, CHEESE). This regression is the same as one of the reduced form regressions; it is Equation (10-5).

$$P = \pi_4 + \pi_5 COMP + \pi_6 WAGE + \pi_7 CHEESE + e \qquad \textbf{(10-5)}$$

Table 10-A

(Continued)

Month	Q	P	COMP	WAGE	CHEESE
14	2011	8.98	6.18	7.25	98.94
15	1792	7.75	6.77	7.50	91.44
16	1892	7.78	7.24	7.50	87.85
17	2180	8.25	9.69	7.75	73.77
18	1928	7.33	8.22	7.80	81.32
19	1918	7.49	8.52	7.90	81.75
20	1897	7.50	10.20	7.80	82.12
21	1892	9.16	9.94	8.00	87.38
22	2034	8.28	10.98	8.20	74.55
23	1980	8.19	11.40	8.25	78.00
24	1967	8.96	11.20	8.50	79.86
25	1927	8.96	9.46	8.50	81.10
26	1718	9.57	5.87	8.60	89.98
27	1764	9.94	6.13	8.70	93.03
28	1674	10.04	6.23	8.75	94.63
29	1760	10.39	9.28	9.00	84.34
30	1836	9.50	11.11	9.00	82.90

Table 10-B

Regression Results for Hausman Test, Equation (10-10)

Dependent variable: Q

Variable	Coefficient	Standard Error	t-Statistic	p-Value
Constant	2,220.61	95.19	23.33	0.00
P	−73.45	9.53	−7.71	0.00
COMP	32.61	5.14	6.34	0.00
$\hat{e}$	168.83	19.81	8.52	0.00

Observations: 30

$R^2 = 0.85$

Adjusted $R^2 = 0.83$

Residual Sum of Squares = 63,281.43

F-statistic = 47.97

Durbin-Watson statistic = 1.76

The results of this regression are not of particular interest here. Running the regression allows us to get the error term observations, completing step 2 of the Hausman test. In step 3, we add the error term observations we just found to the original structural equation, (10-1), as a new independent variable. This gives us Equation (10-10).

$$Q = B_0 + B_1P + B_2COMP + B_3\hat{e} + v \tag{10-10}$$

where $\hat{e}$ represents the error term observations from Equation (10-5). $\hat{e}$ is an independent variable in Equation (10-10) for step 3 of the Hausman test. v is an error term that is assumed to follow OLS assumptions. Table 10-B gives the regression results for Equation (10-10).

The coefficient for $\hat{e}$ is statistically significant; the p-value is less than 0.01. $\hat{e}$ provides explanatory power for Q, which should not happen, since the values of $\hat{e}$ should be random. This indicates simultaneity: P and Q are determined at the same time, so two equations are needed for this model. This result verifies what we know from economic theory: Price and quantity are simultaneously determined by both supply and demand. Ordinary least squares will be biased for this model, so we must use another estimation process.

10-5 INSTRUMENTAL VARIABLES: AN ALTERNATIVE FOR A PROBLEM VARIABLE

Instrumental variables estimation uses a proxy for one of the endogenous variables to estimate an equation with a simultaneity problem. The proxy variable is called an instrumental variable, or instrument. The instrument, often called Z, must meet two important criteria.

1. It should be correlated with the endogenous problem variable.
2. It should be uncorrelated with the error term in the regression.

The instrument must be correlated with the problem variable because we are using the instrument to represent the problem variable in the estimation process. The stronger the correlation, the more the instrument is related to the problem variable and so the better job the instrument does of standing in for the problem variable. Calculating the correlation coefficient gives us the correlation between the instrument and problem variable. We could also run a regression with the problem variable as the dependent variable and the instrument as the independent variable. A coefficient for the instrument that is statistically significant at a 5% error level is evidence that it is highly correlated with the problem variable.

The second criterion is tougher to meet. As discussed in Section 10-3, when simultaneity is present, one of the regression's independent variables will be correlated with the error term. This, of course, violates the classical assumptions. So our instrument must be uncorrelated with the error term in the regression, or we will end up with the exact problem we are trying to eliminate. Ideally, the instrument is not endogenous, but is correlated with the right-hand side endogenous variable. Such an instrument would not be correlated with the error term. Finding such an instrument can be difficult because we have no way to test whether the instrument is correlated with the theoretical error term e in a regression model. The best we can do is to make sure that the instrument is, in theory, exogenous.

Once again let's return to the original pizza demand equation.

$$\text{Demand: } Q = B_0 + B_1P + B_2COMP + e \qquad \text{(10-1)}$$

We need an instrument for P, since it presents a simultaneity problem (P is nonlagged, endogenous, and appears on the right-hand side of the regression). WAGE (used in the supply equation) is a reasonable instrument for P. WAGE and P should be correlated, since an increase in employee wages could be associated with a rise in the average pizza price. The correlation coefficient r for P and WAGE is 0.75 for the data used here (Table 10-A). Using P as the dependent variable, and WAGE as the only independent variable, the coefficient for WAGE is statistically significant at a 1% error level. WAGE is strongly correlated with P, so it meets the first criterion for being an instrument.

WAGE should not be correlated with the error term in Equation (10-1) because it is an exogenous variable. The values of WAGE come from outside the pizzeria's system of demand and supply equations, so it is not simultaneously determined with P and Q. Therefore, there is no reason to believe that WAGE will be correlated with the error term in the demand equation. We can use WAGE as an instrument for P, so Equation (10-1) can be estimated using instrumental variables.

Instrumental variables estimation does not mean that the instrument becomes an independent variable in the regression. When we use instrumental variables to estimate Equation (10-1), P and COMP will still be the only right-hand side variables. Instrumental variables estimation means that the instrument will be used to calculate the coefficient estimates for the independent variables: the instrument will *not* actually appear in the regression equation. In a regression with only one independent variable, the OLS procedure calculates the slope estimate as follows (Section 1-3):

$$B_1 = \frac{(Y - \overline{Y})(X - \overline{X}) \text{ added over all observations}}{(X - \overline{X})(X - \overline{X}) \text{ added over all observations}}$$

Instrumental variables estimation uses the instrumental variable Z in the formula for the slope coefficient. Equation (10-11) calculates the slope estimate for a regression with one independent variable using instrument Z:

$$B_1 = \frac{(Y - \overline{Y})(Z - \overline{Z}) \text{ added over all observations}}{(X - \overline{X})(Z - \overline{Z}) \text{ added over all observations}} \qquad \text{(10-11)}$$

For the usual case when the regression contains more than one independent variable, the calculations are much more complicated.

Let's estimate the pizzeria's demand equation, using WAGE as the instrument. Table 10-C gives the results.

Both independent variables have statistically significant coefficients at a 1% error level. Both slope coefficients have the signs we expect. P has a negative coefficient; the relationship between the price and the quantity of pizzas sold is negative. COMP has a positive coefficient; when the competition raises prices, the pizzeria gets more business. We can also use instrumental variables to estimate the supply equation. We would use a different instrument for P because we have already included WAGE as a predetermined variable in the supply equation.

Using instrumental variables estimation does not guarantee that the estimates will be unbiased. The estimates will be consistent, which means the estimates will come very close to being unbiased for a large sample size. Ordinary least squares is not con-

Table 10-C

Instrumental Variable Regression Results for Pizzeria's Demand, Equation (10-1)

Dependent variable: Q
Instrument variable: WAGE

Variable	Coefficient	Standard Error	t-Statistic	p-Value
Constant	2,086.66	212.78	9.81	0.00
P	−58.16	21.96	−2.65	0.01
COMP	33.65	10.25	3.28	0.00

Observations: 30

$R^2 = 0.37$

Adjusted $R^2 = 0.33$

Residual Sum of Squares = 259,781.34

F-statistic = 10.38

Durbin-Watson statistic = 2.04

sistent when simultaneity is present. If the instrumental variable chosen is good—it comes close to meeting the two criteria given earlier—then instrumental variables estimation deals with simultaneity better than ordinary least squares.

Measurement Error

Sometimes an independent variable is collected or measured improperly. For example, some people do not report all their income when paying taxes. This may cause the government to underestimate the country's total income earned each year. Instrumental variables estimation can be used when an independent variable is measured inaccurately, provided that a good instrument for the problem independent variable can be found. The two criteria discussed earlier still apply to the instrument when it is used to address a measurement error problem, rather than simultaneity. Measurement error in an independent variable causes ordinary least squares to be biased, just as simultaneity does. However, do not use instrumental variables estimation if the *dependent* variable has measurement error. A dependent variable with measurement error does not generate bias in OLS estimates.

10-6 TWO-STAGE LEAST SQUARES: AN ORDERLY APPROACH TO INSTRUMENTAL VARIABLES

Two-stage least squares (2SLS) is a specific type of instrumental variables estimation that uses all of the model's predetermined variables to construct an instrument. It is often difficult to find an instrumental variable that is both highly correlated with the problem variable and not correlated with the error term. Two-stage least squares uses an orderly procedure to form an instrumental variable. Most econometric software can run 2SLS for you with one command, so that you do not have to calculate each stage separately. It is still good to know what those stages are so that you understand what the software is doing and what the results mean.

In the first stage, an instrumental variable is formed for any nonlagged endogenous variable that appears on the right-hand side of the regression. That endogenous variable becomes the dependent variable in a new regression where all the system's predetermined variables are used as explanatory variables. This step is similar to the first step of the Hausman test. As in the Hausman test, the 2SLS regression is a reduced-form regression. The fitted or predicted values for the dependent variable serve as the instrument in the second stage.

The equation must be identified for two-stage least squares to work. This means that for every right-hand side nonlagged endogenous variable in an equation, there has to be at least one predetermined variable in the system that is *not* in that equation. Both Equations (10-1) and (10-2) have one nonlagged right-hand side endogenous variable. For the demand equation (10-1), two predetermined variables are excluded from the equation, WAGE and CHEESE. For the supply equation, COMP is predetermined and is not in the supply equation. We can use two-stage least squares for both equations.

Before we move to the second stage, let's consider how the first stage works when applied to the pizzeria's demand equation. P is taken from the right-hand side of Equation (10-1) and used as a dependent variable with COMP, WAGE, and CHEESE as the independent variables (the three predetermined variables in the simultaneous-equation system). This gives Equation (10-5), the reduced-form equation that we used in the first step of the Hausman test.

$$P = \pi_4 + \pi_5 COMP + \pi_6 WAGE + \pi_7 CHEESE + e \qquad \text{(10-5)}$$

The fitted or predicted values for P, designated $\hat{P}$, are then saved for use as an instrumental variable in the second stage.

The second stage takes the fitted values $\hat{P}$ and uses them in the original structural equation in place of the original P values. So, instead of $Q = B_0 + B_1 P + B_2 COMP + e$, we now have

$$Q = B_0 + B_1 \hat{P} + B_2 COMP + e \qquad \text{(10-12)}$$

with pizza price P replaced by $\hat{P}$. The fitted values $\hat{P}$ are correlated with the actual values P, but $\hat{P}$ will not be correlated with the error term in Equation (10-12). $\hat{P}$ should be a good instrument for P and two-stage least squares should be superior to ordinary least squares for estimating Equation (10-12).

In summary, for each equation in a system with a nonlagged endogenous variable on the right-hand side, the two stages are as follows:

1. Use the endogenous right-hand side variable from the original equation as the dependent variable. Use all the predetermined variables in the original system for the independent variables. Estimate using ordinary least squares. Save the fitted values for the dependent variable for use in the second stage.
2. Take the original equation and replace the endogenous right-hand side variable with the fitted values from stage 1. Estimate using ordinary least squares.

Table 10-D gives the 2SLS results for the pizzeria's demand equation.

Both independent variables have statistically significant coefficients, at a 1% error level. P has a negative coefficient and COMP has a positive coefficient, as expected. The 2SLS results are not all that different from the instrumental variable results presented in Table 10-C (page 218). This makes sense because WAGE, the instrument used in the instrumental variables estimation, is one of the predetermined variables used in the 2SLS procedure. Also, two-stage least squares is a form of instrumental variables estimation.

Next let's estimate the supply equation using two-stage least squares.

$$\text{Supply: } Q = \alpha_0 + \alpha_1 P + \alpha_2 WAGE + \alpha_3 CHEESE + e \qquad \text{(10-2)}$$

In the first stage we take P and use it as a dependent variable with the system's three predetermined variables used as independent variables. This is the same regression we used in the first stage when we estimated demand with two-stage least squares, Equation (10-5).

$$P = \pi_4 + \pi_5 COMP + \pi_6 WAGE + \pi_7 CHEESE + e \qquad \text{(10-5)}$$

In the second stage, $\hat{P}$ (the fitted or predicted values for P) replaces P in Equation (10-2).

$$Q = \alpha_0 + \alpha_1 \hat{P} + \alpha_2 WAGE + \alpha_3 CHEESE + e \qquad \text{(10-13)}$$

Table 10-D

2SLS Results for Pizzeria's Demand Equation

Dependent variable: Q
Predetermined variables: COMP, WAGE, CHEESE[4]

Variable	Coefficient	Standard Error	t-Statistic	p-Value
Constant	2,220.61	201.11	11.04	0.00
P	−73.45	20.14	−3.65	0.00
COMP	32.61	10.86	3.00	0.01

Observations: 30
$R^2 = 0.29$
Adjusted $R^2 = 0.24$
Residual Sum of Squares = 293,301.43
F-statistic = 12.74
Durbin-Watson statistic = 2.05

The 2SLS results for this supply equation are given in Table 10-E.

All three independent variables have statistically significant coefficients at a 5% error level or better. The coefficients all have the expected signs. An increase in pizza price is positively correlated with quantity of pizzas sold. An increase in WAGE or CHEESE represents an increase in costs for the pizzeria, and so these two variables have negative coefficients.

As we would expect, the properties of two-stage least squares are similar to instrumental variables since 2SLS is a form of instrumental variables. Two-stage least squares is consistent, which means it comes very close to giving unbiased estimates for large sample sizes. For smaller sample sizes, there is no promise that the estimates will be unbiased. Two-stage least squares works best when the first stage regression has a high adjusted R^2, indicating a good fit. As noted, most econometrics software can run two-stage least squares with a single command, so that you don't have to run each stage separately. It is important to use the procedure that is built into the software when running two-stage least squares. If each stage is run separately, the standard errors and t-statistics will not be correct. This happens because the software will not realize that the second stage is part of a 2SLS regression.

There is also a three-stage least squares procedure. **Three-stage least squares** adds seemingly unrelated regression to two-stage least squares. The estimation process accounts for correlations between error terms in different equations in the same way that seemingly unrelated regression does (see Section 9-2), and it also includes two-

---

[4] Eviews refers to the list of predetermined variables as the instrument list. Two-stage least squares uses the predetermined variables in the system to construct the instrument. The instrumental variable is the fitted value from the first stage, not the list of predetermined variables.

Table 10-E

2SLS Results for Pizzeria's Supply Equation

Dependent variable: Q
Predetermined variables: COMP, WAGE, CHEESE

Variable	Coefficient	Standard Error	t-Statistic	p-Value
Constant	5,669.75	804.96	7.04	0.00
P	193.95	90.36	2.15	0.04
WAGE	−418.75	128.41	−3.26	0.00
CHEESE	−24.01	6.12	−3.92	0.00

Observations: 30
$R^2 = 0.70$
Adjusted $R^2 = 0.67$
Residual Sum of Squares = 123,428.73
F-statistic = 20.72
Durbin-Watson statistic = 1.76

stage least squares to handle simultaneity. Three-stage least squares is a mathematically complicated procedure, and it will not be covered here.[5]

SUMMARY

1. When a model needs more than one equation because two (or more) dependent variables are determined at the same time, it is called a **simultaneous-equation system**. Ordinary least squares cannot be used to estimate a simultaneous-equation system. The OLS procedure estimates each equation separately, and does not take into account that the equations are part of a larger system. The OLS estimates will be biased.

2. Simultaneous-equation models can be written in two ways. **Structural equations** show the underlying theoretical equations that make up the model; structural equations in a simultaneous-equation system cannot be estimated using ordinary least squares. **Reduced-form equations** only have the predetermined variables on the right-hand side, and can be estimated by ordinary least squares. However, the reduced form is not as useful for learning about the model.

3. A structural equation in a simultaneous-equation system can be estimated only if the equation is identified. **Identification** means there is enough information in a simultaneous-equation system for the equation's coefficients to be estimated. A

[5] Takeshi Amemiya, *Advanced Econometrics* (Cambridge, Massachusetts: Harvard University Press, 1985), pp. 228–231 provides more information about three-stage least squares for interested readers who are familiar with matrix algebra.

simultaneous-equation system can have some equations that are identified and some that are not. For an equation to be identified, it must satisfy the order condition. The **order condition** is a necessary (but not sufficient) condition for an equation to be identified. It requires that for every nonlagged endogenous variable appearing on the right-hand side of the equation, there must be a predetermined variable in the system that has been excluded from the equation.

4. **Simultaneity** occurs when only one equation is used to describe a model that needs two or more equations. A regression equation implies that in theory, the variables on the right-hand side of the equation affect the variable on the left-hand side, but not the other way around. Simultaneity occurs when the left-hand side variable affects a right-hand side variable. Ordinary least squares produces biased estimates if there is simultaneity in the model. The classical assumption that all independent variables are uncorrelated with the error term will not hold true.

5. The Hausman test can be used to see if a variable from the right-hand side of an equation is correlated with the error term. If so, the variable may be endogenous and there could be a simultaneity problem.

6. **Instrumental variables estimation** uses a proxy for one of the endogenous variables to estimate an equation with a simultaneity problem. The proxy, called an instrumental variable, should meet two criteria:
   - It should be correlated with the endogenous problem variable.
   - It should be uncorrelated with the error term in the regression.
   Instrumental variables estimation can also be used to address measurement error.

7. **Two-stage least squares (2SLS)** is a specific type of instrumental variables estimation that uses all the system's predetermined variables to construct an instrument. It is often difficult to find an instrumental variable that is both highly correlated with the problem independent variable and uncorrelated with the error term. Two-stage least squares uses an orderly procedure to form an instrumental variable. The two stages are:
   - Use the endogenous right-hand side variable from the original equation as the dependent variable. For the independent variables, use all the predetermined variables in the original system of equations. Estimate using ordinary least squares. Saved the fitted values for the dependent variable for use in the second stage.
   - Take the original equation and replace the endogenous right-hand side variable with the fitted values from Stage 1. Estimate using ordinary least squares.

EXERCISES

1. Try to explain these terms without looking them up.
   - simultaneous-equation system
   - exogenous variable
   - endogenous variable
   - predetermined variables
   - structural equations
   - reduced-form equations
   - identification

- overidentification
- order condition
- simultaneity
- instrumental variables estimation
- two-stage least squares
- three-stage least squares

2. You are hired by an oil company to study the price of gasoline. Your assistant suggests using the time-series regression:

$$P = B_0 + B_1 Q + B_2 BARREL + e$$

where P is the real price of gasoline, Q is the quantity of gasoline sold, and BARREL is the real price of oil per barrel. What is wrong with this model? What suggestions can you make?

3. Simultaneity causes problems for ordinary least squares regression. Explain the simultaneity problem in a simple way as you would to a friend who doesn't know much about econometrics.

4. If an equation meets the order condition, does that guarantee that the equation is identified? If so, how do you know? If not, then what is the order condition good for?

5. Each of the following four models consists of a two-equation system for the demand and supply of umbrellas. State whether each equation satisfies the order condition or not.

$$Q = \text{number of umbrellas sold each month}$$
$$P = \text{average real price of umbrellas each month}$$
$$INCOME = \text{real average monthly income}$$
$$RAIN = \text{average inches of rain each month}$$
$$WAGE = \text{average real monthly income earned by those assembling the umbrellas}$$
$$PVINYL = \text{average real monthly price of vinyl used to make umbrellas.}$$

Model 1

Demand: $Q = B_0 + B_1 P + B_2 INCOME + B_3 RAIN + e$

Supply: $Q = \alpha_0 + \alpha_1 P + \alpha_2 RAIN + e$

Model 2

Demand: $Q = B_0 + B_1 P + B_2 INCOME + B_3 RAIN + e$

Supply: $Q = \alpha_0 + \alpha_1 P + \alpha_2 WAGE + e$

Model 3

Demand: $Q = B_0 + B_1 P + B_2 INCOME + B_3 RAIN + e$

Supply: $Q = \alpha_0 + \alpha_1 P + \alpha_2 INCOME + \alpha_3 RAIN + e$

> **Model 4**
>
> Demand: $Q = B_0 + B_1P + B_2INCOME + B_3RAIN + e$
>
> Supply: $Q = \alpha_0 + \alpha_1P + \alpha_2INCOME + \alpha_3PVINYL + e$

6. Design supply and demand regressions for a product or service of your choice.
   a. Write out the regressions, along with the definitions of the variables.
   b. Is this model likely to have a simultaneity problem?
   c. Is the demand equation identified?
   d. Is the supply equation identified?
   e. What procedure would you use to estimate the regressions?

7. Sometimes it is advantageous to use instrumental variables estimation instead of ordinary least squares. Instrumental variables estimation is useful when one of the OLS assumptions is violated.
   a. Which assumption is it?
   b. In your own words, explain how the instrumental variables estimator avoids violating this assumption.

8. What is the difference between instrumental variables estimation and two-stage least squares?

9. Without looking it up, explain how the Hausman test checks for simultaneity.

10. In the three-equation system below, every Y variable is endogenous and every X variable is exogenous. Determine which (if any) of the equations satisfy the order condition for identification. (The Greek letter theta, θ, indicates coefficients for the third equation in the same way that B and α are used in the first two equations.)

$$Y_1 = B_0 + B_1Y_2 + B_2Y_3 + B_3X_2 + B_4X_3 + e$$

$$Y_2 = \alpha_0 + \alpha_1Y_1 + \alpha_2X_1 + \alpha_3X_3 + e$$

$$Y_3 = \theta_0 + \theta_1Y_1 + \theta_2Y_2 + \theta_3X_1 + e$$

11. a. Write the reduced-form equations for the model in Exercise 10.
    b. Would it be easier to estimate the reduced form of the model instead of estimating the structural equations shown in Exercise 10? Why or why not?
    c. Consider your answer to part b. Why not just estimate that version of the model, since it is easier?

12. This exercise uses the professional wrestling model given in Equation (5-1) and the data in Table 5-A.

$$HOURS = B_0 + B_1MALE + B_2INCOME + B_3AGE + e \qquad \text{(5-1)}$$

It is possible that INCOME is endogenous and is causing simultaneity. It is possible that the hours spent watching wrestling affect INCOME. Perhaps the following equation should be added to the model so that it is a simultaneous-equation model.

$$INCOME = \alpha_0 + \alpha_1MALE + \alpha_2HOURS + \alpha_3AGE + \alpha_4EDUCATION + e$$

where EDUCATION is the number of years of schooling for each person. For example, 12 indicates the person finished high school, 16 means they completed four years of college. The values for EDUCATION are as follows:

Person	1	2	3	4	5	6	7	8	9	10	11	12	13	14	15	16	17	18	19	20
EDUCATION	18	12	16	12	16	21	10	12	16	22	18	10	12	16	12	14	14	16	12	16

a. Does Equation (5-1) meet the order condition?

b. Does the new equation with INCOME as the dependent variable meet the order condition?

c. Conduct a Hausman test to see if there is evidence that INCOME is endogenous in Equation (5-1). What do the test results tell you?

13. Estimate Equation (5-1) using two-stage least squares, using EDUCATION (from Exercise 12) as one of the predetermined variables, but do not include EDUCATION in Equation (5-1).

a. How do the results compare with the ordinary least squares results given in Table 5-B?

b. Why do the results compare in the way you stated in part a?

14. Consider the following two-equation model:

$$\text{Demand: } P_t = B_0 + B_1 Q_t + B_2 X_t + e$$

$$\text{Supply: } Q_t = \alpha_0 + \alpha_1 P_{t-1} + e$$

where

Q_t = quantity in the current period
X_t = an exogenous variable in the current period
P_t = price in the current time period
P_{t-1} = price in the previous time period

a. What is unusual about this supply and demand model?

b. This type of model is called a recursive model. (The word "recursive" means self-repeating.) Why is the model called recursive? (*Hint:* Assume each time period is a year. What would the model look like if a year goes by and it is now time period t + 1?)

c. Can these equations be estimated using ordinary least squares?

11

Time-Series Models: Using the Past to Consider the Future

In this chapter, you will learn:

- How to estimate different types of time-series models.
- The problems that can occur with these models.
- How to use econometrics for forecasting.
- A test for a special type of causality (whether one variable causes another to change).

Time-series models are of special interest in econometrics because they are often used for forecasting. If you are an executive for a chain of retail stores, you might be interested in forecasting personal consumption expenditures. A bank economist who is interested in macroeconomics and Federal Reserve Bank policy might want to forecast future values of the money supply. Time-series models are used in these types of forecasts. However, econometric forecasting is far from perfect; no one can really predict the future, no matter how good they are at econometrics.

A time-series variable can be thought of as econometric time travel. The variable measures the same thing, but at different points in time. You are staying in the same "place,"—a country, an industry or an individual—but your observations are moving through time. In this chapter, we consider special problems that arise with time-series models. It often takes time for the impact of an independent variable to show up. We can account for this by using independent variables from a previous time period. How much time should we allow for the independent variable to make its mark on the dependent variable? How are such models estimated? These questions are addressed in the next three sections. Then, in Section 11-4, we discuss forecasting problems and procedures. Section 11-5 provides a test to see whether changes in an independent variable tend to occur before changes in the dependent variable. This test, called a Granger causality test, is useful in doing time-series work.

11-1 ESTIMATING DISTRIBUTED LAG MODELS

It takes time for the effect of some independent variables to take place. We model this time gap between when an independent variable changes and when the dependent variable changes with a lagged independent variable. A **lagged independent variable** indicates that the values being used are from previous time periods. We used lagged variables in the Microsoft revenues model in Chapter 7 to account for the time lag between a change in marketing expenditures and a change in revenues. As in Chapter 7, some additional notation will be used in this chapter. Each variable will have a subscript to indicate the time period it represents. (For simplicity, this subscript has been omitted for time-series variables in other chapters.) For example, Y_t represents the value of Y in the current time period, t, and X_t means the same thing for the independent variable X. X_{t-1} represents the value of X from the preceding time period; X_{t-2} is the value of X from two periods ago, and so forth.

Distributed Lag Models

Consider a model of consumption, where the only independent variable is income. Consumption in one year may be influenced by that year's income, the preceding year's income, and even income from several years in the past. Here is one possible regression model:

$$\text{CONSUMPTION}_t = B_0 + B_1 \text{INCOME}_t + B_2 \text{INCOME}_{t-1} + B_3 \text{INCOME}_{t-2} + e_t \tag{11-1}$$

When an independent variable appears in a regression more than once, with different time lags, it is a **distributed lag model**. It has this name because the influence of the independent variable is spread out—or distributed across—several time periods. In Equation (11-1), the influence of income on consumption spreads across three time periods: t (current period), t − 1 (one period ago), and t − 2 (two periods ago). B_1 measures the change in consumption associated with a one-unit change in income in period t, keeping income in periods t − 1 and t − 2 constant. B_2 measures the change in consumption associated with a one-unit change in income in period t − 1, keeping income in periods t and t − 2 constant. The same logic applies to B_3.

As a general rule, independent variables from time periods farther back in time have smaller coefficients than independent variables for more recent periods. Income from last year will likely have a bigger effect on your current consumption than your income from 5 years ago. The coefficient should eventually approach zero as you go farther back in time. If B_1 in Equation (11-1) is 0.8, it is reasonable to expect that B_2 will be smaller than 0.8 (say 0.5) and that B_3 will be even smaller. If we used INCOME_{t-20} in the model (income from 20 years before the consumption took place), it is reasonable to assume that its slope coefficient would be close to zero. Note that we can also include independent variables other than the lagged variable in the model.

Several problems arise when we estimate distributed lag models:

1. Multicollinearity.
2. The degrees of freedom decrease.
3. Effects of lagged variables farther back in time do not always fade out as they should.

Multicollinearity is often a problem in distributed lag models because the same independent variable appears in the model more than once. In Equation (11-1), INCOME from three different time periods appears in the model three times. It is likely that income from three consecutive time periods will be correlated.

The farther back in time the lagged variables go, the more variables there are in the model; this decreases the degrees of freedom. Suppose we have 50 years of annual data, from 1950 through 1999 for Equation (11-1). At first glance, we might think the degrees of freedom are 46, since we have 50 years of data and three slope coefficients (and the intercept) to estimate ($N - k - 1 = 50 - 3 - 1 = 46$). This will not be true in practice. To use the consumption value for 1950 in the regression, we need income values for 1950, 1949, and 1948—for $INCOME_t$, $INCOME_{t-1}$, and $INCOME_{t-2}$—but we don't have values for 1948 and 1949 in the data set. Therefore, the regression has to start with 1952, not 1950. If we start with 1952, then 1952 income can be used for $INCOME_t$, 1951 income for $INCOME_{t-1}$, and 1950 income for $INCOME_{t-2}$. So if we want to estimate Equation (11-1) with 50 years of data, our sample size is really only 48, since the regression must start in 1952, using 1950 and 1951 for the first observation's lagged variables. The degrees of freedom are $48 - 3 - 1 = 44$, not 46 as we initially thought. For any data set, as we add more lagged terms, going farther back in time, we lose more degrees of freedom than if we add a nonlagged independent variable. The farther back the lagged terms go, the more degrees of freedom we lose. If $INCOME_{t-3}$ is added to our model, using the same data set, the degrees of freedom decrease by 2. One degree of freedom would be used up because the slope coefficient for $INCOME_{t-3}$ needs to be estimated. Another degree of freedom would be lost because the regression now starts in 1953 instead of 1952, so that the INCOME value for 1950 can be used as the first value for $INCOME_{t-3}$.

As you include lagged variables from farther back in time, the slope coefficient of the variable should get closer to zero. The third problem with distributed lag models occurs when the effect does not fade out as it should. Multicollinearity can cause this problem. If $INCOME_{t-20}$ is highly correlated with more recent values of INCOME, then the B for $INCOME_{t-20}$ may not be close to zero, *and* it may even be statistically significant. The slope coefficient for $INCOME_{t-20}$ picks up the explanatory power of more recent values of INCOME. The Koyck lag model successfully deals with all three of these problems.

The Koyck Lag Model

The **Koyck lag model** is constructed in a way that makes the slope coefficients automatically get closer to zero as the independent variables go farther back in time.[1] Equation (11-2) shows a generic distributed lag model:

$$Y_t = a + B_0X_t + B_1X_{t-1} + B_2X_{t-2} + \cdots + B_LX_{t-L} + e_t \qquad \textbf{(11-2)}$$

where L represents the number of lags in the model. B_0 is no longer the intercept; it is now the slope coefficient for an independent variable with a time lag of zero. The

---

[1] L. M. Koyck, *Distributed Lags and Investment Analysis* (Amsterdam: North-Holland, 1954).

intercept is represented by a. This notation makes the model easier to follow, since the subscript on B gives the number of lagged time periods for X. For example, B_2 is the slope coefficient for X_{t-2}, the X that is lagged two time periods.

A fraction, referred to as the Greek letter lambda (λ), is used to multiply the base value B_0 so that the slope coefficients decrease as you go back further in time.

$$B_i = B_0\lambda^i \qquad\qquad (11\text{-}3)$$

where i starts at 0 and goes to the number of lags desired, and $0 < \lambda < 1$. Say that $\lambda = 0.5$ and $B_0 = 10$. Then we can find values for the slope coefficients in Equation (11-2) using $B_i = B_0\lambda^i$ and the estimates for λ and B_0 from the Koyck lag model. Table 11-A demonstrates how the $B_i = B_0\lambda^i$ equation is used.

In Table 11-A, the slope coefficients get closer to zero as X comes from a more distant time period. The effect of an independent variable in a Koyck lag model always gets closer to zero as it is lagged farther back in time. Writing this in equation form clarifies that the slope coefficient values in Table 11-A approach zero as you go back farther in time. Assume intercept $a = 15$.

$$\hat{Y}_t = 15 + 10X_t + 5X_{t-1} + 2.5X_{t-2} + 1.25X_{t-3} + 0.625X_{t-4} \qquad (11\text{-}4)$$

Using some mathematical manipulation, Koyck showed that his model, as expressed by Equation (11-2), is the same as Equation (11-5). The math used to get from Equation (11-2) to Equation (11-5) is discussed in Section 11-6.

$$Y_t = a_0 + B_0X_t + \lambda Y_{t-1} + u_t \qquad\qquad (11\text{-}5)$$

where a_0 is an intercept that takes a different value than a in Equation (11-2). B_0 takes the same value as in Equation (11-2), and λ is the same as discussed above. u_t is an error term equal to $e_t - \lambda e_{t-1}$. In practice, (11-5) will often exhibit autocorrelation; This problem will be discussed in more detail later in the chapter. After estimating

Table 11-A

Slope Coefficients Calculated from the Koyck Lag
Model when $B_0 = 10$ and $\lambda = 0.5$

$B_i = B_0\lambda^i$
$B_0 = B_0\lambda^0 = 10 \cdot (0.5)^0 = 10$
$B_1 = B_0\lambda^1 = 10 \cdot (0.5)^1 = 5$
$B_2 = B_0\lambda^2 = 10 \cdot (0.5)^2 = 10 \cdot (0.25) = 2.5$
$B_3 = B_0\lambda^3 = 10 \cdot (0.5)^3 = 10 \cdot (0.125) = 1.25$
$B_4 = B_0\lambda^4 = 10 \cdot (0.5)^4 = 10 \cdot (0.0625) = 0.625$

Equation (11-5), we can use the estimates of B_0 and λ to calculate the B's by using $B_i = B\lambda^i$, as in Table 11-A.

The Koyck model, as expressed by Equation (11-5), successfully deals with the three problems in distributed lag models: (1) Multicollinearity is eliminated, because the only X variable in the regression is X_t. (2) Only two variables show up on the right-hand side of Equation (11-5), and only one of them is a lagged term, Y_{t-1} (and it is lagged only one period). This avoids the large loss in the degrees of freedom that can occur when lags farther back in time are included on the right-hand side of the regression. And (3), the slope coefficients get closer to zero as you go farther back in time (as shown by $B_i = B_0\lambda^i$, in Table 11-A).

We can use ordinary least squares to estimate the Koyck lag model in the form $Y_t = a_0 + B_0X_t + \lambda Y_{t-1} + u_t$. Any other independent variable that we add to the model also ends up being lagged because of the Y_{t-1} term. For example, if we add another independent variable, W_t, to the model, then W_{t-1} becomes part of the equation for Y_{t-1}. Since Y_{t-1} is on the right-hand side of the Koyck model, W_{t-1} is indirectly on the right-hand side of the model also. Thus, W ends up being a lagged variable in the model, whether we want it lagged or not.

The classic example of a Koyck lag model is a consumption model, with income as an independent variable. Writing the model as a distributed lag model (without using the Koyck model) gives a regression similar to the example at the beginning of the chapter.

$$CONSUMPTION_t = a + B_0INCOME_t + B_1INCOME_{t-1} + \cdots$$
$$+ B_LINCOME_{t-L} + e_t \qquad \textbf{(11-6)}$$

where
> CONSUMPTION = quarterly real personal consumption expenditures, per capita
> INCOME = quarterly real personal income, per capita

Applying the Koyck lag model to this example makes it easier to estimate. First we estimate Equation (11-7) using ordinary least squares.

$$CONSUMPTION_t = a_0 + B_0INCOME_t + \lambda CONSUMPTION_{t-1} + u_t \qquad \textbf{(11-7)}$$

This makes it possible to find the slope coefficients, $B_i = B_0\lambda^i$, for the original model, Equation (11-6). The consumption and income data used here are quarterly data from 1959 through 1998.[2] (More recent data will be added to the model for use in the forecasting section of the chapter.) Table 11-B shows the Koyck results for this consumption model.

The next logical step is to use $B_i = B_0\lambda^i$ to find estimates for B_1, B_2, and so on, for the original model, Equation (11-6). Table 11-B gives 0.087 as the B_0 estimate and 0.91

---

[2] Data are from Bureau of Economic Analysis, Department of Commerce, http://www.bea.doc.gov/bea/dn1 .htm. Data are also available at the text website or http://www.economagic.com. Data are adjusted for inflation by using city average CPI where 1982–1984 = 100. CPI data are from Bureau of Labor Statistics at http://www.bls.gov/data/ (click overall most requested BLS Statistics). CPI data are also available at the text website or http://www.economagic.com.

Table 11-B

Regression Results for Koyck Consumption Model

Dependent variable: $CONSUMPTION_t$

Variable	Coefficient	Standard Error	t-Statistic	p-Value
Constant	−10.04	32.52	−0.31	0.76
$INCOME_t$ (B_0)	0.087	0.030	2.92	0.00
$CONSUMPTION_{t-1}$ (λ)	0.91	0.032	28.11	0.00

Observations: 159

$R^2 = 0.99$

Adjusted $R^2 = 0.99$

Residual Sum of Squares = 931,980

F-statistic = 54,321.21

Durbin-Watson statistic = 1.29

Table 11-C

Slope Coefficients Calculated from Koyck
Consumption Model, $B_0 = 0.087$ and $\lambda = 0.91$

$B_i = B_0 \lambda^i$
$B_0 = B_0 \lambda^0 = 0.087 \cdot (0.91)^0 = 0.087$
$B_1 = B_0 \lambda^1 = 0.087 \cdot (0.91)^1 = 0.079$
$B_2 = B_0 \lambda^2 = 0.087 \cdot (0.91)^2 = 0.072$
$B_3 = B_0 \lambda^3 = 0.087 \cdot (0.91)^3 = 0.066$
$B_4 = B_0 \lambda^4 = 0.087 \cdot (0.91)^4 = 0.060$
$B_5 = B_0 \lambda^5 = 0.087 \cdot (0.91)^5 = 0.054$

as the λ estimate. Table 11-C gives slope coefficients calculated using $B_i = B_0 \lambda^i$ for the original model.

If more terms are desired, they can be calculated. Note that the estimates for the slope coefficients become smaller as we go back in time with longer lags. The results can be written in equation form.

$$\hat{CONSUMPTION}_t = -10.04 + 0.087 \; INCOME_t + 0.079 \; INCOME_{t-1}$$
$$+ 0.072 \; INCOME_{t-2} + 0.066 \; INCOME_{t-3} \quad \textbf{(11-8)}$$
$$+ 0.060 \; INCOME_{t-4} + 0.054 \; INCOME_{t-5}$$

We can also use Koyck lag results to find the multipliers often used in macroeconomics. A multiplier gives the total change over time in the dependent variable associated with a one-unit change in the independent variable. In our consumption example, the multiplier gives the total change in consumption over time from a one-unit change in income. The general formula for finding the multiplier is:

$$\text{multiplier} = \hat{B}_0\left(\frac{1}{1 - \hat{\lambda}}\right) \tag{11-9}$$

where $\hat{B}_0$ and $\hat{\lambda}$ are estimates found using the Koyck model. For the consumption example, the multiplier is $0.087 \cdot [1/(1 - 0.91)] = 0.087 \cdot [1/0.09] = 0.97$. This multiplier indicates that a dollar increase in income can generate \$0.97 in consumption over time. There are serious problems with the B_0 and λ estimates used to calculate this multiplier, however. The first problem is autocorrelation.

Koyck Lag Models with Autocorrelation

Most Koyck lag models exhibit autocorrelation. Section 11-6 reveals why. As you will see in Section 11-6, the error term u_t in the typical Koyck model [Equation (11-5)] is clearly related to e_t and e_{t-1} from the original distributed lag model [Equation (11-2)]. The relationship is $u_t = e_t - \lambda e_{t-1}$. The preceding error term is described by $u_{t-1} = e_{t-1} - \lambda e_{t-2}$. e_{t-1} appears in the equations for both u_t and u_{t-1}, so both u_t and u_{t-1} are correlated with e_{t-1}. This means that u_t and u_{t-1} will be correlated with each other, giving us autocorrelation. The $u_t = e_t - \lambda e_{t-1}$ relationship may look familiar. It is almost the same as the first-order autocorrelation process described by Equation (7-7): $e_t - \rho e_{t-1} = u_t$.

If this autocorrelation problem doesn't seem like enough trouble, there is more. In Section 7-3, it was mentioned that the Durbin-Watson statistic is biased toward 2 when a lagged dependent variable shows up on the right-hand side of the model. This means that the Durbin-Watson statistic is biased toward finding no autocorrelation in the Koyck model. Durbin has addressed this problem with the Durbin h-statistic, which corrects for the bias.[3] The **Durbin h-statistic** tests for first-order autocorrelation in models with a lagged dependent variable on the right-hand side, like the Koyck model. The formula for the Durbin h-statistic relies in part on the original Durbin-Watson statistic.

$$h = \left(1 - \frac{\text{D.W.}}{2}\right)\sqrt{\frac{n}{1 - n \cdot [SE(\hat{\lambda})]^2}} \tag{11-10}$$

where D.W. is the regular Durbin-Watson statistic from the regression results, n is the sample size, and $SE(\hat{\lambda})$ is the standard error of the estimate of λ. The Durbin h-statistic

---

[3] J. Durbin, "Testing for Serial Correlation in Least Squares Regression When Some of the Regressors Are Lagged Dependent Variables," *Econometrica*, Vol. 38, 1970, pp. 420–421.

follows the normal distribution. This makes for an easy decision rule. For a two-sided test at the 5% error level, the decision rule is:

- If the Durbin h-statistic is greater than 1.96, reject the null hypothesis of no auto-correlation. There is evidence of autocorrelation.
- If the Durbin h-statistic is equal or less than 1.96, do not reject the null hypothesis of no autocorrelation. Assume that autocorrelation is not a problem.

Note that if the Durbin-Watson statistic is exactly 2, the Durbin h-statistic is zero; the test indicates no evidence of autocorrelation. The closer to 2 the Durbin-Watson statistic is, the less likely we are to reject the null hypothesis of no autocorrelation, keeping the other parts of the h-statistic equation the same. The Durbin-Watson statistic affects the Durbin h-statistic but so does the sample size and the standard error of $\hat{\lambda}$. One problem with the Durbin h-statistic is that if $n \cdot [SE(\hat{\lambda})]^2$ is greater than 1, then the value under the square root sign will end up being negative. This makes it impossible to calculate the Durbin h-statistic in this case. Durbin also has an answer to this problem. His alternative test uses the observed Koyck error term $\hat{u}_t$ as a dependent variable and X_t, Y_{t-1}, and the observed error term lagged one period as independent variables.

$$\hat{u}_t = B_0 + B_1 X_t + B_2 Y_{t-1} + B_3 \hat{u}_{t-1} + e_t \qquad \text{(11-11)}$$

The slope coefficients in Equation (11-11) are not the same as in the Koyck lag model. (For example, B_2 is not λ from the Koyck lag model, since the dependent variable is u_t, not Y_t as in the Koyck model.) If the slope coefficient for $\hat{u}_{t-1}$ is significantly different from zero according to the t-test, then that is evidence of autocorrelation in the Koyck model.

Three actions can be taken when a Koyck model exhibits autocorrelation.

1. Add a missing independent variable.
2. Use instrumental variables to estimate the model (this includes using two-stage least squares).
3. Use a more complicated general least squares procedure.

The best but perhaps hardest solution is to add a missing independent variable. As discussed in Chapter 7, finding and adding a missing independent variable to the model may eliminate the autocorrelation. Then there is no need for more complicated estimation procedures that are harder to interpret.

Instrumental variables estimation is also used to address autocorrelation in Koyck models. A careful reading of Section 11-6 reveals that the $u_t = e_t - \lambda e_{t-1}$ relationship takes place because of the presence of Y_{t-1} in the Koyck model.[4] If a good instrument can be found for Y_{t-1}, instrumental variables estimation is able to manage autocorrelation in Koyck models. (This is a big "if," however; it is often difficult to find a good instrument.) A more complicated general least squares procedure can also be used to address autocorrelation in Koyck lag models, but it will not be covered here.

---

[4] Interested readers can look at the regression featuring Y_{t-1} as a dependent variable, Equation (11-28) in Section 11-6. Equation (11-28) becomes part of the Koyck lag model, and since it contains e_{t-1}, it introduces autocorrelation into the Koyck lag model.

11-2 AUTOREGRESSIVE AND MOVING AVERAGE MODELS: ERRORS THAT LAST OVER TIME

The models we discuss in this section are primarily used for forecasting; they contain only one variable. These models are based on the idea that the best way to predict the variable of interest is to use one or more previous values of the same variable. They do not give us insight into why the variable changes the way it does. These models focus on a mathematical pattern in the data, and then use that pattern to make forecasts about the future. The model's ability to predict future values depends on whether or not the mathematical pattern continues in the future.

Autoregressive Models

In an **autoregressive model** the independent variables are all lagged dependent variables; there are no other independent variables. The dependent variable follows a pattern. A typical autoregressive model is

$$Y_t = B_0 + B_1 Y_{t-1} + e_t \qquad (11\text{-}12)$$

This is an autoregressive model of order 1, or AR(1). The current value of the dependent variable Y_t depends on its value in the preceding period, Y_{t-1}. There is also an intercept and an error term in the model. Chapter 7 described an AR(1) process, but it was for the error terms, not the dependent variable. In Chapter 7, the current error depended on its preceding value. In the AR(1) process here, it is the dependent variable Y_t that depends on its preceding value.

Autoregressive processes can take any order. AR(2) is $Y_t = B_0 + B_1 Y_{t-1} + B_2 Y_{t-2} + e_t$. In general, an autoregressive model is referred to as AR(p), where p is the number of lags. [p is different from rho (ρ), the Greek letter used to symbolize the autocorrelation coefficient in Chapter 7.]

We need a way to decide how many lagged terms we should use in a model. Usually, theory guides us in setting up our initial model. As noted at the beginning of this chapter, however, the models used here are not based on a theory of how changes in the dependent variable are determined. These models are based simply on patterns in the data, patterns that we hope will continue in the future so that forecasts from our models will be accurate. The best number of lagged variables to use can be found by looking at the partial autocorrelation function. The **partial autocorrelation function** gives the correlation coefficients between the dependent variable and this same variable with different lags, while keeping the effect of shorter lags constant. The partial autocorrelation function gives us a series of correlation values. The first correlation value is for Y_t and Y_{t-1}, the second one is for Y_t and Y_{t-2}, then Y_t and Y_{t-3}, and so forth. The correlation between Y_t and Y_{t-2} does not include the effect of the correlation between Y_t and Y_{t-1}. The correlation between Y_t and Y_{t-3} does not include the effect of the correlation between Y_t and Y_{t-2}, nor does it include the effect of the correlation between Y_t and Y_{t-1}. That is why it is known as the *partial* autocorrelation function.

To show how the partial autocorrelation function can be used to decide how many lagged terms to include in a model, we will use the M1 measure of money supply (in

Figure 11-1

Partial Autocorrelation Function for M1. The number on the right side tells which correlation is shown. For example, 3 is the partial correlation between $M1_t$ and $M1_{t-3}$. The dashed lines give the confidence interval for a 5% error level.

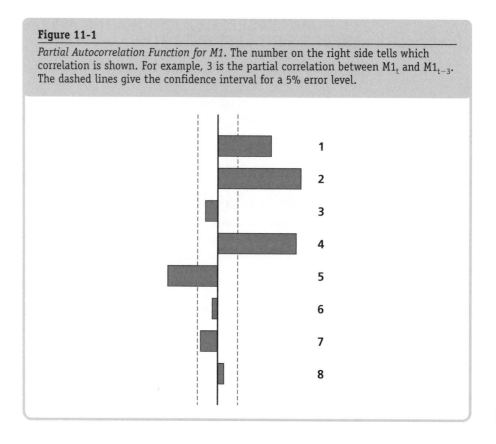

billions of dollars) in an autoregressive model. The data are quarterly, from the first quarter of 1959 through the second quarter of 2001.[5] Figure 11-1 shows the partial autocorrelation function for the M1 money supply data for the first eight lags. (Calling the money supply variable M1, this means it shows the partial correlation for $M1_t$ and $M1_{t-1}$, then $M1_t$ and $M1_{t-2}$, and so on, with the last partial correlation shown being $M1_t$ and $M1_{t-8}$.)

We can use the partial autocorrelation function to see which lagged terms have partial correlations with Y_t that are significantly different from zero. When a partial correlation exceeds the dashed lines on the figure, then it lies outside a 95% confidence interval where the null hypothesis is that the partial correlation is zero. This means the partial correlation is significantly different from zero at a 5% error level. Going backward in time, starting with shorter lags and moving to longer ones, Figure 11-1 shows that the partial correlation coefficients differ significantly from zero when the lag is 1, 2, 4, and 5 periods. Since the longest significant lag is 5, this suggests that an AR(5) model is the best way to run an autoregressive model using this data. Note that we

---

[5] The data are from St. Louis Federal Reserve Board, http://www.stls.frb.org/fred/index.html, and are also available at http://www.economagic.com and the text website.

include a lag of three periods even though it is not significant in the partial autocorrelation function shown above.

$$M1_t = B_0 + B_1 M1_{t-1} + B_2 M1_{t-2} + B_3 M1_{t-3} + B_4 M1_{t-4} + B_5 M1_{t-5} + e_t \quad \text{(11-13)}$$

Like any other autoregressive model, we can estimate Equation (11-13), using ordinary least squares. However, ordinary least squares will not have the same desirable properties that it normally does for small samples, because of the lagged dependent variable(s) on the right-hand side. For larger samples, it will be unbiased. Regression results for Equation (11-13) using 1959–2001 quarterly data are given in Table 11-D.

When we use this type of model, with no right-hand side variables except lagged dependent variables, we are not trying to explain what causes the money supply to change. The idea is simply to find a pattern in the money supply that we can use to make forecasts about the future. Here, the pattern is that preceding values of the money supply (back to $M1_{t-5}$) can predict the current money supply. However, just because a pattern exists in past data, there is no guarantee that it will hold in the future.

The coefficient for $M1_{t-2}$ is *not* statistically significant even though the partial correlation function indicates significance, and the coefficient for $M1_{t-3}$ *is* statistically significant even though the partial correlation indicates otherwise. This shows why it is a good idea to include $M1_{t-3}$ in the model despite an insignificant result in the partial autocorrelation function. Statistical significance in the partial autocorrelation function is not the same as statistical significance in the regression model.

Table 11-D

Regression Results for AR(5) Money Supply Model

Dependent variable: $M1_t$

Variable	Coefficient	Standard Error	t-Statistic	p-Value
Constant	1.50	1.07	1.40	0.16
$M1_{t-1}$	1.23	0.07	17.77	0.00
$M1_{t-2}$	0.04	0.11	0.37	0.71
$M1_{t-3}$	−0.46	0.10	−4.48	0.00
$M1_{t-4}$	0.70	0.11	6.42	0.00
$M1_{t-5}$	−0.51	0.07	−7.27	0.00

Observations: 165

$R^2 = 0.99$

Adjusted $R^2 = 0.99$

Residual Sum of Squares = 8,852.88

F-statistic = 76,942.90

Durbin-Watson statistic = 1.64

Autoregressive models can exhibit a variety of problems. Since all the explanatory variables are really the same variable with different lags, multicollinearity is a potential problem. So is autocorrelation. And, as we discuss in Section 11-3, we may have to confront the dreaded enemy of econometricians everywhere—the unit-root problem. However, before we do that, let's look at moving average models.

Moving Average Models

A **moving average model** uses lagged error terms as independent variables.

$$Y_t = B_0 + B_1 e_{t-1} + B_2 e_{t-2} + B_3 e_{t-3} + \cdots + B_q e_{t-q} + e_t \qquad \textbf{(11-14)}$$

In Equation (11-14) q different lagged error terms are used as independent variables. Independent variables e_{t-1} through e_{t-q} are uncorrelated error terms. e_t is the typical error term found in every regression, and we assume it is not correlated with the other error terms. Moving average models are abbreviated MA(q) where q is the number of lagged error terms present in the model. The name "moving average" comes from the fact that Equation (11-4) gives the moving average of past error terms. We can combine this moving average of past error terms with the mean of the dependent variable to produce a moving average of the dependent variable. Moving average models are estimated using a nonlinear least squares process.[6]

The moving average model given by Equation (11-14) shares an important characteristic with the autoregressive models discussed earlier. Neither tells us anything about what other variables are associated with changes in the dependent variable. At most, we can learn that the dependent variable follows a mathematical pattern in the data we are using. Moving average processes and autoregressive processes can be used along with regular exogenous independent variables in regressions, but like the models shown here, it is not clear what the results can really tell us. As noted earlier, these models are primarily used for forecasting.

We determine the optimal number of lagged error terms to include in a moving average model by its autocorrelation function. An autocorrelation function is different from the partial autocorrelation function used with autoregressive models. An **autocorrelation function** gives correlation coefficients between the dependent variable and the same variable with different lags, but the effect of shorter lags is *not* kept constant. This means that the effect of shorter lags is included in the numbers given with the autocorrelation function. The correlation between Y_t and Y_{t-2} includes the effect of the correlation between Y_t and Y_{t-1}. This is the opposite of the *partial* autocorrelation function used earlier, where the effect of shorter lags is not included.

The Nasdaq stock index is a good candidate for a moving average model. The data are the daily closing values of the index, from January 4, 1999, through December 29, 2000.[7] We will use more recent data and this model in the exercises at the end of the

---

[6] If using Eviews, see nonlinear least squares in the on-line help of student Eviews for more information, or for a more advanced explanation, see G. Judge, W. Griffiths, R. Hill, H. Lutkepohl, and T. Lee, *The Theory and Practice of Econometrics*, 2nd ed. (New York: Wiley, 1985), pp. 307–310.

[7] Data can be found at the text website or http://www.economagic.com.

chapter. Figure 11-2 shows the autocorrelation function for the Nasdaq data, going back eight lags.

Figure 11-2 shows that MA(4) is appropriate for these data. Here is the regression:

$$NASDAQ_t = B_0 + B_1e_{t-1} + B_2e_{t-2} + B_3e_{t-3} + B_4e_{t-4} + e_t \quad \textbf{(11-15)}$$

We used daily data from the text website and nonlinear least squares to estimate this regression; the results are given in Table 11-E.

Autoregressive Moving Average Models

We can use the autoregressive and moving average processes together in **an autoregressive moving average model.** Such a model is abbreviated by ARMA(p, q) where p is the number of lagged dependent variables on the right-hand side, and q is the number of lagged error terms on the right-hand side. For example, ARMA(2, 3) is given by Equation (11-16).

$$Y_t = B_0 + B_1Y_{t-1} + B_2Y_{t-2} + B_3e_{t-1} + B_4e_{t-2} + B_5e_{t-3} + e_t \quad \textbf{(11-16)}$$

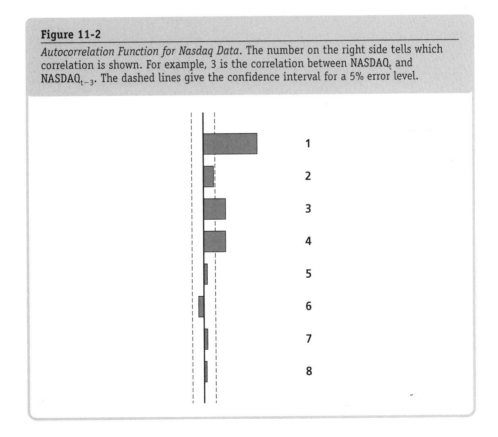

Figure 11-2

Autocorrelation Function for Nasdaq Data. The number on the right side tells which correlation is shown. For example, 3 is the correlation between $NASDAQ_t$ and $NASDAQ_{t-3}$. The dashed lines give the confidence interval for a 5% error level.

Table 11-E

Nonlinear Least Squares Results for MA(4) Nasdaq Model

Dependent variable: $NASDAQ_t$

Variable	Coefficient	Standard Error	t-Statistic	p-Value
Constant	76.65	0.58	132.58	0.00
e_{t-1}	2.18	0.035	62.71	0.00
e_{t-2}	2.54	0.067	37.88	0.00
e_{t-3}	1.74	0.067	26.19	0.00
e_{t-4}	0.60	0.035	17.28	0.00

Observations: 520

$R^2 = 0.97$

Adjusted $R^2 = 0.97$

Residual Sum of Squares = 1,378.98

F-statistic = 4,892.73

Durbin-Watson statistic = 1.33

Used for forecasting, ARMA models are estimated using nonlinear least squares. However, the results of an ARMA model are difficult to interpret.

11-3 STATIONARY VERSUS NONSTATIONARY SERIES: UNIT ROOTS CAN BE HARD TO KILL

A time-series variable is called **stationary** if it does not have an upward or downward trend over time. Mathematically, for a series to be stationary, its mean, variance, and autocorrelation pattern must remain the same over time. A time-series variable that does not meet these requirements and therefore exhibits a trend over time is called **nonstationary**. Autoregressive, moving average, and ARMA models must have stationary variables to be estimated properly. A nonstationary variable causes misleading results. The trend that the nonstationary variable follows is not represented in the model. Since the trend is not controlled for, the estimation process gives the nonstationary variable credit for the trend. It will seem as if the regression has much better goodness of fit than it really does, and the nonstationary variable will seem to have a greater impact in the regression than it really does. When a regression has a very strong goodness of fit and significant t-statistics because of a trend or other factor not accounted for in the model, it is often referred to as a **spurious regression** or a **spurious correlation**. (The word "spurious" refers to something that is different from what it seems to be.[8])

---

[8] A spurious regression also refers to results that occur because of random luck.

Unit-root tests are used to see if a variable is stationary. The term "unit root" comes from the mathematics behind the test. Consider a regression of the form $Y_t = B_0 + B_1 Y_{t-1} + e_t$. If $B_0 = 0$ and $B_1 = 1$, the new value of Y differs from the preceding value by the error term. In this case, Y is called a **random walk** because the values of Y over time will consist of random changes, since the error term is random. If $B_1 = 1$, the variable Y is nonstationary because the value of Y just drifts along over time; it doesn't move back and forth around a constant mean. If B_1 is greater than 1, values of the variable just get larger and larger over time, until the variable explodes. In this case it is clear why the variable is nonstationary. For Y to be stationary, B_1 must lie somewhere between -1 and 1.

The most common unit-root test is the **Dickey-Fuller test**.[9] The Dickey-Fuller test works by taking the variable to be tested, Y, and running this regression:

$$Y_t - Y_{t-1} = B_0 + B_1 Y_{t-1} + e_t \qquad \textbf{(11-17)}$$

Notice that the dependent variable is the difference between the current and preceding values of Y. The null hypothesis for the Dickey-Fuller test is H_0: $B_1 \geq 0$ versus the alternative hypothesis of H_A: $B_1 < 0$. It is a one-sided test. If B_1 in Equation (11-17) is equal to or greater than zero, Y is nonstationary. Therefore, if the Dickey-Fuller test does not reject the null hypothesis of H_0: $B_1 \geq 0$, Y may very well be nonstationary. If the Dickey-Fuller test rejects the null hypothesis, we can assume that Y is stationary. The Dickey-Fuller test statistic does not follow the t-distribution; you must look up critical values in a special table calculated by Dickey and Fuller (see Table H in the Appendix; use the absolute values of the numbers given). Fortunately, some econometrics software packages feature a built-in Dickey-Fuller test command that gives you either the critical value or p-value for the test, so that you don't need to find the Dickey-Fuller critical values manually. There are also augmented Dickey-Fuller tests that account for autocorrelation problems.[10]

Applying the Dickey-Fuller test to the money supply data used to estimate Equation (11-13) gives a Dickey-Fuller test statistic of 1.83.[11] The critical value at a 5% error level is 2.89. The null hypothesis that the variable is nonstationary cannot be rejected; the money supply variable is likely to be nonstationary. The Nasdaq data used to estimate Equation (11-15) is also likely to be nonstationary. The Dickey-Fuller test gives a test statistic of 1.19, and the critical value at a 5% error level is 2.87. This means that the results found for these models (Tables 11-D and 11-E) cannot be trusted. The results have R^2 and adjusted R^2 values that are higher than they should be. The adjusted R^2 is 0.99 for the money supply model, and 0.97 for the Nasdaq model. (Thinking back,

---

[9] D. Dickey and W. Fuller, "Distribution of the Estimators for Autoregressive Time-Series with a Unit Root," *Journal of the American Statistical Association*, Vol. 74, 1979, pp. 427–431. W. Fuller, *Introduction to Statistical Time Series* (New York: Wiley, 1976), pp. 546–638.

[10] S. Said and D. Dickey, "Testing for Unit Roots in Autoregressive Moving Average Models of Unknown Order," *Biometrika*, Vol. 71, 1984, pp. 599–607.

[11] This test was conducted on Eviews, setting the number of lags in the dialogue box to zero to do a regular Dickey-Fuller test. To conduct an augmented test in Eviews, set the number of lags in the dialogue box to a value greater than zero. If using Eviews, see the on-line help under Augmented Dickey-Fuller test, if you are interested in additional information.

didn't it seem too good to be true?) Also, the t-statistics given in Tables 11-D and 11-E are misleading; they are too large.

Keeping a Nonstationary Variable in Its Place

Like a stubborn weed, unit roots are difficult to get rid of. One way to make a nonstationary variable stationary is to use first differences. Instead of using Y_t as the variable, we use the first difference (the change in the variable from one period to the next), $Y_t - Y_{t-1}$, as the variable. Suppose you want to estimate an AR(1) process $Y_t = B_0 + B_1 Y_{t-1} + e_t$, but you discover Y is nonstationary. You can try $Y_t - Y_{t-1} = B_0 + B_1 (Y_{t-1} - Y_{t-2}) + e_t$ instead. You still have to use the Dickey-Fuller test to see if $Y_t - Y_{t-1}$ is stationary, though. Sometimes the process is done more than once, taking second differences, which means the difference of the differences![12]

Unfortunately, taking first differences to make a variable stationary has two serious problems. First, the meaning of the variable changes. Instead of the money supply, we will have the change in money supply. Interpreting these different regression results will be more difficult. Secondly, by taking the first difference in the variable, we lose information on how the variable moves over time. By trying to force it to be stationary, we lose information about what is actually happening. A better approach would be to find additional independent variables that account for why the trend occurs in the first place. However, finding such variables can be problematic.

Taking first differences of the money supply data and running a Dickey-Fuller test gives a test statistic of 8.99; the critical value for a 5% error level is approximately 2.89. We can reject the null hypothesis of nonstationary. We assume that the difference or change in money supply, $M1_t - M1_{t-1}$, is stationary. Taking first differences of the Nasdaq index leads to the same conclusion. The test statistic for the first difference of NASDAQ is 16.04 and the critical value with a 5% error level is 2.87. We assume that $NASDAQ_t - NASDAQ_{t-1}$ is stationary.

Earlier in the chapter, we used money supply data to estimate an AR(5) process. The Dickey-Fuller test reveals that the variable used, M1, is *not* stationary. Table 11-F shows what happens when the stationary first differences are used in the AR(5) model.

Compare the results from Table 11-F to the original ones in Table 11-D (page 237) where we used M1 without taking first differences. The adjusted R^2 is only 0.58 when we take first differences, not 0.99 as in the model with the nonstationary M1 variable. The 0.99 value from Table 11-D is misleadingly high. Three out of the five slope coefficients have lower t-statistics when we use first differences. The change in t-statistics is not as dramatic as we might have expected, though. Keep in mind that the model that generated the results for Table 11-F is not the same model that generated the results for Table 11-D. One model uses the change in the money supply for its variables; the other uses the regular money supply.

Cointegration

Cointegration occurs when the variables in a model are nonstationary, but the trends of the variables are related in a way so that the error term observations are stationary.

---

[12] The difference of the differences is $(Y_t - Y_{t-1}) - (Y_{t-1} - Y_{t-2})$.

Table 11-F

Regression Results for AR(5) Money Supply Model Using First Differences

Dependent variable: $M1_t - M1_{t-1}$

Variable	Coefficient	Standard Error	t-Statistic	p-Value
Constant	1.49	0.75	2.00	0.05
$M1_{t-1} - M1_{t-2}$	0.45	0.08	5.72	0.00
$M1_{t-2} - M1_{t-3}$	0.20	0.07	2.75	0.01
$M1_{t-3} - M1_{t-4}$	−0.07	0.07	−0.90	0.37
$M1_{t-4} - M1_{t-5}$	0.61	0.07	8.26	0.00
$M1_{t-5} - M1_{t-6}$	−0.41	0.08	−5.04	0.00

Observations: 142

$R^2 = 0.60$

Adjusted $R^2 = 0.58$

Residual Sum of Squares = 5,487.79

F-statistic = 39.99

Durbin-Watson statistic = 1.98

The presence of cointegration allows the researcher to proceed as if the variables were stationary. For cointegration to take place, the variables must be nonstationary to the same extent, and this nonstationary aspect from the different variables must cancel each other out. Think of it this way: If two people having a pillow fight try to hit each other at exactly the same time and with the same force, the pillows hit each other and cancel each other out.

You can adapt the Dickey-Fuller test to check for cointegration. Run the Dickey-Fuller test as usual, using the error term observations from the regression as the variable you are testing. If the null hypothesis of the Dickey-Fuller test is rejected, indicating that the error term observations may be stationary, you can assume that cointegration exists for the variables in your regression.

11-4 FORECASTING: THERE IS NO CRYSTAL BALL

The models presented in this chapter are primarily used for forecasting. The idea is to estimate the model and then use the results to make predictions about the future behavior of the dependent variable. Forecasting is not a crystal ball; no one can really predict the future. Econometric forecasting is just a way to use available historical data to make your best *guess* about the future. No matter what you call it though, it is still a guess, albeit an educated one. Think of forecasting as using previous information to say something about the likelihood of future events.

Forecasting usually involves two or three steps, which we summarize here, then examine more fully below.

1. Estimate a regression using the variable you want to predict as the dependent variable.
2. Using the intercept and slope estimates found in the first step, put in values for independent variables and then calculate a value for the dependent variable. This is the forecast or predicted value for the dependent variable. In this step, you are not running a regression; you are doing a calculation.
3. The forecasts found in step 2 convey more information if a confidence interval is given.

Suppose you want to predict how long a caller has to wait on hold when ordering from a catalog store over the telephone.

$$\text{WAIT}_t = B_0 + B_1\text{HOLD}_t + B_2\text{STAFF}_t + e_t \qquad\qquad \textbf{(11-18)}$$

where
WAIT_t = average number of minutes a caller waits on hold for service, for hour t
HOLD_t = average number of other callers on hold during that hour
STAFF_t = number of people taking phone calls during that hour

To predict the waiting time, WAIT_t, the first step is to estimate this regression using available data. Suppose the results are $\hat{\text{WAIT}}_t = 8 + 6 \cdot \text{HOLD}_t - 5 \cdot \text{STAFF}_t$. If we want to forecast a value for WAIT in the next time period, t + 1, we use $\hat{\text{WAIT}}_{t+1} = 8 + 6 \cdot \text{HOLD}_{t+1} - 5 \cdot \text{STAFF}_{t+1}$. We use the same notation to write this forecast as we use for a fitted dependent variable in a regression, with a hat over it: $\hat{\text{WAIT}}_{t+1}$. We don't know what the actual value of WAIT_{t+1} is, if time period t + 1 is in the future. Values for HOLD_{t+1} and STAFF_{t+1} must be used to compute the forecast. We can estimate values for independent variables in the future by extrapolating from past values. Alternatively, other regressions can be used to forecast a value for one of the independent variables, using that variable as a dependent variable in this new regression. The regression estimated to forecast HOLD_{t+1} might look like $\text{HOLD}_t = B_0 + B_1X_t + e_t$ where X_t is an independent variable relevant to HOLD_t. (Now, however, there may be the problem of forecasting a value for X_{t+1} so that we can predict HOLD_{t+1}! Suppose we use 4 for the HOLD_{t+1} and 3 for STAFF_{t+1}.[13] Then the forecast for WAIT_{t+1} is $8 + (6 \cdot 4) - (5 \cdot 3) = 17$.

A forecast based on estimated values for the model's independent variables is called a **conditional forecast**. Here, the forecast is conditional on the values of HOLD_{t+1} and STAFF_{t+1} used. The forecast of $\hat{\text{WAIT}}_{t+1} = 17$ depends on values of 4 for HOLD_{t+1} and 3 for STAFF_{t+1}. We could make a set of conditional forecasts for WAIT_{t+1}. We could assume different values for average number of people on hold in time period t + 1, HOLD_{t+1}, keeping STAFF_{t+1} at 3, and see how the different values for $\hat{\text{WAIT}}_{t+1}$ come out. We could also try different values for STAFF_{t+1} and see what values $\hat{\text{WAIT}}_{t+1}$ will take. Table 11-G demonstrates this idea.

If the actual values of the independent variables are known at the time the forecast is made, then it is an **unconditional forecast**. Forecasts can be unconditional under two

---

[13] STAFF_{t+1} is an estimate because a member of the staff may not show up when scheduled.

Table 11-G

Conditional Forecasts for $\widehat{WAIT}_{t+1}$ for Different Values of $HOLD_{t+1}$ and $STAFF_{t+1}$

If $HOLD_{t+1}$ is:	If $STAFF_{t+1}$ is:	$8 + 6 \cdot HOLD_{t+1} - 5 \cdot STAFF_{t+1} =$	$\widehat{WAIT}_{t+1}$
2	3	$8 + (6 \cdot 2) - (5 \cdot 3) = 5$	5
3	3	$8 + (6 \cdot 3) - (5 \cdot 3) = 11$	11
4	3	$8 + (6 \cdot 4) - (5 \cdot 3) = 17$	17
4	4	$8 + (6 \cdot 4) - (5 \cdot 4) = 12$	12
4	6	$8 + (6 \cdot 4) - (5 \cdot 6) = 2$	2

circumstances. The first occurs when all independent variables in the model are lagged. If the model is $Y_t = B_0 + B_1 X_{t-1} + B_2 W_{t-1} + e_t$ where X_{t-1} and W_{t-1} are independent variables, then Y_{t+1} can be forecast unconditionally using $\hat{Y}_{t+1} = B_0 + B_1 X_t + B_2 W_t$. At time t, both X_t and W_t are known, so an unconditional forecast can be found.

The second way to do an unconditional forecast is to deliberately refrain from using all of the available data. If we have 200 months of data, we might estimate the regression using only the first 180 months of data. When data at the end of the sample are purposely omitted from the initial regression run so that it can be used later, that omitted portion is called a **hold-out sample**. The hold-out sample can be used to check the model's forecasting ability. After estimating the regression using the first 180 months of data, we would use these results to forecast the dependent variable for the remaining 20 months of data. The forecast is unconditional, since values for the independent variables in those last 20 months are known. Then we can compare the forecast values (the $\hat{Y}$ values) with the actual values that occurred in the hold-out sample (the Y values) for the 20 months of the hold-out sample.

Confidence Intervals for Forecasts

A forecast that is a single number is called a **point forecast** (since it is one point on a graph). Point forecasts do not convey much information and can be misleading unless the researcher states the precision of the forecast. This involves using a confidence interval. For any error level, say a 5% error level, if the confidence interval comes out smaller, it indicates the forecast is more precise. If the confidence interval comes out wider (or larger) it indicates a less precise forecast. To find a 95% confidence interval for a point forecast, use this formula:

$$\hat{Y}_{t+1} - S_{forecast} t_c \leq Y_{t+1} \leq \hat{Y}_{t+1} + S_{forecast} t_c \qquad \textbf{(11-19)}$$

where $\hat{Y}_{t+1}$ is the point forecast for which you are constructing the confidence interval. t_c is the critical value from a t-table for a 95% confidence interval. The error level is

5%, and the confidence interval is the equivalent to a two-sided test, so the appropriate critical value is half of the error level, 2.5%. For a 99% confidence interval, t_c would be the critical value for 0.5%, or $t_{0.005}$. Y_{t+1} is the true, unknown value of the variable you are trying to predict. (Y_{t+1} is known if you have a hold-out sample, but you don't use it to construct the confidence interval. You are testing your model's ability to forecast, so you need to know if the confidence interval contains the true value to test the ability of your model to forecast.) $S_{forecast}$ is the standard error of the forecast, shown in Equation (11-20) for a regression with only one independent variable.

$$S_{forecast} = \sqrt{s_e^2 \left[1 + \frac{1}{n} + \frac{(\hat{X}_{t+1} - \overline{X})^2}{(X_t - \overline{X})^2 \text{ totaled over each time period}} \right]} \qquad \textbf{(11-20)}$$

where s_e^2 is the estimated standard error of the error term squared. n is the sample size, which is equal to the number of time periods for a time-series model. $\hat{X}_{t+1}$ is the estimated or extrapolated value for the independent variable in time period $t+1$, the period you are forecasting for. $\overline{X}$ is the sample mean for the independent variable. "$(X_t - \overline{X})^2$ totaled over each time period" indicates that for each time period, a value is calculated using $(X_t - \overline{X})^2$, and then those numbers are added to get a single total.

Several interesting facts can be found from examining Equation (11-20). Since n appears in the denominator of a term, larger samples will give a smaller forecast standard error $S_{forecast}$. This means that larger samples will give us a smaller forecast confidence interval, and therefore a more precise forecast. The more the independent variable X varies over the sample, the larger $(X_t - \overline{X})^2$ totaled over each time period will be. This gives a smaller $S_{forecast}$ and a more precise forecast. If there is a variety of experiences in the sample, if X changes a lot, that means the forecast is likely to be more precise, compared to a sample where X didn't change much. More variation in X allows us to better estimate the relationship between X and Y and this allows for a more precise forecast.

If the estimated independent variable for the forecast period, $\hat{X}_{t+1}$, varies a lot from historical experience, if it is far from the mean, then the standard error of the forecast is bigger; this indicates a less precise forecast. You can see this in Equation (11-20), because $(\hat{X}_{t+1} - \overline{X})^2$ will be relatively large.

To demonstrate the calculation of a forecast confidence interval, consider a model using variables introduced in Chapter 5.

$$SCORE_t = B_0 + B_1 STUDY_t + e \qquad \textbf{(11-21)}$$

where SCORE is Mia's test scores, and STUDY is the number of hours she studies for each exam. Think of each exam as a separate time period, so that t is the number of the exam, from 1 to 15. The data in Table 5-A are used to estimate this regression *except* for the last exam.[14] The data for the last exam serves as a very small hold-out sample. The results are written $\hat{SCORE}_t = 58.20 + 1.96 \cdot STUDY_t$. $STUDY_{15}$, the number of hours studied for the fifteenth exam, is equal to 14. The forecast value for the score then is $58.2 + (1.96 \cdot 14) = 85.64$.

---

[14] LIBRARY is left out of the model as an independent variable, because Equation (11-20) can only be used to calculate the standard error of the forecast if there is one independent variable in the model.

We can use Equation (11-19) to form a 95% confidence interval for the forecast, but first we need to find an estimate of the standard error of the forecast, $S_{forecast}$. The first 14 data points from Table 5-A are our sample, and the number of hours studied for the fifteenth exam (14 hours) is the value of the independent variable in time period $t + 1$ $(\hat{X}_{t+1})$; these values are used in Equation (11-20). Most econometrics software gives you s_e^2 or s_e.[15] The other squared terms can be calculated from the data (the first 14 rows of Table 5-A). n and $\hat{X}_{t+1}$ both happen to be equal to 14 in this example.

$$S_{forecast} = \sqrt{s_e^2\left[1 + \frac{1}{n} + \frac{(\hat{X}_{t+1} - X)^2}{(X_t - X)^2 \text{ totaled over each time period}}\right]} =$$

$$S_{forecast} = \sqrt{(8.70)^2\left[1 + \frac{1}{14} + \frac{(14 - 9.79)^2}{388.36}\right]}$$

$$= \sqrt{75.69(1 + 0.071 + 0.046)} = \sqrt{84.55} = 9.19$$

Next we use Equation (11-19) to find a 95% confidence interval. Recall the predicted value for the fifteenth test score is 85.64. For 12 degrees of freedom ($n - k - 1 = 14 - 1 - 1 = 12$), t_c is 2.18.[16]

$$\hat{Y}_{t+1} - S_{forecast} t_c \leq Y_{t+1} \leq \hat{Y}_{t+1} + S_{forecast} t_c$$

$$[85.64 - (9.19 \cdot 2.18)] \leq Y_{t+1} \leq [85.64 + (9.19 \cdot 2.18)]$$

$$65.61 \leq Y_{t+1} \leq 105.67$$

Given that Mia studied 14 hours for this exam, there is a 95% chance her score will end up being between 66 and 106. This is a large confidence interval; it tells us the forecast of 85.64 is not very precise. This forecast has such a large confidence interval that it includes scores that aren't even possible on a 100-point exam! This is because the sample size and degrees of freedom are so small that the regression results are not very precise. In reality, Mia scored an 86 on the exam, and our predicted value is 85.64. We were very lucky to be so close in our prediction. The actual value of 86 falls inside the 66-to-106 confidence interval as it should, with 95% probability.

Evaluating Forecasts

The consumption, Nasdaq, and money supply models we examined earlier were all estimated without using all of the data. Keeping a hold-out sample allows us to compare our forecasts to actual values.[17] This allows us to see how well the models performed for forecasting. Most econometrics software can calculate forecast values along with statistics about performance if you use a hold-out sample. One such measure is the percent

---

[15] For those using Eviews, the standard error of the regression given with the regression results can be used for s_e.

[16] Remember that for a confidence interval, the critical value for the t-statistic should be the same one used for a two-sided test.

[17] The exercises at the end of the chapter provide an opportunity to use the Nasdaq hold-out sample.

forecast error, which calculates the difference between the forecast and the actual value as a percentage. To summarize the percent forecast error for a hold-out sample, use the average of the absolute values. This keeps negative and positive forecasting errors from canceling each other out and making the average forecast error appear better than it really is. For the consumption model, using a hold-out sample from the first quarter of 1999 through the first quarter of 2000 gives the average absolute value for the forecast error as 2.25%. The consumption model does a good job of forecasting levels of consumption for the hold-out sample. Using a hold-out sample for the money supply model (the first differences model, Table 11-F) from the first quarter of 1996 through the second quarter of 2001 gives the average absolute value for the forecast error as 171%, which is not very good.

Forecasting with Autocorrelation

Autocorrelation is a problem for regression estimation, but there is a way to incorporate the existence of autocorrelation into forecasts. It would, of course, be better if there were no autocorrelation in the first place, but if it is present, we can use it to improve our forecasts. To estimate a model with autocorrelation, we must estimate the autocorrelation coefficient ρ. Since we have to find an estimate for ρ anyway, we might as well use it in making the forecast. This is better than assuming that ρ is zero, since, because of the autocorrelation, we know that ρ is not zero. Most econometrics software allows you to forecast using an estimate of ρ when autocorrelation is present.

Forecasting with Simultaneous-Equation Models

Simultaneous-equation models can be used in forecasting, although it is complicated mathematically. Forecasts are made for both exogenous and endogenous variables in the system; these are then used to forecast values for subsequent years. This means that forecasts for two years from now will be based on forecasts for next year. This allows the simultaneity of the equations in the model to be accounted for, as you forecast farther and farther into the future. It also means that a forecast for one variable that is way off throws off the whole system, making forecasts for later years worse than they would have been otherwise. The Federal Reserve Bank and private consulting firms use complex simultaneous-equation models to make forecasts about the economy.

11-5 TESTING FOR CAUSALITY: WHAT CAME FIRST, THE CHICKEN OR THE EGG?

Regression analysis can never *prove* that one variable causes another. However, when time-series data are used, a weaker type of causality can be useful. **Granger causality** occurs when X changes and changes in Y follow thereafter.[18] We say that X "Granger-causes" Y.

---

[18] C. Granger, "Investigating Causal Relations by Econometric Models and Cross-Spectral Methods," *Econometrica*, Vol. 37, 1969, pp. 24–36.

The most popular version of the Granger test for causality involves an F-test. Suppose we want to see if X Granger-causes Y. The unrestricted model for the test has lagged X's and Y's on the right-hand side of the equation.

$$Y_t = B_0 + [B_1 Y_{t-1} + B_2 Y_{t-2} + \cdots + B_p Y_{t-p}]$$
$$+ [B_{p+1} X_{t-1} + B_{p+2} X_{t-2} + \cdots + B_{p+p} X_{t-p}] + e_t \tag{11-22}$$

The researcher chooses the number of lags, p. To illustrate how the subscripts on the coefficients and variables in Equation (11-22) work, suppose p is 4. Equation (11-22) then becomes

$$Y_t = B_0 + [B_1 Y_{t-1} + B_2 Y_{t-2} + B_3 Y_{t-3} + B_4 Y_{t-4}]$$
$$+ [B_5 X_{t-1} + B_6 X_{t-2} + B_7 X_{t-3} + B_8 X_{t-4}] + e_t$$

The null and alternative hypotheses used for the Granger test are:

H_0: All the slope coefficients for the lagged X variables are zero.

H_A: At least one slope coefficient for the lagged X variables is not zero.

The restricted model for the F-test is

$$Y_t = B_0 + B_1 Y_{t-1} + B_2 Y_{t-2} + \cdots + B_p Y_{t-p} + e_t \tag{11-23}$$

After running these two regressions, our next step is to proceed with the F-test presented in Chapter 5. If the null hypothesis is rejected, there is evidence that X Granger-causes Y.

Granger causality is a weaker statement than saying "X causes Y." It is possible that statistically, X can Granger-cause Y at the same time that Y Granger-causes X. If this occurs, it makes the importance of Granger causality dubious for the model in question. It is always a good idea to run the test the other way, as confirmation. In other words, suppose our hypothesis is that X Granger-causes Y, and the test above rejects the null hypothesis and supports the idea that X Granger-causes Y. We should make sure that Y does *not* Granger-cause X. This is easily done by switching the dependent and independent variables in Equations (11-22) and (11-23). Now the unrestricted model is

$$X_t = B_0 + B_1 X_{t-1} + B_2 X_{t-2} + \cdots + B_p X_{t-p} + B_{p+1} Y_{t-1}$$
$$+ B_{p+2} Y_{t-2} + \cdots + B_{p+p} Y_{t-p} + e_t \tag{11-24}$$

The null and alternative hypotheses are

H_0: All the slope coefficients for the lagged Y variables are zero.

H_A: At least one slope coefficient for the lagged Y variables is not zero.

Here is the restricted model:

$$X_t = B_0 + B_1 X_{t-1} + B_2 X_{t-2} + \cdots + B_p X_{t-p} + e_t \tag{11-25}$$

If the null hypothesis is rejected, then there is evidence that Y Granger-causes X. If the null hypothesis is not rejected, there is *no* evidence that Y Granger-causes X. Therefore, if the null hypothesis is not rejected in this second test, the initial hypothesis that X Granger-causes Y is still supported by the available evidence. It is a good idea to do both these tests a few times specifying a different number of lags (p) to make sure that the tests come out the same way regardless of how many lags are chosen.

Some believe there is a strong link between energy prices and the economy. Let's use the Granger test to see if electricity prices Granger-cause real gross domestic product (GDP). Quarterly data for the electrical power producer price index (PPI) and real GDP from the first quarter of 1967 through the second quarter of 2001 are used here.[19] Some econometrics programs have the Granger test built-in. You simply list the variables and number of lags desired. We want to see if electricity prices Granger-cause real GDP. Following Equations (11-22) and (11-23), using real GDP as the dependent variable Y and the electrical power index as X, the null hypothesis is rejected at a 5% error level. This means that at least one slope coefficient for the lagged electric power index variables is statistically significant. This result holds true for several different choices for the number of lags (8, 12, and 16). There is evidence that electricity prices Granger-cause real GDP.

For the second test, we want to see if real GDP Granger-causes electricity prices. Now the variables are switched around as in Equations (11-24) and (11-25) so that the price of electricity serves as the dependent variable. This time, the null hypothesis cannot be rejected at any reasonable level of significance. This holds true whether the number of lags is 8, 12, or 16. There is no evidence that real GDP Granger-causes electricity prices. Our previous conclusion, that there is evidence that electricity prices Granger-cause real GDP, remains intact.

SUMMARY

1. Time-series models are of special interest in econometrics because they are often used for forecasting. Econometric forecasting is far from perfect; no one can really predict the future no matter how good they are at econometrics.

2. It takes time for the effect of some independent variables to take place. A time gap between when an independent variable changes and when the dependent variable changes can be modeled using a lagged independent variable. When an independent variable appears in a regression more than once, with different time lags, it is a **distributed lag model**. Several problems arise when estimating distributed lag models:

   1. Multicollinearity.
   2. A decrease in the degrees of freedom.
   3. As variables are lagged farther back in time, the effect of the lagged independent variables may not fade out as it should.

---

[19] The data are available at the text website or http://www.economagic.com. The electrical power producer price index data are also available from U.S. Bureau of Labor Statistics at http://www.bls.gov.ppi/.

3. The **Koyck lag model** successfully deals with all three problems listed above. The Koyck lag model is constructed in a way that the farther back in time the lag goes, the closer the slope coefficients automatically get to zero [See Equation (11-2).] Koyck lag models can be estimated using $Y_t = a_0 + B_0 X_t + \lambda Y_{t-1} + u_t$. However, most Koyck lag models exhibit autocorrelation.

4. An **autoregressive model** contains only lagged dependent variables on the right-hand side; there are no other independent variables. A typical autoregressive model is $Y_t = B_0 + B_1 Y_{t-1} + e_t$. This is an autoregressive model of order 1, or AR(1). Autoregressive processes can take any order. The partial autocorrelation function helps determine how many lagged terms should be used in the model.

5. A **moving average model** uses previous error terms as the independent variables [see Equation (11-14)]. Moving average models are abbreviated by MA(q), where q is the number of lagged error terms present in the model. The optimal number of lagged error terms for a moving average model can be determined by its autocorrelation function.

6. The autoregressive and moving average processes can be used together in an autoregressive moving average model. Such a model is abbreviated by ARMA(p, q), where p is the number of lagged dependent variables on the right-hand side, and q is the number of lagged error terms on the right-hand side.

7. A time-series variable is **stationary** if it does not have an upward or downward trend over time. Autoregressive, moving average, and ARMA models must have stationary variables to be estimated properly. A nonstationary variable causes misleading results. **Unit-root tests** are used to see if a variable is stationary. The most common unit-root test is the **Dickey-Fuller test**. One way to make a nonstationary variable stationary is to use first differences. There are two serious problems with taking first differences to make a variable stationary. First, the meaning of the variable changes. Secondly, taking the first difference in the variable causes information on how the variable moves over time to be lost.

8. The models presented in this chapter are primarily used for forecasting. Forecasting is not a crystal ball; no one can really predict the future. Using econometrics to forecast future events is just a way of using available historical data to make your best guess about the future. Forecasting typically involves two or three steps.
   1. Estimate a regression using the variable you want to predict as the dependent variable.
   2. Using the intercept and slope estimates found in the first step, put in values for independent variables and then calculate a value for the dependent variable. This is the forecast or predicted value for the dependent variable. In this step, you are not running a regression; you are doing a calculation.
   3. The forecasts found in Step 2 will convey more information if a confidence interval is given.

9. Regression analysis can never *prove* that one variable causes another. However, when time-series data are used, a weaker type of causality can be useful. If X changes and changes in Y follow thereafter, there is **Granger causality**. The most popular version of the Granger test for causality uses an F-test.

EXERCISES

1. Try to explain these terms without looking them up.
   - lagged independent variable
   - distributed lag model
   - Koyck lag model
   - Durbin h-statistic
   - autoregressive model
   - partial autocorrelation function
   - moving average model
   - autocorrelation function
   - autoregressive moving average model
   - stationary variable
   - nonstationary variable
   - spurious regression
   - unit-root test
   - random walk
   - Dickey-Fuller test
   - cointegration
   - conditional forecast
   - unconditional forecast
   - hold-out sample
   - point forecast
   - Granger causality

2. Suppose that Equation (11-1) is altered so that it includes lagged terms for income going back to $t - 10$:

$$\text{CONSUMPTION}_t = B_0 + B_1\text{INCOME}_t + B_2\text{INCOME}_{t-1}$$
$$+ B_3\text{INCOME}_{t-2} + \cdots + B_{11}\text{INCOME}_{t-10} + e_t$$

   a. If you use annual data from 1950 to 1999 to estimate this equation, what are the degrees of freedom?
   b. Suppose the regression is changed again, so that it is

$$\text{CONSUMPTION}_t = B_0 + B_1\text{INCOME}_t + B_2\text{INCOME}_{t-1}$$
$$+ B_3\text{INCOME}_{t-2} + \cdots + B_{21}\text{INCOME}_{t-20} + e_t$$

   Using the same 1950–1999 data, what are the degrees of freedom now?
   c. What are the degrees of freedom if the model is estimated as a Koyck lag model, using the same data?

3. Clarence Darrow (a well-known lawyer) once said, "History repeats itself; that's one of the things that's wrong with history."[20]

---

[20] The quote can be found at http://www.quotegallery.com.

a. Suppose that history really does repeat itself. Would an econometrician who uses time-series models for forecasting agree with the second part of Darrow's statement, "that's one of the things that's wrong with history?" Explain.

b. If the first part of Darrow's statement is wrong and history does not repeat itself, what does this imply for forecasting with time-series models?

4. Quarterly consumption and income data from 1959 through 1998 are used to estimate Equation (11-7). (The data are available at the text website.[21]) Use these same data to estimate this version of the consumption model:

$$\text{CONSUMPTION}_t = B_0 + B_1 \text{INCOME}_t + B_2 \text{INCOME}_{t-1}$$
$$+ B_3 \text{INCOME}_{t-2} + B_4 \text{INCOME}_{t-3} + e_t$$

The slope coefficient estimates should get closer to zero as the time lags get longer.

a. Do the slope estimates follow the expected pattern?

b. Do you see any problems with the results?

5. Every January before the Super Bowl, the business press runs stories concerning the "Super Bowl Predictor." (For recent examples, use Google or any other search engine to search for "Super Bowl Predictor.") The Super Bowl Predictor says that whenever a team from the National Football Conference wins the Super Bowl, the stock market goes up. If a team from the American Football Conference wins, the stock market goes down. The Super Bowl Predictor has been right approximately 80% of the time.

a. Should financial advisors use the Super Bowl Predictor?

b. The Super Bowl Predictor is not a regression. However, what concept from this chapter could be useful here?

6. For parts a–d, find four values B_1 through B_4 for a distributed lag model when the Koyck model gives estimates of $B_0 = 20$ and

a. $\lambda = 0.01$

b. $\lambda = 0.25$

c. $\lambda = 0.75$

d. $\lambda = 0.99$

e. What pattern emerges when the values for λ in parts a–d change?

7. a. In the Koyck lag model, λ should be between 0 and 1. Find B_1 through B_4 for a distributed lag model when the Koyck model gives estimates of $B_0 = 20$ and $\lambda = 2.0$.

b. What problem arises when $\lambda = 2.00$?

8. a. If a confidence interval is smaller (more narrow), does that mean that the estimate is more or less precise? Explain.

Use Equation (11-20) to answer the following questions. What do your answers tell you about the precision of the estimate?

b. Does a larger value for s_e^2 give a smaller or larger confidence interval? How about

c. A larger value for n?

d. A larger value for $(\hat{X}_{t+1} - \bar{X})^2$?

e. A larger value for $(X_t - \bar{X})^2$ totaled over each time period?

9. a. Use the Durbin h-test to see if the results given by the Koyck consumption model in Table 11-B exhibit autocorrelation.

b. If the Durbin h-statistic indicates autocorrelation, what can be done to improve the model?

10. Suppose you want to use the Durbin h-statistic to check a Koyck model for autocorrelation, but the standard error for the estimate of λ is relatively high (perhaps the model didn't fit the data very well). How might this affect the Durbin h-statistic?

11. Explain what happens in a moving average or autoregressive model if a variable is not stationary.

12. a. How are the statements "X causes Y" and "X Granger-causes Y" different?

b. Explain how to test for Granger causality.

13. Recall the simple DVD expenditures model from Chapter 1:

$$DVDEXP = B_0 + B_1 INCOME + e$$

a. Use the data in Table 1-A to estimate this model. (The hand-calculated results in Chapter 1 are not sufficient; you will need to find s_e^2 to calculate the forecasting confidence interval in part c.)

b. Use your results in part a to find a point forecast for DVDEXP if INCOME is 800 next month.

c. Form a 95% confidence interval for your forecast in part b. (*Hint*: The $X - \bar{X}$ column in Table 1-A is useful in doing one of the necessary calculations.)

d. Does the confidence interval contain zero? What does this tell you?

e. What should be done differently to make the forecast more accurate?

14. a. In Section 11-2, an MA(4) model is used for the Nasdaq data.[22] However, the Dickey-Fuller test indicates that NASDAQ is nonstationary. Using the same Nasdaq data, take the first differences of NASDAQ. What is the best number of lags for a moving average model when using the first differences of NASDAQ? Estimate this model.

b. Use the Dickey-Fuller test to see if the first differences of NASDAQ are stationary.

15. Use the regression you estimated in Exercise 14 and the Nasdaq data from January 4, 1999, through December 29, 2000, to forecast for the hold-out sample from January 1, 2001, to August 31, 2001.[23] Look over the forecasted values. What is odd about these results? Can you explain why they came out this way?

---

[22] Data can be found at the text website or http://www.economagic.com.
[23] Data can be found at the text website or http://www.economagic.com.

APPENDIX

11-6 THE MATH BEHIND THE KOYCK LAG MODEL

In this section we examine the mathematical steps required to turn Equation (11-2) into Equation (11-5). Starting from

$$Y_t = a + B_0X_t + B_1X_{t-1} + B_2X_{t-2} + \cdots + B_LX_{t-L} + e_t \qquad \textbf{(11-2)}$$

we want to end up with

$$Y_t = a_0 + B_0X_t + \lambda Y_{t-1} + u_t \qquad \textbf{(11-5)}$$

Here is how to do it:

Step 1. Replace all the slope coefficients in Equation (11-2) with terms that include only B_0 and λ. Use Equation (11-3), $B_i = B_0\lambda^i$, to do this. For example, B_2 can be replaced with $B_0\lambda^2$.

$$Y_t = a + B_0X_t + B_0\lambda X_{t-1} + B_0\lambda^2X_{t-2} + \cdots + B_0\lambda^LX_{t-L} + e_t \qquad \textbf{(11-26)}$$

Since B_0 appears in every right-hand side term except the intercept and the error term, we can simplify Equation (11-26) as

$$Y_t = a + B_0(X_t + \lambda X_{t-1} + \lambda^2X_{t-2} + \cdots + \lambda^LX_{t-L}) + e_t \qquad \textbf{(11-27)}$$

Step 2. Create a new equation similar to Equation (11-27) except that the dependent variable is Y_{t-1} instead of Y_t. Now all the independent variables and the error term are lagged one time period back compared to Equation (11-26).

$$Y_{t-1} = a + B_0(X_{t-1} + \lambda X_{t-2} + \lambda^2X_{t-3} + \cdots + \lambda^{L-1}X_{t-L}$$
$$+ \lambda^LX_{t-(L+1)}) + e_{t-1} \qquad \textbf{(11-28)}$$

Step 3. Multiply both sides of Equation (11-28) by λ.

$$\lambda Y_{t-1} = \lambda a + B_0(\lambda X_{t-1} + \lambda^2X_{t-2} + \lambda^3X_{t-3} + \cdots + \lambda^LX_{t-L}$$
$$+ \lambda^{L+1}X_{t-(L+1)}) + \lambda e_{t-1} \qquad \textbf{(11-29)}$$

Step 4. To arrive at our final destination, Equation (11-5), subtract Equation (11-29) from Equation (11-27). Take the left-hand side of Equation (11-27) and subtract the left-hand side of Equation (11-29), and do the same thing for the right-hand side of the equation. This gives

$$Y_t - \lambda Y_{t-1} = a - \lambda a + B_0[X_t + (\lambda X_{t-1} - \lambda X_{t-1}) + (\lambda^2X_{t-2} - \lambda^2X_{t-2})$$
$$+ (\lambda^LX_{t-L} - \lambda^LX_{t-L}) + \lambda^{L+1}X_{t-(L+1)}] + e_t - \lambda e_{t-1} \qquad \textbf{(11-30)}$$

The terms inside the square brackets cancel out except for X_t and $\lambda^{L+1}X_{t-(L+1)}$. The $\lambda^{L+1}X_{t-(L+1)}$ term will be small compared to X_t. λ is a fraction less than 1, and λ taken to the $L + 1$ power makes the $\lambda^{L+1}X_{t-(L+1)}$ small enough to be ignored. Equation (11-30) can be simplified:

$$Y_t - \lambda Y_{t-1} = a - \lambda a + B_0 X_t + e_t - \lambda e_{t-1} \qquad \textbf{(11-31)}$$

Define a new intercept $a_0 = a - \lambda a$ and a new error term $u_t = e_t - \lambda e_{t-1}$. Then add λY_{t-1} to both sides of Equation (11-31) to get Equation (11-5).

$$Y_t = a_0 + B_0 X_t + \lambda Y_{t-1} + u_t \qquad \textbf{(11-5)}$$

12

Qualitative Choice Models: The Dependent Variable Is a Dummy

This chapter will show you:

- How to set up and estimate a model when the dependent variable is a dummy variable.

- How to interpret the results of this type of model and measure its performance.

- An overview of two data problems that can occur when information is missing for some observations.

There are a variety of situations where you may want to build a regression model around a dependent variable that is not originally a number; the dependent variable may describe a characteristic, choice, or category that is not numerical. For example, you may want to study how voting decisions are made, whether someone will take the bus or drive to work, or how people decide to go to graduate school or not. In these three examples, the appropriate regression models feature a dummy dependent variable and are called **qualitative choice models**. In the voting study, the dependent variable could be defined as equal to 1 if the voter chooses the incumbent candidate and equal to 0 if the voter chooses the challenger. In the commuting study, the dependent variable could be set to 1 if the individual takes public transportation to work, and 0 if he or she drives a car. The regressions for these examples are called **binary choice models** because each model features only two choices. In Section 12-1, we examine how to estimate and interpret binary choice models.

If there are more than two candidates in an election, or if you consider more than two ways to get to work (bus, train, carpool, drive alone), then your model needs to accommodate more choices. **Multinomial choice models** have dependent variables that are dummy variables, but there are more than two choices included in the model. Multinomial choice models will be discussed in Section 12-2. In Section 12-3, we give an overview of two special problems that can occur if some values of the dependent variable cannot be observed.

12-1 BINARY CHOICE: THE DEPENDENT VARIABLE IS 0 OR 1

In this section, we look at three different ways to estimate a binary choice model: the linear probability model, probit, and logit. We can estimate linear probability models using ordinary least squares, but not probit and logit models. However, several serious problems arise with linear probability models that can lead researchers to use the probit or logit models.

Linear Probability Model

The **linear probability model** looks like a typical OLS regression at first, but it is not. The linear probability model is estimated using ordinary least squares, but we must interpret the results differently. The interpretation differs because the dependent variable in a binary choice model can take only two predefined values. The difference between the initial formulation of a linear probability model and a typical OLS model lies with the dependent variable.

$$Y = B_0 + B_1X_1 + B_2X_2 + \cdots + B_kX_k + e \qquad \text{(12-1)}$$

where $Y = 1$ if the individual makes one choice and $Y = 0$ if the individual takes the other choice.[1] The independent variables can include both dummy variables and typical independent variables. Also, the observations don't have to be individuals; they can be firms, countries, or any entity that is making a decision.

An example concerning the decision to go to graduate school will show how to interpret the results of a linear probability model.

$$GRADSCHOOL = B_0 + B_1GPA + B_2INCOME + e \qquad \text{(12-2)}$$

where

GRADSCHOOL = 1 if student goes to graduate school within 3 years of
receiving a bachelor's degree; 0 otherwise
GPA = student's undergraduate grade point average
INCOME = student's family annual income, in thousands of dollars

Suppose we find the following results, where the coefficient estimates are all statistically significant at a 1% error level:

$$GRADSCHOOL = -0.7 + 0.4 \cdot GPA + 0.002 \cdot INCOME + e \qquad \text{(12-3)}$$

For every observation, a fitted or predicted value for the dependent variable can be calculated using the values for that observation's independent variables and the estimated coefficients from the regression (the $\hat{B}$'s).[2] In a typical OLS regression, the fitted or predicted value for the dependent variable tells us what value we can expect the dependent variable to take on average, given the values of the independent variables. However, this interpretation does not work here. Suppose Phoebe has a 3.5 grade point aver-

---

[1] The dependent variable does not always have to represent a choice. For example, the dependent variable could indicate whether an individual contracts an illness.
[2] Fitted values are discussed in Chapter 1.

age and comes from a family with an annual income of $50,000. The fitted value of GRADSCHOOL for Phoebe is

$$0.8 = -0.7 + 0.4 \cdot 3.5 + 0.002 \cdot 50 \qquad \text{(12-4)}$$

(Recall that INCOME is in thousands of dollars, so the fitted value is calculated using 50, not 50,000.) Although the dependent variable Y in this binary choice model takes only two values, 0 or 1, the fitted or predicted value of GRADSCHOOL for Phoebe is 0.8. Most of the time, the fitted value will not be 0 or 1. We therefore interpret the fitted value as an *estimate of the probability* that Phoebe decides to go to grad school. The 0.8 value is the model's estimate of the chance that Phoebe will decide to go to grad school.

Bart, with a 2.2 GPA and a family income of $60,000, has a fitted value for GRADSCHOOL of 0.3. We can conclude that Bart is less likely to go to grad school than Phoebe (with the 0.8 fitted value). The regression results estimate that the chance that these two students will decide to go to graduate school is 80% for Phoebe and 30% for Bart. These probabilities reflect what we expect individual decision-makers to choose, considering the characteristics captured by the independent variables. Notice that these probabilities are not numbers we can observe. Only the actual decision to go to graduate school or not can be observed.

We also interpret the slope coefficients differently here. In a typical OLS regression, the slope coefficient represents the change in the dependent variable for a one-unit change in the independent variable, keeping the other independent variables in the regression constant. In the linear probability model, the slope coefficient represents the change in *probability* that the dependent variable will be equal to 1 that occurs with a one-unit change in the independent variable, keeping the other independent variables in the model constant. The 0.4 slope estimate for GPA in Equation (12-4) means that if a student's GPA increases by a whole point (say from 2.0 to 3.0), the estimated probability that the student will decide to go to grad school increases by 0.4, keeping family income constant. The 0.002 slope estimate for INCOME in Equation (12-4) indicates that if the student's family's income increases by $1000 (INCOME increases by 1), the estimated probability the student will decide to go to grad school increases by 0.002, keeping GPA constant. A negative slope estimate would indicate the decrease in the estimated probability that the dependent variable is 1 with a one-unit increase in the independent variable, keeping the other independent variables constant. If the slope estimate for an independent variable X_1 is -0.3, it means that if X_1 increases by 1, the estimated probability that the individual chooses $Y = 1$ decreases by 0.3, keeping the other independent variables in the model constant. Changes in the independent variables are linearly related to the probability that the dependent dummy variable is 1, so the name **linear probability model** makes sense.

Unfortunately, there are problems with the linear probability model. In general, this model is often not the best estimation method for a qualitative choice model, because it assumes a linear relationship between the independent variables and the probability that $Y = 1$. Often this relationship is not linear. Perhaps the most bothersome problem with the linear probability model is that the fitted values can be less than 0 or greater than 1, but a probability has to be bounded by 0 and 1. If the probability of something occurring is 1, it is a sure thing. The probability can never be larger than 1. That would mean there is a greater than 100% chance it will happen. Also, if the probability of something occurring is 0, there is no way it can happen. A probability can never be less than 0.

Consider again the results shown for the grad school model in Equation (12-3). Suppose Malcolm has a GPA of 4.0 and a family income of $200,000. The fitted value of GRADSCHOOL for Malcolm is

$$1.3 = -0.7 + 0.4 \cdot 4.0 + 0.002 \cdot 200$$

This is, of course, impossible because a 1.3 probability means a 130% chance; it can never be greater than 100%. Likewise, Ian, with a 1.0 grade point average and family income of $50,000, has a fitted value for GRADSCHOOL of -0.2, indicating the probability he will go to graduate school is negative. Give the guy a break; the lowest the probability can be is 0, indicating there is no chance; it can't be negative.

One simple way to resolve this problem is to set all the negative fitted values equal to zero and set all the fitted values greater than 1 equal to 1. However, this is not very satisfying. In real life, it is rare that we would know before the decision is made that the probability of someone going to graduate school is 1. This holds true for other situations that you might study using a linear probability model. At the other end of the spectrum, even someone who doesn't have the best grades could still have a greater than zero chance of going to graduate school. The linear probability model tends to give too many extreme results—too many cases where the estimated probability is equal to or very close to 0 or 1.

Another problem is that the errors will not be normally distributed, violating an OLS assumption. A third problem is that the linear probability model will have heteroskedasticity. The variance of the error term is $p(1 - p)$ where p is the probability that the dependent variable is equal to 1.[3] This probability is different for each observation. The error term variance will not be constant, causing heteroskedasticity in the model. Weighted least squares can be used, but it is not efficient and it changes the meaning of the results.

The final problem is that R^2 (and adjusted R^2) will not be an appropriate measure of the goodness of fit in the linear probability model. In fact, this is a problem for all qualitative choice models, not just the linear probability model. The dependent variable allows only for values of 0 or 1, nothing in between, but the fitted value for the dependent variable often falls between 0 and 1. If the fitted value is 0.8, we would predict that the student would decide to go to grad school. If the student decides this way, we will be correct, but GRADSCHOOL will equal 1, not 0.8. R^2 will only give the model partial credit for its prediction, not full credit, since the fitted value of 0.8 does not equal the actual value of 1. Since the fitted value led us to correctly predict the outcome, the model should be given full credit for making the correct prediction. R^2 underestimates performance for models with a dependent dummy variable.

---

[3] Because the dependent variable takes only values of 0 or 1, the error term is not normally distributed. It is binomially distributed, giving it a variance of $p(1 - p)$, where p is the probability that the dependent variable is 1, and $(1 - p)$ is the probability that the dependent variable is 0.

A better measure of performance is the percentage of observations that the model correctly predicts. In the first step, we classify each prediction as 1 or 0. If a fitted value is 0.5 or larger, consider that to be a prediction that the dependent variable will be equal to 1. Consider a fitted value of less than 0.5 to be a prediction that the dependent variable will be 0. Next, we compare these predictions to what actually occurred, counting the number of correct predictions. Then we use this number to calculate the percentage predicted correctly.

$$\text{percentage of observations predicted correctly}$$
$$= \frac{\text{number of observations predicted correctly}}{\text{total number of observations}} \cdot 100 \qquad \textbf{(12-5)}$$

It is best to break this measure down even further, finding the percentages predicted correctly for $Y = 1$ and $Y = 0$ separately. To see why, suppose we have 100 observations for the grad school model, where 25 students decided to go to grad school. This gives us 75 cases where the dependent variable GRADSCHOOL is 0 and 25 cases where it is 1. Let's assume the model correctly predicts all the cases where GRADSCHOOL is 0 but only predicts 5 correctly for the 25 cases where GRADSCHOOL is 1. Overall, this gives us 80 cases predicted correctly (the 75 students who decided against graduate school and 5 of the 25 who decided for it). If you just saw the 80% figure, you would think the model is doing a good job of predicting, but this would be somewhat misleading. For the cases where GRADSCHOOL is 0, the model made correct predictions 100% of the time. For the cases where GRADSCHOOL is 1, the model predicted the correct outcome only 20% of the time (5 out of 25 cases). Seen in this light, the 80% figure calculated earlier makes the model seem better than it really is. The model doesn't do very well at predicting who decides to go to grad school, even though it correctly predicted all the students who decided against grad school. However, note that predicting outcomes is not necessarily what qualitative choice models are all about; they are often used to investigate what factors affect individuals in making a particular decision.

Suppose Clark Kent and Bruce Wayne are running for President of the United States. We can use a binary choice model to study what factors influence voters' decisions.

$$\text{WAYNE} = B_0 + B_1\text{INCOME} + B_2\text{AGE} + B_3\text{MALE} + e \qquad \textbf{(12-6)}$$

where
$\quad$ WAYNE = 1 if individual votes for Bruce Wayne; 0 otherwise
$\quad$ INCOME = individual's household income, in thousands of dollars
$\quad$ AGE = individual's age in years
$\quad$ MALE = 1 if individual is male; 0 otherwise

Table 12-A gives data from a random sample of voters. (There is a third-party candidate in the election; those in the random sample who support the third-party candidate have been omitted in Table 12-A and will be accounted for later in the chapter.) Table 12-B gives the linear probability model results using these data.

Table 12-A

Data for Two-Candidate Voting Model

Observation	WAYNE	INCOME	AGE	MALE
1	0	10	18	0
2	1	58	48	1
3	1	64	51	0
4	0	14	19	0
5	0	11	22	1
6	0	16	23	0
7	1	60	44	1
8	0	19	26	0
9	1	110	37	0
10	1	44	68	1
11	0	21	28	0
12	0	29	25	1
13	0	28	27	0
14	1	40	45	0
15	0	26	32	0
16	0	33	32	1
17	1	46	28	1
18	0	12	42	0
19	0	30	41	0
20	1	40	38	1
21	0	35	40	1
22	1	18	48	0
23	0	14	19	1

(continued)

Table 12-A

(Continued)

Observation	WAYNE	INCOME	AGE	MALE
24	1	50	40	0
25	1	72	31	0
26	0	38	18	0
27	1	55	43	1
28	0	50	50	1
29	1	22	62	0
30	1	85	62	0

Table 12-B

Linear Probability Results for Two-Candidate Voting Model

Dependent variable: WAYNE

Variable	Coefficient	Standard Error	t-Statistic	p-Value
Constant	−0.51	0.19	−2.65	0.01
INCOME	0.0098	0.0030	3.25	0.00
AGE	0.016	0.0053	3.08	0.00
MALE	0.0031	0.13	0.02	0.98

Observations: 30

$R^2 = 0.58$

Adjusted $R^2 = 0.53$

Residual Sum of Squares = 3.15

F-statistic = 11.87

As Table 12-B indicates, the slope estimate for INCOME is positive and significant at a 1% error level. A $1000 increase in income (INCOME is in thousands) means that the estimated probability the voter will choose Bruce Wayne for president increases by 0.0098, keeping AGE and MALE constant. The slope estimate for AGE is also significant at a 1% error level. For every additional year of age, the estimated probability that a voter will choose Bruce Wayne increases by 0.016, keeping INCOME and MALE constant. The slope coefficient for MALE is not statistically significant, so there is no evidence that men and women vote differently in this sample. We can conclude that older, richer voters are more likely to vote for Bruce Wayne than for Clark Kent.

As we noted earlier, R^2 and adjusted R^2 don't measure model performance in qualitative choice models very well. It is better to look at the percentage of observations predicted correctly. Table 12-C gives the fitted values for WAYNE for each observation. Every fitted value of 0.5 or higher is counted as a prediction that WAYNE will be 1 for that observation. Every fitted value that is less than 0.5 is counted as a prediction that WAYNE will be 0 for that observation.

Of the 30 observations, 27, or 90.0%, are predicted correctly. Of the people who voted for Bruce Wayne, 12 out of 14, or 85.7%, are predicted correctly. For those who

Table 12-C

Fitted Values, Predictions, and Actual Values for WAYNE in Two-Candidate Voting Model

Observation	WAYNE			Prediction correct?
	Fitted Value	Prediction	Actual Value	
1	−0.12	0	0	Yes
2	0.84	1	1	Yes
3	0.95	1	1	Yes
4	−0.06	0	0	Yes
5	−0.04	0	0	Yes
6	0.02	0	0	Yes
7	0.80	1	1	Yes
8	0.10	0	0	Yes
9	1.17	1	1	Yes
10	1.03	1	1	Yes
11	0.15	0	0	Yes
12	0.18	0	0	Yes
13	0.20	0	0	Yes
14	0.61	1	1	Yes
15	0.26	0	0	Yes
16	0.34	0	0	Yes

(*continued*)

voted for Clark Kent, 15 out of 16, or 93.8%, were predicted correctly. In this particular example, breaking down the percent predicted correctly into two categories, observations where WAYNE = 1 and where WAYNE = 0 didn't matter much; the percentage predicted is not dramatically different. That will not always be the case. The R^2 is 0.58, meaning that the model explains 58% of the variation in the dependent variable. This is low compared to the 90.0% predicted correctly. Using R^2 would lead you to conclude that the model does not perform as well as it actually does.[4] Notice how some of the fitted values for WAYNE in Table 12-C are below 0 or above 1. This demonstrates one of the problems with linear probability models that we pointed out earlier. These fitted values are estimates of probabilities, but probabilities can never be less than zero or greater than one.

Table 12-C
(Continued)

Observation	WAYNE			Prediction correct?
	Fitted Value	Prediction	Actual Value	
17	0.40	0	1	No
18	0.29	0	0	Yes
19	0.45	0	0	Yes
20	0.50	1	1	Yes
21	0.49	0	0	Yes
22	0.45	0	1	No
23	−0.06	0	0	Yes
24	0.63	1	1	Yes
25	0.70	1	1	Yes
26	0.16	0	0	Yes
27	0.73	1	1	Yes
28	0.80	1	0	No
29	0.71	1	1	Yes
30	1.33	1	1	Yes

[4] Note that 90.0% predicted correctly is remarkably high, considering the small sample size and that voting behavior can be difficult to explain.

Probit

The probit model resolves many of the problems encountered with the linear probability model. In many cases, the linear probability model is not the best way to estimate a qualitative choice model. As noted, the linear probability model can give estimated probabilities that lie below 0 or above 1, values that we know are impossible. A better model would account for the fact that probabilities must not be less than 0 or greater than 1. The model should also account for the fact that often, you are less likely to have probabilities close to 0 or 1. As you get closer to an extreme value, 0 or 1, the chance of getting a probability that low or that high should taper off. The **probit model**, which is based on the cumulative normal probability distribution, will not give probabilities less than zero or greater than one, and is less likely to give probabilities close to 0 or 1 than is the linear probability model. Compared to the linear probability model, the probit model more accurately describes many of the decision-making processes we might want to study. Figure 12-1 compares the probit and linear probability models.

Although the probit model is actually nonlinear, it can be written in a way that resembles other econometric models. First, we need Equation (12-7), which represents the transformation performed by the cumulative normal probability function.

$$\text{probability} = F(Z) \tag{12-7}$$

In Equation (12-7), F is a mathematical function, the cumulative normal probability function that transforms a value from the normal probability function (Z) into a probability, where the values are bounded by 0 and 1. The probit model uses the inverse cumulative normal probability function; it transforms a probability into a value for Z.

$$Z = F^{-1}(\text{probability}) \tag{12-8}$$

Figure 12-1

Linear Probability Model and Probit Model.

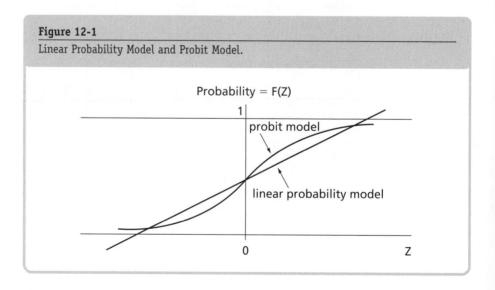

The -1 superscript on F indicates that an inverse mathematical function is being used. The probit model is

$$Z = F^{-1}(\text{probability}) = B_0 + B_1 X_1 + B_2 X_2 + \cdots + B_k X_k + e \quad \textbf{(12-9)}$$

Although at first glance Equation (12-9) looks like a typical regression model, it is a nonlinear model, because of the F^{-1}(probability) term. The probit model cannot be estimated by ordinary least squares. Probit is estimated using maximum likelihood; **maximum likelihood** estimates coefficients by finding the estimates that maximize the chance you would see the values that actually occurred in the sample. Maximum likelihood is an iterative technique. It runs a regression over and over until it finds the estimates that maximize the likelihood that you would see the values observed in the sample.

The probit model (and the logit model that we cover next) work best for large sample sizes, often in the hundreds. Also, it helps if both of the possible choices are adequately represented in the sample. For example, suppose that for the grad school example, you have a sample of 200, but only 3% decide to go to graduate school, which is only 6 people out of the 200. There may not be enough information in the sample to give you good estimates when so few people choose grad school, and the regression results may not be very reliable.

We can estimate the two-candidate voting model as a probit model, using the same variables as before, and the same data from Table 12-A. The results are given in Table 12-D.

The results using probit estimation are somewhat different than with the linear probability model (compare Table 12-B). The coefficient estimates for INCOME and AGE are statistically significant at a 5% error level with the probit model; they were significant at a 1% error level with the linear probability model. Because we know linear

Table 12-D

Probit Results for Two-Candidate Voting Model

Dependent variable: WAYNE

Variable	Coefficient	Standard Error	t-Statistic	p-Value
Constant	-5.19	1.70	-3.06	0.00
INCOME	0.071	0.034	2.10	0.04
AGE	0.073	0.034	2.18	0.03
MALE	-0.70	0.90	-0.78	0.44

Observations: 30

McFadden pseudo-$R^2 = 0.61$

Residual Sum of Squares $= 2.62$

probability models have several problems, these probit results could be more accurate. (However, a much larger sample size would be preferred for an actual study.) The coefficient estimates from the probit model cannot be interpreted as a change in probability, as we did with the linear probability model.[5] The interesting way to use probit results is to find fitted values to make predictions, as we did with the linear probability model in Table 12-C.

The percent of observations predicted correctly gives us information about the probit model's performance. Calculating the percentages predicted correctly using the same method as was used with the linear probability model, the probit model results give us 86.7% correct, compared to 90% correct with the linear probability model.[6] Of the people in the sample who voted for Bruce Wayne, 78.6% are predicted correctly by the probit model, compared to 85.7% by the linear probability model. For those who voted for Clark Kent, 93.8% are predicted correctly by the probit model, the same by the linear probability model. These differences are small, but in some cases differences in results between the two models can be substantial.

Instead of R^2 to measure the goodness of fit in probit models, the McFadden pseudo-R^2 is reported. **Pseudo-R^2** is the name of a goodness-of-fit measure that is used instead of R^2 for models with a dependent dummy variable. Normally, "pseudo" means that something is fake; here, however, it indicates that pseudo-R^2 is a different measure that seems to be like R^2, but really isn't. Several useful pseudo-R^2 measures have been developed for qualitative choice models.[7] Many econometrics programs that estimate probit or logit models calculate a pseudo-R^2 measure along with the rest of the results. Here, the pseudo-R^2 measure tells us that the probit model explains 61% of the variation in the dependent variable.

Logit

The **logit model** is based on the cumulative logistic distribution, instead of the cumulative normal distribution that the probit model uses. For any one regression, the results from the probit and logit estimation methods are often similar in terms of statistical significance. The logit model, if thought of in terms of probabilities, will give probability estimates that are bounded by 0 and 1, just like the probit model. Also like the probit model, the logit model avoids extreme probability values that are close to 0 or

---

[5] Some econometrics software programs convert the coefficient estimates into probability changes that are comparable to linear probability model coefficients.

[6] Eviews gives the percent predicted correctly for probit and logit models under the "View" menu for the equation.

[7] McFadden developed one of the most common pseudo-R^2 measures; Eviews automatically calculates it for probit and logit binary choice models. For details, see D. McFadden, "Conditional Logit Analysis of Qualitative Choice Behavior" in P. Zarembka (ed.), *Frontiers in Econometrics* (New York: Academic Press, 1974). For a discussion of pseudo-R^2 measures, see G. S. Maddala, *Limited-Dependent and Qualitative Variables in Econometrics* (New York: Cambridge University Press, 1983), pp. 37–41.

1. Both models circumvent the main problems encountered with the linear probability model.

The dependent variable is set up differently in the logit model. Equation (12-10) shows what the logit model looks like.[8]

$$\ln\left(\frac{Y}{1 - Y}\right) = B_0 + B_1X_1 + B_2X_2 + \cdots + B_kX_k + e \qquad \textbf{(12-10)}$$

Fitted values for the dependent variable now represent the logarithm of the odds that Y will equal 1. The terms *probability* and *odds* do not mean the same thing. If the probability of an event is 0.25, the odds will be:

$$\frac{\text{probability}}{1 - \text{probability}} = \frac{0.25}{1 - 0.25} = \frac{1}{3}$$

(often written 1:3 or said "1 to 3"). If the probability is 0.5 or 50%, the odds will be $0.5/(1 - 0.5) = 1/1$, or 1:1. We can give the slope coefficients in the logit model a specific interpretation: A change in an independent variable affects the logarithm of the odds that Y equals 1. A coefficient estimate from a logit model tells us the change in the logarithm of the odds for a one-unit change in an independent variable, keeping other independent variables constant.

Like probit, logit cannot be estimated using ordinary least squares. We use maximum likelihood instead. We can estimate the two-candidate voting model using logit, utilizing the same data from Table 12-A. The regression results for the logit estimation are given in Table 12-E.

The McFadden pseudo-R^2 and the levels of statistical significance are similar for the logit and probit results (compare Tables 12-D and 12-E). The coefficient estimates for INCOME and AGE are statistically significant at a 5% error level in both regressions. The coefficient estimate for MALE is statistically insignificant in both regressions. The values of the slope estimates are different, however, because their meaning is different. For example, the 0.13 slope estimate for AGE means that a one-year increase in age increases the logarithm of the odds of voting for Bruce Wayne by 0.13, keeping INCOME and MALE constant. As a practical matter, besides the interpretation of the slope coefficients, there is not that much difference between using the probit and logit models.

---

[8] When running logit, you do not calculate the $\ln[Y/(1 - Y)]$ term for the dependent variable, you use Y as the dependent variable, as always. If the software includes a logit procedure, it uses maximum likelihood estimation based on the idea that the form of the dependent variable is $\ln[Y/(1 - Y)]$. It does not literally use $\ln[Y/(1 - Y)]$ as the dependent variable; $\ln[Y/(1 - Y)]$ cannot be used literally as the dependent variable because if $Y = 1$, $\ln[Y/(1 - Y)] = \ln[1/0]$, which is the natural logarithm of an undefined number (it approaches infinity), and if $Y = 0$, $\ln[Y/(1 - Y)] = \ln(0)$, which is also undefined (it approaches negative infinity).

Table 12-E

Logit Results for Two-Candidate Voting Model

Dependent variable: WAYNE

Variable	Coefficient	Standard Error	t-Statistic	p-Value
Constant	−8.96	3.23	−2.77	0.01
INCOME	0.12	0.06	1.98	0.05
AGE	0.13	0.06	2.03	0.04
MALE	−1.03	1.54	−0.67	0.51

Observations: 30

McFadden pseudo-R^2 = 0.60

Residual Sum of Squares = 2.59

12-2 MULTIPLE CHOICE: MORE THAN TWO POSSIBLE ANSWERS

We may want to estimate a qualitative choice model for a situation with more than two possible choices. In the voting model example, there could be more than two candidates. The estimation methods discussed so far can't handle more than two choices. If a third candidate, Peter Parker, is added, then we must adapt the previous methods of estimation to account for this third choice. It is best if we don't order the choices in the voting model. That means we should avoid defining Y as 0 if the choice is Clark Kent, 1 if it is Bruce Wayne, and 2 if it is Peter Parker. Doing so implies that Wayne somehow falls between Kent and Parker. This might make sense if Kent and Parker are at opposite ends of the political spectrum and Wayne is a middle-of-the-road candidate, but it is often difficult to rank choices in this manner. If we were studying other situations—such as how people get to work, by car, bus, or train—the same idea applies. There is no reasonable way to order these choices. The good news is, there are estimation methods that can be used with unordered choices.

In some research, however, the choices *can* be ordered. For example, a model concerning education could have a dependent variable defined such that Y is 0 if the individual does not have a high school diploma, 1 if he has a high school diploma but no bachelor's degree, 2 if he has a bachelor's degree but no graduate degree, and 3 if he has a graduate degree. Qualitative models with ordered dependent variables can be estimated using special models that we won't discuss here. Proper interpretation of ordered model results can be difficult.[9]

---

[9] See G. S. Maddala, *Limited-Dependent and Qualitative Variables in Econometrics* (New York: Cambridge University Press, 1983), pp. 46–51, and Peter McCullagh, "Regression Models for Ordinal Data," *Journal of the Royal Statistical Society*, Vol. 42, No. 2, 1980, pp. 109–142.

A Linear Probability Model for More than Two Choices

We can adapt the linear probability model for situations with more than two choices. To include a third candidate in our voting model, we use two equations instead of one. (In general, the number of equations needed is one less than the number of choices.)

$$WAYNE = B_0 + B_1 INCOME + B_2 AGE + B_3 MALE + e \qquad \textbf{(12-11)}$$

$$PARKER = B_4 + B_5 INCOME + B_6 AGE + B_7 MALE + e \qquad \textbf{(12-12)}$$

where PARKER is 1 if the individual prefers Peter Parker for president; 0 otherwise. The B's in Equation (12-12) are given different subscripts from those in Equation (12-11) to show that they can take different values. We use ordinary least squares to estimate these regressions, so the linear probability model will have the same problems here as it does when there are two choices.

The estimated probabilities must add to one for any observation. The estimated probability that an individual will vote for Bruce Wayne is given by the fitted value of WAYNE for Equation (12-11) for that individual. Likewise, the estimated probability that an individual will vote for Parker is given by the fitted value of PARKER for Equation (12-12) for that individual. If the estimated probability that an individual will vote for Bruce Wayne is 0.5, and the estimated probability that the same individual will vote for Peter Parker is 0.3, then we know the estimated probability that this person will vote for Clark Kent must be 0.2. The three estimated probabilities must add up to 1. Because of this, we do not have to run a third regression for Clark Kent. The estimated intercepts for all three candidates sum to 1, so once we find estimates for B_0 and B_4, we can figure out what the intercept estimate will be in an equation for Clark Kent, without actually running the regression. Likewise, the slope estimates for any variable will sum to zero across the three candidates, so once we have estimates for the slope coefficients in the Bruce Wayne and Peter Parker equations, we can also find the slope estimates for AGE and INCOME for Clark Kent without actually running a third regression.

This adaptation of the linear probability model for more than two choices works only if the independent variables in each equation are the same. Otherwise, a more complicated generalized least squares procedure must be used.[10]

Individuals who supported Peter Parker are not included in the data we used for the binary choice models. Table 12-F adds this data for individuals who were surveyed who support Parker. It is not a coincidence that these last 10 observations all supported Parker; they may not have been the last 10 observations in the original sample because they were omitted from Table 12-A. Adding these data to the data in Table 12-A gives us a data set with three different choices in it. Notice that the observations start with 31, since Table 12-A contains observations 1–30. When adding these data to the other thirty observations, the PARKER variable should also be added to the original 30 observations. PARKER takes a value of zero for the first 30 observations since those individuals voted for either Bruce Wayne or Clark Kent.

---

[10] A. Zellner and T. H. Lee, "Joint Estimation of Relationships Involving Discrete Random Variables," *Econometrica*, Vol. 33, 1965, pp. 382–394.

Table 12-F

Additional Observations for the Voting Model: Individuals Who Support Peter Parker for President

Observation	WAYNE	INCOME	AGE	MALE	PARKER
31	0	22	19	1	1
32	0	24	20	1	1
33	0	30	22	1	1
34	0	21	24	1	1
35	0	26	21	1	1
36	0	30	34	0	1
37	0	29	24	1	1
38	0	33	25	1	1
39	0	28	27	1	1
40	0	32	30	1	1

We can use the 30 observations in Table 12-A and the 10 additional observations in Table 12-F to estimate Equations (12-11) and (12-12), the two equations for the linear probability model in this example. The results are given in Tables 12-G and 12-H.

Table 12-G shows that the results using WAYNE as the dependent variable are similar to the results with the binary choice linear probability model (compare to Table 12-B). We also interpret the slope estimates the same way as with the binary choice model. For example, the 0.017 slope estimate for AGE means that if someone is a year older, the estimated probability that they will vote for Bruce Wayne increases by 0.017, keeping INCOME and MALE constant.

The results for Peter Parker given in Table 12-H are very different from those for Bruce Wayne. The slope estimate for INCOME is significant in the Wayne equation, but it is insignificant in the Parker equation. Those with more income tend to vote for Bruce Wayne, but income doesn't seem to affect whether you vote for Peter Parker or not. Those with more moderate income tend to vote for Peter Parker *or* Clark Kent. The slope estimate for AGE is significant at a 5% error level, and it is negative. This means that younger voters tend to choose Peter Parker. This is in contrast to the positive AGE slope in the Wayne equation, which indicates that older people tend to vote for Bruce Wayne. MALE has a significant positive slope estimate at a 1% error level, and it is relatively large. The estimated probability of a male voting for Peter Parker is 0.33 higher than that for a female voter, if they have the same age and income. That is a big difference. Women apparently find Parker the least acceptable of the three can-

Table 12-G

Linear Probability Results for Three-Candidate Voting Model

Dependent variable: WAYNE

Variable	Coefficient	Standard Error	t-Statistic	p-Value
Constant	−0.58	0.16	−3.71	0.00
INCOME	0.010	0.0027	3.74	0.00
AGE	0.017	0.0043	4.05	0.00
MALE	−0.035	0.099	−0.35	0.73

Observations: 40

$R^2 = 0.62$

Adjusted $R^2 = 0.59$

Residual Sum of Squares $= 3.41$

F-statistic $= 19.99$

Table 12-H

Linear Probability Results for Three-Candidate Voting Model

Dependent variable: PARKER

Variable	Coefficient	Standard Error	t-Statistic	p-Value
Constant	0.48	0.19	2.50	0.02
INCOME	−0.00085	0.0033	−0.26	0.80
AGE	−0.011	0.0053	−2.06	0.05
MALE	0.33	0.12	2.69	0.01

Observations: 40

$R^2 = 0.30$

Adjusted $R^2 = 0.25$

Residual Sum of Squares $= 5.19$

F-statistic $= 5.35$

didates. There is no evidence that women prefer Bruce Wayne to Clark Kent or that they prefer Clark Kent to Bruce Wayne, since MALE is insignificant in the Wayne equation. The next step is to look at the percent of observations predicted correctly in the two equations, which you are asked to do in an exercise at the end of the chapter.

Multinomial Logit

Multinomial logit is used to estimate qualitative choice models with more than two choices, when the choices are not ordered.[11] This technique avoids problems that occur with the linear probability model. Like the linear probability model, the number of equations you need is one less than the number of choices. One of the choices is used as the base choice, and it does not have its own equation. Applying multinomial logit to the three-candidate voting model using Clark Kent as the base choice gives two equations.[12]

$$\ln\left(\frac{WAYNE}{KENT}\right) = B_0 + B_1 INCOME + B_2 AGE + B_3 MALE + e \quad \textbf{(12-13)}$$

$$\ln\left(\frac{PARKER}{KENT}\right) = B_4 + B_5 INCOME + B_6 AGE + B_7 MALE + e \quad \textbf{(12-14)}$$

where KENT $= 1$ if the individual prefers Clark Kent, 0 otherwise.

Equations in a multinomial logit model must be estimated simultaneously, using maximum likelihood. Most student versions of econometrics software and even some full versions do not feature this type of estimation. The slope coefficients are interpreted differently than with the binomial logit model. Here, the meaning of each slope is interpreted relative to the base choice. Suppose the estimate of B_2 is 0.02. For each additional year of age, the logarithm of the probability of a Bruce Wayne vote increases by 0.02, compared to the logarithm of the probability of a Clark Kent vote (keeping INCOME and MALE constant). More formally, increasing AGE by one year increases the difference between the logarithm of the probability of voting for Bruce Wayne and the logarithm of the probability of voting for Clark Kent by 0.02.[13] The other slope coefficients are interpreted in the same manner.[14]

12-3 AN OVERVIEW OF CENSORED AND TRUNCATED DATA: OBSERVATIONS YOU CAN'T SEE CAN HURT YOU

There are two data problems that come up when information is missing for some of the observations: censored and truncated data. These problems can occur even if the dependent variable is not a dummy variable. These problems can occur when data we

---

[11] See McFadden, *op. cit.*

[12] Like the binomial logit model, the software would not literally use ln(WAYNE/KENT) or ln(PARKER/KENT) as the dependent variable. It uses maximum likelihood estimation based on the idea that the form of the dependent variable is ln(WAYNE /KENT) or ln(PARKER/KENT).

[13] This is true because ln(WAYNE/KENT) = ln(WAYNE) − ln(KENT).

[14] In the example used here, all the independent variables reflect characteristics of the individual decision-maker. If an independent variable reflects characteristics of the choices, then for multinomial logit, it should be defined such that it reflects the difference of the characteristics for the two choices represented in the regression. For example, if a new variable is added to Equation (12-13) to capture the amount of campaign spending in each voter's area, it should be defined as the amount of spending done by Wayne's campaign minus the amount spent by Kent's campaign in the area. For Equation (12-14), the variable would be defined as the amount of spending done by Parker's campaign minus the amount spent by Kent's campaign in the area.

would typically use to estimate the regression are unavailable, because the values cannot be observed. Ordinary least squares will give biased and inconsistent estimates when either censored or truncated data are used, because the error term for such a regression violates the classical OLS assumptions. In this section we give a brief overview of censored and truncated data.

Censored Data

Censored data are missing some values for the dependent variable because they cannot be observed. However, all the values for the independent variables are still available. Suppose you work for a housing developer and you want to study what factors affect how much people will pay for a new house. Your firm has just completed a new development where all the houses are the same. You conduct a survey, gathering information from each prospective buyer who sees the houses; this information will be used for independent variables in your regression model. Your company gives you the price that each buyer ends up paying for the house. However, there is a problem. Some of the prospective buyers decide not to buy a house. You have values for the independent variables for them, but no value for the dependent variable. You don't know what price they are willing to pay for a house, because they didn't buy one. There is some price they are willing to pay, but it is in their heads and you cannot observe it. What they are willing to pay is hidden, or "censored" from you. Ordinary least squares cannot estimate models with censored data. Because of the missing data, it is unlikely that the mean of the error term will be zero. The classical assumptions will not hold and OLS estimation will be biased and inconsistent. The Tobit model, developed by James Tobin, is used to estimate regressions with censored data.[15] The Tobit model is estimated using maximum likelihood.

Truncated Data

Truncated data are missing observations where the dependent variable falls above or below a certain value. This means that values for *both* the dependent and independent variables are missing for some of the observations. This differs from censored data, where only the dependent variable is missing for some of the observations. With truncated data, complete observations are missing because the dependent variable took a value either above or below a certain line that makes it impossible to observe any of the variables for that observation. Suppose you are conducting a study concerning household medical expenditures. You could use the amounts people deduct from their taxes for medical expenses as a measure of their medical expenses, but even if you can get access to this data, you will still have a problem. Some households with very low incomes do not have to file federal income tax returns, so those households will be missing from your sample. Your sample won't be random; households with low incomes will be missing. These households will be cut off, or "truncated," from your sample. As with censored data, ordinary least squares cannot estimate regressions with

---

[15] See Maddala, *op. cit.*, pp. 151–156 for details on censored data and on how the Tobit model works. The original paper on this work is J. Tobin, "Estimation of Relationships for Limited Dependent Variables," *Econometrica*, Vol. 26, 1958, pp. 24–36.

truncated data. The truncated data causes heteroskedasticity, and bias arises because of the missing observations for the independent variables. Special estimation methods that incorporate maximum likelihood must be used to estimate regressions with truncated data.[16]

SUMMARY

1. If the dependent variable in a regression is not originally a number—if it describes a characteristic or category that is not numerical—then the model is a **qualitative choice model**.

2. If the purpose of a model is to predict which of two possibilities will be chosen, the model is called a **binary choice model**. Three main estimation methods are used to estimate binary choice models.

3. In a **linear probability model**, the dependent variable takes only two values, 1 or 0. This model is estimated using ordinary least squares. The slope coefficient represents the change in probability that the dependent variable will be 1 that occurs with a one-unit change in the independent variable, keeping remaining independent variables constant. There are three problems with the linear probability model.
    *   The fitted values, which can take values less than zero or greater than 1 even though a probability cannot be less than 0 or greater than 1.
    *   Heteroskedasticity.
    * R^2 is not an appropriate measure of goodness of fit.

4. The **probit model** resolves many of the problems encountered with the linear probability model. Based on the cumulative normal probability distribution, this model will not give fitted values less than zero or greater than one. Probit is estimated using **maximum likelihood**, which estimates coefficients by finding the estimates that maximize the chance you would see the values that actually occurred in the sample.

5. The **logit model** is based on the cumulative logistic distribution. This model gives probability estimates that are bounded by 0 and 1, just like the probit model. The results from both estimation methods are often similar in terms of statistical significance. With the logit model, a change in an independent variable affects the logarithm of the odds that Y equals 1. Logit is estimated using maximum likelihood.

6. For models with more than two choices, a **multinomial choice model** is necessary. The linear probability model can be adapted for more than two choices by using more than one equation, with different dependent variables. The number of equations needed is one less than the number of choices. Logit can also be adapted to estimate a multinomial choice model in a similar manner.

7. Censored and truncated data occur when information is missing for some of the observations. Ordinary least squares will give biased and inconsistent estimates, because the error term violates the classical OLS assumptions.

---

[16] More information about these estimation methods can be found in Maddala, *op. cit.*, pp. 165–170.

- **Censored data** are missing some values for the dependent variable because they cannot be observed but all values for the independent variables are available. The Tobit model is used to estimate regressions with censored data.
- **Truncated data** are missing observations where the dependent variable falls above or below a certain value. This means that values for both the dependent variable and independent variables are missing for some of the observations.

EXERCISES

1. Try to explain these terms without looking them up.
    - qualitative choice model
    - binary choice model
    - multinomial choice model
    - linear probability model
    - probit model
    - maximum likelihood
    - pseudo-R^2
    - logit model
    - multinomial logit
    - censored data
    - truncated data
2. Think of a decision people make that you could study using a binary choice model. What will your dependent and independent variables be?
3. Why is ordinary least squares often a poor estimation method for qualitative choice models?
4. The slope estimates for the two-candidate voting model are different depending on whether probit or logit is used. Compare the slope estimates given in Tables 12-D and 12-E. Do the different slope estimates mean something is wrong? Why are the estimates different?
5. What is the difference between odds and probability? Why is this difference relevant in discussing qualitative choice models?
6. The following cross-section model concerns the decision to rent or own a home. The sample was randomly selected 2 years ago from households that were renting at the time.

$$HOME = B_0 + B_1 INCOME + B_2 PRICE + B_3 CHILDREN + e$$

where

$HOME$ = 1 if household members bought a house within 2 years; 0 otherwise

$INCOME$ = household's income, in thousands of dollars

$PRICE$ = average price of a house in area, in thousands of dollars

$CHILDREN$ = number of children in household

Suppose the linear probability model is used, and for one household, the fitted value for HOME is 0.48.

    a. Is the model predicting that the household will try to buy approximately half a house? Explain.

    b. Based on the fitted value of 0.48, do you think the household will buy a home?

    c. How surprised would you be if your answer to part b turns out to be wrong?

7. Suppose the household in Exercise 6 does not buy a house. Use the 0.48 fitted value as an example to explain why R^2 underestimates the performance of qualitative choice models.

8. The following estimates have been found for the rent decision model in Exercises 6 and 7; all estimates are statistically significant at a 5% error level.

$$\text{HOME} = 0.4 + 0.005\text{INCOME} - 0.008\text{PRICE} + 0.3\text{CHILDREN} + e$$

Interpret the slope estimates if these results were found using:

a. the linear probability model

b. the logit model

9. An elitist UFO-watching club requires all potential members to pass a test to show how much they know about UFOs before they can join the club. The test is pass or fail; there are no letter grades. The following table gives how many hours each person studied for the test, and whether or not they passed. (PASS = 1 if person passed the test, 0 otherwise)

Observation	PASS	HOURS
1	1	42
2	0	27
3	0	5
4	1	35
5	0	7
6	0	21
7	1	40
8	0	10
9	1	25
10	0	12
11	1	40
12	1	23
13	1	14
14	1	38

Observation	PASS	HOURS
15	0	15
16	0	27
17	1	36
18	1	15
19	1	27
20	0	16
21	1	34
22	0	17
23	1	18
24	0	32
25	0	20
26	1	31
27	0	20
28	1	29
29	1	30
30	0	30

a. Use the data to run the following models: linear probability, probit, and logit. Summarize your results. (You may want to save the fitted values for use in part b.)

b. Choose one of the three estimation methods, and for that set of results find the percent predicted correctly for:
   - all observations
   - observations in which the person passed the test
   - observations in which the person failed the test

c. Which gives you a better indication of the model's performance, your answer to part b or the R^2 or psuedo-R^2? Why?

10. a. Explain why truncated or censored data are a problem for ordinary least squares estimation.

b. How do truncated and censored data differ?

c. Give examples of censored data and truncated data that are not in the chapter.

11. Use the data in Table 12-A to estimate the two-candidate model using logit. Your results should match those in Table 12-E.
   a. What is the percent of total observations predicted correctly?
      What is the percent of observations predicted correctly when
   b. WAYNE = 1?
   c. WAYNE = 0?
   d. How do your answers compare to the percent of observations predicted correctly with the probit and linear probability models when these same data are used?

12. Using the data given Tables 12-A and 12-F, estimate the two linear probability regression equations (12-11) and (12-12) for the three-candidate voting model. (You will need to save the fitted values from the regressions.)
   Find the percent of observations predicted correctly for those who supported:
   a. Bruce Wayne
   b. Peter Parker
   c. Clark Kent (*Hint:* This can be done without estimating a third regression.)
   d. Find the overall percentage of observations predicted correctly.

13. Consider the following regression for the three-candidate voting model, to be estimated using the linear probability model.

$$\text{VOTE} = B_0 + B_1\text{INCOME} + B_2\text{AGE} + B_3\text{MALE} + e$$

where VOTE = 0 if the individual prefers Peter Parker, 1 if Clark Kent is preferred, and 2 if Bruce Wayne is preferred. This regression is simpler than the model given by Equations (12-11) and (12-12) because only one regression is used.
   a. Is the regression shown here a good idea? Explain.
   b. If your answer to part a is yes, explain the circumstances under which it would not be a good idea. If your answer to part a is no, explain the circumstances under which it would be a good idea.

13

Econome-"tricks": Misleading Uses of Econometrics[1]

This chapter presents:

- Examples of misleading econometric results.

- Questions that should be asked about any set of econometric results.

- A table summarizing problems and situations that occur in econometrics.

Econometrics can be used for good or for evil. No one can ever be perfectly objective, but a researcher can attempt to be as objective as possible by giving full disclosure of the results and information. Or, one can be misleading, playing games with the model specification, with the data sample, or with the way the results are reported, so that the evidence appears to support what the researcher wants. This is unethical. Misleading results, results that fool the reader, are often unintentional. Sometimes inexperienced researchers are not rigorous in their work and present misleading results, not because they mean to be dishonest, but simply because they don't know enough about econometrics.

This chapter serves as a warning that econometrics can be used to learn from what has happened in the past, or it can be used to mislead, often unintentionally. Sections 13-1 through 13-6 demonstrate how econometric results can be deceptive. In the examples given, something is amiss that causes the results to differ from what they should be. Many of the ideas in this chapter have been mentioned elsewhere in the book, but here we examine them in detail. Section 13-7 sums up what to look for when reading econometric results and gives points to keep in mind when doing your own work so that you do not mistakenly mislead anyone. Section 13-8 summarizes the different econometric problems and situations that we have covered in this book.

---

[1] This chapter's title was inspired by the classic article "Let's Take the Con Out of Econometrics" by Edward E. Leamer, *American Economic Review*, March 1983, Vol. 73, No. 1, pp. 31–43.

13-1 STATISTICAL SIGNIFICANCE DOES NOT PROVE CAUSALITY: HENDRY'S THEORY OF INFLATION

Hendry's theory of inflation is that a specific, publicly known variable is the true cause of inflation.[2] Hendry uses the following regression model to test his theory:

$$P = B_0 + B_1C + B_2C^2 + e \qquad (13\text{-}1)$$

where P is a measure of the price level in the United Kingdom. Hendry estimates Equation (13-1) using quarterly data from 1958 to 1975, and gets the results shown in Equation (13-2).

$$\hat{P} = 10.9 - 3.2C + 0.39C^2$$

$$\text{t-statistics} = (19.8)(-13.9)(19.5) \quad R^2 = 0.982 \qquad (13\text{-}2)$$

The numbers in parentheses underneath Equation (13-2) are t-statistics; the estimates are all statistically significant at a 1% error level.[3] The R^2 is an impressive 0.98. Has Hendry made an important breakthrough in explaining inflation? What do you think C is? Take a guess.

Remember, theory is important in formulating a regression model (Chapter 4). The independent variables in a regression model should always be consistent with a coherent theory that you are testing. In Hendry's theory of inflation, the independent variable C is cumulative rainfall in the United Kingdom! Now that you know this, the results are not as impressive. No reasonable theory claims rain causes inflation. Nor can Hendry's regression results be used to make this claim. He got these results because P and C both rise during the period from 1958 to 1975. This example illustrates why theory is so important in formulating regression models. Hendry's real point is that statistical significance does not prove that changes in an independent variable cause changes in the dependent variable. As we noted in Section 1-2, statistical significance does not prove causality.

Consider another example, a time-series model where the dependent variable is the quantity of diamonds sold or exchanged in a regional market.

$$Q = B_0 + B_1\text{PRICE} + B_2\text{INCOME} + B_3\text{ENGAGE} + e \qquad (13\text{-}3)$$

where

Q = number of diamonds bought and sold in each time period
PRICE = index that expresses real average price of diamonds used for engagement rings in each time period
INCOME = real average household income in each time period
ENGAGE = number of marriage engagements in region in each time period

---

[2] David F. Hendry, "Econometrics—Alchemy or Science?" *Economica*, Nov. 1980, Vol. 47, No. 188, pp. 387–406. The theory of inflation is on pages 391–395.

[3] These results are from Hendry (*op. cit.*) p. 394. In Hendry's paper, standard errors are reported in parentheses below the estimates. The standard errors have been used to calculate the t-statistics shown here in Equation (13-2).

Suppose that the slope estimate for PRICE comes out positive ($\hat{B}_1 > 0$) and is statistically significant at a 1% error level. At first glance, this seems to support the idea that if the price of diamonds goes up, keeping INCOME and ENGAGE constant, people will buy more diamonds![4] When interpreting econometric results, it is always a good idea to ask yourself if the interpretation passes a commonsense test: Is the interpretation of these results reasonable? The answer is no. People do not buy more diamonds if the price is higher, keeping income and the number of engagements constant.

Equation (13-3) looks like a demand equation. It contains price, income, and the number of engagements, three independent variables that would be in a demand equation for diamonds. The demand equation alone does not determine the number of diamonds bought and sold, though. We need a simultaneous-equation system so that we can estimate the supply equation for diamonds at the same time. We cannot interpret the $\hat{B}_1 > 0$ result as meaning people will buy more diamonds when the price goes up, because the supply equation is missing from the model. Since the supply equation is missing, violating the classical assumptions, ordinary least squares will be biased (see Chapter 10).

13-2 DIFFERENT COMBINATIONS OF INDEPENDENT VARIABLES CAN GIVE CONTRADICTORY RESULTS

Changing a model's independent variables can lead to very different results. We demonstrate this by changing the gasoline revenue model that we used for the Chow test in Chapter 5. Here is the original model:

$$\text{GASREV} = B_0 + B_1\text{PRICE} + B_2\text{UNEMPLOY} + B_3\text{SUMMER}$$
$$+ B_4\text{FALL} + B_5\text{WINTER} + e \qquad \text{(5-21)}$$

where

$\quad$ GASREV = real retail gasoline sales revenues, in millions of 1983 dollars, per quarter-year

$\quad$ PRICE = price index for gasoline, averaged over each quarter

$\quad$ UNEMPLOY = average unemployment rate for each quarter

$\quad$ SUMMER = 1 during summertime, 0 otherwise

$\quad$ FALL = 1 during fall, 0 otherwise

$\quad$ WINTER = 1 during winter, 0 otherwise

What happens if we leave PRICE out of the model? This would be a mistake. Economic theory indicates the price of gasoline should be included, so omitting it violates the first classical assumption.[5] Here it is omitted anyway, to make a point.

$$\text{GASREV} = B_0 + B_2\text{UNEMPLOY} + B_3\text{SUMMER}$$
$$+ B_4\text{FALL} + B_5\text{WINTER} + e \qquad \text{(13-4)}$$

---

[4] You may know that in this case, if people did buy more diamonds when the price goes up, diamonds would be a Giffen good. (See any intermediate microeconomics textbook for more details about the Giffen good concept.)

[5] Recall the first classical assumption: "The dependent variable is linearly related to the coefficients, and the model contains the right independent variables."

Equation (13-4) can be estimated for 1967–1972 using the same quarterly data we used in Chapter 5. Table 5-J is reproduced here as Table 13-A to show the original results with PRICE included in the model; Table 13-B shows what happens when PRICE is missing. In Table 13-A, the slope estimate for UNEMPLOY is *not* statistically significant at a 5% error level. In Table 13-B, UNEMPLOY *is* significant at a 5% error level (and a 1% error level also). This shows that changing the model specification, omitting one independent variable, can change the results. When PRICE is included, there is no evidence that the unemployment level affects gasoline revenues. Exclude PRICE and it looks like the unemployment level may be relevant in determining gasoline revenues.

Perhaps when PRICE is omitted, UNEMPLOY simply picks up some of the effect of PRICE. Remember, each slope estimate gives the average change in the dependent variable for a one-unit change in its independent variable, keeping other independent variables constant. When we omit PRICE, the slope coefficient of UNEMPLOY is estimated without holding PRICE constant. That could be why UNEMPLOY becomes statistically significant at a 1% error level when PRICE is not in the regression. The results in Table 13-B are misleading because PRICE is missing from the regression. An exercise at the end of the chapter asks you to investigate this idea in more detail. Section 4-3 discusses the effects of omitting a relevant independent variable or including an extra one in a regression. It is especially important to remember the discussion in Section 4-4 concerning objectivity in econometrics. It is dishonest to run several versions of the regression model and then report only the results that show what you want.

Table 13-A

Results for Gasoline Revenue Model

Dependent variable: GASREV
1967–1972, Quarterly Data

Variable	Coefficient	Standard Error	t-Statistic	p-Value
Constant	−11,271.76	4,165.63	−2.71	0.02
PRICE	998.94	165.78	6.03	0.00
UNEMPLOY	206.58	120.59	1.71	0.10
SUMMER	1,544.89	246.20	6.28	0.00
FALL	1,727.66	251.54	6.87	0.00
WINTER	1,092.07	255.94	4.27	0.00

Observations: 24

$R^2 = 0.92$

Adjusted $R^2 = 0.89$

Residual Sum of Squares = 3,264,647

F-statistic = 38.92

Table 13-B

Results for Gasoline Revenue Model Excluding PRICE

Dependent variable: GASREV
1967–1972, Quarterly Data

Variable	Coefficient	Standard Error	t-Statistic	p-Value
Constant	13,701.92	708.66	19.34	0.00
UNEMPLOY	720.28	144.18	5.00	0.00
SUMMER	1,613.39	415.80	3.88	0.00
FALL	2,039.24	416.18	4.90	0.00
WINTER	1,508.30	416.65	3.62	0.00

Observations: 24

$R^2 = 0.74$

Adjusted $R^2 = 0.69$

Residual Sum of Squares $= 9,850,106$

F-statistic $= 13.84$

13-3 EXTRAPOLATION CAN STRETCH THINGS TOO FAR

Extrapolating or projecting regression results past the range of values taken by the variables in the data is dangerous; it can give you misleading conclusions. We discussed this briefly in Section 2-1. Here, an example based on Quinn's DVD model from Chapters 1 and 2 demonstrates the problem. The results shown in Table 2-B can be written in equation form as

$$\widehat{DVDEXP} = 89.09 + 0.064 \, INCOME - 3.18 \, PRICE + 6.05 \, RAINFALL \quad \textbf{(13-5)}$$

where
$DVDEXP$ = amount Quinn spends each month on DVDs, in dollars
$INCOME$ = Quinn's monthly income, in dollars
$PRICE$ = average monthly price of DVDs, in dollars
$RAINFALL$ = total monthly rainfall in Quinn's town, in inches

One month, Quinn takes time off from work so she can appear on three L.A. game shows: "Wheel of Classical Assumption Violations," "Who Wants to Be an Econometrician?" and "Hollywood Ordinary Least Squares." She wins a total of $500,000 on the three shows; needless to say, she doesn't work at her regular job that month. During this same month, the average price of DVDs is $23.00, and the rainfall in her hometown is 4 inches. We can use the regression results for the model, shown in Equation

(13-5), along with the given values of the independent variables to predict how much Quinn will spend on DVDs the month she wins the $500,000.

$$\hat{DVDEXP} = 89.09 + (0.064 \cdot 500,000) - (3.18 \cdot 23.00)$$
$$+ (6.05 \cdot 4) = \$32,040.15 \tag{13-6}$$

That's a lot of money to spend on DVDs! It's unlikely that Quinn can come up with enough movies that she likes to spend $32,040.15 on DVDs in one month. This predicted value of $32,040.15 is far too high. We originally estimated the DVD model with data where income ranged between $320 and $1,264 (see Table 2-A). Quinn's $500,000 winnings are far away from any experience contained in the sample. It is unlikely that the linear relationship between income and DVD expenditures estimated by the model will hold for an income of $500,000 since none of the income values used to estimate the model in the first place even come close to such a high value. Using regression results to extrapolate, to extend past the range of sample data as we did here, can give you deceptive predictions and conclusions. It is highly unlikely that Quinn will spend anything close to $32,040.15 on DVDs that month, even with her windfall of $500,000.

13-4 CONNECTING THE DOTS: FORCING THE REGRESSION LINE TO FIT THE DATA

Regression analysis is meant to test whether a theoretical relationship between variables is supported by the data. It is *not* supposed to be just a complicated game of "connect the dots." For any data set, there is some complicated curve that can be drawn to fit the data; there is a mathematical way to connect the dots. An experienced econometrician might use a fancy econometric model to draw a curve that fits the data. The econometrician can "connect the dots," but this doesn't prove anything. It doesn't give us any real information about the general relationship between the variables, because the regression probably won't fit well when estimated with a different data set. If the regression model is specifically built to fit one data set, it is probably unsuitable for forecasting future events. It is also doubtful that the results can be used to make conclusions that can be utilized elsewhere with different data. As soon as you change the sample, and use a different time period or different cross-section, the results don't hold anymore. We demonstrate this idea with an example concerning airline ticket pricing.

The price of airline tickets seems to have some correlation with the distance of the trip, but the relationship is not clear to the casual observer. With discounts for buying tickets early, staying over on a Saturday night, and other pricing schemes, it is difficult to design a simple model that explains ticket prices. Both supply and demand factors determine airline ticket prices in a free market. However, suppose you find an article on the Internet that claims it can explain or predict airline ticket prices based on the distance of the trip. The regression equation used in the article is

$$PRICE = B_0 + B_1(DISTANCE)^2 + B_2(DISTANCE)^3 + e \tag{13-7}$$

where

PRICE = price of a round-trip ticket, in dollars
DISTANCE = distance between airports, in miles

This regression can be estimated by ordinary least squares, since the coefficients enter the regression in a linear fashion (see Section 2-2). The data are given in Table 13-C.

If we use the data from Table 13-C to estimate the airfare model expressed by Equation (13-7), we get the results shown in Table 13-D. At first glance, the model seems to fit the data well and appears to explain differences in airline ticket prices reasonably. Both independent variables, the distance squared and the distance cubed, have coefficients that are statistically significant at a 1% error level. The goodness of fit seems strong, with an R^2 of 0.88 and an adjusted R^2 of 0.86.

Although the independent variables have statistically significant coefficients and the goodness of fit is high, something about this model is peculiar. The design of the model, the specification, is odd. Why would the distance squared and the distance cubed be relevant independent variables, but not just the distance? What happens if we run a regression using DISTANCE as the only independent variable?

$$PRICE = B_0 + B_1 DISTANCE + e \qquad \text{(13-8)}$$

Table 13-C

Data for Airfare Model

Observation	PRICE	DISTANCE	Observation	PRICE	DISTANCE
1	573	887	13	468	1,482
2	500	1,030	14	592	1,078
3	172	202	15	122	1,686
4	565	789	16	143	1,658
5	305	320	17	246	270
6	291	413	18	653	836
7	352	1,558	19	463	603
8	151	116	20	594	973
9	268	1,620	21	422	1,460
10	498	1,560	22	483	677
11	358	510	23	456	1,502
12	446	483			

Table 13-D

Regression Results for Airfare Model

Dependent variable: PRICE

Variable	Coefficient	Standard Error	t-Statistic	p-Value
Constant	179.02	27.36	6.54	0.00
$(DISTANCE)^2$	0.0011	0.000095	11.56	0.00
$(DISTANCE)^3$	-0.00000066	0.000000055	-11.82	0.00

Observations: 23

$R^2 = 0.88$

Adjusted $R^2 = 0.86$

F-statistic = 70.76

Table 13-E

Regression Results for Simple Airfare Model

Dependent variable: PRICE

Variable	Coefficient	Standard Error	t-Statistic	p-Value
Constant	372.34	70.57	5.28	0.00
DISTANCE	0.026	0.066	0.39	0.70

Observations: 23

$R^2 = 0.01$

Adjusted $R^2 = -0.04$

F-statistic = 0.15

The results are given in Table 13-E.

The coefficient for DISTANCE is not significant at any reasonable error level; Table 13-E gives its p-value as 0.70. The R^2 is 0.01 and the adjusted R^2 is negative! This means that when DISTANCE is the lone independent variable, the regression does not work at all. Also, no relevant theory explains why using $(DISTANCE)^2$ and $(DISTANCE)^3$ as independent variables will predict ticket prices. Perhaps the researcher ran different models and chose the one that fit the data! If so, this is bad econometrics. If the researcher chose Equation (13-7), the regression with $(DISTANCE)^2$ and $(DISTANCE)^3$ in it, because it was the only way he could get the regression to fit well, then the regression is just connecting the data points. These regression results tell us nothing about any general relationship between distance and price that might exist. The results don't give us insight into how pricing in the airline industry works.

Figure 13-1 shows the situation. In Figure 13-1, DISTANCE is plotted on the horizontal axis and PRICE is on the vertical axis (see Table 13-C for exact numerical val-

Figure 13-1

Plot of DISTANCE and PRICE Data.

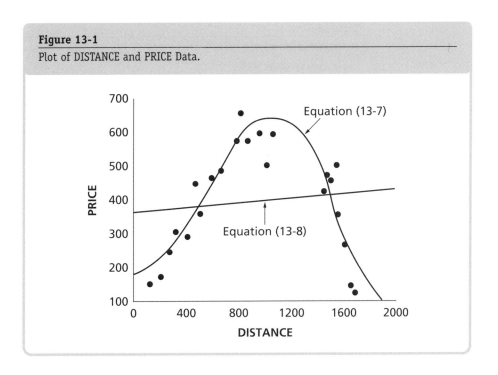

ues). Each dot represents one trip or observation from the sample. You can see why a linear regression doesn't work well here. The data points trace out an upside-down U shape. Perhaps the researcher plotted the data and then built a regression model to fit the data points. This would give the statistically significant results in Table 13-D, but there is no reason to believe that the relationship between DISTANCE and PRICE always forms an upside-down U. In fact, there are two data points on the right-hand side of the figure where the distance is relatively large and the price is relatively low. Most long-distance flights not that cheap, so this observation could just be the "luck of the draw" for this sample.

To show why Equation (13-7) fails to be useful, we should estimate (13-7) with a different data sample, to test its robustness. Table 13-F gives the results for a different data sample.

The results in Table 13-F show that Equation (13-7), with $(DISTANCE)^2$ and $(DISTANCE)^3$, is not robust. As soon as we estimate this regression with another data set, the results fall apart. Equation (13-7) cannot be used to describe the relationship between trip distances and airplane ticket prices. A better model would have simultaneous equations in it, and even then, formulating a good working model will be difficult. Besides distance, we would have to consider the number of airlines that compete for passengers along the same route, how many flights each airline has, what the demand is for travel along that route, how the time of year affects demand, and so on. The supply and demand for airline tickets is relatively difficult to model. The main point here, though, is that an econometric model should not be formulated simply to fit one set of data points. Use theory to construct your models. Also, a good model should be able to perform well when estimated with other data samples. That way you

Table 13-F

Regression Results for Airfare Model, Estimated Using a Second Data Sample

Dependent variable: PRICE

Variable	Coefficient	Standard Error	t-Statistic	p-Value
Constant	452.89	168.72	2.68	0.01
$(DISTANCE)^2$	−0.0018	0.0036	−0.48	0.64
$(DISTANCE)^3$	0.000003	0.0000058	0.52	0.61

Observations: 23

$R^2 = 0.02$

Adjusted $R^2 = -0.08$

F-statistic $= 0.16$

will know that your model describes a relationship between variables that holds true in general; it is not just a fancy way of connecting the dots in a data set.

13-5 SMALL SAMPLE SIZES DON'T GIVE YOU MUCH INFORMATION

The more degrees of freedom there are for running a regression, the more information you have available for the regression process, and the better your chances that the estimates will be accurate. (Degrees of freedom are discussed in Section 2-1.) When the degrees of freedom are small, the results may not be representative of what you would get if you had more information—that is, more degrees of freedom. The results won't be accurate. Recall that the degrees of freedom in a regression model are $n - k - 1$ where n is the sample size, k is the number of slope coefficients in the regression, and the 1 is for the intercept. For any regression, a larger sample size will give you more degrees of freedom, making it more likely you will get better estimates.

Here, the simple version of the airfare model from Section 13-4 demonstrates how a small sample size can give misleading results. Suppose that instead of the 23 observations given in Table 13-C, only 8 observations were collected for the sample. For this example, 8 observations were chosen at random from the data in Table 13-C. The numbers of the observations chosen are: 1, 3, 5, 6, 8, 12, 19, and 22 (column 1 of Table 13-C). The simple version of the airfare model, Equation (13-8), PRICE = B_0 + B_1DISTANCE + e, is then estimated using these eight observations; the results are given in Table 13-G.

Just looking at the results in Table 13-G, we might think that the simple version of the airfare model has promise—that airplane tickets really can be predicted by the distance between destinations. At second glance though, you might notice that the number of observations is only 8. Eight observations means that the degrees of freedom are only 6 ($n - k - 1 = 8 - 1 - 1 = 6$). The results in Table 13-G are based on a *very* small amount of information. From the previous section, we already know that this

Table 13-G

Regression Results for Simple Airfare Model, Estimated with a Small Sample

Dependent variable: PRICE

Variable	Coefficient	Standard Error	t-Statistic	p-Value
Constant	91.58	32.79	2.79	0.03
DISTANCE	0.58	0.063	9.23	0.00

Observations: 8
$R^2 = 0.93$
Adjusted $R^2 = 0.92$
F-statistic $= 85.23$

Table 13-H

Regression Results for Simple Airfare Model, Estimated Using a Second Data Sample

Dependent variable: PRICE

Variable	Coefficient	Standard Error	t-Statistic	p-Value
Constant	368.88	131.33	2.81	0.01
DISTANCE	0.062	0.36	0.17	0.87

Observations: 23
$R^2 = 0.00$
Adjusted $R^2 = -0.05$
F-statistic $= 0.029$

regression doesn't perform well when the 23-observation sample is used. Our new results in Table 13-G use a substantially smaller sample size, so we know that the original results in Table 13-E are more reliable. If we estimate the regression using other samples, we will very likely get a weak goodness of fit (like Table 13-E), rather than the strong goodness of fit displayed in Table 13-G when only eight observations were used. If we use the second 23-observation sample from the previous section to estimate the simple version of the airfare model, we get the results shown in Table 13-H.[6]

With this larger second sample, the coefficient for DISTANCE is statistically insignificant, and the goodness of fit is terrible, with a negative adjusted R^2. These results support the idea that small-sample results are often misleading. Note that in this example, even 23 observations is not that large a sample. If you were a consultant doing a serious study of airline ticket pricing, you would want a sample size in the thousands to improve your chances of getting accurate estimates. (Recall from the last section that a simultaneous-equation system is also needed here.)

---

[6] Note that in Section 13-4, it was the airfare model itself that had problems, not the data sample.

13-6 SELF-SELECTION: INDIVIDUAL CHOICE DETERMINES WHO IS IN THE SAMPLE

Suppose a brochure for a Masters in Business Administration program gives statistics showing that students who earn MBAs make more money than those who don't attend graduate school at all. The brochure implies that earning an MBA at their institution will give you the knowledge and skills you need to be successful. However, students who decide to earn MBAs are not chosen at random. For the most part, they decided to go back to school to advance their careers. On average, then, the typical MBA student probably has a higher level of ambition and drive, compared to someone who doesn't attend grad school. This brings up an interesting question: Why do MBAs make more money? Is it what they learned in their MBA program, or are they simply more ambitious than those who do not pursue a graduate degree? It is difficult to answer this question since people with MBAs are often more ambitious.[7] The larger salaries going to MBAs could be because of their drive, not because they learned important information in their MBA program. This is an example of self-selection.

Self-selection occurs when a sample is not representative of the population because individuals determine by their own choices whether they are in the sample or not. Setting up an econometric model that determines whether MBAs make more money because of what they learned in school or because of ambition will be difficult. The researcher will have to find ambitious people who didn't go on to some form of graduate school. Then ambitious people without graduate degrees and ambitious people with MBAs can be compared to see who made more money. If those with MBAs still make more money, then maybe they did learn something valuable from their additional education. Otherwise, maybe it is ambition that helps MBAs succeed, not the MBA program itself. The problem is, how do we measure ambition? Out of those who did not get an MBA, how do you determine who are ambitious and who are not? Self-selection is one of the most perplexing problems in econometrics.[8]

An example about TV-viewing habits will show the problem with self-selection. An advertising agency conducts a survey to study adult TV-watching habits. The agency wants to estimate the following regression model:

$$TV = B_0 + B_1 AGE + B_2 INCOME + B_3 MALE + e \qquad (13\text{-}9)$$

where

$$TV = \text{hours of television watched in one week, for each person}$$
$$AGE = \text{person's age}$$
$$INCOME = \text{individual's annual income}$$
$$MALE = 1 \text{ if male, 0 otherwise}$$

---

[7] Note that in this discussion, "ambitious" is used to describe someone who is willing to spend time and effort to pursue an MBA in order to advance in a business career. No value judgment is intended.

[8] Dale and Krueger provide an instructive approach to a specific self-selection problem in their paper, "Estimating the Payoff to Attending a More Selective College: An Application of Selection on Observables and Unobservables," Working Paper #409, Industrial Relations Section, Princeton University, 1999. In order to investigate the returns to attending a selective college, Dale and Krueger compare the earnings of those who attended a selective college to those who were accepted by a selective college but chose not to attend.

The agency contacts 1200 people from different households for the survey and 500 respond. The results are given in Table 13-I. The slope estimate for AGE is statistically significant at a 5% error level, but those for INCOME and MALE are not.

The sample used to estimate the TV-viewing model has a self-selection problem. People who are very busy with work were less likely to participate in the survey. Therefore, those who did participate are not a random sample of the population; for example, higher-income viewers are underrepresented in the sample because they are more likely to be busy. This may explain why the estimated B for INCOME is not statistically significant. Since higher-income viewers are underrepresented, there is not enough variation in INCOME to get an accurate estimate of its slope. Also, the ordinary least squares process will give biased estimates in this case, since the sample is biased toward lower-income viewers. This means that the slope estimate for INCOME will not be as good as it could be. The other slope estimates are also likely to be biased. Because people tend to make more income as they get older, older people are also underrepresented in the sample; this affects the slope estimate for AGE. (Another problem, separate from the self-selection problem, is that people don't always answer surveys accurately. This is why economists often avoid using survey data.)

The self-selection problem could be corrected if the agency could somehow compel people to participate in the survey, regardless of their income. Suppose the agency conducts the survey again, paying 500 individuals a substantial amount of money to participate. Also, the agency picks 500 individuals by income level and age that represent the population the agency wants to study. This does away with the self-selection problem. Using the data from this survey to reestimate the TV-viewing model gives the results in Table 13-J.

Notice the difference in the results now that there is no self-selection problem. The slope estimate for INCOME is farther from zero than before and is statistically significant at a 1% error level. Presumably, the estimates that come from the new sample

Table 13-I

Results for TV-Viewing Model (Sample Is Self-Selected)

Dependent variable: TV

Variable	Coefficient	Standard Error	t-Statistic	p-Value
Constant	5.10	0.69	7.39	0.00
AGE	0.23	0.11	2.09	0.04
INCOME	−0.030	0.034	−0.88	0.38
MALE	−4.20	3.76	−1.12	0.26

Observations: 500

$R^2 = 0.53$

Adjusted $R^2 = 0.53$

F-statistic = 186.50

Table 13-J

Results for TV-viewing Model (No Self-Selection Problem in Sample)

Dependent variable: TV

Variable	Coefficient	Standard Error	t-Statistic	p-Value
Constant	17.25	2.64	6.53	0.00
AGE	0.27	0.12	2.25	0.02
INCOME	−0.45	0.17	2.65	0.01
MALE	−0.98	1.22	0.80	0.42

Observations: 500

$R^2 = 0.83$

Adjusted $R^2 = 0.83$

F-statistic = 806.81

(Table 13-J) are more accurate than those from the sample with self-selection (Table 13-I), but there is no way to verify this because we cannot know the true values. Note that the goodness of fit has improved, from an adjusted R^2 of 0.53 (with self-selection), to 0.83 (without self-selection).

13-7 "TRUTH-IN-ADVERTISING" IS THE KEY TO HONEST ECONOMETRICS

The key to honest econometrics is to make sure that you reveal all your results and everything you learned during your research. (See Section 4-4.) In this section, we present four questions you should ask about any econometric results before you accept the researcher's conclusions. Also, when writing up your own work, be sure to keep these four questions in mind, by checking that the four questions are clearly addressed in your paper.

1. Is the model's specification justified by theory?
2. Is the sample a reasonable size and is there any reason to believe that it does not represent the relevant population?
3. Are the results robust?
4. Are the conclusions justified by the evidence presented?

1. IS THE MODEL'S SPECIFICATION JUSTIFIED BY THEORY? Hendry's econometric theory of inflation, discussed in Section 13-1, shows what happens if proper theory is ignored. The slope estimate for cumulative rainfall came out statistically significant because both the cumulative rainfall and the price level increased over time. Remember that a statistically significant result does not prove causation. In this example, rain did not cause the price level to go up.

The airfare model in Section 13-4 is another example of a regression model that is not supported by theory. It was specifically designed to fit one sample. Not surprisingly, the model didn't work well when estimated with a different sample. Basic economic theory tells us that a simultaneous-equation model should have been used, since both supply and demand determine airline ticket prices.

2. IS THE SAMPLE A REASONABLE SIZE AND IS THERE ANY REASON TO BELIEVE THAT IT DOES NOT REPRESENT THE RELEVANT POPULATION? A sample size that is too small does not contain enough information. It makes it much less likely that the econometric process will give us accurate estimates, because the process doesn't have enough information to work with. This idea was illustrated in Section 13-5 when we estimated a simple linear version of the airfare model with a very small sample size.

A random sample is not guaranteed to represent the population you want to study. However, larger sample sizes are more likely to be representative. The sample must really be random, though, or constructed in a way such that it is representative of the population being studied. If the sample is collected in a way that excludes a relevant portion of the population, this will bias the results. Self-selection is a troublesome source of this type of error, as the survey of TV viewers in Section 13-6 demonstrated.

3. ARE THE RESULTS ROBUST? Would the conclusions based on the results be the same if the model were formulated a little differently? Does the researcher give you information about different versions of the model that were estimated? If not, be careful about placing too much reliance on the results. The researcher may have tried several versions of the model and wrote only about the one version that came out the way he wanted. In writing about your own research, always indicate what you found with different versions of the model. That way your readers will know whether your results hold in general, or only under specific conditions. Giving your readers this information signals to them that you were thorough in doing your research.

4. ARE THE CONCLUSIONS JUSTIFIED BY THE EVIDENCE PRESENTED? Once again, remember that statistical significance does not prove causation. Also, as discussed in Section 3-2, there are situations in which statistical significance can be trivial. The fact that a coefficient is statistically significant doesn't mean that it is important. Finally, does the researcher extrapolate far outside the data used when making her conclusions? If so, be wary of taking the conclusions too seriously. Section 13-3 provides an example of this, when Quinn's DVD model predicted she would spend over $32,000 on DVDs in one month.

A controversial use of extrapolation lies outside of economics, in health studies. If a substantial dosage of a substance is shown to cause cancer in rats, does that mean that it will cause cancer in humans? Animal rights activists argue that this type of testing does not teach us anything, because results from experiments on rats cannot be extrapolated to make conclusions about humans. Many scientists disagree, pointing out it is dangerous to conduct such experiments on humans, and that valuable information can be gained from the experiments that may save human lives.[9]

---

[9] For a website that opposes animal research, see the New England Anti-Vivisection Society at http://www.neavs.org. For a website that defends animal research, see the Foundation for Biomedical Research at http://www.fbresearch.org.

13-8 A TABLE OF ECONOMETRIC SITUATIONS AND PROBLEMS

Table 13-K will help you recall different problems and situations that can occur as you do econometric work. Each issue appears in the order in which it appears in the book.

Table 13-K

Summary of Common Econometric Problems and Situations

Problem or Situation	Recognizable Characteristics	Violation of Classical Assumptions (Section 2-2)	
Causality: Regression cannot prove that X causes Y	This is always true for every regression.	None	
Small sample size	This is easily recognizable since you know the sample size before you run the regression.	None	
Selection bias	Can be hard to recognize; think about how the data were collected: Is there a bias?	None	
Type I or Type II error	Can't be recognized; Type I and II errors are always a risk.	None	
Statistical significance can be trivial	Slope estimate is statistically significant, but when you interpret it, its effect is very small.	None	
Tautology	The regression fits perfectly, $R^2 = 1$.	Since the regression always fits perfectly, there is no error term. (Assumptions 3–7 presume an error term is present).	
Inflation	A time-series regression where at least some variables are measured in money so that they are affected by general increases in the price level.	Assumption 4, if more than one independent variable is strongly affected by inflation and the inflation is not accounted for, there could be multicollinearity.	
Omitted independent variables	Theory indicates a variable should be included, but it is not.	Assumption 1 (. . . the model contains the right independent variables) and assumption 3 (none of the independent variables are correlated with the error term.) The estimates will be biased.	

Solution	2nd Best Solution	Section and/or Example
No real solution, but estimating the model with different data samples provides additional evidence.		Section 1-2; Section 13-1, Hendry's inflation model
Increase sample size.	Be very careful about interpreting the results, since they are based on a small amout of information.	Section 2-3 [discussion of $\text{V}\hat{\text{A}}\text{R}(\hat{\text{B}}_1)$]; Section 13-5, airplane example, Table 13-G
Use a random sample.		Section 3-1, Dewey vs. Truman
No real solution, but try estimating the model with different data to get more evidence.	When you interpret regression results, remember that Type I and II errors do exist.	Section 3-1 (Table 3-A)
In interpreting the slope coefficient, make it clear that statistical significance does not mean the independent variable is necessarily important.		Section 3-2, trucker example (Table 3-C)
Develop a new regression that addresses a hypothesis that is not automatically true by definition.		Section 4-3, GDP example
Adjust variables measured in money by dividing by an index that measures inflation, such as a CPI index. (*Note*: This should be done even if only one variable is affected by inflation.)		Section 4-3, see Equation (4-2) and Table 4-A
Include the omitted variable.	If the omitted variable is not available, try to find something close to it.	Section 4-3, see Equation (4-9) and Table 4-B for the DVD model with a missing independent variable

(*continued*)

Table 13-K

(Continued)

Problem or Situation	Recognizable Characteristics	Violation of Classical Assumptions (Section 2-2)	
Extra or unnecessary independent variables	The presence of the variable in the model is not justified by theory.	Assumption 1 (. . . the model contains the right independent variables)	
Robustness	Changing the model slightly changes the results dramatically; slightly different versions of the model lead to very different conclusions.	None	
Outlier	An observation or value for one variable lies far outside the range of the other observations for this variable.	None	
Dummy variable trap	Software is unable to estimate model.	Assumption 2 (None of the independent variables have a linear relationship. There will be perfect multicollinearity.)	
Joint hypotheses	Hypothesis involves more than one B.		
Combining two data sets	Increases the sample size.		
Multicollinearity	Slope estimates unexpectedly appear insignificant, but R^2 and F-test still indicate strong goodness of fit. Also, model is not robust. (Section 6-2)	Assumption 2 (None of the independent variables have a linear relationship.)	
Autocorrelation	Observed errors follow a pattern; the Durbin-Watson statistic can often detect first-order autocorrelation. Note that the t-statistics are larger than they should be. (Sections 7-1, 7-3)	Assumption 4 (Observed errors are independent of each other, so they are not correlated with each other.)	
Heteroskedasticity	Observed errors come from different distributions with different variances. (Use Park test or White test.) Note that t-statistics are larger than they should be. (Sections 8-1, 8-2, 8-3)	Assumption 6 (Error term has a constant variance.)	

Solution	2nd Best Solution	Section and/or Example
Remove the unnecessary variable.		Section 4-3, see Equation (4-10) and Table 4-C for the DVD model with an unnecessary independent variable
Reveal all results when reporting research. Take special care not to overstate the importance or rigor of the results.		Section 4-3; Section 13-2; Section 13-4, airfare model; Section 13-7
Check that the observation was recorded correctly. If so, it stays in the sample. If not, correct it or eliminate it from the sample.		Section 4-5, example with $100,000,000 income
Remove one dummy variable.		Section 5-1, see Equation (5-6): Professional wrestling model with an extra dummy.
Design your own F-test to test joint hypotheses.		Section 5-3 Equation (5-15): seasonal DJIA model
The Chow test tells whether you can combine two data sets.		Section 5-3, Equation (5-20): gasoline revenue model
Possible solutions: 1. Do nothing (only good under certain conditions; see Section 6-4). 2. Eliminate a correlated independent variable. 3. Redesign model. 4. Increase sample size.		Chapter 6, exam score model
Redesign model to include any missing variables, such as seasonal dummy variables, that would account for the autocorrelation. (Section 7-4)	Generalized difference equation/AR(1) method. (Section 7-5)	Chapter 7, Microsoft revenue model
Redesign model to account for the different sizes of the observations. (Section 8-4)	Weighted least squares, or corrected standard error and t-statistics method. (Section 8-5)	Chapter 8, concert tour model

(continued)

Table 13-K

(Continued)

Problem or Situation	Recognizable Characteristics	Violation of Classical Assumptions (Section 2-2)	
Pooled-data model estimation	Pooled data combine cross-section and time-series data. Use special techniques, such as seemingly unrelated regression, fixed effects, or random effects to estimate pooled-data regressions.		
Simultaneity	Theory indicates that more than one equation is necessary. (Section 10-1) Also, use the Hausman test to see if simultaneity is a potential problem. (Section 10-4)	Assumption 3 (None of the independent variables are correlated with the error term.)	
Measurement error	Can be hard to recognize. You need to know how the data were collected, and whether the collection method was reliable.	Assumption 1 (. . . the model contains the right independent variables.) If a variable is measured incorrectly, it is not really the right variable.	
Causality in time-series (Granger causality test)			
Dependent variable is a dummy			

SUMMARY

1. Econometrics can be used to learn from what has happened in the past, or it can be used to mislead, often unintentionally. If the model is not based on theory, the results may not make sense, even if the t-statistics show statistical significance.

2. Changing a model's independent variables can dramatically alter the results. It is dishonest to run several versions of a regression model and then report only results that show what you wanted.

3. Extrapolating or projecting regression results past the range of values taken by the variables in the data can be dangerous; it can give misleading conclusions.

4. Regression analysis is meant to test whether a theoretical relationship between variables is supported by data. It is not supposed to be a complicated game of "connect the dots." For any data set, some complicated curve can be drawn to fit the data; there is always a mathematical way to connect the dots. Drawing a curve to fit the data doesn't prove anything. It doesn't give us any real information about the general relationship between the variables because the regression is unlikely

Solution	2nd Best Solution	Section and/or Example
		Section 9-5 provides a comparison of Seemingly Unrelated Regression, Fixed Effects, and Random Effects estimation techniques.
Use a simultaneous-equation system. Instrumental variables estimation including two-stage least squares can also be used. (Sections 10-5, 10-6)		Chapter 10 pizza model
Get new data that has been collected properly, without measurement error.	Use instrumental variable estimation, which included two-stage least squares. (Sections 10-5, 10-6).	Sections 10-5, 10-6
Granger test looks for Granger causality: When changes in Y follow changes in X.		Section 11-5
Use probit, logit, or multinomial logit models.		Chapter 12 Voting example

to fit well when estimated with a different data set. A regression model specifically built to fit one data set is unsuitable for forecasting what happens in the future.

5. The more degrees of freedom, the more information there is available for the regression process, and the better the chance the estimates will be accurate.

6. **Self-selection** occurs when a sample does not represent the population because individuals, by their own choices, determine whether or not they are in the sample. Regression results are likely to be biased when there is self-selection.

7. The key to honest econometrics is to make sure that you reveal all your results and everything you learned during your research. Keep in mind four questions when you do your own econometric work and when you read work by others:
   - Is the model's specification justified by theory?
   - Is the sample a reasonable size and is there any reason to believe that it does not represent the relevant population?
   - Are the results robust?
   - Are the conclusions justified by the evidence presented?

EXERCISES

1. What is self-selection? Why is it a problem?

2. There are four questions you should consider when reading econometrics results and when writing your own work. Without looking at the text, state the four questions and briefly explain each one.

3. This chapter presents several different problems that make econometric results misleading. Without looking at the text or your notes, write a short description of as many of the different problems as you can remember.

4. Why is it wrong to find a model that fits the data the best? Isn't that the point of doing econometrics? Explain.

5. Suppose you collected 20 more samples of data to test the simple linear version of the airfare model (PRICE $= B_0 + B_1$ DISTANCE $+ e$) (*Note*: 20 more samples, meaning 20 more sets of observations, not just 20 more data points.)
   a. Would you be surprised if the estimate of B_1 is statistically significant at a 5% error for one of the samples? Why or why not?
   b. What if DISTANCE is statistically significant for 19 out of the 20 samples? How would you interpret this?

6. Download the 1973–2000 data for the gasoline revenue model from the text website to answer the following questions.
   a. Estimate the gasoline revenue model with the 1973–2000 data, omitting PRICE as an independent variable. Compare this to the original results where PRICE was included in the model (Table 5-K).
   b. Why do you think these results differ from those described in Section 13-2?
   c. Back up your answer to part b with evidence.

7. As mentioned in Section 13-4, the airfare model needs a simultaneous-equation system to be estimated properly.
   a. Write a supply equation and a demand equation for the airfare model, including additional variables that are not mentioned in the text.
   b. Are the equations identified? If not, redesign the model so that both equations are identified.
   c. Do you think you would be able to collect the data you need for these variables?

8. An amateur researcher finds that when air conditioning use is higher than average, so is the crime rate. The researcher estimates a simple cross-section regression model with a measure of the crime rate as the dependent variable and a measure of air conditioner use as the independent variable. The results show the air conditioner variable has a statistically significant coefficient estimate at a 1% error level. He concludes that the air conditioning must be doing something to the air that causes crime to rise.
   a. Comment on this conclusion.
   b. What should be done to investigate the matter further?

9. In 1798, Thomas Robert Malthus wrote "An Essay on the Principle of Population." In this famous essay, he noted that the rate of population growth was greater than the rate of growth in the food supply. Malthus feared that this would have

disastrous effects for the English economy, and that starvation could result. Since 1789, England, along with many other nations, has enjoyed a dramatic increase in its standard of living.

a. Why did things turn out better than Malthus feared?

b. Malthus did not use an econometric model, but what econometric mistake is relevant here?

Glossary

A

adjusted $\bar{R}^2$ R^2 with degrees of freedom taken into account

AR(1) method can be used when autocorrelation is present; can be thought of as a method to simultaneously estimate the B's and the autocorrelation coefficient ρ from a generalized difference equation

autocorrelation occurs when observed errors follow a pattern so that they are correlated; also called *serial correlation*

autocorrelation function gives correlation coefficients between the dependent variable and the same variable with different lags, but the effect of the shorter lags is not kept constant; used to determine the number of lags in a moving average model

autoregressive model model in which the independent variables are all lagged dependent variables; there are no other independent variables

autoregressive moving average model a model that combines autoregressive and moving average processes

B

binary choice model regression model with a dependent dummy variable that allows only two choices

BLUE Best Linear Unbiased Estimator

C

censored data data that are missing some values for the dependent variable because they cannot be observed; no values missing for independent variables

Chow test type of F-test that checks if coefficients estimated using different data but the same model are equal; if they are equal, the two data sets can be combined

classical assumptions seven requirements that must be true of a linear regression model for ordinary least squares to work best (the seventh assumption is optional)

Cochrane-Orcutt method can be used when autocorrelation is present; method of estimating a generalized difference equation, estimates the autocorrelation coefficient ρ and the B's several times until the estimates of ρ converge

coefficient a parameter or value in a regression that does not change from one observation to another

cointegration occurs when variables in a model are nonstationary to the same extent, in a way that allows the researcher to proceed as if the variables are stationary

consistent estimator an estimator whose estimates approach the true value when the sample size becomes very large

correlation coefficient r measures the extent to which two variables move together

critical value value of a test statistic that marks the beginning of the rejection region

cross-section data information on many people, countries, firms, or entities for the same period of time

D

decision rule rule that tells how to use a test statistic to decide whether to reject the null hypothesis

degrees of freedom a measure of the amount of information available to estimate a regression model; degrees of freedom = sample size (n) − number of coefficients to be estimated (k) − 1 (one degree of freedom subtracted for the intercept), or n − k − 1

dependent variable variable that typically appears on the left-hand side of a regression equation; in theory, its values depend upon the independent variables in the regression

Dickey-Fuller test most common unit-root test

distributed lag model model in which an independent variable appears more than once, with different time lags

double-log model model that takes the natural logarithm of the dependent and independent variables

dummy variable variable that allows us to include a non-numerical variable in a regression

Durbin h-statistic tests for first-order autocorrelation in models with a lagged dependent variable on the right side, like the Koyck model

Durbin-Watson statistic test for first-order autocorrelation

E

econometric model one or more equations that are used in econometrics to estimate the relationship between different factors or variables

efficient estimator when two estimators are unbiased, the estimator with the lower variance

endogenous variable a variable that is in theory explained by the model

estimator method for finding estimates

exogenous variable the variable's values are determined outside the model—the model does not try to explain why the variable takes the values it does

explained sum of squares (ESS) one of the two parts of TSS; the movement in Y that is explained by the regression equation

explanatory variable explains or predicts the value of the dependent variable; independent variable

extrapolation projecting beyond the range of the sample

F

first-order autocorrelation a type of autocorrelation that occurs when an observed error is influenced by the observed error from the preceding time period

fixed effects model model that incorporates differences between firms, states, people, or other entity by allowing the intercept to change; the intercept is different for each entity but stays constant over time

G

Gauss-Markov theorem when six of the classical assumptions (assumptions 1–6) all hold true, then ordinary least squares is the best linear unbiased estimator

generalized difference equation used to estimate a regression when there is autocorrelation, found by taking the difference of two equations

Granger causality a weaker type of causality that occurs when X changes and changes in Y follow thereafter

H

heteroskedasticity the error term in a regression model does not have a constant variance

hold-out sample portion of the sample that is intentionally omitted from the initial regression run so that it can be used later to check the model's forecasting ability

homoskedasticity the error term variance is constant

I

identification occurs when there is enough information in a simultaneous equation system to estimate an equation's coefficients

independent variable variable that is considered independent of other variables in the regression

instrumental variables estimation method that uses a proxy for an endogenous variable to estimate an equation with a simultaneity problem

interaction variable accounts for the possibility that the relationship between an independent and a dependent variable may be influenced by another independent variable

J

joint hypothesis hypothesis that involves more than one coefficient at a time

K

Koyck lag model model in which the slope coefficients automatically get closer to zero as the independent variables go farther back in time; used to estimate a distributed lag model

L

lagged independent variable a variable for which the values being used come from previous time periods

linear probability model binary choice model estimated with ordinary least squares; assumes the probability that $Y = 1$ is linearly related to the independent variables

logit model binary choice model that uses the cumulative logistic distribution to give probabilities bounded by 0 and 1, thereby avoiding some of the problems inherent in the linear probability model; its coefficient estimates give the change in the logarithm of the odds for a one-unit change in an independent variable, keeping other independent variables constant

M

maximum likelihood iterative technique that estimates coefficients by finding estimates that maximize the chance of seeing the values that actually occurred in the sample

Monte Carlo study uses made-up data to examine the properties of different estimators

moving average model model that uses previous error terms as independent variables

multicollinearity occurs when two (or more) independent variables are highly correlated in a linear fashion

multinomial choice model regression model with a dependent dummy variable that allows for more than two choices

multinomial logit technique for estimating qualitative choice models with more than two choices, when the choices are not ordered

multiple or multivariate regression model regression model with more than one independent variable

N

negative autocorrelation autocorrelation in which the errors tend to alternate in sign

nonstationary variable a time-series variable that does not have the same mean, variance, or autocorrelation pattern over time

O

observation set of numbers for different variables that go together; can be for one time period, country, firm, or other entity included in the data sample

one-sided test test in which the alternative hypothesis features either a "greater than" or a "less than" symbol

order condition a necessary but not sufficient condition for an equation to be identified

ordinary least squares (OLS) method for estimating a regression line in which values are found for the coefficient estimates that minimize the sum of $\hat{e}^2$

outlier an observation for a variable that lies far away from the other observations

overidentification occurs when there is more than enough information in a simultaneous-equation system to estimate an equation's coefficients

P

panel data pooled data set that contains observations from the same entities over time

Park test statistical test for heteroskedasticity in which the researcher specifies a size factor Z

partial autocorrelation function gives the correlation coefficients between the dependent variable and this same variable with different lags, while keeping the effect of shorter lags constant; used to determine the number of lags in an autoregressive model

perfect multicollinearity occurs when two independent variables have a perfect linear relationship

point forecast single-number forecast

polynomial model regression model used to estimate curves

pooled data data set that contains cross-section data and time-series data

population the entire set of possible data points

positive autocorrelation autocorrelation in which the errors tend to have the same sign from one period to the next

predetermined variables exogenous and lagged endogenous variables; they are not determined by the model

probit model binary choice model that uses the cumulative normal probability distribution to give probabilities bounded by 0 and 1, thereby avoiding some of the problems inherent in the linear probability model; estimated using maximum likelihood

pseudo-R^2 goodness-of-fit measure that is used instead of R^2 for models with a dependent dummy variable

p-value statistic that gives the probability of Type I error

Q

qualitative choice model regression model in which the dependent variable is a dummy variable

qualitative variable variable that represents a property or feature that is not numerical

quantitative variable variable that represents a number

R

R^2 ratio of the explained sum of squares to the total sum of squares; $R^2 = ESS/TSS$, also called the coefficient of determination (measures goodness of fit)

random effects model model that incorporates differences between cross-sectional entities by allowing the intercept to change randomly

random walk changes in a variable are completely random over time

reduced-form equation method of stating a simultaneous-equation system in which only predetermined variables appear on the equations' right-hand side

replicable results occur when others can use the same data and regression model and obtain the same results

residual observed error; the difference between the actual value of the dependent variable and the predicted value

residual sum of squares (RSS) one of the two parts of TSS, the movement in Y that is *not* explained by the regression equation

restricted model used in an F-test, model in which the values of some of the coefficients have been changed or restricted by assuming the null hypothesis is true

robustness ability of a model to give similar results when small changes are made in it

S

sample members of a group who are chosen to represent the whole group (can be firms, countries, people, etc.)

sampling distribution probability distribution for a set of coefficient estimates

seemingly unrelated regression (SUR) an estimation method that allows the error terms of separate but related regressions to be correlated

selection bias occurs when a particular group is under- or overrepresented in a sample

self-selection occurs when a sample does not represent the population because individuals, by their own choices, determine whether or not they are in the sample

semi-log model an adaptation of the double-log model in which only some of the variables are transformed by the natural logarithm

serial correlation occurs when observed errors follow a pattern so that they are correlated; also called *autocorrelation*

simple regression model contains only one independent variable

simultaneity occurs when a single-equation model is used to describe a model that needs two or more equations

simultaneous-equation system a model that requires two or more equations because there are two or more dependent variables that are determined at the same time

size factor Z typically a measure of each observation's size; also called the *proportionality factor*

specification the form a model will take, and the independent variables that will be included

spurious regression a regression that shows good fit and significant t-statistics because of a trend or other factor not accounted for in the model

stationary variable a time-series variable that has the same mean, variance, and autocorrelation pattern over time

stochastic random

structural equation method method of stating a simultaneous-equation system that shows the model's underlying theory

T

tautology a statement or equation that is true by definition

three-stage least squares type of instrumental variables estimation that adds seemingly unrelated regression to two-stage least squares

time-series data data that follow one person, country, firm, or other entity across different time periods

total sum of squares (TSS) a measure of the total movement in the dependent variable

truncated data data that are missing observations for both the dependent and independent variables when the dependent variable falls above or below a certain value

two-sided test test in which the null hypothesis is rejected if it seems likely the true value of the slope coefficient B is greater or less than the null hypothesis

two-stage least squares type of instrumental variables estimation that uses all of the model's predetermined variables to construct an instrument

Type I error situation in which the null hypothesis is true but it is rejected

Type II error situation in which the null hypothesis is false but it is not rejected

U

unbiased estimator expected value or mean of estimator is equal to its true value—that is, the sampling distribution of the estimator is centered on the true value

unconditional forecast forecast in which the values of the independent variables are known at the time the forecast is made

unit-root test used to see if a variable is stationary

unrestricted model used in an F-test, model in which no changes or restrictions have been forced on the regression

V

variable quantity in a regression that changes from one observation to another

variance inflation factor (VIF) a measure of multicollinearity based upon regressing one of the independent variables on *all* of the remaining independent variables

W

weighted least squares (WLS) an estimation method that corrects for heteroskedasticity by dividing all the variables by a size factor Z

White test statistical test for heteroskedasticity in which the size factor Z is not specified ahead of time

Appendix of Statistical Tables

Table A

Critical Values for the t-statistic

	Level of Significance				
One-sided **Two-sided**	**10%** **20%**	**5%** **10%**	**2.5%** **5%**	**1%** **2%**	**0.5%** **1%**
1	3.078	6.314	12.706	31.821	63.656
2	1.886	2.920	4.303	6.965	9.925
3	1.638	2.353	3.182	4.541	5.841
4	1.533	2.132	2.776	3.747	4.604
5	1.476	2.015	2.571	3.365	4.032
6	1.440	1.943	2.447	3.143	3.707
7	1.415	1.895	2.365	2.998	3.499
8	1.397	1.860	2.306	2.896	3.355
9	1.383	1.833	2.262	2.821	3.250
10	1.372	1.812	2.228	2.764	3.169
11	1.363	1.796	2.201	2.718	3.106
12	1.356	1.782	2.179	2.681	3.055
13	1.350	1.771	2.160	2.650	3.012
14	1.345	1.761	2.145	2.624	2.977
15	1.341	1.753	2.131	2.602	2.947
16	1.337	1.746	2.120	2.583	2.921
17	1.333	1.740	2.110	2.567	2.898
18	1.330	1.734	2.101	2.552	2.878
19	1.328	1.729	2.093	2.539	2.861
20	1.325	1.725	2.086	2.528	2.845
21	1.323	1.721	2.080	2.518	2.831
22	1.321	1.717	2.074	2.508	2.819

Degrees of Freedom (row label)

(*continued*)

Table A

(Continued)

	Level of Significance				
One-sided Two-sided	10% 20%	5% 10%	2.5% 5%	1% 2%	0.5% 1%
23	1.319	1.714	2.069	2.500	2.807
24	1.318	1.711	2.064	2.492	2.797
25	1.316	1.708	2.060	2.485	2.787
26	1.315	1.706	2.056	2.479	2.779
27	1.314	1.703	2.052	2.473	2.771
28	1.313	1.701	2.048	2.467	2.763
29	1.311	1.699	2.045	2.462	2.756
30	1.310	1.697	2.042	2.457	2.750
40	1.303	1.684	2.021	2.423	2.704
50	1.299	1.676	2.009	2.403	2.678
60	1.296	1.671	2.000	2.390	2.660
70	1.294	1.667	1.994	2.381	2.648
80	1.292	1.664	1.990	2.374	2.639
90	1.291	1.662	1.987	2.368	2.632
100	1.290	1.660	1.984	2.364	2.626
110	1.289	1.659	1.982	2.361	2.621
120	1.289	1.658	1.980	2.358	2.617
Infinity	1.282	1.645	1.960	2.326	2.576

Degrees of Freedom

The t-distribution is symmetrical. For a negative t-statistic, take the absolute value before using this table. The values in the table are generated using the TINV function in Microsoft Excel.

Table B

Standardized Normal Distribution

z	0.00	0.01	0.02	0.03	0.04	0.05	0.06	0.07	0.08	0.09
0.0	0.5000	0.4960	0.4920	0.4880	0.4840	0.4801	0.4761	0.4721	0.4681	0.4641
0.1	0.4602	0.4562	0.4522	0.4483	0.4443	0.4404	0.4364	0.4325	0.4286	0.4247
0.2	0.4207	0.4168	0.4129	0.4090	0.4052	0.4013	0.3974	0.3936	0.3897	0.3859
0.3	0.3821	0.3783	0.3745	0.3707	0.3669	0.3632	0.3594	0.3557	0.3520	0.3483
0.4	0.3446	0.3409	0.3372	0.3336	0.3300	0.3264	0.3228	0.3192	0.3156	0.3121
0.5	0.3085	0.3050	0.3015	0.2981	0.2946	0.2912	0.2877	0.2843	0.2810	0.2776
0.6	0.2743	0.2709	0.2676	0.2643	0.2611	0.2578	0.2546	0.2514	0.2483	0.2451
0.7	0.2420	0.2389	0.2358	0.2327	0.2296	0.2266	0.2236	0.2206	0.2177	0.2148
0.8	0.2119	0.2090	0.2061	0.2033	0.2005	0.1977	0.1949	0.1922	0.1894	0.1867
0.9	0.1841	0.1814	0.1788	0.1762	0.1736	0.1711	0.1685	0.1660	0.1635	0.1611
1.0	0.1587	0.1562	0.1539	0.1515	0.1492	0.1469	0.1446	0.1423	0.1401	0.1379
1.1	0.1357	0.1335	0.1314	0.1292	0.1271	0.1251	0.1230	0.1210	0.1190	0.1170
1.2	0.1151	0.1131	0.1112	0.1093	0.1075	0.1056	0.1038	0.1020	0.1003	0.0985
1.3	0.0968	0.0951	0.0934	0.0918	0.0901	0.0885	0.0869	0.0853	0.0838	0.0823
1.4	0.0808	0.0793	0.0778	0.0764	0.0749	0.0735	0.0721	0.0708	0.0694	0.0681
1.5	0.0668	0.0655	0.0643	0.0630	0.0618	0.0606	0.0594	0.0582	0.0571	0.0559
1.6	0.0548	0.0537	0.0526	0.0516	0.0505	0.0495	0.0485	0.0475	0.0465	0.0455
1.7	0.0446	0.0436	0.0427	0.0418	0.0409	0.0401	0.0392	0.0384	0.0375	0.0367
1.8	0.0359	0.0351	0.0344	0.0336	0.0329	0.0322	0.0314	0.0307	0.0301	0.0294
1.9	0.0287	0.0281	0.0274	0.0268	0.0262	0.0256	0.0250	0.0244	0.0239	0.0233
2.0	0.0228	0.0222	0.0217	0.0212	0.0207	0.0202	0.0197	0.0192	0.0188	0.0183
2.1	0.0179	0.0174	0.0170	0.0166	0.0162	0.0158	0.0154	0.0150	0.0146	0.0143
2.2	0.0139	0.0136	0.0132	0.0129	0.0125	0.0122	0.0119	0.0116	0.0113	0.0110

(continued)

Table B

(Continued)

z	0.00	0.01	0.02	0.03	0.04	0.05	0.06	0.07	0.08	0.09
2.3	0.0107	0.0104	0.0102	0.0099	0.0096	0.0094	0.0091	0.0089	0.0087	0.0084
2.4	0.0082	0.0080	0.0078	0.0075	0.0073	0.0071	0.0069	0.0068	0.0066	0.0064
2.5	0.0062	0.0060	0.0059	0.0057	0.0055	0.0054	0.0052	0.0051	0.0049	0.0048
2.6	0.0047	0.0045	0.0044	0.0043	0.0041	0.0040	0.0039	0.0038	0.0037	0.0036
2.7	0.0035	0.0034	0.0033	0.0032	0.0031	0.0030	0.0029	0.0028	0.0027	0.0026
2.8	0.0026	0.0025	0.0024	0.0023	0.0023	0.0022	0.0021	0.0021	0.0020	0.0019
2.9	0.0019	0.0018	0.0018	0.0017	0.0016	0.0016	0.0015	0.0015	0.0014	0.0014
3.0	0.0013	0.0013	0.0013	0.0012	0.0012	0.0011	0.0011	0.0011	0.0010	0.0010

Each value in the table represents the area (or probability) to the right of z for the right-hand tail of the standard normal probability distribution. The distribution is symmetrical, so for the left-hand tail, take the absolute value of z before using this table. The values in the table are generated using the NORMDIST function in Microsoft Excel, and then subtracting these values from 1.

Table C

Critical Values for the F-statistic (5% Significance Level)

				Degrees of Freedom in the Numerator									
	1	2	3	4	5	6	7	8	9	10	15	20	Infinity
1	161	200	216	225	230	234	237	239	241	242	246	248	254
2	18.5	19.0	19.2	19.3	19.3	19.3	19.4	19.4	19.4	19.4	19.4	19.5	19.5
3	10.1	9.55	9.28	9.12	9.01	8.94	8.89	8.85	8.81	8.79	8.70	8.66	8.53
4	7.71	6.94	6.59	6.39	6.26	6.16	6.09	6.04	6.00	5.96	5.86	5.80	5.63
5	6.61	5.79	5.41	5.19	5.05	4.95	4.88	4.82	4.77	4.74	4.62	4.56	4.37
6	5.99	5.14	4.76	4.53	4.39	4.28	4.21	4.15	4.10	4.06	3.94	3.87	3.67
7	5.59	4.74	4.35	4.12	3.97	3.87	3.79	3.73	3.68	3.64	3.51	3.44	3.23
8	5.32	4.46	4.07	3.84	3.69	3.58	3.50	3.44	3.39	3.35	3.22	3.15	2.93
9	5.12	4.26	3.86	3.63	3.48	3.37	3.29	3.23	3.18	3.14	3.01	2.94	2.71
10	4.96	4.10	3.71	3.48	3.33	3.22	3.14	3.07	3.02	2.98	2.85	2.77	2.54
11	4.84	3.98	3.59	3.36	3.20	3.09	3.01	2.95	2.90	2.85	2.72	2.65	2.40
12	4.75	3.89	3.49	3.26	3.11	3.00	2.91	2.85	2.80	2.75	2.62	2.54	2.30
13	4.67	3.81	3.41	3.18	3.03	2.92	2.83	2.77	2.71	2.67	2.53	2.46	2.21
14	4.60	3.74	3.34	3.11	2.96	2.85	2.76	2.70	2.65	2.60	2.46	2.39	2.13
15	4.54	3.68	3.29	3.06	2.90	2.79	2.71	2.64	2.59	2.54	2.40	2.33	2.07
16	4.49	3.63	3.24	3.01	2.85	2.74	2.66	2.59	2.54	2.49	2.35	2.28	2.01
17	4.45	3.59	3.20	2.96	2.81	2.70	2.61	2.55	2.49	2.45	2.31	2.23	1.96
18	4.41	3.55	3.16	2.93	2.77	2.66	2.58	2.51	2.46	2.41	2.27	2.19	1.92
19	4.38	3.52	3.13	2.90	2.74	2.63	2.54	2.48	2.42	2.38	2.23	2.16	1.88
20	4.35	3.49	3.10	2.87	2.71	2.60	2.51	2.45	2.39	2.35	2.20	2.12	1.84
21	4.32	3.47	3.07	2.84	2.68	2.57	2.49	2.42	2.37	2.32	2.18	2.10	1.81
22	4.30	3.44	3.05	2.82	2.66	2.55	2.46	2.40	2.34	2.30	2.15	2.07	1.78

Degrees of Freedom in the Denominator

(*continued*)

Table C

(Continued)

Degrees of Freedom in the Denominator

	Degrees of Freedom in the Numerator												
	1	**2**	**3**	**4**	**5**	**6**	**7**	**8**	**9**	**10**	**15**	**20**	**Infinity**
23	4.28	3.42	3.03	2.80	2.64	2.53	2.44	2.37	2.32	2.27	2.13	2.05	1.76
24	4.26	3.40	3.01	2.78	2.62	2.51	2.42	2.36	2.30	2.25	2.11	2.03	1.73
25	4.24	3.39	2.99	2.76	2.60	2.49	2.40	2.34	2.28	2.24	2.09	2.01	1.71
26	4.23	3.37	2.98	2.74	2.59	2.47	2.39	2.32	2.27	2.22	2.07	1.99	1.69
27	4.21	3.35	2.96	2.73	2.57	2.46	2.37	2.31	2.25	2.20	2.06	1.97	1.67
28	4.20	3.34	2.95	2.71	2.56	2.45	2.36	2.29	2.24	2.19	2.04	1.96	1.65
29	4.18	3.33	2.93	2.70	2.55	2.43	2.35	2.28	2.22	2.18	2.03	1.94	1.64
30	4.17	3.32	2.92	2.69	2.53	2.42	2.33	2.27	2.21	2.16	2.01	1.93	1.62
40	4.08	3.23	2.84	2.61	2.45	2.34	2.25	2.18	2.12	2.08	1.92	1.84	1.51
50	4.03	3.18	2.79	2.56	2.40	2.29	2.20	2.13	2.07	2.03	1.87	1.78	1.44
60	4.00	3.15	2.76	2.53	2.37	2.25	2.17	2.10	2.04	1.99	1.84	1.75	1.39
70	3.98	3.13	2.74	2.50	2.35	2.23	2.14	2.07	2.02	1.97	1.81	1.72	1.35
80	3.96	3.11	2.72	2.49	2.33	2.21	2.13	2.06	2.00	1.95	1.79	1.70	1.32
90	3.95	3.10	2.71	2.47	2.32	2.20	2.11	2.04	1.99	1.94	1.78	1.69	1.30
100	3.94	3.09	2.70	2.46	2.31	2.19	2.10	2.03	1.97	1.93	1.77	1.68	1.28
110	3.93	3.08	2.69	2.45	2.30	2.18	2.09	2.02	1.97	1.92	1.76	1.67	1.27
120	3.92	3.07	2.68	2.45	2.29	2.18	2.09	2.02	1.96	1.91	1.75	1.66	1.25
Infinity	3.84	3.00	2.60	2.37	2.21	2.10	2.01	1.94	2.01	1.83	1.67	1.57	1.00

The values in the table are generated using the FINV function in Microsoft Excel.

Table D

Critical Values for the F-statistic (1% Significance Level)

	Degrees of Freedom in the Numerator												
	1	**2**	**3**	**4**	**5**	**6**	**7**	**8**	**9**	**10**	**15**	**20**	**Infinity**
1	4052	4999	5404	5624	5764	5859	5928	5981	6022	6056	6157	6209	6366
2	98.5	99.0	99.2	99.3	99.3	99.3	99.4	99.4	99.4	99.4	99.4	99.5	99.5
3	34.1	30.8	29.5	28.7	28.2	27.9	27.7	27.5	27.3	27.2	26.9	26.7	26.1
4	21.2	18.0	16.7	16.0	15.5	15.2	15.0	14.8	14.7	14.6	14.2	14.0	13.5
5	16.3	13.3	12.1	11.4	11.0	10.7	10.5	10.3	10.2	10.1	9.72	9.55	9.02
6	13.8	10.9	9.78	9.15	8.75	8.47	8.26	8.10	7.98	7.87	7.56	7.40	6.88
7	12.3	9.55	8.45	7.85	7.46	7.19	6.99	6.84	6.72	6.62	6.31	6.16	5.65
8	11.3	8.65	7.59	7.01	6.63	6.37	6.18	6.03	5.91	5.81	5.52	5.36	4.86
9	10.6	8.02	6.99	6.42	6.06	5.80	5.61	5.47	5.35	5.26	4.96	4.81	4.31
10	10.0	7.56	6.55	5.99	5.64	5.39	5.20	5.06	4.94	4.85	4.56	4.41	3.91
11	9.65	7.21	6.22	5.67	5.32	5.07	4.89	4.74	4.63	4.54	4.25	4.10	3.60
12	9.33	6.93	5.95	5.41	5.06	4.82	4.64	4.50	4.39	4.30	4.01	3.86	3.36
13	9.07	6.70	5.74	5.21	4.86	4.62	4.44	4.30	4.19	4.10	3.82	3.66	3.17
14	8.86	6.51	5.56	5.04	4.69	4.46	4.28	4.14	4.03	3.94	3.66	3.51	3.00
15	8.68	6.36	5.42	4.89	4.56	4.32	4.14	4.00	3.89	3.80	3.52	3.37	2.87
16	8.53	6.23	5.29	4.77	4.44	4.20	4.03	3.89	3.78	3.69	3.41	3.26	2.75
17	8.40	6.11	5.19	4.67	4.34	4.10	3.93	3.79	3.68	3.59	3.31	3.16	2.65
18	8.29	6.01	5.09	4.58	4.25	4.01	3.84	3.71	3.60	3.51	3.23	3.08	2.57
19	8.18	5.93	5.01	4.50	4.17	3.94	3.77	3.63	3.52	3.43	3.15	3.00	2.49
20	8.10	5.85	4.94	4.43	4.10	3.87	3.70	3.56	3.46	3.37	3.09	2.94	2.42
21	8.02	5.78	4.87	4.37	4.04	3.81	3.64	3.51	3.40	3.31	3.03	2.88	2.36
22	7.95	5.72	4.82	4.31	3.99	3.76	3.59	3.45	3.35	3.26	2.98	2.83	2.31

Degrees of Freedom in the Denominator

(*continued*)

Table D

(Continued)

	Degrees of Freedom in the Numerator												
	1	2	3	4	5	6	7	8	9	10	15	20	Infinity
23	7.88	5.66	4.76	4.26	3.94	3.71	3.54	3.41	3.30	3.21	2.93	2.78	2.26
24	7.82	5.61	4.72	4.22	3.90	3.67	3.50	3.36	3.26	3.17	2.89	2.74	2.21
25	7.77	5.57	4.68	4.18	3.85	3.63	3.46	3.32	3.22	3.13	2.85	2.70	2.17
26	7.72	5.53	4.64	4.14	3.82	3.59	3.42	3.29	3.18	3.09	2.81	2.66	2.13
27	7.68	5.49	4.60	4.11	3.78	3.56	3.39	3.26	3.15	3.06	2.78	2.63	2.10
28	7.64	5.45	4.57	4.07	3.75	3.53	3.36	3.23	3.12	3.03	2.75	2.60	2.06
29	7.60	5.42	4.54	4.04	3.73	3.50	3.33	3.20	3.09	3.00	2.73	2.57	2.03
30	7.56	5.39	4.51	4.02	3.70	3.47	3.30	3.17	3.07	2.98	2.70	2.55	2.01
40	7.31	5.18	4.31	3.83	3.51	3.29	3.12	2.99	2.89	2.80	2.52	2.37	1.80
50	7.17	5.06	4.20	3.72	3.41	3.19	3.02	2.89	2.78	2.70	2.42	2.27	1.68
60	7.08	4.98	4.13	3.65	3.34	3.12	2.95	2.82	2.72	2.63	2.35	2.20	1.60
70	7.01	4.92	4.07	3.60	3.29	3.07	2.91	2.78	2.67	2.59	2.31	2.15	1.54
80	6.96	4.88	4.04	3.56	3.26	3.04	2.87	2.74	2.64	2.55	2.27	2.12	1.49
90	6.93	4.85	4.01	3.53	3.23	3.01	2.84	2.72	2.61	2.52	2.24	2.09	1.46
100	6.90	4.82	3.98	3.51	3.21	2.99	2.82	2.69	2.59	2.50	2.22	2.07	1.43
110	6.87	4.80	3.96	3.49	3.19	2.97	2.81	2.68	2.57	2.49	2.21	2.05	1.40
120	6.85	4.79	3.95	3.48	3.17	2.96	2.79	2.66	2.56	2.47	2.19	2.03	1.38
Infinity	6.63	4.61	3.78	3.32	3.02	2.80	2.64	2.51	2.64	2.32	2.04	1.88	1.00

The values in the table are generated using the FINV function in Microsoft Excel.

Degrees of Freedom in the Denominator

Table E

Critical Values for the Durbin-Watson Statistic (5% Significance Level)

n	k = 1		k = 2		k = 3		k = 4		k = 5		k = 6		k = 7		k = 8		k = 9		k = 10	
	d_l	d_u	d_l	d_u	d_l	d_u	d_l	d_u	d_l	d_u	d_l	d_u	d_l	d_u	d_l	d_u	d_l	d_u	d_l	d_u
10	0.88	1.32	0.70	1.64	0.53	2.02	0.38	2.41	0.24	2.82	—	—	—	—	—	—	—	—	—	—
11	0.93	1.32	0.76	1.60	0.60	1.93	0.44	2.28	0.32	2.65	0.20	3.01	—	—	—	—	—	—	—	—
12	0.97	1.33	0.81	1.58	0.66	1.86	0.51	2.18	0.38	2.51	0.27	2.83	0.17	3.15	—	—	—	—	—	—
13	1.01	1.34	0.86	1.56	0.72	1.82	0.57	2.09	0.45	2.39	0.33	2.69	0.23	2.99	0.15	3.27	—	—	—	—
14	1.05	1.35	0.91	1.55	0.77	1.78	0.63	2.03	0.51	2.30	0.39	2.57	0.29	2.85	0.20	3.11	0.13	3.36	—	—
15	1.08	1.36	0.95	1.54	0.81	1.75	0.69	1.98	0.56	2.22	0.45	2.47	0.34	2.73	0.25	2.98	0.18	3.22	0.11	3.44
16	1.11	1.37	0.98	1.54	0.86	1.73	0.73	1.94	0.62	2.16	0.50	2.39	0.40	2.62	0.30	2.86	0.22	3.09	0.16	3.30
17	1.13	1.38	1.02	1.54	0.90	1.71	0.78	1.90	0.66	2.10	0.55	2.32	0.45	2.54	0.36	2.76	0.27	2.98	0.20	3.18
18	1.16	1.39	1.05	1.54	0.93	1.70	0.82	1.87	0.71	2.06	0.60	2.26	0.50	2.46	0.41	2.67	0.32	2.87	0.24	3.07
19	1.18	1.40	1.07	1.54	0.97	1.69	0.86	1.85	0.75	2.02	0.65	2.21	0.55	2.40	0.46	2.59	0.37	2.78	0.29	2.97
20	1.20	1.41	1.10	1.54	1.00	1.68	0.89	1.83	0.79	1.99	0.69	2.16	0.60	2.34	0.50	2.52	0.42	2.70	0.34	2.89
21	1.22	1.42	1.13	1.54	1.03	1.67	0.93	1.81	0.83	1.96	0.73	2.12	0.64	2.29	0.55	2.46	0.46	2.63	0.38	2.81
22	1.24	1.43	1.15	1.54	1.05	1.66	0.96	1.80	0.86	1.94	0.77	2.09	0.68	2.25	0.59	2.41	0.50	2.57	0.42	2.73
23	1.26	1.44	1.17	1.54	1.08	1.66	0.99	1.79	0.90	1.92	0.80	2.06	0.72	2.21	0.63	2.36	0.55	2.51	0.47	2.67
24	1.27	1.45	1.19	1.55	1.10	1.66	1.01	1.78	0.93	1.90	0.84	2.04	0.75	2.17	0.67	2.32	0.58	2.46	0.51	2.61

n	d_L	d_U	d_L	d_U	d_L	d_U	d_L	d_U	d_L	d_U	d_L	d_U	d_L	d_U	d_L	d_U	d_L	d_U	d_L	d_U
25	1.29	1.45	1.21	1.55	1.12	1.65	1.04	1.77	0.95	1.89	0.87	2.01	0.78	2.14	0.70	2.28	0.62	2.42	0.54	2.56
26	1.30	1.46	1.22	1.55	1.14	1.65	1.06	1.76	0.98	1.87	0.90	1.99	0.82	2.12	0.74	2.25	0.66	2.38	0.58	2.51
27	1.32	1.47	1.24	1.56	1.16	1.65	1.08	1.75	1.00	1.86	0.93	1.97	0.85	2.09	0.77	2.22	0.69	2.34	0.62	2.47
28	1.33	1.48	1.26	1.56	1.18	1.65	1.10	1.75	1.03	1.85	0.95	1.96	0.87	2.07	0.80	2.19	0.72	2.31	0.65	2.43
29	1.34	1.48	1.27	1.56	1.20	1.65	1.12	1.74	1.05	1.84	0.98	1.94	0.90	2.05	0.83	2.16	0.75	2.28	0.68	2.40
30	1.35	1.49	1.28	1.57	1.21	1.65	1.14	1.74	1.07	1.83	1.00	1.93	0.93	2.03	0.85	2.14	0.78	2.25	0.71	2.36
40	1.44	1.54	1.39	1.60	1.34	1.66	1.29	1.72	1.23	1.79	1.18	1.85	1.12	1.92	1.06	2.00	1.01	2.07	0.95	2.15
50	1.50	1.59	1.46	1.63	1.42	1.67	1.38	1.72	1.34	1.77	1.29	1.82	1.25	1.88	1.20	1.93	1.16	1.99	1.11	2.04
60	1.55	1.62	1.51	1.65	1.48	1.69	1.44	1.73	1.41	1.77	1.37	1.81	1.34	1.85	1.30	1.89	1.26	1.94	1.22	1.98
70	1.58	1.64	1.55	1.67	1.53	1.70	1.49	1.74	1.46	1.77	1.43	1.80	1.40	1.84	1.37	1.87	1.34	1.91	1.31	1.95
80	1.61	1.66	1.59	1.69	1.56	1.72	1.53	1.74	1.51	1.77	1.48	1.80	1.45	1.83	1.43	1.86	1.40	1.89	1.37	1.93
90	1.64	1.68	1.61	1.70	1.59	1.73	1.57	1.75	1.54	1.78	1.52	1.80	1.49	1.83	1.47	1.85	1.45	1.88	1.42	1.91
100	1.65	1.69	1.63	1.72	1.61	1.74	1.59	1.76	1.57	1.78	1.55	1.80	1.53	1.83	1.51	1.85	1.48	1.87	1.46	1.90
150	1.72	1.75	1.71	1.76	1.69	1.77	1.68	1.79	1.67	1.80	1.65	1.82	1.64	1.83	1.62	1.85	1.61	1.86	1.59	1.88
200	1.76	1.78	1.75	1.79	1.74	1.80	1.73	1.81	1.72	1.82	1.71	1.83	1.70	1.84	1.69	1.85	1.68	1.86	1.67	1.87

Adapted from N. E. Savin and Kenneth J. White, "The Durbin-Watson Test for Serial Correlation with Extreme Sample Sizes or Many Regressors," *Econometrica*, Vol. 45, No. 8, November 1977, pp. 1989–1996.

Table F
Critical Values for the Durbin-Watson Statistic (1% Significance Level)

n	k=1 d_l	k=1 d_u	k=2 d_l	k=2 d_u	k=3 d_l	k=3 d_u	k=4 d_l	k=4 d_u	k=5 d_l	k=5 d_u	k=6 d_l	k=6 d_u	k=7 d_l	k=7 d_u	k=8 d_l	k=8 d_u	k=9 d_l	k=9 d_u	k=10 d_l	k=10 d_u
10	0.60	1.00	0.47	1.33	0.34	1.73	0.23	2.19	0.15	2.69	–	–	–	–	–	–	–	–	–	–
11	0.65	1.01	0.52	1.30	0.40	1.64	0.29	2.03	0.19	2.45	0.12	2.89	–	–	–	–	–	–	–	–
12	0.70	1.02	0.57	1.27	0.45	1.58	0.34	1.91	0.24	2.28	0.16	2.67	0.11	3.05	–	–	–	–	–	–
13	0.74	1.04	0.62	1.26	0.50	1.53	0.39	1.83	0.29	2.15	0.21	2.49	0.14	2.84	0.09	3.18	–	–	–	–
14	0.78	1.05	0.67	1.25	0.55	1.49	0.44	1.76	0.34	2.05	0.26	2.35	0.18	2.67	0.12	2.98	0.08	3.29	–	–
15	0.81	1.07	0.70	1.25	0.59	1.46	0.49	1.70	0.39	1.97	0.30	2.24	0.23	2.53	0.16	2.81	0.11	3.10	0.07	3.37
16	0.84	1.09	0.74	1.25	0.63	1.45	0.53	1.66	0.44	1.90	0.35	2.15	0.27	2.41	0.20	2.68	0.14	2.94	0.09	3.20
17	0.87	1.10	0.77	1.26	0.67	1.43	0.57	1.63	0.48	1.85	0.39	2.08	0.31	2.32	0.24	2.57	0.18	2.81	0.13	3.05
18	0.90	1.12	0.81	1.26	0.71	1.42	0.61	1.60	0.52	1.80	0.44	2.02	0.36	2.24	0.28	2.47	0.22	2.70	0.16	2.93
19	0.93	1.13	0.84	1.27	0.74	1.42	0.65	1.58	0.56	1.77	0.48	1.96	0.40	2.17	0.32	2.38	0.26	2.60	0.20	2.81
20	0.95	1.15	0.86	1.27	0.77	1.41	0.69	1.57	0.60	1.74	0.52	1.92	0.44	2.11	0.36	2.31	0.29	2.51	0.23	2.71
21	0.98	1.16	0.89	1.28	0.80	1.41	0.72	1.55	0.63	1.71	0.55	1.88	0.47	2.06	0.40	2.24	0.33	2.43	0.27	2.62
22	1.00	1.17	0.91	1.28	0.83	1.41	0.75	1.54	0.67	1.69	0.59	1.85	0.51	2.02	0.44	2.19	0.37	2.37	0.30	2.55
23	1.02	1.19	0.94	1.29	0.86	1.41	0.78	1.53	0.70	1.67	0.62	1.82	0.55	1.98	0.47	2.14	0.40	2.31	0.34	2.48
24	1.04	1.20	0.96	1.30	0.88	1.41	0.81	1.53	0.73	1.66	0.65	1.80	0.58	1.94	0.51	2.10	0.44	2.26	0.38	2.41

n	dL	dU	dL	dU	dL	dU	dL	dU	dL	dU	dL	dU	dL	dU	dL	dU	dL	dU	dL	dU
25	1.06	1.21	0.98	1.31	0.91	1.41	0.83	1.52	0.76	1.65	0.68	1.78	0.61	1.91	0.54	2.06	0.47	2.21	0.41	2.36
26	1.07	1.22	1.00	1.31	0.93	1.41	0.86	1.52	0.78	1.64	0.71	1.76	0.64	1.89	0.57	2.03	0.51	2.17	0.44	2.31
27	1.09	1.23	1.02	1.32	0.95	1.41	0.88	1.52	0.81	1.63	0.74	1.74	0.67	1.87	0.60	2.00	0.54	2.13	0.47	2.27
28	1.10	1.24	1.04	1.33	0.97	1.42	0.90	1.51	0.83	1.62	0.76	1.73	0.70	1.85	0.63	1.97	0.57	2.10	0.50	2.23
29	1.12	1.25	1.05	1.33	0.99	1.42	0.92	1.51	0.86	1.61	0.79	1.72	0.72	1.83	0.66	1.95	0.60	2.07	0.53	2.19
30	1.13	1.26	1.07	1.34	1.01	1.42	0.94	1.51	0.88	1.61	0.81	1.71	0.75	1.81	0.68	1.93	0.62	2.04	0.56	2.16
40	1.25	1.34	1.20	1.40	1.15	1.46	1.10	1.52	1.05	1.58	1.00	1.65	0.95	1.72	0.90	1.80	0.84	1.88	0.80	1.96
50	1.32	1.40	1.29	1.45	1.25	1.49	1.21	1.54	1.16	1.59	1.12	1.64	1.08	1.69	1.04	1.75	1.00	1.81	0.96	1.86
60	1.38	1.45	1.35	1.49	1.32	1.52	1.28	1.56	1.25	1.60	1.21	1.64	1.18	1.68	1.14	1.73	1.11	1.77	1.07	1.82
70	1.43	1.49	1.40	1.52	1.37	1.55	1.34	1.58	1.31	1.61	1.28	1.65	1.25	1.68	1.22	1.72	1.19	1.75	1.16	1.79
80	1.47	1.52	1.44	1.54	1.42	1.57	1.39	1.60	1.36	1.62	1.34	1.65	1.31	1.68	1.29	1.71	1.26	1.75	1.23	1.78
90	1.50	1.54	1.47	1.56	1.45	1.59	1.43	1.61	1.41	1.64	1.38	1.66	1.36	1.69	1.34	1.71	1.31	1.74	1.29	1.77
100	1.52	1.56	1.50	1.58	1.48	1.60	1.46	1.63	1.44	1.65	1.42	1.67	1.40	1.69	1.38	1.72	1.36	1.74	1.34	1.77
150	1.61	1.64	1.60	1.65	1.58	1.67	1.57	1.68	1.56	1.69	1.54	1.71	1.53	1.72	1.52	1.74	1.50	1.75	1.49	1.77
200	1.66	1.68	1.65	1.69	1.64	1.70	1.63	1.72	1.62	1.73	1.61	1.74	1.60	1.75	1.59	1.75	1.58	1.77	1.57	1.78

Adapted from N. E. Savin and Kenneth J. White, "The Durbin-Watson Test for Serial Correlation with Extreme Sample Sizes or Many Regressors," *Econometrica*, Vol. 45, No. 8, November 1977, pp. 1989–1996.

> Null; reject
< Null; Accept

Table G

Critical Values for the Chi-Squared Distribution χ^2 (one-sided)

Degrees of Freedom	Significance Level					Degrees of Freedom	Significance Level			
	10%	5%	2.50%	1%			10%	5%	2.50%	1%
1	2.71	3.84	5.02	6.63		20	28.41	31.41	34.17	37.57
2	4.61	5.99	7.38	9.21		21	29.62	32.67	35.48	38.93
3	6.25	7.81	9.35	11.34		22	30.81	33.92	36.78	40.29
4	7.78	9.49	11.14	13.28		23	32.01	35.17	38.08	41.64
5	9.24	11.07	12.83	15.09		24	33.20	36.42	39.36	42.98
6	10.64	12.59	14.45	16.81		25	34.38	37.65	40.65	44.31
7	12.02	14.07	16.01	18.48		26	35.56	38.89	41.92	45.64
8	13.36	15.51	17.53	20.09		27	36.74	40.11	43.19	46.96
9	14.68	16.92	19.02	21.67		28	37.92	41.34	44.46	48.28
10	15.99	18.31	20.48	23.21		29	39.09	42.56	45.72	49.59
11	17.28	19.68	21.92	24.73		30	40.26	43.77	46.98	50.89
12	18.55	21.03	23.34	26.22		40	51.81	55.76	59.34	63.69
13	19.81	22.36	24.74	27.69		50	63.17	67.50	71.42	76.15
14	21.06	23.68	26.12	29.14		60	74.40	79.08	83.30	88.38
15	22.31	25.00	27.49	30.58		70	85.53	90.53	95.02	100.43
16	23.54	26.30	28.85	32.00		80	96.58	101.88	106.63	112.33
17	24.77	27.59	30.19	33.41		90	107.57	113.15	118.14	124.12
18	25.99	28.87	31.53	34.81		100	118.50	124.34	129.56	135.81
19	27.20	30.14	32.85	36.19						

The values in the table are generated using the CHIINV function in Microsoft Excel.

Smaller nonstat Do Not Rej

lgr stat Rej

Table H

Critical Values for the Dickey-Fuller Test*

Degrees of Freedom	Level of Significance (One-sided Test)			
	10%	**5%**	**2.5%**	**1%**
25	–2.64	–2.99	–3.33	–3.75
50	–2.60	–2.93	–3.23	–3.59
100	–2.59	–2.90	–3.17	–3.50
250	–2.58	–2.88	–3.14	–3.45
500	–2.57	–2.87	–3.13	–3.44
Infinity	–2.57	–2.86	–3.12	–3.42

*These critical values are for a regression that contains a constant and no trend term. See Wayne A. Fuller, *Introduction to Statistical Time Series,* 2nd ed. (New York: John Wiley & Sons, Inc., 1996), p. 642.

Index